Cognitive Carpentry

Cognitive Carpentry:
A Blueprint for How to Build a Person

John L. Pollock

A Bradford Book
The MIT Press
Cambridge, Massachusetts
London, England

This book was was printed and bound in the United States of America.

Library of Congress Cataloging-in-Publication Data

Pollock, John L.
  Cognitive carpentry : a blueprint for how to build a person / John L. Pollock.
  p.   cm.
  "A Bradford book."
  Includes bibliographical references and index.
  ISBN 0-262-16152-4 (alk. paper)
  1. Reasoning. 2. Cognition. 3. OSCAR (Computer file) 4. Pollock, John L. How to build a person. 5. Artificial intelligence—Philosophy. 6. Machine learning. I. Title.
BC177.P599   1995
006.3'3—dc20   94-48106
                                                                          CIP

For Cynthia—
the mother of OSCAR

Contents

4 An Architecture for Epistemic Cognition

5 Plan-Based Practical Reasoning

6 The Logical Structure of Plans

7 An Architecture for Planning

8 Acting

9 OSCAR

References

Index

Preface

OSCAR is an architecture for an autonomous rational agent; it is the first such architecture capable of sophisticated rational thought. This book presents the theory underlying OSCAR and gives a brief description of the actual construction of OSCAR. That construction is presented in full detail in *The OSCAR Manual*, available, with the LISP code for OSCAR, by anonymous FTP from aruba.ccit.arizona.edu, in the directory /pub/oscar. Help in obtaining the files or running OSCAR can be secured by sending an email message to oscar-help@arizona.edu. The readers of this book are encouraged to retrieve a copy of this material and experiment with OSCAR. (For this purpose, access to a computer running Common LISP is required.)

It has long been my contention that work in artificial intelligence has made less progress than expected because it has been based upon inadequate foundations. AI systems are supposed to behave rationally, but their creators have not generally come to the problem equipped with an account of what it is to behave rationally. Progress in AI has been made by relying upon unformulated intuitions about rationality, and they can carry us only so far. As the tasks required of a rational agent become more difficult, our untutored intuitions become less clear and eventually fail us altogether. The foundation required for further progress is a philosophical theory of rationality.

Philosophy has seen many theories of rationality. Perhaps most such theories are criticizable on grounds of computational infeasability. If they constituted correct theories of rationality, then rationality would be impossible. But, I insist, rationality is not impossible, because human beings are for the most part rational. I have defended this claim to some extent in *How to Build a Person*, and a more extensive defense could be mounted by appealing to the account of rationality propounded in this book.

There are, of course, psychologists who claim to have shown that human beings are not rational. Although that claim still finds favor in psychology, it has largely been repudiated in philosophy on the grounds that it is based upon an inadequate understanding of what it is to be rational. For instance, some psychologists seem to think that the mere fact that a person has false beliefs (about, for example, probability) and reasons in accordance with them shows him to be irrational. Once stated clearly, such a view requires little refutation.

The implementability of a theory of rationality is a necessary condition for its correctness. This amounts to saying that philosophy needs

AI just as much as AI needs philosophy. A partial test of the correctness of a theory of rationality is that it can form the basis for an autonomous rational agent, and to establish that conclusively, one must actually build an AI system implementing the theory. It behooves philosophers to keep this in mind in when constructing their theories, because it takes little reflection to see that many kinds of otherwise popular theories are not implementable.

OSCAR is based upon my own work in epistemology and practical reasoning. That work has evolved over the years, partly in response to pressures from the desire to construct an implementable theory. The work has come to fruition in OSCAR, the first AI system capable of performing reasoning that philosophers would regard as epistemologically sophisticated. It is to be emphasized that OSCAR is an *architecture* for a rational agent, and not by itself a complete rational agent. OSCAR provides the framework for cognition and the reasoning engine for a rational agent. To get this architecture to perform sophisticated cognitive tasks, it must be given additional resources in the form of reason-schemas, Q&I modules (see chapter 1), and so forth.

The task of providing reason-schemas sufficient to allow OSCAR to perform various kinds of reasoning—for instance, perceptual reasoning, inductive reasoning, probabilistic reasoning, or inference to the best explanation—is essentially the same task as the traditional one of giving an epistemological analysis of such reasoning. One of the exciting features of OSCAR is that a user can experiment with accounts of such reasoning without being a programmer. OSCAR is designed with a simple user interface that allows a would-be cognitive carpenter to type in proposed reason-schemas in a simple format and then investigate how OSCAR treats problems using those reason-schemas. Thus, if one accepts the general picture of rationality underlying OSCAR, one can use OSCAR as an aid in investigating more specific aspects of rationality. In a somewhat different vein, there is also interdisciplinary work underway at the University of Arizona to use OSCAR as the basis for a system of language processing. This work is being performed jointly by cognitive psychologists, computational linguists, and philosophers.

OSCAR is based upon simple and familiar philosophical principles. Cognition is divided loosely into practical cognition and epistemic cognition. Practical cognition aims at choosing plans for acting, and plans are compared in terms of their expected values. Practical cognition presupposes epistemic cognition, which supplies the beliefs used by practical cognition in its search for good plans. Epistemic cognition begins with perception (broadly construed) and forms further beliefs through various forms of defeasible reasoning. The details of both the theory of defeasible reasoning and the theory of plan search and plan selection are novel, but the general outline of the theory will be familiar to all philosophers.

OSCAR is not incompatible with most of the work that has been done in AI on problems like planning, automated theorem proving, and probabilistic reasoning via Bayesian networks. Most of that work can be incorporated into OSCAR in the form of Q&I modules or reason-schemas. OSCAR supplies a framework for integrating such work into a single architecture.

Much of the material presented in this book has been published, in preliminary form, in a other places, and I thank the publishers of that material for allowing it to be reprinted here in modified form. Chapter 1 is based upon material originally published in *Cognitive Science* ("The phylogeny of rationality") and *The Journal of Experimental and Theoretical AI* ("OSCAR: a general theory of rationality"). Chapter 2 summarizes material from a number of my books on epistemology, the most noteworthy being *Contemporary Theories of Knowledge* (Princeton) and *Nomic Probability and the Foundations of Induction* (Oxford). Chapter 3 presents the theory of defeasible reasoning developed in a series of earlier articles ("Defeasible reasoning" in *Cognitive Science*, "A theory of defeasible reasoning" in *The International Journal of Intelligent Systems*, "Self-defeating arguments" in *Minds and Machines*, "How to reason defeasibly" in *Artificial Intelligence*, and "Justification and defeat" in *Artificial Intelligence*). Chapter 4 contains material from "How to reason defeasibly" and "Interest-driven suppositional reasoning" (*The Journal of Automated Reasoning*). Chapter 5 is based upon "New foundations for practical reasoning" (*Minds and Machines*). Some of the material in chapters 7 and 8 was published in "Practical Reasoning in OSCAR" (*Philosophical Perspectives*). Some of chapter 9 is taken from "OSCAR—a general purpose defeasible reasoner" (*Journal of Applied Non-Classical Logics*). The rest of the material is seeing the light of day for the first time in this book.

I also thank the University of Arizona for its steadfast support of my research, and Merrill Garrett in particular for his continued enthusiasm for my work and the help he has provided in his role as Director of Cognitive Science at the University of Arizona. I am indebted to numerous graduate students for their unstinting constructive criticism, and to my colleagues for their interactions over the years. In the latter connection, I have profited more than I can say from years of discussion with Keith Lehrer.

Chapter 1
Rational Agents

1. Two Concepts of Rationality

There are two ways of approaching the topic of rationality. The philosophical tradition has focused on *human* rationality. As human beings, we assess our own thought and that of our compatriots as rational to varying degrees. In doing this, we apply "standards of rationality", and our judgments appear to be normative. We compare how people think with how they *should* think. Many philosophers have thus concluded that epistemology and the theory of practical rationality are normative disciplines—they concern how people should reason rather than how they do reason. But the source of such normativity becomes problematic. What could make it the case that we should reason in a certain way?

I have proposed a naturalistic theory of epistemic norms [1986] that I now want to apply more generally to all of rationality. This account begins with the observation that rules are often formulated in normative language, even when the rules are purely descriptive. For example, in describing a physical system that has been built according to a certain design, we may observe that whenever one state of the system occurs, another state "should" follow it. Thus, I might observe that when I turn the steering wheel of my truck, it should change direction. The use of normative language reflects the fact that we are formulating rules governing the operation of the system (*functional descriptions*, in the sense of my [1990]), but such functional descriptions do not formulate invariant generalizations. These rules describe how the system "normally" functions, but it is also possible for the system to behave abnormally. For instance, my truck may skid on an icy road, in which case it may fail to change direction despite my turning the steering wheel. In a sense made precise in my [1990], functional descriptions are descriptions of how a system will function *under certain conditions*, where these conditions are both common and stable.

Applying these observations to rationality, my proposal was that we *know how* to reason. In other words, we have procedural knowledge for how to do this. As with any other procedural knowledge, we must make a competence/performance distinction. Although we know how to do something, we may fail to do it in a way conforming to the rules describing our procedural knowledge. The most familiar example in cognitive science is linguistic knowledge, but the same point applies to knowledge of how to reason. So my proposal is that rules for rationality are descriptive of our procedural knowledge for how to reason (or perhaps more generally, for how to think). The use of normative language in the formulation of these rules reflects no more than the fact that we do not always act in accordance with our procedural knowledge.

An important fact about procedural knowledge is that although we are rarely in a position to articulate it precisely, we do have the ability to judge whether, in a particular case, we are conforming to the rules describing that knowledge. Thus, in language processing, although I cannot articulate the rules of my grammar, I can tell whether a particular utterance is grammatical. Similarly, in swinging a golf club, although I may be unable to describe how to do it properly ("properly" meaning "in accordance with the rules comprising my procedural knowledge"), I can nevertheless judge in particular cases that I am or am not doing it properly. It just "feels right" or "feels wrong". And similarly, in reasoning, although we may be unable to articulate the rules for reasoning with any precision, we can still recognize cases of good or bad reasoning. These "intuitive" or "introspective" judgments provide the data for constructing a theory about the content of the rules governing our reasoning. In this respect, the construction of philosophical theories of reasoning is precisely parallel to the construction of linguistic theories of grammar. In each case, our data are "intuitive", but the process of theory construction and confirmation is inductive, differing in no way from theory construction and confirmation in any other science.

This account has the consequence that when we describe human rationality, we are describing contingent features of human beings and so are really doing psychology by non-traditional means. The fact that we are employing non-traditional means rather than conventional experimental methods does not seem to be particularly problematic. Again, compare linguistics. In principle, standard psychological experimental methods are applicable in either case, but at this stage of investigation it is difficult to see how to apply them. The only reasonably direct access we have to our norms is through our introspection of conformity or non-conformity to the rules. We cannot simply investigate what people do when they reason, because people do not always reason correctly. The current methodology of cognitive psychology is too blunt an instrument to be applied to this problem with much success. No doubt, this will eventually change, and when it does, philosophers must be prepared to have one more field of inquiry pulled out from under their feet, but in the meantime standard philosophical methodology is the best methodology we have for addressing these problems.[1]

I have been urging that the task of eliciting the human norms for rationality is essentially a psychological one. However, this leads to a perplexing observation. Some features of human rationality may be strongly motivated by general constraints imposed by the design problem rationality is intended to solve, but other features may be quite idiosyncratic, reflecting rather arbitrary design choices. This leads to an anthropocentric view of rationality. These idiosyncratic design features may prove to be of considerable psychological interest, but they may be of less interest in understanding rationality per se.

These considerations suggest a second way of approaching the topic of rationality, which may ultimately prove more illuminating. This is to approach it from the "design stance", to use Dennett's [1987] felicitous term. We can think of rationality as the solution to certain design problems. I will argue that quite general features of these problems suffice to generate much of the structure of rationality. General logical and feasibility constraints have the consequence that there is often only one obvious way of solving certain design problems, and this is the course taken by human rationality.

Approaching rationality from the design stance is more common in artificial intelligence than it is in philosophy. This methodology will suffice to generate much of the general architecture of rational thought, but as the account becomes increasingly detailed, we will find ourselves making arbitrary design decisions or decisions based upon marginal comparisons of efficiency. At that stage it becomes

---

[1] Some psychological investigations of reasoning provide convincing evidence for conclusions about the rules governing human reasoning competence. For example, I find the evidence that humans do not employ *modus tollens* as a primitive rule quite convincing [see Wason 1966 and Cheng and Holyoak 1985]). But most psychological work that aims to elicit the content of these rules is less convincing. For example, most uses of protocol analysis assume that humans have access to what rules govern their reasoning, an assumption that seems obviously wrong in the light of the difficulties philosophers have had in articulating those rules. See the discussion in Smith, Langston, and Nisbett [1992]. Furthermore the results of protocol analysis often seem crude when compared to familiar philosophical theories about the structure of particular kinds of reasoning.

somewhat problematic just what our topic is. We can either take the traditional philosophical/psychological course and try to give an accurate description of human cognition, or we can take the engineering approach of trying to describe some system or other that will solve the design problem, without requiring that it be an exact model of human cognition. I find both approaches interesting. My overarching goal in this book is to give a general description of rational thought applicable to all rational agents. But a constraint on this enterprise must be that it is possible for a rational agent to function in the way described. The only way to be certain that this constraint is satisfied is to provide a sufficiently precise and detailed account that it becomes possible to build an agent implementing it. This book will attempt to provide large parts of such an account, although by no means all of it. No claim will be made that the rational agent described is in every respect an accurate model of human rationality. On the other hand, I will be guided in my theory construction by the general desire not to stray too far from the human exemplar, partly because I want this theory to throw some light on why human cognition works in the way it does and partly because this is a good engineering strategy. In trying to solve a design problem, it can be very useful to look at a functioning system that already solves the problem, and in the case of rationality the only such system to which we currently have access is human beings.

To ensure that a rational agent could actually function in the way described, I will impose the general requirement on my theory that it be implementable. The result of such implementation will be part of an artificial rational agent. In this connection, it is to be emphasized that a rational agent consists of more than an intellect. It must also have a perceptual system, a system of extensors for manipulating its environment, and, for many purposes, linguistic abilities. It is possible that linguistic abilities will come free given the rest of the system, but the received view in contemporary linguistics is that language requires special subsystems dedicated to language processing. All of these topics must be addressed before a complete artificial rational agent can be produced. However, this investigation will focus exclusively on the intellect. The objective is to construct a theory of rationality of sufficient precision to produce an artificial intellect—an *artilect* for short.[2]

Not all of artificial intelligence has so grand an objective as that of

---

[2] The term "artilect" was coined by de Garis [1989].

building an artilect. Most work in AI is directed at more mundane problems of data processing and decision making. But even such projects have an intimate connection with the theory of rationality. A general constraint on any such system is that the conclusions drawn and decisions made be "reasonable" ones. To a certain extent, we can judge the reasonableness of conclusions just by using our intuitions. But as the systems get more complex and the questions harder, we outstrip our ability to make such judgments without the backing of a general theory of rationality. Ultimately, all work in AI is going to have to presuppose a theory of rationality.

My aim is to construct a sufficiently precise theory of rationality that it can be used to provide the basis for constructing an artilect. That is the objective of the OSCAR project, and OSCAR is the computer system that results. Implementing a theory of cognition on a computer can be regarded as either an exercise in computer modeling or an attempt to build a machine that thinks. This is the difference between weak and strong AI. I favor the latter construal of the enterprise and have defended it at length in my book *How to Build a Person*. The present book is the sequel to that book. In *How to Build a Person*, I defended what might be called the "metaphysical foundations" of the project. These consist of three theses: *agent materialism*, according to which persons are physical objects; *token physicalism*, according to which mental states are physical states; and *strong AI*, in the particular form claiming that a system that adequately models human rationality will be a person and have the same claim to thoughts and feelings as a human being. This book takes its title from the last chapter of *How to Build a Person*, entitled "Cognitive Carpentry" and comprising an initial sketch of the theory of rationality envisioned by the OSCAR project. This book aims to redeem the promissory notes proffered in the earlier book.

Although this book does not complete the OSCAR project, I believe that it does establish that it can be completed. This has important implications throughout philosophy and cognitive science. First, it should lay to rest the numerous claims that "symbol-processing AI" is impossible. It must be possible, because this book does it. Second, the theory underlying OSCAR is based upon my own somewhat old-fashioned epistemological theories. Although I prefer not to call them "foundations theories", they are the foundations-like theories defended in my [1974] and [1986] under the label "direct realism". This book establishes that these theories can provide the epistemological basis for a rational agent. Providing such a basis becomes a severe challenge to competing theories. I do not believe that any of them can provide a similarly satisfactory basis, in which case they cannot be correct descriptions of human rationality. This book throws down the gauntlet to competing epistemological theories to show that they too can spawn functioning artilects. Finally, although for the reasons discussed in the final chapter, this book does not yet produce a fully functional artilect, it makes it reasonably clear that such an artilect can be produced, and this has implications for the philosophical arguments against strong AI. I sought to answer those arguments in *How to Build a Person*, but the most powerful answer will be OSCAR itself. Once OSCAR is fully functional, the argument from analogy will lead us inexorably to attribute thoughts and feelings to OSCAR with precisely the same credentials with which we attribute them to human beings. Philosophical arguments to the contrary will be passé.

2. The Goal of Rationality

My general strategy is to begin with a description of the design problem for which I take rationality to provide a solution and then argue that a considerable amount of the structure of rationality can be elicited as providing the only apparent solutions to various logical and feasibility problems that arise in the course of trying to design a rational agent that satisfies this design specification. What then *is* the design problem for which rationality is a solution?

The world contains many relatively stable structures. These can be roughly categorized as of two kinds. Some are stable by virtue of being hard to destroy. A rock is a good example of such *passive stability*. Others achieve stability by interacting with their immediate surroundings to make them more congenial to their continued survival. Plants and animals are the obvious examples of such *active stability*. Rationality (in a very general sense) represents one solution to the problem of active stability. A rational agent has beliefs reflecting the state of its environment, and it likes or dislikes its situation. When it finds the world not entirely to its liking, it tries to change that. Its *cognitive architecture* is the mechanism whereby it chooses courses of action aimed at making the world more to its liking.[3]

---

[3] Stating the problem as one of survival is a bit simplistic for biological agents designed by evolution. For such agents, rationality might be better viewed as a partial solution to survival of the species, or some even more sophisticated biological objective. However, this will not affect the theory adumbrated in this book.

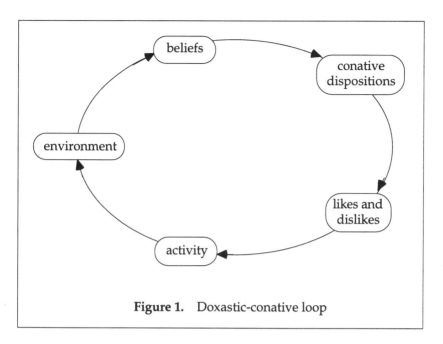

Figure 1.   Doxastic-conative loop

This is the general conception of rationality that I am concerned to investigate, and should be understood as a partial stipulation regarding what I mean here by "rationality". As I have described it, a rational agent has beliefs and likes or dislikes. At the moment, I am using these terms loosely. A rational agent must have some internal "doxastic" states that are at least fairly well correlated with some states of its environment, and some *conative dispositions* to "like or dislike" its situation. The agent must in addition have cognitive mechanisms whereby all of this leads it to engage in activity that has a tendency to change its immediate environment so that it acquires new doxastic states that interact with its conative dispositions in such a way that the agent likes its situation better. This *doxastic-conative loop* is diagrammed in figure 1. This is the mechanism of stability characteristic of rational agents.

Cognition can be roughly divided into *epistemic cognition*, which concerns what to believe, and *practical cognition*, which concerns what to do. Practical cognition presupposes beliefs about one's situation, and these are provided by epistemic cognition. In an important sense, epistemic cognition is subservient to practical cognition. The principal function of cognition is to direct activity (practical cognition), and the role of epistemic cognition in rationality is to provide the factual background required for practical cognition.

The objective of this book is to investigate the way in which a rational agent implements the doxastic-conative loop—to investigate the structure of rational thought. The best way to begin is by examining simpler agents that do not quite have the credentials to be considered rational.

3. Precursors of Rationality

As I will use the term, an *agent* is any system capable of acting on its environment to render it more congenial to its continued survival. This is a very broad notion of an agent that includes both plants and animals and even viruses. The simplest kind of agent is a *non-cognitive agent*. Rather than directing activity by anything approximating thought and reasoning, a non-cognitive agent simply reacts. The simplest kind of non-cognitive agent has built-in reflexes that respond directly to perceptual input. The behavior of such an agent is entirely hardwired. It is incapable of learning.

A more complex kind of non-cognitive agent is capable of acquiring new reflexes through something like operant conditioning. This represents a significant step upward. For operant conditioning to be possible, there must be states of the agent-cum-environment that act as positive or negative reinforcers when they follow actions taken by the agent. Speaking loosely, these are situation types that are "liked" or "disliked" by the agent. Such conative responses to situation types are not required in a simpler non-cognitive agent that is incapable of learning. They represent the first step along the road to rationality.

Non-cognitive agents respond directly to perceptual input. The next step toward rationality results from adding more sophisticated mental representations of the world. *Cognitive agents* have both mental representations of the world and likes and dislikes. When their representations indicate that the world is not entirely to their liking, they engage in activity aimed at changing that. *Epistemic cognition* is the mechanism responsible for the formation of these mental representations. Once they become sufficiently sophisticated, we regard the mental representations as beliefs.

There are different solutions to the problem of generating activity in response to beliefs coupled with likes or dislikes. The simplest mechanism would consist of built-in reflexes, as in a simple non-cognitive agent. A more sophisticated cognitive agent will also exhibit conditioned reflexes. The difference between conditioning in a cognitive agent and conditioning in a non-cognitive agent is that in the former responses can be conditioned to arbitrary mental representations of the world and not just to perceptual input. It is worth noticing that in order for conditioning to be possible, some initial dispositions to act have to be built-in. Otherwise, the agent would engage in no activity prior to conditioning, and hence no conditioning could occur.

In principle, there could be cognitive agents capable of sophisticated epistemic cognition but capable only of directing their activity through built-in or conditioned reflexes. I will refer to such an agent as a *reactive agent*. More sophisticated cognitive agents add *practical cognition* to epistemic cognition. Practical cognition directs activity on the basis of the agent's beliefs about its environment and does so in more sophisticated ways than by built-in or conditioned reflexes. Practical cognition enables the agent to direct its activity by thinking about how best to act given its beliefs about its situation and its likes and dislikes. Practical cognition can vary in complexity. A "short-sighted" agent may direct its activity one act at a time, on the basis of the observation that one act is more likely to produce a situation the agent likes than is some alternative act. A more sophisticated agent can engage in complex planning. A simple plan may require performing several acts in a fixed order. The execution of a more complicated plan might span a lifetime.

4. Mechanisms of Cognition

Among the mechanisms of epistemic and practical cognition are some we recognize as *reasoning*. The reasoning involved in epistemic cognition has generally been called "theoretical reasoning", but that label is somewhat misleading, so I will call it *epistemic reasoning*. The reasoning involved in practical cognition is *practical reasoning*. I will refer to epistemic and practical reasoning jointly as *ratiocination*.[4] Without yet trying to characterize reasoning, we can nonetheless recognize that there are other cognitive mechanisms that also produce beliefs and direct activity. This is required because reasoning is slow. Many

---

[4] In Pollock [1986 and 1989], I used the term "intellection" instead of "ratiocination".

aspects of reasoning are essentially serial. Whenever possible, human cognition is accelerated by employing our inherently slow hardware in parallel processing. Unfortunately, much of reasoning cannot be done in parallel, so human cognition includes many nonratiocinative processes that also issue in beliefs and actions. For instance, a human being does not have to pull out a pocket calculator and compute trajectories in order to catch a baseball or get out of the way of a bus. We have a built-in mechanism that allows us to estimate such trajectories very quickly.

Such nonratiocinative processes have sometimes been called "quick and dirty", but that is a misnomer because they need not be at all dirty. For example, our built-in procedures for computing trajectories are incredibly accurate. Their shortcoming is not inaccuracy but inflexibility. They achieve their speed by building in assumptions about the environment, and when those assumptions fail, the processes may yield wildly inaccurate answers. For instance, if we see that a baseball is going to bounce off a telephone pole, we had best wait until it ricochets before predicting its trajectory. Our built-in "trajectory module" cannot handle this situation accurately, so we use ratiocination to override it temporarily, until the situation becomes one that can be handled accurately by the trajectory module. I will refer to modules like the trajectory module as *Q&I modules* ("quick and inflexible").

It must not be supposed that human Q&I modules are concerned exclusively with motor skills. Psychological evidence strongly suggests that most everyday inductive and probabilistic inference is carried out by Q&I modules.[5] In this case, the modules really are rather dirty. Accurate probabilistic reasoning is in many cases computationally infeasible, and so humans appear to rely upon processes like Tversky's "representativeness heuristic", which often yield results incompatible with the probability calculus.[6] This is not to say, however, that it is unreasonable to rely upon such approximation methods. The alternative of explicit reasoning is too slow for many practical purposes, and rough approximations often suffice for the purposes for which we need the probabilities.

Much ordinary inductive inference is also the result of Q&I modules. Inductive inference *can* Be carried out ratiocinatively—by explicit reasoning from explicitly stated data—and scientists try to do that. But

---

[5] Tversky and Kahneman [1974].

[6] Tversky [1977].

this requires the storage and processing of huge databases, which is exhaustive of system resources and computationally expensive. Only in science do we tend to accumulate a large body of data, peruse it, and then engage in explicit inductive reasoning about it. In ordinary life, we tend to employ procedures that allow us to use the data as we acquire them and then forget the data, forming provisional generalizations that we modify as we go along. This is much more efficient, but it is subject to pitfalls having to do with the possibility of non-independent data that cannot be judged non-independent because they are no longer recalled.[7]

Thus far I have talked about Q&I modules only for belief formation, but Q&I modules are equally important in practical cognition. In addition to the practical Q&I modules that will be discussed below, I suspect that in at least some cases, emotions constitute Q&I modules for practical reasoning. For instance, being afraid of tigers initiates quick avoidance responses without our having to think about it—a very useful reaction for anyone who is likely to encounter tigers unexpectedly. Embarrassment, indignation, and so forth, may similarly be practical Q&I modules whose purpose is to supplement explicit practical reasoning in social situations. This provides a computational role for these emotions and throws light on why human beings are subject to them. This account is not applicable to all emotions. For instance, it seems unlikely that depression can be viewed as a practical Q&I module. But perhaps what this shows is that what have been called "emotional states" constitute a grab bag of different kinds of states playing different roles in human beings.

The advantage of Q&I modules is speed. The advantage of ratiocination, on the other hand, is extreme flexibility. It seems that ratiocination can in principle deal with any kind of situation, but it is slow. In complicated situations we may have no applicable Q&I modules, in which case we have no choice but to undertake explicit reasoning about the situation. In other cases, human beings accept the output of the Q&I modules *unless* they have some explicit reason for not doing so. Ratiocination is used to monitor the output and override it when necessary. In sum, the role of ratiocination should be (1) to deal with cases to which Q&I modules do not apply and (2) to monitor and override the output of Q&I modules as necessary. A rational agent can be viewed as a bundle of Q&I modules with ratiocination sitting on top and tweaking the output as necessary.

---

[7] This will be discussed further in chapter 2.

A cognitive agent could be devoid of ratiocination. Its cognition could consist entirely of Q&I modules. It is quite possible that many moderately sophisticated animals work in this way. I will take the defining characteristic of rationality to be the supremacy of ratiocination over Q&I modules. A *fully rational agent* is one in which ratiocination has total overall control. This is not to denigrate the importance of Q&I modules. It is doubtful that any agent could survive in a hostile world relying upon ratiocination as its exclusive means of cognition, but what sets rational agents apart from others is that ratiocination provides the court of last appeal. Given time to make the appeal, the agent will direct its activity in accordance with the pronouncements of ratiocination insofar as these differ from the pronouncements of its Q&I modules. We can divide rationality into *epistemic rationality* and *practical rationality*. In a *fully epistemically rational agent*, epistemic reasoning takes ultimate precedence over Q&I modules in belief formation, and in a *fully practically rational agent*, practical reasoning takes ultimate precedence over Q&I modules in directing activity. It will become apparent that human beings are closer to being fully epistemically rational than they are to being fully practically rational.

5. The Logical Structure of Practical Rationality

Situation-Likings

The design objective of rational cognition is to facilitate the agent's survival by implementing the doxastic-conative loop, that is, by directing the agent's activity so as to make the world more to the agent's liking. What the agent likes, in this sense, is its total (token) situation-at-a-time. It likes "the way things are". I will refer to these as *situation-likings*. We can, accordingly, evaluate a system of cognition in terms of its probable success in bringing about situations that are to the agent's liking. In doing this we are taking an "external" or "instrumental" perspective on cognition. We are viewing cognition from the design stance. I will argue that a considerable amount of the structure of rationality can be elicited as providing the only apparent solutions to various logical and feasibility problems that arise in the course of trying to design a rational agent that satisfies this design specification.

Situation-likings provide the ultimate starting point for rational deliberation. These are not representational states—the agent need not be thinking about the way things are. Situation-liking is a feeling rather than a propositional attitude. Instead of saying that a rational agent seeks to make its situation more to its liking, the same point could probably be made by saying that the agent seeks to make itself happier, or seeks pleasure. I have avoided these more traditional formulations because the terms "happiness" and "pleasure" have connotations not intended by the theory. Situation-liking is perhaps best described as a "pro-attitude" toward one's current situation. This is explanatory only insofar as it is understood as pointing toward a fuller functional explanation of situation-likings, and that is the way they ultimately should be understood. The claim is simply that *there is* a mental state, here called "situation-liking", that plays a certain functional role in practical cognition, and the rest of the theory of practical cognition fills out the description of that functional role. It will emerge below that, as human beings, we have introspective access to situation-likings. This access gives us a grasp of them that is largely independent of their functional role and makes them more familiar to us than if we simply had to postulate them as "unobserved states that play a certain role in cognition".

An agent's liking or disliking for its current situation is affected by its beliefs about that situation. In trying to improve its situation, it is trying to render more likable the way the situation *actually is*—not just the way the situation is believed to be. This introduces a complication in the doxastic-conative loop. The agent seeks to render its situation more likable, not just better liked. The objective is to change the situation so that it would be better liked *if* the agent had true beliefs about all the relevant aspects of it. I will express this by saying that the agent seeks to improve the "objective likability" of its situation.

I have avoided formulating the objective of rationality as one of "maximizing" the likability of its situation, because I do not want to assume that there is a maximally likable alteration of every situation. Rather, a rational agent considers various ways of altering its situation and chooses between them on the basis of their comparative likabilities. There may always be other, more likable alternatives, but rationality cannot require an agent to think of all of them. Resource constraints make that impossible. Rationality just requires an agent to engage in a "rationally satisfactory search". I will say much more about this later, but it should be obvious even at this early stage of the investigation that such a search need not (indeed, cannot) be exhaustive.

Plans
As I shall use the term, *to live the good life* is to live so that, insofar as possible, the situation one is in is likable. Practical cognition seeks to

direct the agent in its pursuit of the good life. It does this by selecting and executing courses of action that are likely to contribute to this objective. Such a course of action is a *plan*.

Planning aims at the construction or discovery of plans whose execution is likely to put the agent in a situation more likable than the one it would otherwise be in. An agent may be faced with a choice between several plans, each likely to improve the agent's situation. In choosing among them, the agent must balance their likelihood of improving its situation against the degree of improvement they make likely. More generally, in evaluating a plan, an agent should ideally consider each possible outcome and how likable it would be, and weight the outcome proportional to the agent's estimate of the probability of that being the actual outcome. To use standard mathematical terminology, plans should be evaluated in terms of the mathematical expectation of the likability of the situation resulting from adopting the plan. In thus evaluating a plan, an agent is never in a position to predict what (infinitely specific) situation token will result from its execution. All that can be predicted is that, with various probabilities, certain *types* of situations will result, the types being defined in terms of their features. The plan is evaluated by evaluating those different situation types and forming a weighted average, weighting each according to the agent's estimate of the probability that it will be the situation type resulting from executing the plan. It should be emphasized, however, that this is the *ideal* of plan evaluation. Resource constraints often force a real agent to compromise on this ideal.

Expected Likabilities

To evaluate plans in this way, an agent must first be able to evaluate situation types. This leads to a kind of type/token problem. The likes and dislikes that define the goal of practical reasoning pertain to situation tokens, but the reasoning itself can proceed only in terms of situation types. Such reasoning is made possible by the fact that our liking or disliking a situation token is caused by general features of the situation. For example, after a strenuous hike into a beautiful mountain valley, being hungry and tired disposes me toward disliking the current situation, but being in a spectacular place disposes me toward liking it. The only way a rational agent can pursue likable situation tokens is by identifying features causally relevant to their being liked or disliked and then pursuing or avoiding those features. The objective of practical reasoning is to render the actual situation token likable (or as likable as possible), but the only way to do this is to try to ensure that it has features that tend to render situation tokens likable.[8] Accordingly, a situation type must be evaluated in terms of its "expected likability", i.e., the mathematical expectation of the degree of liking of situation tokens of that type.[9] Only by employing such evaluations can practical reasoning aim at rendering the actual situation token likable.

The general goal of rationality is to improve the likability of the agent's situation. For this to be well-defined, all we need is a comparative relation of liking one situation token more than another. But now we find that the only way a rational agent can attempt to improve the likability of its situation is by reasoning about situation types in terms of their expected likabilities. This introduces a serious complication. In order for the expected likability of a situation type to be well defined, it is no longer sufficient to have a comparative relation of situation-liking; it must be possible to assign numerical values to the degree of liking an agent has for its current situation. That there are such numbers does not seem particularly problematic because the degree of liking is a physical parameter of some sort that plays a certain role in the agent's cognitive architecture. However, there remains a problem of "scale". Mathematical expectations require not just numerical measures but *cardinal* measures. The result of adding or averaging such measures must make sense. This is not guaranteed by the mere existence of a measure. For example, given one measure of the degree of situation-

---

[8] Philip Pettit [1991] makes similar observations, although he identifies likes with desires.

[9] The expected likability of a situation type is a weighted average of the likabilities of situation tokens of that type, whereby the weighting is determined by the probability of tokens of the type being liked to any particular degree. If we make the simplifying assumption that there are just finitely many possible values $r_1,...,r_n$ for the likability of tokens of type F, then the expected liking of tokens of type F is the sum

$$\sum_{i \leq n} r_i \cdot \text{prob(the likability of } x \text{ is } r_i \text{ / } x \text{ is a situation token of type } F).$$

In the general case the expected-liking is

$$\int_{-\infty}^{+\infty} r \cdot d\text{prob(the likability of } x \text{ is } \leq r \text{ / } x \text{ is a situation token of type } F).$$

liking, the logarithm of that measure is also a measure, but adding
one of the measures is equivalent to multiplying the other. The consequence is that these two measures can yield different comparisons of
expected likability, so that on the first measure, a situation type S_1
may have a higher expected likability than a second situation type S_2,
while on the second measure S_2 will have a higher expected likability
than S_1. In the standard theory of measurement, the problem of choosing
a scale is solved by supposing there is a physical composition process
that corresponds to applying addition to the measurements, but no
such process presents itself in the case of situation-likings. How then
are we to choose a particular measurement scale for situation-likings?

The key to this first problem is to realize that there is a second
problem that must also be solved. If a rational agent is to employ
expected situation-likings in its rational deliberations, it must be able
to form beliefs about their values. This means that it is not enough for
there merely to *exist* a numerical measure of situation-likings. The
agent must also be able to form beliefs about the values of this measure.
The only obvious way to do this is through introspection. An ideally
designed rational agent would be able to introspect its situation-likings,
and the introspection would yield a number that could then be employed
in computing expected situation-likings. Such introspection would
simultaneously solve the scale problem and the problem of forming
beliefs about situation-likings. In effect, the proper scale becomes
defined functionally as the scale used by introspection, and the results
of introspection are then employed in various ways in cognition.

It must be emphasized, however, that the preceding remarks are
about introspection in an "ideally designed" rational agent. Two observations are in order about introspection. First, introspection tends
to be in disfavor these days, partly as a legacy of logical positivism,
and partly as a result of psychological experiments that show introspection to be unreliable as a guide to certain aspects of cognition.[10]
In the latter connection, it should be emphasized that the psychological
investigations focus primarily on our ability to introspect causes. It is
hardly surprising that we are unable to introspect causes, because
causes are not the sort of thing that can ever be perceived—they must
be inferred from simpler facts that can be perceived.[11] I have argued

---

[10] See Lackner and Garrett [1972].

[11] The investigations actually presupposed that the subjects could tell introspectively what they were thinking, because in order to determine what their subjects
were thinking, the investigators simply *asked* them.

[1989] that introspection plays an essential functional role in epistemic cognition, and now I am arguing that it plays an equally essential functional role in practical cognition. As much as one's philosophical prejudices might incline one to eschew introspection, it cannot be done. Introspection is an essential part of cognition.

From a computational point of view, there is nothing mysterious about introspection. For instance, in designing a system of automated reasoning that runs on a digital computer, if a certain numerical parameter is used to guide some bit of reasoning and it is also desirable for the reasoner to have a belief about the value of the parameter, it is computationally trivial to have the reasoning program determine the value of the parameter and insert a belief about it into the reasoner's set of beliefs. That is all that introspection need amount to. There is, accordingly, no obstacle (at this point) to constructing a rational agent capable of the kind of introspection of situation-likings that was described above. But at the same time it must be acknowledged that such introspection is problematic for human beings. We are certainly capable of telling introspectively whether we like our situation, but introspection does not provide us with a number. I suspect that this reflects, in part, the fact that computation in human beings works quite differently from computation in digital computers, and so the introspection of numerical values more difficult. However, a numerical measure of situation-liking must somehow be forthcoming if we are to be able to compute expected situation-likings.[12]

I will now suggest a solution to this problem. It lies in the fact that although introspection does not provide us with a number directly, it does provide us with more than a preference ordering. In a rough sense introspection also apprises us of how much we like or dislike our situation. We might more accurately (but somewhat obscurely) say that introspection provides us with a "quantitative feel". It is quantitative in the sense that it not only generates comparisons—we like one situation better than another—but it also makes sense to ascribe

---

[12] One of the impressive accomplishments of "rational choice theory" is that the methods of Ramsey [1926] and von Neumann and Morgenstern [1944] provide a way of obtaining numerical measures of preference from nonnumerical preference and indifference orderings, and it might be supposed that this provides the solution to the problem of obtaining a cardinal measure of situation-liking. However, this work is not applicable to the present problem. It requires preferences between situation types (specifically, situation types consisting of gambles), but the preferences generated by situation-likings are between situation tokens.

rough magnitudes to the comparisons. We may like situation A a *lot* better than situation B, while liking situation C only a *little* better than situation D. If these quantitative feels are to be used to make sense of expected situation-likings, they must somehow be transformed into numbers. It appears that there is, in fact, a way of doing this, as I will now explain.

We can define a quaternary preference relation $\rho(A,B,C,D)$ as holding iff the agent would prefer having B to having A more than it would prefer having D to having C. The observation that introspection provides us with a quantitative feel can now be expressed less obscurely as the observation that it informs us of this quaternary relation on situation tokens. A binary preference relation can be defined in terms of ρ by saying that B is preferred to A iff $\rho(A,B,A,A)$ holds. An ordinal measure of situation-liking is simply a function $u(x)$ such that for any x and y, x is preferred to y iff $u(x) > u(y)$. If we make reasonable assumptions about binary preference, this ensures that infinitely many ordinal measures of situation-liking exist. The scale problem is then the problem of choosing a "privileged" ordinal measure to use in computing expected likabilities. This can be done by requiring an appropriate measure $u(x)$ also to represent the quaternary preference relation, in the sense that for any x,y,z,w, $\rho(x,y,z,w)$ holds iff $u(y)-u(x) > u(w)-u(z)$. Nonlinear transformations of measures will have the effect of reversing quaternary preference relations provided there are "enough" items in the domain of the preference relation, so if we make some reasonable assumptions about the set of possible situation tokens, the result will be that $u(x)$ is uniquely determined up to linear transformation. That is sufficient to yield unique comparisons of expected likabilities.

This is not yet a complete solution to the problem. A complete solution must exhibit the constraints on ρ that guarantee the existence of a cardinal measure, and I am unsure what the precise set of constraints should be. I am going to assume, however, that there is some such set of constraints, and hence expected likability is well-defined.[13]

---

[13] One triple of assumptions that, when added to the ordering assumption, appears to be sufficient is as follows, where '<' symbolizes binary preference between situation tokens:

If Γ and Λ are sets of situation tokens such that for every $x \in \Gamma$ and $y \in \Lambda$, $x < y$, then there is a z such that for every $x \in \Gamma$ and $y \in \Lambda$, $x < z < y$.

The Identification Problem and Feature-Likings

Given a solution to the logical problem of assigning numerical values to situation-likings and thereby rendering expected likabilities well-defined, a rational agent who wants to use these numbers in practical reasoning still faces the problem of identifying features or combinations of features that are causally relevant to situations' being liked or disliked and determining their degree of causal relevance, that is, evaluating their expected likabilities. I will refer to this as the *identification problem*. Let us call these causally relevant features "value-laden features". As I have described it, the identification problem is, in principle, an empirical problem to be solved by epistemic reasoning aimed at discovering how such features and their combinations affect our likings for situation tokens. An ideal rational agent, unconstrained by time or resource limitations, and able to survive in the real world for an extended period of time without engaging in any practical reasoning, could solve this problem in this way and use the resulting solution to drive its subsequent practical reasoning.[14] However, human beings are not ideally situated in the world and do not have the luxury of waiting until they have solved such complex empirical problems before they can begin engaging in practical reasoning for the first time. Nor, most likely, will any rational agent have that luxury. For this reason, human beings do not work in the way described, and it is probably impossible for any real agent to work in this way. This is a feasibility problem. Even if an ideally rational agent could solve this problem by empirical investigation of the causal structure of the world, real agents must take shortcuts vitiating the need to acquire all this theoretical knowledge prior to engaging in practical reasoning. By definition, any such shortcut procedure constitutes a Q&I module.

Exactly how human beings solve this problem is an empirical question requiring psychological investigation. Armchair philosophy cannot

---

For any situation tokens x,y,z such that $x < y$ and $x < z$, there are situation tokens w,v such that $z < w < v$ and $\sim\!\rho(x,y,w,v)$ and $\sim\!\rho(x,y,v,w)$.

For any situation tokens x,y,z such that $x < y$ and $z < y$, there are situation tokens w,v such that $w < v < z$ and $\sim\!\rho(x,y,w,v)$ and $\sim\!\rho(x,y,v,w)$.

However, there may be other sets of assumptions that would be preferable for various reasons.

[14] This may be overly optimistic. Empirical investigation is typically driven by practical reasoning regarding how to find the answers to certain questions. Accordingly, it might be impossible for even an ideal rational agent to acquire the requisite knowledge of expected likabilities before engaging in practical cognition.

provide a definitive answer, but introspection suggests a mechanism. Human beings have the ability to imagine a situation and then exhibit conative responses to the imagined situation. For example, imagining a situation in which I am being torn apart on a torture rack, I exhibit an introspectible dislike for the imagined situation. It is a brute fact about human beings that they have such conative reactions to imagined situations. Their ability to react conatively to imagined situations is essential to their enjoyment of literature, and I have even suggested elsewhere that moral judgments may be based in part on this ability.[15] It is important to recognize that imagined situations are always inherently general. Imagined situations can never incorporate more than finitely many features. As such, our reaction to these imagined situations constitutes a conative response to situation types rather than situation tokens. We might call these *feature-likings*, in contrast to situation-likings, to emphasize that they are conative responses to types rather than tokens, although it is not clear that these two kinds of likings should be regarded as genuinely different kinds of mental states. One can conjecture that the way feature-likings work neurologically is by marshaling the ordinary mechanisms that give rise to situation-likings and applying them to imagined situations, the result being an introspectible liking for an imagined situation *type* rather than a situation token. Human beings employ these introspectible feature-likings to make an intuitive assessment of how much they would like being in situations of the type imagined, that is, to assess expected situation-likings of situation types. There is, however, no logical connection between such introspectible likings for imagined situations and the expected likabilities of the type of situation imagined, so the former cannot provide a logically good reason for the latter. Accordingly, this kind of assessment must be regarded as constituting a Q&I module.

It is a consequence of my stipulative definition of rationality that situation-likings are the basic evaluative states in terms of which plans are to be assessed. However, we could explore an alternative conception of rationality that begins with feature-likings. On this conception a rational agent pursues liked features and seeks to avoid disliked features. This is the conception of rationality underlying contemporary rational choice theory. This approach must provide a solution to several problems. First, we need a mechanism for combining the likings of

---

[15] Pollock [1986a].

individual features to compute a liking for combinations of features. We cannot just sum the individual feature-likings, because features may interact. For instance, I like dill pickles and I like vanilla ice cream, but I do not care much for the combination. Second, a distinction must be made between the "primitive" liking for a combination of features and the "all-things-considered" liking. The former just measures how much the agent likes those features by themselves and independent of their tendencies to be accompanied by or to cause other features. The all-things-considered liking takes such tendencies into account. Notice that plans must be evaluated in terms of the all-things-considered liking for adopting the plan. Typically, the agent's primitive liking for adopting a plan is neutral, and value attaches to the plan only indirectly by way of tendencies that it has to bring about other features the agent likes or dislikes. It looks as if these all-things-considered likings must be computed in terms of expected values, which in turn requires a cardinal measure for primitive feature-likings. The logical, mathematical, and epistemological problems faced by this approach are no less onerous than those that arise from taking situation-likings to be basic.

I see no reason in principle why an agent could not be made to conform to either conception of rationality. The overall structure of the agent would be the same on either conception, but somewhat different mechanisms would be used for evaluating plans. Which sort of agent is a human being? There is reason to believe that the norms of rationality incorporated into the functional description of human cognition give precedence to situation-likings over feature-likings. A feature might seem desirable to a person in the abstract, despite the fact that getting it invariably makes the person unhappy (and not because of concomitant features that the person dislikes). For instance, a person might imagine in the abstract that she would greatly enjoy foreign travel, but observe that whenever she engages in it she is thoroughly bored. Under these circumstances, we would regard it as irrational for her to continue pursuing that feature. This suggests that human beings conform to the first conception of rationality, according to which situation-likings provide the court of last appeal. This is the model of rationality that will be embodied in OSCAR, but the fact that human beings work in this way is not, as far as I can see, a reason for thinking this is a "better" conception of rationality.

Regardless of whether an agent begins with feature-likings or situation-likings, it is still faced with the problem of using those to compute the expected values of plans. This is, in principle, a complex

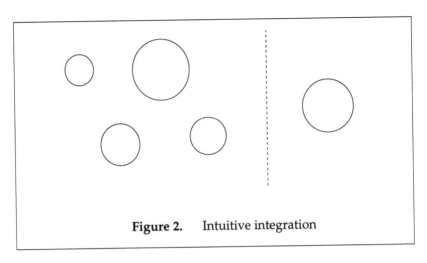

Figure 2.   Intuitive integration

integration problem. The necessity of being able to solve such a problem seems particularly puzzling in the light of the fact that human beings do not generally engage in any such complicated mathematics in the course of making practical decisions. What this indicates is the presence of another, quite important, Q&I module. Human beings are often able to solve integration problems without doing mathematics. Suppose, for instance, that I present you with the array of circles depicted on the left side of figure 2, and ask you to draw a single circle whose size is approximately the average of the given circles. You would have no difficulty drawing a circle approximately the size of that on the right side of figure 2. But how did you do it? You certainly did not measure the circles, compute the areas, average them, and then compute the diameter for the new circle. Furthermore, you can do this exercise just as readily with irregular figures. Human beings have a built-in ability to compare areas without performing precise measurements. Furthermore, the comparisons generate more than an ordinal ranking, because we are able to do things like averaging the areas. This seems to involve a Q&I module that takes non-numerical "analogue" inputs and approximates the results of computations which, in explicit form, involve integration. It is this same ability that is involved in estimating the expected value of a plan. What I referred to earlier as the "quantitative feel" produced by introspection of situation-likings is another instance of "non-numerical analogue outputs" produced by human cognitive mechanisms. It seems likely that the Q&I modules we employ for estimating probabilities produce similar non-numerical outputs, and all of these together are manipulated by Q&I modules that, in effect, solve integration problems. This feature of human cognition turns in part on the fact that introspection of what are in fact real-valued parameters does not provide human cognizers with numbers. This suggests that artificial agents that are not so constrained might be able to solve these integration problems explicitly without relying upon Q&I modules, but this is a matter to be resolved by experimentation.

Plans and Goals
Recall that "to live the good life" is to live so that, insofar as possible, the situation one is in is likable. Rationality is a tool for living the good life. A rational agent directs its activity on the basis of its beliefs about the expected values of combinations of features, trying always to better its situation, that is, render it more likable. It does this by choosing goals whose achievement will have that effect and then selecting and executing courses of action that aim at the achievement of those goals. For the sake of logical uniformity, we can identify goals with combinations of features of situations. Note that these goals need not be feature combinations that the agent values highly. A rational agent may pursue things that it actively dislikes, provided it likes them better than what it already has. Similarly, a rational agent may decline to pursue things it likes, because it likes what it already has better.

An agent tries to achieve goals by designing and executing courses of action aimed at realizing them. Designing such a course of action is *planning*. The simplest planning may involve selecting a single act to perform in order to achieve some readily attainable goal. More complex plans may involve multiple steps, each prescribing an act subject to conditions that may depend upon both the current situation and the outcome of the previous steps of the plan. For example, a plan for driving across town might involve taking one route if the traffic is light and another route if it is heavy. Chapter 6 investigates the logical structure of plans. It is argued there that in their most general form, plans can have all the logical structure of parallel computer programs.

This commonsensical description of planning involves two distinct elements: goals and plans. The relationship between goals and plans is more complicated than might initially be supposed. Goals are chosen on the basis of their expected likabilities, but the mere fact that a plan successfully achieves such a goal is not sufficient to make it a good plan. The situation token that results from executing the plan must invariably exemplify more features than those included in the combination of features constituting the goal, and some of these may reverse the likability of the situation. For example, it may be that, in the abstract, I would like being rich. But it may also be that the only way I could become rich is by doing things I would despise doing, and I would not like a situation that includes my being rich as a result of my doing those things.

Goals are chosen *before* plans are adopted for achieving them, so goals can be selected only on the basis of expected likabilities in the abstract. Accordingly, the expected value of a plan may not be a function of the abstract values of the goals it aims at achieving. So what use are goals? Why not dispense with them altogether? Perhaps a rational agent should just survey possible plans and select those having high expected values. Goals would play no role in this process.

This suggestion, however, runs afoul of feasibility considerations. The construction and evaluation of plans is a difficult and time-consuming process. An ideal rational agent, unconstrained by time or resource limitations, could systematically generate all possible plans and select for execution those having high expected values. However, agents subject to realistic limitations must focus their attention more efficiently on plans that are likely to be relevant to their current situation. They do not have the luxury of being able to pick systematically through an infinite list of plans, most of which are irrelevant and of no value anyway.

It is useful to compare planning with automated theorem proving. It has often been observed that it would be possible to build an automated theorem prover that systematically generates all possible proofs in the predicate calculus. Then if we want to know whether some particular formula is a theorem of the predicate calculus, we just wait and see whether a proof of it is generated. This is the so-called British Museum algorithm. Such a theorem prover would be hopelessly inefficient for any practical purposes. By contrast, human reasoning is *interest-driven* in the sense that the course of our reasoning is determined in part by what questions we are trying to answer. If we want to know what time it is in Moscow, we reason quite differently than if we want to know the sum of 14 and 87. In other words, our reasoning involves a control structure that makes it more directly germane to the questions we want to answer.

A similar control structure is required for practical reasoning. A scattergun approach to planning is as impractical as the British Museum algorithm. Goals focus planning in two ways. First, if a plan is able to attain a goal having an expected likability higher than the expected likability of the situation that would otherwise result, that creates a presumption in favor of the plan having a positive expected value, because the outcome of the plan will be a situation of a general type that tends to be better liked than situations of the type that would otherwise result. Thus by directing planning at such goals, the rational agent is guaranteed to focus its attention on plans that *tend* to be good. Second, whether a particular plan is likely to achieve a specific goal is a factual question of the sort that falls within the purview of epistemic cognition. Accordingly, the construction of plans aimed at specific goals is an exercise of epistemic cognition. As such, it can be directed by the general control structures governing interest-driven epistemic reasoning, and need not proceed at random. This would not be possible unless planning aimed at specific goals.

To summarize, feasibility constraints require the use of goals to direct the course of planning. Goals can be evaluated only in terms of expected likabilities and without reference to any way of achieving the goals. This guarantees that the plans that achieve goals having high expected values will tend to be good ones, in the sense of producing situation tokens the rational agent likes. However, once produced, plans must be evaluated not just in terms of the values of their goals but in terms of all predictable features of their outcomes.[16] In other words, the expected values of plans must be computed in terms of the difference between the expected likability of the situation type that consists of adopting the plan and the expected likability of the situation type that consists of not adopting the plan. (This will be discussed further in chapter 6.)

Goals and Desires

Adopting a goal initiates planning for its achievement. It does this by passing interest in discovering such plans to the system of epistemic cognition. When an agent selects a goal, it comes to *want* or *desire* it. Desires constitute a functionally (and, in humans, introspectibly) different state from likings or valuings. Their purpose is to encode goals. Their functional role is to move the agent to act or plan, or more generally to initiate practical cognition.

Goals are adopted as a result of being judged suitable. The suitability of a goal is a function of the agent's current situation, because goals

---

[16] In chapter 6, this is handled by expanding the set of goals for a plan to include all value-laden features whose probabilites are known to be affected by the plan.

are chosen in an attempt to better that situation, rendering it more to the agent's liking. It is to be emphasized that goals are not the same thing as feature combinations believed to have high expected likabilities. As indicated above, an agent's goal may be to achieve something it dislikes as long as it likes it better than what would happen otherwise. Suitability is a matter of relative expected value rather than absolute expected value.

A rational agent should adopt a goal whenever it is judged suitable in the preceding sense,[17] but this does not guarantee that anything will actually happen as a result of adopting the goal because the agent may not have any information at its disposal that will enable it to make progress in planning for the achievement of the goal. Typically, progress in planning results only when the agent recognizes an opportunity to improve its lot. For example, I like eating ice cream, but I do not spend all my days plotting how to find and eat some ice cream. As a general rule, I engage in planning for the eating of ice cream only when I encounter a concrete opportunity for doing so. For instance, finding ice cream available as dessert at a dinner party may cause me to fabricate the plan to say "yes" when my hostess asks whether I would like some. Of course, sometimes we create our own opportunities. If there is no ice cream readily available and I want some badly, I might make my own, but under ordinary circumstances a plan to achieve the eating of ice cream in this way would not be a good plan because the effort involved would outweigh the benefits achieved.

On the preceding account, goals are adopted (desires are formed) as a result of beliefs about their expected values, and these beliefs are produced by epistemic cognition. There is a problem here, however. How does the agent know which combinations of features to evaluate as potential goals? If features are selected randomly for evaluation, few will turn out to be suitable goals. An agent must have a more efficient mechanism for *proposing* potential goals. The agent can then go on to evaluate these potential goals and decide which to adopt. This amounts to a control structure for that part of an agent's reasoning devoted to the evaluation of potential goals.

---

[17] This oversimplifies a bit. Sometimes a goal that would be suitable in this sense is nevertheless rejected on the grounds that it is not achievable. For example, a person might like being ruler of the world or having a love affair with a movie star, but a rational agent will not usually form an active desire for these things because it recognizes that they are unattainable. I attribute this filtering of desires to the action of reflexive reasoners, in the sense of section 8, and not to the basic planar structure of a rational agent.

A second problem, analogous to some already discussed, is that a real agent cannot wait until it has acquired a lot of knowledge about the causal structure of the world before it begins to adopt goals and engage in practical cognition. Accordingly, a real agent must incorporate a Q&I module for desire formation, which gets practical cognition started without the need for large amounts of theoretical knowledge.

These two problems can be solved simultaneously by (1) having a Q&I module that proposes potential goals and leads to their default adoption, and (2) giving ratiocination the power to evaluate these goals explicitly and override their adoption if they are judged unsuitable. This amounts to having *overridable* dispositions to form desires. I will refer to these as *optative dispositions*. In order to enable desire formation in situations of minimal knowledge, some of these optative dispositions must be built-in. Others can then be acquired through conditioning. For example, we have built-in optative dispositions to try to alleviate our hunger, to try to avoid pain, and to pursue pleasure. We have a number of such "hedonistic" dispositions that give rise to desires automatically, without our having to engage in any reasoning about their expected values. Conditioning can then lead to the establishment of new optative dispositions. When a combination of features tends to be followed by the satisfaction of desires, a conditioning mechanism can use that to create a new disposition. Thus we may come to desire money, or we may acquire the disposition to desire to read an interesting book when we hear about it, or the disposition to desire to see certain kinds of new films.

The general mechanism of built-in and conditioned optative dispositions constitutes a Q&I module for desire formation. In a rational agent, there must also be a purely ratiocinative basis for desire formation. The sole ratiocinative basis for desiring something should be the belief that it is a suitable goal. In a fully rational agent, ratiocination must have the power to override any Q&I modules. Accordingly, if an optative disposition produces a desire in me but I have the belief that I would not like having the desire satisfied (i.e., its relative expected value is negative), this *should* dispel the desire. In human beings, this does not always happen, as is illustrated by compulsions. For example, a compulsive smoker may believe that the expected value of smoking is negative but desire to smoke nonetheless. In a fully rational agent, that belief would cancel the desire to smoke. Obviously, human beings are less than fully rational in this respect. Such beliefs may serve to depress the strength of the desire, but they do not dispel the desire entirely.

Conversely, if a fully rational agent believes that some combination of features has a high relative expected situation-liking, that should automatically produce a desire. Failure to form the requisite desire is a mark of irrationality, but people are sometimes irrational in precisely this way. For example, I enjoy skiing, but for some reason I can rarely get myself to go skiing. I know that if I went, I would enjoy it, and I am often in a position where I can take a day off and go skiing if I so choose, but I cannot get myself motivated to do it. In other words, despite having all of the requisite beliefs, I lack the desire. This is irrational but perhaps not terribly unusual. Once again, human beings are not fully rational agents.

Intentions, Plans, and Instrumental Desires

Desires provide the trigger for planning. Constructing a plan is a matter of epistemic cognition. Whether a plan will, with a certain probability, achieve some goal is a factual question of the sort that falls within the purview of epistemic cognition. So is the evaluation of the plan in terms of expected situation-likings. However, once all that has been done, the agent still has to decide what plan to adopt. A satisfactory plan must be at least minimally good, in the sense that the expected situation-liking of the situation type consisting of adopting the plan is at least as great as the expected situation-liking of the situation type consisting of not adopting the plan. Equivalently, the plan must have a non-negative expected value. However, this is not automatically sufficient to make it rational for an agent to adopt the plan, because sometimes the agent will have to choose between several competing plans, and one of the competitors may be better than the others. In that case, the optimal competitor should be adopted. The logic of such choices is more complicated than it may seem at first. (This constitutes the subject matter of chapter 5.) When, as a result of such deliberation, a plan is adopted, this must be encoded in the agent somehow. The states that do this are *intentions*. The functional role of intentions is to encode plan adoption.[18]

A plan is typically a "partial" solution to the problem of achieving a goal.[19] For instance, given the goal of being in Los Angeles on Friday, I may plan to fly on Friday morning. However, in order to

---

[18] This observation was perhaps first made by Bratman [1987].

[19] This is a familiar observation in AI planning theory. It is due originally to Sacerdotti [1975].

execute this plan, I may have to engage in further practical reasoning. I will have to make plans about when and where to buy a ticket, what airline to use, what flight to take, and so forth. When an agent adopts a partial plan some of whose steps require further planning, something must initiate that further planning. The state having this functional role is what we call an *instrumental desire*. It is a desire because its role is to initiate further planning, but it is not a desire produced by any of the mechanisms so far discussed. That is, it is the result of neither optative dispositions nor beliefs about the relative values of potential goals. Let us call desires produced in either of those ways *primitive desires*. Primitive desires provide the starting points for planning. In contrast to primitive desires, instrumental desires are produced by practical reasoning itself. Whenever a plan is adopted, rationality dictates that the agent form the desire to execute the plan steps at the appropriate time, and these desires in turn act either as triggers for action if the plan step is one that can be executed directly or as triggers for further practical reasoning. (The details of this will be investigated in chapter 7.)

Action Initiation

Once some plans are adopted there must still be something further that gets an agent to act. There is a temptation to think of the adoption of a plan as beginning a process that grinds inexorably to the execution of the plan unless the plan is subsequently retracted (i.e., unless we change our minds). But things don't really work that way. Adopting a plan is not like setting a train moving on rigid rails. Although I plan to do something and never explicitly change my mind, the plan may never be executed just because I never feel like executing it. There may always be other things I want to do more, including doing nothing. For example, I might adopt the plan to go to the grocery store this afternoon. As the afternoon progresses, it occurs to me at various times that I planned to go to the grocery store, but each time my reaction is, "Oh, I don't feel like going just now. I will do it later." Finally the afternoon is over, and I have not gone, but there was never a point at which I explicitly retracted my plan to go. I just didn't do it. Furthermore, not only lethargy can keep plans from being executed. I may have planned to go to the grocery store, but I got engrossed in writing this chapter, and every time I thought about going to the grocery store I decided that I would rather keep writing and go later. Eventually the afternoon was over, and I had not gone.

The possibility of such procrastination arises from the fact that planning typically leaves the scheduling of plan steps rather indefinite.

The advantage of this is that it minimizes conflicts between adopted plans and unforeseen opportunities that arise later. But the disadvantage is that some further mechanism is required for deciding when to execute a plan step.

The basis for such a mechanism lies in a distinction between two kinds of primitive desires—desires for the future and desires for the present. Only the former can be the subject of planning. You cannot plan for the present. Planning takes time, and you cannot plan ahead for a situation that is already here. In order to play any role in directing action, desires for the present must be desires *to do* something. I will refer to such desires as *present-tense action desires*.

Recall that a reactive agent guides its actions solely on the basis of built-in and conditioned reflexes generating immediate action. However, there is a problem regarding reactive agents that I have so far ignored: more than one reflex can be triggered simultaneously, and it may be impossible to perform the actions dictated by them all. A reactive agent must have some mechanism for adjudicating disputes in such cases. The only obvious mechanism is to assign strengths to reflexes, and when two reflexes compete, the stronger wins. We can, at least metaphorically, think of such reflexes as generating present-tense action desires, and in deciding what to do when there is a conflict, all the reactive agent can do is act on the desire that is strongest, that is, do what it most wants to do.

An agent capable of planning can do better. It can, in many cases, adjust its plans so as to avoid such conflicts. However, planning can never entirely replace reacting to present-tense action desires. Planning is applicable only insofar as we can predict what is likely to befall us. If the unexpected happens, it may be too late to plan for it, and all we can do is react. Basic reflexes like withdrawing from pain are going to be essential ingredients in any rational agent. Ratiocination can only supplement such pre-rational mechanisms.

Just as a reactive agent can experience conflicting reflexes, a rational agent can encounter conflicts between plans and reflexes. The plan to retrieve a valuable object that fell into a fire may conflict with the reflex of withdrawing one's hand from the fire. Sometimes the plan wins out. This requires that there be an adjudication mechanism in a rational agent that can choose not only between actions prescribed by present-tense action desires but also actions prescribed by plans. This must be done in terms of the value of some parameter of the actions between which the agent is choosing. In the case of actions prescribed by present-tense action desires, the relevant parameter is how much the agent wants to perform the action—in other words, the strength of the desire. Accordingly, we can use the same language in talking about the parameter attaching to actions prescribed by plans. The agent *wants*, more or less strongly, to perform such an action, and it can decide which action to perform by selecting the one it wants most strongly to perform.[20] How much an agent wants to perform such an action can be regarded as the strength of the agent's desire to perform it, where this desire is the instrumental desire produced by adopting the plan.

The degree to which an agent wants to perform an action prescribed by a primitive present-tense action desire is determined by the optative disposition producing that desire. There must also be a mechanism determining the degree to which an agent wants to perform an action prescribed by a plan. Ideally, this should result in choices being made so that the plans having higher expected values are the ones that get executed. The way to do this is to have the strength of an instrumental desire correspond to the expected value of the plan. More accurately, when a plan prescribes a sequence of acts and A is one of those acts, let the *tail* of the plan relative to A be the remainder of the plan after the steps preceding A have been executed. The tail of a plan is itself a plan, and we can talk about its expected value in the same way we talk about the expected value of any plan. Once the first part of a plan has been executed, the degree to which an agent wants to execute the next step should correspond to the expected value of the tail of the plan relative to that next step.

Given this understanding of degrees of wanting to perform actions, my proposal is that a rational agent should, at any given time, perform the action it most wants to perform. This amounts to marshaling the pre-rational machinery of the reactive agent and extending it to the results of planning. However, there are what appear initially to be counterexamples to this account. Sometimes it is rational to postpone doing what I most want if I know that I can do it later and something else I want to do cannot be postponed. Suppose I am out of the house, and I plan to telephone a friend when I get back and before she leaves for work. There will be only a short interval in which I can do that. As I am driving home, I become increasingly hungry and want to have lunch. If I had to choose between (1) eating lunch and not calling my friend and (2) calling my friend and not eating lunch, I

---

[20] Jean Hampton has pointed out to me that this is essentially a Hobbesian view of deliberation. See *The Leviathan*, chapter 6, paragraph 29.

would unhesitatingly choose lunch. So it seems that I want to eat lunch more than I want to call my friend. But what I may actually do is postpone lunch just long enough to call my friend, because I know that I will not be able to call her later. This appears to be a counterexample to the account just proposed for the rational initiation of action.

However, this putative counterexample confuses the strength of the instrumental desire to eat lunch (my present-tense action desire) with the strength of my primitive desire to eat lunch. It is quite true that my primitive desire to eat lunch is stronger than my primitive desire to telephone my friend. That is what is shown by the observation that if I had to choose between them, I would choose lunch. However, in the technical sense defined above, the strength of my wanting to eat lunch and the strength of my wanting to telephone my friend are determined not by the strengths of the primitive desires but rather by the expected values of the plans in which they are embedded. What actually happens is that I begin by adopting the plan to telephone my friend when I get home. Then I get hungry. I consider two plans. The first is to eat lunch immediately upon returning home. The second is to telephone my friend immediately upon returning home and then eat lunch. The second plan is preferable to the first, so it is adopted. As the execution of that plan unfolds, telephoning my friend is the first action mandated. It thus becomes a candidate for performance. At that point, eating lunch has not even been prescribed by an adopted plan. That step will not be prescribed until after I have telephoned my friend. Eating lunch is prescribed only by a primitive desire to alleviate my hunger forthwith, but that desire (we can suppose) is weaker than my instrumental desire to call my friend, because the latter derives from a plan for both eating lunch and calling my friend. Accordingly, I will choose to telephone my friend first, and then to have lunch.

6. An Overview of Practical Rationality

Approaching rationality from the design stance suffices to generate a great deal of the structure governing how a rational agent must function. The account has been rather complex, so let me provide a brief recapitulation:

- The objective of rationality is to live so that, insofar as possible, one likes the situations one is in—in other words, seek to maximize the likability of one's situation, where this is the degree to which one would like one's situation if one had true beliefs about all the relevant aspects of it. Thus **situation-likings** become the fundamental states in terms of which rationality is to be understood.

- A rational agent tries to accomplish this objective by discovering courses of action (plans) whose execution will result in its liking its situation better. Adopted plans are stored as **intentions**.
- In discovering such plans, the agent must reason about situations in terms of general features of them. The prediction that the execution of a plan will result in a situation the agent likes must be based on general beliefs about the expected likability of general types of situations. In particular, the agent must assess plans in terms of beliefs about the **expected likability** of the situation type consisting of adopting the plan.
- Evaluating the expected likabilities of situation types is an extremely difficult problem. Any agent subject to realistic constraints must use Q&I modules to help it solve this problem. At least in human beings, these generate **feature-likings**, which are used non-ratiocinatively to produce estimates of expected likabilities.
- In searching for plans having high expected values, some mechanism is required to focus the search on plans that are antecedently likely to have high expected values. This is done by selecting as goals highly valued situation types and then searching for plans to achieve these goals. The search can then be constrained by using familiar techniques like goal reduction. Adopted goals are encoded as **desires**.
- Rational action is not just a matter of mechanically executing adopted plans. The agent must decide when to execute a plan and must choose among competing actions available at any given time. A rational agent does this by forming **present-tense action desires**, which are desires to perform currently available actions. Some of these desires are produced by optative dispositions, and others are derivative from adopted plans. Rationality then dictates performing the action prescribed by the strongest such desire.

Philosophical theories of rationality have been based primarily upon the belief/desire psychology inherited from Hume. One of the simple consequences of the preceding account is that such a psychology is inadequate for the construction of a rational agent. A rational agent must have beliefs, situation-likings, feature-likings, intentions, primitive desires, instrumental desires, and present-tense action desires. Each of these states plays an importantly different functional role in rationality. It is particularly important to distinguish likings from desires, because most theories of rationality fail to make this distinction. The role of desires is to encode the goals whose adoption initiates acting and planning; the role of likings is to provide both the comparisons used in selecting the goals that supply the focus for planning and the basis for evaluating plans.

One of the most important consequences of this account is that only an ideally situated agent, unconstrained by limited computational resources and able to engage in large amounts of epistemic reasoning without doing any practical reasoning, could rely upon ratiocination for all of its practical cognition. Any real agent must make heavy use of Q&I modules in order to produce practical conclusions within a reasonable amount of time. In other words, ratiocination is not a general solution to cognition. Rationality must be built on top of pre-rational mechanisms. In a fully rational agent, the output of these Q&I modules is in principle correctable by ratiocination, although it is doubtful that human beings are always capable of making full corrections.

Practical cognition begins with various kinds of evaluative attitudes. Philosophers have disagreed about whether these evaluative attitudes are themselves subject to rational assessment.[21] It is a consequence of the present theory of rationality that primitive desires, instrumental desires, feature-likings, and present-tense action desires are all subject to rational evaluation. Feature-likings are produced by a special mechanism, but their purpose is to serve as a Q&I module for finding situation types having high expected situation-likings. If it is ascertained that the expected likability of a situation type is not high, then a fully rational agent will either give up the feature-liking or ignore it in practical reasoning. Obviously, instrumental desires can be criticized by criticizing the plan from which they are derived. Perhaps more surprising, primitive desires are also criticizable. Primitive desires can be produced either by optative dispositions or by ratiocination on the basis of the belief that a situation type has a high relative expected value. In the latter case, the desire is criticizable if the grounds for the

---

[21] Nagel [1970] and Gauthier [1986] both argue that desires can be criticized rationally. Parfit [1984] maintains that they cannot.

belief are criticizable. If instead the desire is produced by an optative disposition, then (as we have already seen) it can be criticized if it is ascertained that the object of the desire does not have a high relative expected value (you wouldn't like it if you had it). Some present-tense action desires are derived from plans, and these can obviously be criticized by criticizing the planning. But others are produced nonratiocinatively by optative dispositions, and it may seem that they are immune from criticism. However, recall that the objective of practical cognition is to help the agent live a good life, where that consists of living in such a way that the situation tokens one is in are likable. The pre-rational optative dispositions that produce present-tense action desires can still be evaluated by asking whether they contribute to this goal. The present-tense action desires produced by these dispositions do not themselves have any automatic claim to fulfillment. It is particularly obvious that optative dispositions produced by conditioning can be harmful when judged by this standard. If it is determined that a particular desire of this sort does not contribute to leading the good life, that *should* serve to dispel it. If an agent retains that desire despite having this belief, the desire is irrational. (Of course, this is one respect in which human beings are not fully rational. Acquiring such beliefs does not automatically dispel the irrational desires.)

On the theory of rationality constructed here, reasoning includes not just epistemic reasoning but also practical reasoning wherein desires are adopted on the basis of beliefs about the expected situation-likings of potential goals, intentions are adopted on the basis of beliefs about the relative values of plans, and actions are produced by choosing the strongest present-tense action desires. In contrast, the traditional Humean picture of reasoning recognizes only epistemic reasoning. Such a restriction seems to me to be unduly narrow. All of these state transitions between beliefs, desires, and intentions are dictated by the functional architecture of a rational agent. They are part of the makeup of a rational agent, so why not call them "reasoning"? They are certainly part of rationality, and insofar as an agent fails to perform these state transitions, the agent is subject to the criticism that it is being irrational in the sense of not behaving as a fully rational agent would behave. We can decline to call these state transitions "reasoning" if we like, but that can be no more than a linguistic convention and does not indicate any deep difference between these state transitions and those involved in epistemic reasoning. As far as I can see, they are all on a par as being part of the functional description of a fully rational agent.

7. Interfacing Epistemic and Practical Cognition

Epistemic cognition produces the beliefs used by the rational agent in the course of practical cognition. This includes beliefs about the nature of the agent's current situation and about the general structure of the world. These beliefs are used in choosing goals, evaluating and adopting plans, and directing activity on the basis of those plans and present-tense action desires.

The distinction between epistemic and practical cognition is a useful one, but I doubt that it can be made absolutely precise. The difficulty is that epistemic and practical cognition are highly interdependent. Within philosophy, it has tended to be the case that either epistemic cognition is discussed in isolation from practical cognition, or the attempt is made to reduce epistemic cognition to practical cognition by identifying it with practical cognition about what to believe.[22] But neither strategy can be completely successful. First, practical cognition must be based upon beliefs about the agent's current situation. For instance, it may require a prior estimate of the probability of actions having different outcomes. Such beliefs are the result of epistemic cognition. Thus any practical cognition must presuppose prior epistemic cognition. This has the immediate consequence that epistemic cognition cannot be viewed as just a special kind of practical cognition, because that would lead to an infinite regress.

By and large, epistemologists have tried to ignore practical cognition in their investigations of epistemic cognition, but that cannot be entirely satisfactory either. The whole point of epistemic cognition is to help the agent solve practical problems. Epistemic cognition comes into play only in response to questions posed by practical cognition. It does not proceed at random; it is interest-driven in the sense that it tries to answer specific questions. It begins with questions posed by practical cognition. In trying to answer these questions, epistemic cognition may be led to pose other questions for itself that are only indirectly connected with practical cognition, but ultimately it must be practical cognition that directs the interests of epistemic cognition. I will take the questions posed by practical cognition to comprise the set of *ultimate-epistemic-interests*.

The connections between epistemic cognition and practical cognition do not stop there. It has often been insufficiently appreciated by

---

[22] An example of the latter is Levi [1980]. This has also been urged in AI by Jon Doyle [1988 and 1988a].

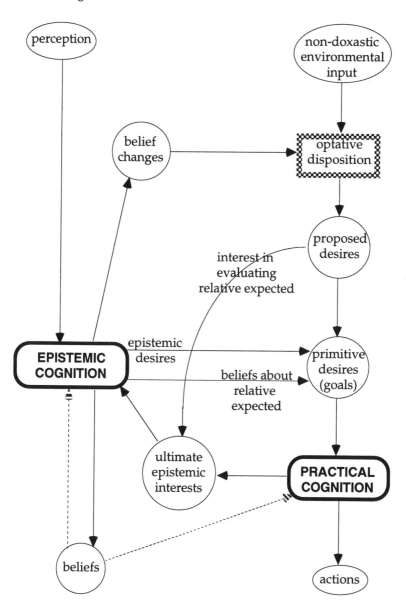

Figure 3. Flow of data in ratiocination

epistemologists that epistemic cognition will be unable to answer many of the questions posed by practical cognition just by thinking. If I want to know what time it is, I cannot just think about it—I have to look at a clock. Generally, answering practically motivated questions requires investigating the world empirically. This requires *taking action*. The actions can range from focusing my eyes, to examining the contents of my immediate surroundings, to asking someone else a question, to engaging in a multi-year research project involving high-energy linear accelerators. These are activities of the sort directed by practical cognition. So we get a loop from practical cognition through epistemic cognition and back to practical cognition. The mechanism for this involves epistemic cognition's producing new goals for practical cognition to try to achieve—goals of acquiring certain kinds of knowledge. Goals are encoded in desires, and I will refer to these epistemically driven desires as *epistemic desires*. Given an epistemic desire, practical cognition can produce reasoning about how to acquire the desired knowledge. That practical cognition may pose further questions for epistemic cognition, which may produce further epistemic desires, and so on.

The preceding observations can be combined into the general architecture of rationality that is diagrammed in figure 3. Circles represent databases, and rectangles represent data-processing modules. Solid arrows indicate the flow of new data that drives the operation of the modules, and dashed arrows indicate the retrieval of previously stored data. Expanded versions of the diagram will be constructed as the book progresses. Epistemic and practical cognition include both ratiocination and the operation of Q&I modules. These are of equal importance in the construction of a rational agent. However, I have more to say about ratiocination, so that will be the main topic of discussion as this investigation progresses.

8. Reasons, Arguments, and Defeasibility

In epistemic reasoning, we adopt new beliefs as a result of either perceptual input or inference from previously held beliefs. In the latter case, the previously held beliefs constitute "good reasons" for believing the conclusions. If we string together the reasoning by which we arrive at a belief via earlier beliefs, the result is an *argument*, so we can regard reasoning as the construction of arguments. This does not mean that the argument is itself an object represented in the agent's thought. Perhaps it would be better to say that the agent *instantiates* an argument. The argument is a record of the state transitions involved in the agent's reasoning.

Epistemic reasoning starts with premises that are input to the reasoner. In human beings, these are provided by perception. For now I will assume that the input premises are propositions, but I will propose a somewhat different view in the next chapter. The input premises comprise the set *input*. The system then makes inferences from those premises. *Reasons* provide the atomic links in arguments. Reasons always comes in schemas. For example, for any propositions P and Q, $\ulcorner (P\&Q) \urcorner$ is a reason for P, and for any term x, $\ulcorner x$ looks red to me $\urcorner$ is a reason for me to believe $\ulcorner x$ is red $\urcorner$. Reasons are combined in various patterns to form arguments. The simplest arguments are *linear* arguments. These can be viewed as finite sequences of propositions, each of which is either a member of *input* or inferable from previous members of the sequence in accordance with some reason schema. Arguments can also have more complex nonlinear forms. (This will be discussed at greater length in chapter 3.)

Although it seems obvious that in epistemic reasoning we instantiate defeasible arguments, this is a substantive claim, and it is illuminating to ask why reasoning takes this form. A rudimentary answer can be gleaned from thinking about the role of mental representations in a rational agent. Thoughts constructed out of mental representations are supposed to provide the triggers for action. In a rational agent whose environment is unpredictable, it will be desirable to have great diversity in mental representations so that fine discriminations can be made and used in guiding action. However, this desideratum must be balanced by one of computational feasibility. Updating the agent's beliefs must be something that can be done in real time. Maximum discriminability would be achieved by having the agent's beliefs produced by a one-one function from the entire set of perceptual inputs the agent has experienced throughout its existence. However, updating beliefs on that basis is much too difficult a computational task. A feasible alternative would be to have each of an agent's beliefs reflect some small subset of its perceptual history. This would be to treat the beliefs as deduced from the sets of perceptual beliefs reflecting the perceptual history. This, however, does not allow sufficiently fine discriminations. It amounts to a particularly simple form of phenomenalism, whereby all beliefs are deduced from perceptual beliefs.[23] It

---

[23] For a discussion of phenomenalism and its failings, see Pollock [1986, 39ff].

would not allow any non-deductive inferences, like induction or abduction. The categorizations of its environment that an agent could
make in this way are not sufficiently rich to enable it to direct its
actions in very useful ways.

To get sufficiently fine discriminations, it must be possible for an
agent's mental representations to take account of unlimited amounts
of perceptual input, but it cannot be required that the agent survey
huge arrays of perceptual inputs before forming beliefs. The only
obvious way to achieve these two desiderata simultaneously is to enable
the agent to adopt beliefs on the basis of small sets of perceptual
inputs but then retract them in the face of additional perceptual inputs
if those additional inputs conflict in various ways with the original
bases for the beliefs. This is a description of *defeasible reasoning*. Beliefs
are adopted on the basis of arguments that appeal to small sets of
previously held beliefs, but the beliefs can later be retracted in the face
of new information.

It is now a commonplace of both philosophical epistemology and
artificial intelligence that epistemic reasoning can lead not only to the
adoption of new beliefs but also to the retraction of old beliefs. Similarly,
practical reasoning can lead to the formation of intentions but also to
the retraction of intentions. In philosophy, reasoning is said to be
"defeasible" in the sense that correct reasoning can lead first to the
adoption of a conclusion and subsequently to its retraction. Both
practical reasoning and epistemic reasoning are defeasible. This aspect
of reasoning has been called "nonmonotonic" in AI work.[24]

Reasoning proceeds in terms of reasons. Within epistemic reasoning,
some reasons are *conclusive reasons*, in the sense that they logically
entail their conclusions. The defeasibility of epistemic reasoning results
from the fact that there are non-conclusive reasons that support their
conclusions only defeasibly. These are *prima facie reasons*. Considerations that defeat prima facie reasons are *defeaters*. There are two
importantly different kinds of defeaters. Where *P* is a prima facie
reason for *Q*, *R* is a *rebutting defeater* iff *R* is a reason for denying *Q*.

---

[24] The work on defeasible reasoning in philosophy stems mainly from the publications of Roderick Chisholm and myself. See Chisholm [1957], [1966], [1977], and
Pollock [1965, 1967, 1970, 1974, 1986, 1987, 1990]. See also Kyburg [1974, 1983]. For
a sampling of the work in AI, see Delgrande [1988], Etherington [1987], Etherington
and Reiter [1983], Loui [1987], McCarthy [1980 and 1984], McDermott and Doyle
[1980], Moore [1985], Nute [1988], Pearl [1988], Pollock [1987, 1990c, 1991, 1992a],
Poole [1985, 1988], Reiter [1980], and Reiter and Criscuolo [1981].

All work on nonmonotonic logic and defeasible reasoning has recognized the existence of rebutting defeaters, but there was a time when it was often overlooked that there are other defeaters too.[25] For instance, suppose x looks red to me, but I know that x is illuminated by red lights and red lights can make objects look red when they are not. Knowing this defeats the prima facie reason, but it is not a reason for thinking that x is *not* red. After all, red objects look red in red light too. This is an *undercutting defeater*. Undercutting defeaters attack the connection between the reason and the conclusion rather than attacking the conclusion directly. My claim, discussed in chapter 2, is that rebutting defeaters and undercutting defeaters are the only kinds of defeaters necessary for describing the full logical complexity of defeasible reasoning.

In philosophy the concept of a prima facie reason has served primarily as a tool for the analysis of different kinds of epistemological problems, and that is the origin of my own work on defeasible reasoning. Prima facie reasons and defeaters have served as the main logical tools for my work in epistemology since 1965. Within philosophy, defeasible reasoning has not, until quite recently, been the subject of much logical investigation in its own right. In sharp contrast, nonmonotonic reasoning has been the subject of intensive logical investigation in AI. It will be my contention, however, that the AI work has been done without sufficient attention to actual epistemological examples of defeasible reasoning, with the consequence that the resulting theories are inadequate for the description of complex defeasible reasoning. (This claim will be defended in chapter 3.)

A common impression in AI is that defeasible reasoning consists of jumping to conclusions or making "tentative guesses".[26] It is supposed that defeasible reasoning is less secure than normal reasoning, and should be countenanced only for the sake of computational efficiency. What is overlooked is that defeasible reasoning *is* normal reasoning. Its use is not just a matter of computational efficiency. It is logically impossible to reason successfully about the world around us using only deductive reasoning. All interesting reasoning outside mathematics involves defeasible steps. For instance, our basic information about the world comes from sense perception. Things appear certain

---

[25] I first pointed out the existence of defeaters other than rebutting defeaters in my [1970].

[26] Doyle [1979].

ways to us, and we take that to be a reason for believing that they are that way. Clearly this reasoning is defeasible, but our reasoning in this way is no mere matter of convenience. As years of work in epistemology has made clear, there is in principle no way to logically deduce the state of the world from the way it appears.[27] Moving up the epistemic ladder, we use induction to form general beliefs summarizing observed regularities. If a regularity has been observed to hold in every case, that gives us a reason for thinking that it holds in general. If it has only been observed to hold in most cases, that gives us a reason for thinking it will continue to hold in most cases. Such inductive reasoning is defeasible, and it cannot be replaced by deductive reasoning. There is no way to deduce general conclusions from finitely many observations. Given that a generalization holds most of the time, we can use that to infer that it will hold in further unobserved cases. This inference is also defeasible. It takes "Most A's are B's, and this is an A" to be a defeasible reason for "This is a B". The upshot is that defeasible reasoning is not just common; it is thoroughly pervasive and absolutely essential. Almost everything we believe is believed at least indirectly on the basis of defeasible reasoning, and things could not have been any other way.

The next three chapters will be devoted to a study of defeasible reasoning. In studying reasoning, we can divide the subject into three parts: semantics, the study of correct arguments, and procedural theories of reasoning. Semantics is concerned with what conclusions are "ultimately reasonable" given any initial set of premises. The study of correct arguments concerns the structure of arguments aimed at establishing those ultimately reasonable conclusions, without any concern for how the arguments might be found or constructed. Procedural theories of reasoning deal with the control structure of a reasoner (the "architecture" of the reasoner) that governs its actual reasoning behavior. The study of correct arguments is often called "proof theory", but that is not a very good label for reasoning that includes non-deductive inferences like induction or abduction. Perhaps the main difference between theories of reasoning in AI and theories of reasoning in philosophy is that the latter have not traditionally attended to the architecture of the reasoner. I cannot, however, see any principled reason why that should be the case. I suspect that philosophers just did not think of this problem or else thought that it could not be profitably investigated.

---

[27] For further discussion of this point, see my [1986, 39ff].

9. Reflexive Cognition

Although epistemic cognition is initiated by practical cognition, it need not be *directed* by practical cognition about how to answer questions. That would lead to an infinite regress, because practical cognition always requires beliefs about the world. If we could not acquire some such beliefs without first engaging in practical cognition, we could never get started. This indicates that there must be a *default control structure* governing epistemic cognition, and in particular, governing the way in which it tries to answer questions. However, in human beings it is also possible to override the default control structure. For example, suppose I know a lot of calculus, and I am faced with an integration problem. Purely a priori reasoning, directed by my default reasoning strategies, may suffice to solve the problem. But if it is a complicated problem, a better way of solving it may be to look it up in an integration table. Solving the problem in this way involves practical cognition intervening in the course of epistemic cognition, providing an alternative strategy for answering the question and using that to override the default reasoning strategies.

Clearly it is a good idea for a sophisticated rational agent to be able to modify the course of its own epistemic endeavors by engaging in practical cognition about how best to pursue them. This allows practical cognition to affect the strategies employed in attempting to answer questions. An agent can learn that certain natural (default) strategies are unlikely to be effective in specific circumstances, and new strategies may be discovered that are more effective. The latter are often obtained by analogy from previous problem solving. It must be possible for the rational agent to use practical cognition in this manner to direct the course of epistemic cognition (and also to direct the course of practical cognition itself). I will refer to this as *reflexive cognition*. But it cannot be emphasized too strongly that reflexive cognition is not an essential part of all epistemic cognition. Because practical cognition presupposes epistemic cognition, some epistemic cognition must be possible without practical cognition. A rational agent must have built-in default control strategies for both epistemic cognition and practical cognition, and the agent must be able to employ these default strategies without engaging in reflexive cognition about how to reason.

In order to perform reflexive cognition, an agent must be able to think about its own reasoning. An agent with such capabilities is a *reflexive cognizer*. The construction of a reflexive cognizer is a tricky process. It involves the ability to reason and then "move up a level" to form beliefs about what reasoning has occurred. We want the cognizer to direct future reasoning by relying upon generalizations it has formed about the efficacy of certain kinds of reasoning in the past. This requires the ability to monitor ongoing reasoning introspectively and make judgments about it. A number of different kinds of judgments will be involved in reflexive cognition. Reasoning strategies are affected by judging that one way of attacking a problem is more likely to produce an answer than another way of attacking the problem. Another kind of reflexive cognition is involved in overriding Q&I modules. There, the cognizer discovers inductively that relying upon Q&I modules is unreliable under certain circumstances. To discover this, the cognizer must judge introspectively that it was relying upon Q&I modules on particular occasions, it must be able to tell introspectively what conclusion was produced, and it must be able to judge that the conclusion was false. This knowledge enables the cognizer to form a generalization about the reliability of Q&I modules. Then to apply this generalization, the cognizer must be able to judge in a particular case that it is relying upon Q&I modules. A similar kind of reflexive cognition is important in defeasible reasoning. There, the cognizer may discover inductively that reasoning in accordance with a certain prima facie reason is unreliable under specifiable circumstances, and that constitutes a defeater for the reasoning. Discovering and applying this defeater involves essentially the same mechanisms of reflexive cognition as that used in overriding Q&I modules.

Reasoning requires a system of mental representation—what in the philosophical literature is called a *language of thought*.[28] Reasoning consists of manipulating sentences in the language of thought. A reflexive cognizer must be able to think about the sentences in its own language of thought and observe their manipulation. For this to be possible, the cognizer's system of mental representation must incorporate something analogous to quotation names of those sentences. If p is a sentence in the language of thought, let «p» be its quotation name.

The construction of a reflexive cognizer will begin with a *planar reasoner* that lacks the ability to move up a level and observe itself. A planar reasoner can still reason about reasoning, in the same way it reasons about anything else, but it will have no special mechanisms for use in reasoning specifically about reasoning. To this planar reasoner we must then add an *introspective module* and a *truth-evaluation module*. The default epistemic reasoning module can be viewed as consisting

---

[28] The term is from Fodor [1975].

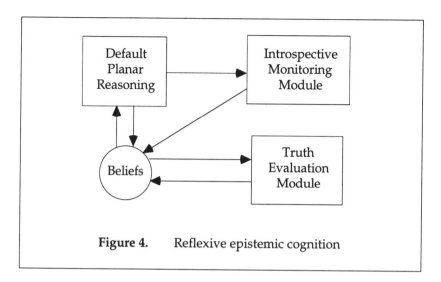

Figure 4.   Reflexive epistemic cognition

of a planar reasoning module, the introspective monitoring module, and the truth-evaluation module, combined as in figure 4. Note that this is all part of default epistemic reasoning, because the system must perform this much reasoning *before* it can apply practical reasoning to the question of how to reason. A full-fledged reflexive cognizer then results from giving practical cognition the ability to alter the course of epistemic cognition in various ways and using the results of reflexive epistemic cognition in choosing how to do that.

The introspective module enables the cognizer to acquire beliefs about its own reasoning. It will accomplish this by adding procedures to the cognizer that, under appropriate circumstances, lead the cognizer to adopt beliefs of the form

> I believe «p»;
> I believe «p» on the basis of «q_1»,...,«q_n»;

when it does in fact hold that belief on that basis.[29]

From a computational point of view, the addition of such an intro-spective module to a planar reasoner creates no obvious difficulties, but there are grave difficulties associated with the addition of a truth-

---

[29] These procedures must be interest driven, in the sense of section 10. The reasoner should adopt these beliefs only if it is previously interested in them.

evaluation module. The obvious proposal is to adopt an analogue of Tarski's T-schema:[30]

From p, infer $\ulcorner$«p» is true$\urcorner$.
From $\ulcorner$«p» is true $\urcorner$, infer p.[31]

The problem is that incorporating these rules into a reasoner will lead immediately to the liar paradox. The resulting inconsistency will be catastrophic in any reasoner that is compelled to draw all possible deductive consequences from its beliefs. There is a massive literature in philosophical logic regarding how to avoid the liar paradox, and that all becomes relevant here.[32] Thus the liar paradox, which initially appears to be a purely logical puzzle, becomes resurrected as an obstacle to AI. I think that this will not be unusual. A great many familiar philosophical problems arise in a new guise when we start modeling reasoning.

10. Interest-Driven Reasoning

In searching for arguments, a reflexive cognizer can bring to bear the full power of its practical reasoning, as informed by all of its prior experience. However, a reflexive cognizer must be built on top of a planar reasoner, and the searches of the latter are guided exclusively by the built-in procedures that constitute the default strategies for the reflexive cognizer. Let us focus on the native reasoning strategies of the default non-reflexive cognizer. I have noted that we could build a reasoning system that systematically generates all possible arguments, and it would be complete for, say, the predicate calculus. Using this system, if we want to establish a certain conclusion we must just wait until the system gets to it. This is the so-called British Museum algorithm.

---

[30] Tarski [1956].

[31] These must also be interest-driven. In the sense of section ten, the first would be a backward reason and the second a forward reason.

[32] For a sampling of the literature on the liar paradox, see Martin [1970, 1984]. For an extremely interesting proposal from AI, see Perlis [1985]. For my own suggestion regarding how to manage the reasoning involved in the liar paradox, see Pollock [1990b].

But such a system would be hopelessly inefficient. The behavior of any satisfactory reasoner must be guided by the conclusions it is trying to establish rather than just reasoning randomly until it happens upon its desired conclusion. All actual reasoners, human or artificial, are guided in some way or other. There is a rather obvious general account of how this works in default human reasoning. The basic idea is that reasoning proceeds both forward and backward (it uses forward chaining and backward chaining). We reason forward from our existing beliefs, and backward from what we are interested in establishing, and try to bring the two chains of reasoning together. Reasoning backward can be regarded as deriving interests from interests. A reasoning system that combines such forward and backward reasoning will be said to be *interest-driven*. (The logical structure of interest-driven reasoning will be investigated further in chapter 4.)

The bidirectional structure of interest-driven reasoning is extremely important for understanding the way in which epistemic and practical cognition interact. I have argued that epistemic cognition gets its point from practical reasoning. Practical cognition passes questions to epistemic cognition, which the latter tries to answer. The mechanism for this is the set of *ultimate-epistemic-interests*. These are questions posed by practical cognition for the sake of deciding what to do. In turn, these provide the initial interests for epistemic cognition. Epistemic cognition reasons backward from these interests, deriving interest in other questions whose answers would facilitate answering those in *ultimate-epistemic-interests*. This is just goal reduction applied to reasoning. Perception provides the premises in *input* from which epistemic cognition reasons forward, and the aim of epistemic reasoning is to bring these two chains of reasoning together so that questions of interest can be answered.

Interests come in degrees, reflecting the practical importance of the questions of interest. For instance, I may simultaneously want to see a certain movie tonight and avoid getting hit by a car while crossing the street. Both require practical reasoning, but I place greater importance on avoiding being hit than on seeing the movie. Accordingly, I have a higher degree of interest in questions pertaining to how to avoid being hit than I do in questions pertaining to how to see the movie. One of the main functions of such degrees of interest is to prioritize reasoning. Human beings and other rational agents have limited computational powers. There is typically more reasoning for them to do than they can do at any one time. They need some mechanism for deciding which reasoning to do first, and degrees of interest provide part of the mechanism for such prioritization.

Just as degrees of interests vary, so do the strengths of reasons. Some reasons are better than others. For example, knowing that all A's are B's and this is an A gives me a better reason for believing that this is a B than does knowing that most A's are B's and this is an A. Similarly, something's looking clearly red to me in good light gives me a better reason for thinking it is red than does its looking vaguely red to me in dim light. The strengths of the reasons employed in an argument affect the *degree of justification* of the conclusion of the argument. The better the reasons, the higher the degree of justification. (The precise way in which the strengths of reasons affect the degree of justification of the conclusion will be investigated in chapter 3.)

Degrees of justification have a role to play in adjudicating disputes in epistemic reasoning. For example, if I have a reason for believing P but also have a significantly better reason for believing $\sim P$, then it is $\sim P$ that I should believe. But if I have equally good reasons for believing P and $\sim P$, then I should withhold belief in both. This is a purely "internal" function for degrees of justification in epistemic reasoning. Degrees of justification are also important in connecting epistemic reasoning and practical reasoning. The practical importance of a question (i.e., our degree of interest in it) determines how justified we must be in an answer before we can rest content with that answer. For example, consider a ship's captain on a busman's holiday. He is taking his wife on a Caribbean cruise on a ship where he has no official status other than being a passenger. The ship seems well equipped, and he idly wonders how many lifeboats are on board. To answer this question, he might simply consult the descriptive brochure that was passed out to all the passengers. But now suppose things change catastrophically. An accident occurs, disabling all of the ship's officers and putting the ship in jeopardy. The visiting captain is pressed into duty to run the ship. The ship is in danger of sinking. At this point it becomes very important for him to know whether there are enough lifeboats aboard for all the passengers. To answer this question, it is no longer sufficient to consult the descriptive brochure. That is not a good enough reason. He must either count them himself or have them counted by someone he regards as reliable. The importance of the question makes it incumbent upon him to have a very good reason for his believed answer. Thus the degree of interest in a question determines the degree of justification a rational agent must have for an answer.

11. The Project

This investigation began with a very general conception of a rational agent as an agent that likes or dislikes its situation to varying degrees and when it finds the world not entirely to its liking it tries to change that. General logical considerations and considerations of computational feasibility suffice to dictate a great deal of the structure of a rational agent. We were led to the picture of a rational agent as a planning agent whose planning is directed by defeasible epistemic cognition and initiated and evaluated by a complicated structure of evaluative attitudes. This structure was not elicited by reflecting on human cognition but was the only obvious solution to a number of logical problems and problems of computational feasibility. Although the enterprise has been to describe rationality in general, and not just human rationality, I take it that this throws considerable light on the nature of human rationality and explains why human cognition has much of the structure that it does.

The rest of the book will be concerned with working out the details of the theory of rationality that has been sketched in this chapter. The book divides roughly into two parts. The first part is concerned with epistemic reasoning and the second with practical reasoning. Chapter 2 gives a general description of human epistemology, formulated in terms of prima facie reasons and defeaters. Chapter 3 investigates the logical structure of defeasible reasoning. Chapter 4 formulates a procedural theory of interest-driven defeasible reasoning—an account of how to perform the reasoning rather than just an account of the results we would like the reasoning to produce. This account forms the basis for an implemented general-purpose defeasible reasoner intended to provide the inference engine for the artilect that is the goal of the OSCAR project.

Chapter 5 turns to the theory of practical reasoning and provides a general defense of a "plan-based theory of practical reasoning". Chapter 6 investigates the logical structure of plans, and chapter 7 addresses the computational architecture of a rational agent capable of plan-based practical reasoning. Chapter 8 investigates the way in which actions are directed on the basis of the plans the agent has adopted. Chapter 9 summarizes the theory produced in the earlier chapters and describes the detailed architecture that results from it. This architecture has been implemented and provides the basis for an assault on the problems that remain for the production of a fully functional artilect. Chapter 9 closes with a survey of those problems.

Chapter 2
Epistemology from the Design Stance

1. Epistemology and Cognition

Chapter 1 sketched some general features of the cognitive architecture of a rational agent. Those features concern both epistemic and practical cognition and are motivated by quite general aspects of rationality. The rest of the book will be concerned with filling in details, beginning with an account of epistemic cognition. Epistemic cognition proceeds via both epistemic reasoning and some important Q&I modules that accelerate those aspects of epistemic cognition that can be performed only very slowly by ratiocination. This account will focus primarily on reasoning rather than the Q&I modules, although I will point out where Q&I modules are of particular importance and what some of them might look like.

A description of epistemic reasoning must give a general account of those aspects of epistemic reasoning that are common to all subject matters, and supplement that account with specific details governing particular kinds of epistemic reasoning. We can make a distinction between *theoretical epistemology* and *applied epistemology*. Theoretical epistemology describes the inference engine for epistemic reasoning. The inference engine will be an interest-driven deductive and defeasible reasoner, and it will be described in detail in the next two chapters. A constraint on the design of the inference engine is that it must be capable of handling all of the complex reasoning required by a realistic applied epistemology. Accordingly, this chapter will provide a sketch of some of the central elements of the applied epistemology that will be presupposed by the OSCAR project. The applied epistemological theories presented in this chapter have all been developed and defended elsewhere. For the most part, the purpose of this chapter is not to do new work in epistemology but rather to present previously constructed theories in capsule form so that they can be usedthroughout the rest of the book. For the purposes of building an artilect, these applied epistemological theories will have to undergo further development in various ways, filling in details that are required for implementing the reasoning they describe. That will be the next stage of the OSCAR project. The current stage concentrates on getting the general architecture right.

In philosophy, the term "epistemology" includes much that is not of interest in the current context. My concern here is with "epistemology from the design stance". A rough distinction can be made between epistemological questions that bear on the design of a rational agent and those that bear on the description of the rational agent once it is running. Many traditional epistemological problems fall into the latter category. For example, the analysis of ⌜S knows P⌝ is of no interest in this investigation. What is of interest is how a rational agent should reason in acquiring perceptual knowledge, performing inductive generalizations, and so forth. Epistemology from the design stance is concerned exclusively with the structure of epistemic reasoning.

Leaving aside Q&I modules for the moment, the beliefs of a rational agent are produced by a combination of perception and reasoning. Perception produces beliefs about the agent's immediate surroundings. Inductive reasoning from those beliefs produces general beliefs. There are several different kinds of inductive reasoning. *Enumerative induction* produces conclusions of the form ⌜All F's are G's⌝ as a result of observing a sample of F's all of which are G's. *Statistical induction* produces probabilistic generalizations of the form ⌜The probability of an A being a B is approximately r⌝ as a result of observing a sample of F's in which the proportion of G's is r. Reasoning from these generalizations produces further singular beliefs, beliefs in causal connections, subjunctive conditionals, and so forth. Reasoning from exceptionless generalizations of the form ⌜All F's are G's⌝ is just a matter of deduction, but reasoning from probabilistic generalizations of the form ⌜The probability of an A being a B is approximately r⌝ is more complicated. The inference is defeasible and proceeds in terms of the *statistical syllogism*, which says roughly that if the probability of an A's being a B is high then it is defeasibly reasonable to expect a particular A to be a B. I turn now to a more detailed account of some of this.

2. Perception

The starting point for belief formation is perception. Perception is a causal process that produces beliefs about an agent's surroundings. The construction of a rational agent requires a complete account of this causal process, and that is a formidable task. Very schematically, we can think of perception as beginning with the activation of sensors, whose signals are processed in complex ways to produce a sensory image, and then beliefs are produced in response to that image. I suspect that the most difficult part of constructing a complete theory of perception lies in describing the computations leading from sensory input to the production of an image, and that is where most of the work is being done in the psychology of vision and in machine vision. Fortunately, the epistemologist can largely ignore all of that, because we can think of epistemology as beginning with the image and concerning itself with how beliefs are produced from that.

Perception apprises us of some of the properties of our surroundings, including the existence and position of objects of varying colors, shapes, and textures. I will refer to these as *perceptible properties*. Most properties are not perceptible. I cannot tell simply by looking at something how much it weighs, its age, or its marital status. I can, of course, perceive other properties that may constitute contingent clues regarding these non-perceptible properties.

Where φ is an appropriate perceptible property, we can talk about an agent's "having a φ image". For instance, an agent may have an image of a red object positioned in the left side of the visual field. This gives the agent a reason to think that *there is* a red object so positioned. In general, for perceptible φ, having a φ image gives an agent a reason to think that its circumstances exemplify φ. Clearly the agent's justification for holding this belief is defeasible. For example, the agent may have very good reason to believe that there is no pink elephant before him, and that may make it unreasonable to believe that there is a pink elephant before him despite the fact that he has a visual image of one. It is tempting to describe this by saying that, in perception, we employ the following prima facie reason scheme:

(2.1)   Where φ is a perceptible property, ⌜I have a φ image⌝ is a prima facie reason for an agent to believe ⌜My circumstances exemplify φ⌝.[1]

An interesting twist arises in understanding this principle, however. It is most natural to think of reasons for beliefs as being other beliefs and accordingly to understand (2.1) as telling us that when an agent has a belief of the form ⌜I have a φ image⌝, that gives the agent a defeasible reason for believing ⌜My circumstances exemplify φ⌝. However, in two ways, this is an inadequate account of the way in which

---

[1] For further discussion and defense of this principle, see my [1986, 39ff]. Variants of this principle also formed the basis of my account of perceptual knowledge in my [1965, 1967, 1971, and 1974].

perceptual images give us reasons for beliefs about our surroundings. First, it would leave a gap in the account. A computational theory of perception ends with the production of an image, but the epistemological theory would begin with a belief about an image. How do we get from the existence of the image to the belief about the image? It might be supposed that this gap is filled by a mechanism ensuring that whenever we have a φ image, we automatically form the belief that we do. On this account, the justification of my beliefs about my surroundings "passes through" beliefs about my visual images. However, that is simply false. Human beings rarely have any beliefs at all about their images. The first beliefs they form on the basis of perception are typically about physical objects. When I walk around campus, I form beliefs to the effect that there are trees and buildings around me, there are people hurrying by, and so forth. I rarely form any beliefs about my visual images. I *can* form beliefs about my visual images, but that normally involves a deliberate change of attention—not something that I do ordinarily. In the normal course of events, perceptual images give rise directly to beliefs about our surroundings, without this being mediated by any beliefs about the images.

Throughout much of the history of epistemology, there was an assumption that went unquestioned. This is the *doxastic assumption*, according to which the only thing that can be relevant to whether an agent ought to hold a belief is what other beliefs the agent holds. But the doxastic assumption must be rejected, because it makes it impossible to explain how human beings can have perceptual knowledge when they lack beliefs about their perceptual images.[2] A correct account of perceptual knowledge must acknowledge that the mere existence of a perceptual image, independent of any beliefs about it, can lead the agent to form beliefs about its surroundings, and when such beliefs are formed on that basis, they are reasonable beliefs, that is, they are epistemically justified. I propose to describe this by saying that *having the image* constitutes a prima facie reason for holding the belief. This amounts, in part, to a convention regarding how I am going to use the term "reason". In particular, I am going to use it rather broadly so that cognitive states other than beliefs can be reasons for beliefs. In principle, any cognitive states to which the reasoner has "direct access"

---

[2] See my [1986, 58-64 and 87-91] for further discussion of this claim.

can be reasons.[3] Of course, the most common kinds of reasons will be beliefs, but these are not the only possible kinds of reasons. I propose then to reformulate (2.1) as follows:

(2.2)   Where φ is a perceptible property, an agent's having a φ image constitutes a prima facie reason for the agent to believe ⌐My circumstances exemplify φ⌐.

It is customary to talk about reasons as if they are propositions. For example, we may say that a conjunction is a reason for each conjunct. However, endorsing (2.2) requires us to take the reason-relation to relate mental states rather than their propositional contents. For instance, rather than saying that ⌐(P&Q)⌐ is a reason for P, we must say that *believing* ⌐(P&Q)⌐ is a reason for *believing P*. Usually, however, the mental states that are reasons will be beliefs, and in that case I will usually write as if it is the contents of the beliefs rather than the beliefs themselves that are reasons for each other. Bear in mind, however, that this is just a convenient shorthand.

A further complication must be addressed. Although we rarely have beliefs about our perceptual images, we sometimes do. Furthermore, when we have such beliefs, it is possible for them to be mistaken.[4] For example, a common mistake is to suppose that shadows in snow look grey. In fact, as every artist knows, they have a distinct bluish cast. But most people are unaware of this, and if you ask a person standing before a snow-covered landscape what color the shadows look to him, he may answer by appealing to his general belief that such shadows look grey rather than by attending introspectively to his image. If he does, he will form the false belief that the shadows look grey to him.

Now consider a person who has a false belief about his perceptual image. Think, for instance, of the person with the false belief about the shadow in the snow. On the basis of his belief that the shadow looks grey, the might conclude that it is grey. What should we say about the reasonableness of this conclusion? He does not have a reason of the form of (2.2) for his belief, but nevertheless, given his false belief about how the shadow looks, it seems defeasibly reasonable

---

[3] This amounts to an endorsement of what is called "internalism" in epistemology.

[4] For further discussion of this point, see my [1986, 58-64].

for him to believe that the shadow is grey. This suggests that (2.2) should be supplemented with:

(2.3)　　Where φ is a perceptible property, an agent's believing he has a φ image constitutes a prima facie reason for him to believe ⌜My circumstances exemplify φ⌝.

Furthermore, the preceding example indicates that reasons of the form of (2.3) take precedence over conflicting reasons of the form of (2.2). This can be captured by saying that reasons of the form of (2.3) constitute undercutting defeaters for conflicting reasons of the form of (2.2). Precisely:

(2.4)　　Where θ is a perceptible property, an agent's believing he has a θ image and believing that if his circumstances exemplify θ then they do not exemplify φ constitutes an undercutting defeater for (2.2).

It should be observed that an agent's believing he has a θ image and believing that if his circumstances exemplify θ then they do not exemplify φ also constitutes a rebutting defeater for (2.2). This is automatic, because by (2.2) this gives the agent a reason to believe that his circumstances exemplify θ and hence that they do not exemplify φ. However, this observation is not sufficient to accommodate our reasoning in this case, because the agent's having a φ image and believing that if his circumstances exemplify θ then they do not exemplify φ also constitutes a rebutting defeater for the inference, in accordance with (2.3), to the conclusion that his circumstances exemplify θ. In other words, the rebutting relationship between θ and φ is symmetrical. In order to give the inference in accordance with (2.3) precedence over the inference in accordance with (2.2), we must break the symmetry by acknowledging the undercutting defeater formulated in (2.4).

There is another kind of defeater for (2.2) that is of considerable importance. Suppose that I see an object and it looks red to me. By (2.2), that gives me a prima facie reason for thinking that it is red. But suppose I also know that the object is illuminated by red lights, and such illumination can make objects look red when they are not. Surely this makes it unreasonable for me to conclude that the object is red. On the other hand, the inference is not defeated by a rebutting defeater, because I have no reason for thinking that the object is not red. Although non-red objects can look red in red light, red objects also look red in red light. Accordingly, this example must be taken to illustrate the presence of an undercutting defeater. The undercutting defeater consists of observing that under the present circumstances, an object's looking red is not a reliable indicator of its being red. More generally:

(2.5) The belief:
  the present circumstances are of a general type C such that the probability is not high of being in circumstances exemplifying φ given that one has a φ image under circumstances of type C
is an undercutting defeater for both (2.2) and (2.3).

I will refer to defeaters of this form as *reliability defeaters* for (2.2) and (2.3).[5]

Reliability defeaters represent a general phenomenon in defeasible reasoning. Whenever belief in P is a prima facie reason for belief in Q, discovering that under the present circumstances, P's being true is not a reliable indicator of Q's being true, constitutes an undercutting defeater for the prima facie reason. More precisely:

(2.6) If belief in P is a prima facie reason for belief in Q, the belief:
  the present circumstances are of a general type C such that the probability is not high of Q's being true given that P is true under circumstances of type C
is an undercutting defeater for this prima facie reason.

The application of (2.5) to (2.3) is assimilated by (2.6). Note, however, that the application of (2.5) to (2.2) is not assimilated by (2.6), because (2.6) talks only about prima facie reasons that are beliefs. Furthermore, (2.6) cannot be reformulated so as to include the application of (2.5) to (2.2), because there is an important disanalogy. The prima facie reason formulated by (2.2) consists of *having a φ image*, and the defeater formulated by (2.5) consists of discovering that *having a φ image* is not a reliable indicator of being in circumstances exemplifying φ. By contrast, the prima facie reason to which (2.6) applies consists of *believing P*, but the defeater formulated in (2.6) does not consist of discovering that *believing P* is not a reliable indicator of Q's being true.

---

[5] This characterization of reliability defeaters is simplistic in one respect. I have argued [1990, pg. 198], that a "projectibility constraint" must be imposed on C.

3. Justification and Warrant

The rules governing epistemic reasoning are rules for updating the cognizer's set of beliefs, in response to both further perceptual input and further reasoning. Given a set of beliefs, the rules for epistemic reasoning describe how it should be altered, either by adopting new beliefs or retracting beliefs currently held. Accordingly, we can think of the epistemic reasoner as being described by a function *update*, which is applied repeatedly to the agent's set of beliefs and current perceptual states to generate the new set of beliefs that become reasonable as a result of a single step of reasoning. Philosophers talk about *epistemic justification*. This term has been used in several importantly different ways, but in one sense of the term, the beliefs that are epistemically justified at any given time are just those that it is reasonable to hold. In other words, if an agent's beliefs comprise a set **B**, and **P** is the set of all the agent's current perceptual states, a belief is currently justified iff it is in *update*(**B**,**P**). A belief can be justified at one time and become unjustified at a later time as a result either of additional reasoning or new perceptual input. Justification has to do with what beliefs the agent ought to hold at any given time.

A complication arises from the fact that we can be justified to varying degrees in holding different beliefs. In chapter 3, it will be argued that to fully implement rationality, beliefs must be stored with their associated degrees of justification. These degrees are used in computing degrees of justification for new conclusions produced by *update*. A specification of *update* must include a description of how this works. Formally, however, the set **B** on which *update* operates can be taken to be a set of pairs $\langle P, \alpha \rangle$ of propositions and their associated degrees of justification. The value of *update*(**B**,**P**) must also have this form. Then an agent is justified to degree α in believing a proposition P iff $\langle P, \alpha \rangle \in$ *update*(**B**,**P**).

The beliefs that an agent is justified in holding change as a function of both reasoning and perceptual input. Sometimes we are interested in holding the perceptual input fixed and asking whether a belief is justified after a certain amount of reasoning. This can be described by supposing the agent begins with a set $\mathbf{B}_0$ of beliefs, and then applying *update* repeatedly without any new perceptual input. Define:

$$J_0 = \mathbf{B}_0;$$
$$J_{n+1} = update(J_n, \varnothing).$$

Then J_n is the set of beliefs justified after n steps of reasoning.[6] Because reasoning is defeasible, a belief may be justified at one stage, unjustified at a later stage, justified again still later, and so on.

For some purposes we are interested in a less transitory notion of justification. Let us say that a proposition is *warranted* iff it is "justified in the limit". More precisely, a warranted proposition is one that eventually becomes justified and stays justified:

> P is *warranted to degree* α iff there is an n such that for every $m > n$, $\langle P, \alpha \rangle \in J_m$.

Warrant and justification are closely connected concepts, but they are also importantly different. A proposition can be warranted without being justifiably believed, because it may become justified only later as a result of constructing an argument that has not yet been constructed. Similarly, a currently justified belief may fail to be warranted because further reasoning may reveal a defeater for some defeasible inference used in its justification.

4. The Statistical Syllogism

We believe very few exceptionless generalizations. Most of the generalizations we believe and in terms of which we guide our behavior are statistical, of the form ⌜Most F's are G's⌝. In order to function in a world like ours, a rational agent must be equipped with rules (1) enabling it to form beliefs in statistical generalizations, and (2) enabling it to make inferences from those statistical generalizations to beliefs about individual matters of fact. The latter rules are called *acceptance rules*. I will begin the discussion of probabilistic reasoning by focusing on acceptance rules. I have argued [1990] that the most fundamental acceptance rule is the *statistical syllogism*. The non-numerical version of the statistical syllogism is very familiar in AI, comprising the most common example of defeasible reasoning. It can be formulated roughly as follows:

---

[6] It is argued in chapter 4 that this picture must be made more complicated. *Update* must operate on "conclusions" rather than beliefs, where conclusions can be either defeated or undefeated. Then the set of beliefs justified after n stages of reasoning is the set of undefeated conclusions after n stages of reasoning.

Most F's are G's.
This is an F.
This is a G.

We often reason in roughly this way. For instance, on what basis do I believe what I read in the newspaper? Certainly not that everything printed in the newspaper is true. No one believes that. But I do believe that most of what is printed in the newspaper is true, and that justifies me in believing individual newspaper reports. I take it that what ⌜Most F's are G's⌝ requires is that the probability is high of an arbitrary G's being an F. Accordingly, this can be rewritten as:

$\text{prob}(G/F) \geq r$.
This is an F.
This is a G.

The choice of r will vary from one situation to another, depending upon the degree of certainty that is demanded. It was argued in chapter one that when questions are passed to the epistemic reasoner, the associated degrees of interest reflect their importance in practical reasoning, and these degrees of interest determine the degree of justification the cognizer must have in order to accept an answer. In the case of the statistical syllogism, this degree of justification determines the value of r. I will say more about this in the next chapter.

The probabilities to which the statistical syllogism appeals are indefinite (general) probabilities; that is, the probabilities relate properties. They are to be distinguished from definite (single case) probabilities, which attach to propositions. There is, however, more than one kind of indefinite probability, and correspondingly we can formulate different versions of the statistical syllogism. I have argued [1990] that the most fundamental version of the statistical syllogism proceeds in terms of *nomic probabilities*. These are the probabilities involved in statistical laws of nature. At least heuristically, one can think of $\text{prob}(G/F)$ as a measure of the proportion of all physically possible F's that would be G's. Nomic probability is discussed at length in Pollock [1990], and the reader is referred to that book for more details. It is shown there that other versions of the statistical syllogism, formulated in terms of different kinds of indefinite probabilities, can be derived from the fundamental version that appeals to nomic probabilities. In particular, where freq$[A/B]$ is the relative frequency with which G's are F's, that is, the proportion of actual G's that are F's, a frequency-based version of the statistical syllogism can be derived from the version that appeals to nomic probabilities:

$$\text{freq}[G/F] \geq r.$$
$$\underline{\text{This is an } F.}$$
$$\text{This is a } G.$$

Obviously, the inference described by the statistical syllogism is a defeasible one. This suggests that the statistical syllogism could be formulated more precisely as follows:

(4.1)   If $r > 0.5$ then $\ulcorner Fc$ and $\text{prob}(G/F) \geq r \urcorner$ is a prima facie reason for $\ulcorner Gc \urcorner$, the strength of the reason depending upon the value of r.

It is illuminating to consider how this rule handles the lottery paradox.[7] Suppose you hold one ticket in a fair lottery consisting of 1 million tickets, and suppose it is known that one and only one ticket will win. Observing that the probability is only .000001 of a ticket's being drawn given that it is a ticket in the lottery, it seems reasonable to accept the conclusion that your ticket will not win. But by the same reasoning, it will be reasonable to believe, for each ticket, that it will not win. However, these conclusions conflict jointly with something else we are warranted in believing, namely, that some ticket will win. Assuming that we cannot be warranted in believing each member of an explicitly contradictory set of propositions, it follows that we are not warranted in believing of each ticket that it will not win.

Not everyone agrees with this diagnosis of the lottery paradox. Kyburg [1970] and Etherington, Kraus, and Perlis [1991] urge that it is reasonable to conclude of any individual ticket that it will not be drawn. However, there is a simple argument that seems to show that this is wrong. If I am justified in believing, not just that it is improbable that ticket n will be drawn, but that ticket n will definitely not be drawn, and I am presented with the opportunity of purchasing ticket n, then it is unequivocally true that I should not purchase it. However, it would be unreasonable to draw this conclusion. No matter how improbable it is that ticket n will be drawn, if the payoff is sufficiently great, then I *should* buy the ticket. For instance, if the probability of ticket n's being drawn is one in a million, but the ticket costs one

---

[7] The lottery paradox is due to Kyburg [1961].

dollar and the payoff is one billion dollars, then rationality clearly dictates that I should buy the ticket. On the other hand, if I am justified in believing that the ticket will not be drawn, and not just that it is improbable that it will be drawn, then I am precluded from reasoning in this way. It would be irrational for me to buy the ticket, no matter what the payoff, if I am justified in believing that it will not be drawn. Accordingly, that cannot be a justified belief in the case of a fair lottery.

This is no problem for the statistical syllogism as long as it provides only a prima facie reason for concluding that a ticket will not be drawn. What is happening in the lottery paradox is that the prima facie reason is defeated. The lottery paradox is a case in which we have prima facie reasons for a number of conclusions, but they collectively defeat one another. This illustrates the *principle of collective defeat*. This principle will turn out to be of considerable importance, so I will say a bit more about it. Suppose we are warranted in believing some proposition R and we have equally good prima facie reasons for each of $P_1,...,P_n$, where $\{P_1,...,P_n\}$ is a minimal set of propositions deductively inconsistent with R (i.e., it is a set deductively inconsistent with R and has no proper subset that is deductively inconsistent with R). Then for each i, the conjunction $\ulcorner R$ & P_1 & ... & P_{i-1} & P_{i+1} & ... & $P_n \urcorner$ entails $\sim P_i$. Thus by combining this entailment with the arguments for R and $P_1,...,P_{i-1},P_{i+1},...,P_n$ we obtain an argument for $\sim P_i$ that is as good as the argument for P_i. It follows that we have equally strong support for both P_i and $\sim P_i$, and hence we could not reasonably believe either on this basis; neither is warranted. This holds for each i, so none of the P_i is warranted. They collectively defeat one another. Thus, the simplest version of the principle of collective defeat can be formulated as follows:

(4.2)   If we are warranted in believing R and we have equally good independent prima facie reasons for each member of a minimal set of propositions deductively inconsistent with R, and none of these prima facie reasons is defeated in any other way, then none of the propositions in the set is warranted on the basis of these prima facie reasons.

Collective defeat will be discussed at greater length in chapter 3.

Collective defeat is familiar in AI from the discussion of *skeptical* and *credulous* reasoners [Touretzky, Horty, and Thomason 1987]. Roughly, skeptical reasoners withhold belief when they have equally good reasons for and against a conclusion, and credulous reasoners choose a conclusion at random. It has sometimes been urged that the choice between skeptical and credulous reasoners is more a matter of taste than a matter of logic, but my own view is that credulous reasoners are just wrong. Suppose you have two friends, Smith and Jones, whom you regard as equally reliable. Smith approaches you in the hall and says, "It is raining outside." Jones then announces, "Don't believe him. It is a fine sunny day." If you have no other evidence regarding the weather, what should you believe? It seems obvious that you should *withhold* belief, believing neither that it is raining nor that it is not. If you were to announce, "I realize that I have no better reason for thinking that it is raining than for thinking that it is not, but I choose to believe that it is raining", no one would regard you as rational.

I have heard credulous reasoners defended on the grounds that if an agent is making practical decisions, it is better to do something rather than nothing.[8] Sometimes this seems right. For instance, if the agent is deciding where to have a picnic and the considerations favoring two sites are tied, it seems reasonable to choose at random.[9] But there are other situations in which such a policy could be disastrous. If the agent is performing medical diagnosis and the evidence favoring two diseases is tied, we do not want the agent to decide randomly to treat the patient for one disease rather than the other. It could happen that the diseases are not serious if left untreated, but if the patient is treated for the wrong disease, that treatment will gravely exacerbate his condition. In such a case we want the agent to reserve judgment on the matter and not proceed blindly.

The difference between these two examples is that in the case of the picnic, the agent's epistemic ignorance makes the expected values of both plans for where to hold the picnic equal, and either plan is preferable to not holding the picnic at all. But in the medical diagnosis case, the agent's ignorance makes the expected value of doing nothing higher than the expected value of either plan for treatment. If the agent resolved its ignorance by resolving epistemic ties at random and then acting on the basis of the conclusions thus drawn, it could not distinguish between these two kinds of cases. Instead, a rational agent

---

[8] Both Jon Doyle and Richmond Thomason have argued this way in recent conversations.

[9] This example is due to Jon Doyle (in conversation).

should acknowledge its ignorance and take that into account in computing the expected values of plans.

The preceding considerations suggest that the controversy over skeptical and credulous reasoning stems from a confusion of epistemic reasoning with practical reasoning. In practical reasoning, if one has no basis for choosing between two alternative plans, one should choose at random. The classical illustration is the medieval tale of Buridan's ass who starved to death standing midway between two equally succulent bales of hay because he could not decide from which to eat. This marks an important difference between practical reasoning and epistemic reasoning. An agent making practical decisions must first decide what to believe and then use those beliefs in deciding what to do, but these are two different matters. If the evidence favoring two alternative hypotheses is equally good, the agent should record that fact and withhold belief. Subsequent practical reasoning can then decide what to do given that epistemic conclusion. In some cases it may be reasonable to choose one of the hypotheses at random and act *as if* it is known to be true, and in other cases more caution will be prescribed. But what must be recognized is that the design of the system of practical reasoning is a separate matter from the design of the system of epistemic reasoning that feeds information to the practical reasoner. Epistemic reasoning should acknowledge ignorance when it is encountered rather than drawing conclusions at random. This is what the principle of collective defeat mandates.

Although the principle of collective defeat allows the principle (4.1) of statistical syllogism to escape the lottery paradox, it turns out that the very fact that (4.1) can handle the lottery paradox in this way shows that it cannot be correct. The difficulty is that every case of high probability can be recast in a form that makes it similar to the lottery paradox. We need only assume that $\text{prob}(G/F) < 1$. Pick the smallest integer n such that $\text{prob}(G/F) < 1 - 1/2^n$. Now consider n fair coins, unrelated to each other and unrelated to c's being F or G. Let T_i be $\ulcorner$ is a toss of coin $i\urcorner$ and let H be $\ulcorner$ is a toss that lands heads$\urcorner$. There are 2^n *Boolean conjunctions* of the form $\ulcorner(\sim)Hx_1 \;\&\; ... \;\&\; (\sim)Hx_n\urcorner$ where each tilde in parentheses can be either present or absent. For each Boolean conjunction $\beta_j x_1...x_n$,

$$\text{prob}(\beta_j x_1...x_n / T_1 x_1 \;\&\; ... \;\&\; T_n x_n) = 2^{-n}.$$

Consequently, because the coins were chosen to be unrelated to F and G,

$$\text{prob}(\sim\beta_j x_1 ... x_n / Fx \ \& \ T_1 x_1 \ \& \ ... \ \& \ T_n x_n) = 1 - 2^{-n}.$$

By the probability calculus, a disjunction is at least as probable as its disjuncts, so

$$\text{prob}(\sim Gx \ \vee \sim\beta_j x_1 ... x_n / Fx \ \& \ T_1 x_1 \ \& ... \ \& \ T_n x_n) \geq 1 - 2^{-n} > \text{prob}(Gx / Fx).$$

Let $t_1, ..., t_n$ be a sequence consisting of one toss of each coin. As we know $\ulcorner Fc \ \& \ T_1 t_1 \ \& \ ... \ \& \ T_n t_n \urcorner$, (4.1) gives us a prima facie reason for believing each disjunction of the form

$$\sim Gc \ \vee \sim\beta_j t_1 ... t_n.$$

By the propositional calculus, the set of all these disjunctions is equivalent to, and hence entails, $\sim Gc$. Thus we can construct an argument for $\sim Gc$ in which the only defeasible steps involve the use of (4.1) in connection with probabilities at least as great as that used in defending Gc. Hence, we have a situation formally identical to the lottery paradox. Therefore, the principle of collective defeat has the consequence that if $\text{prob}(G/F)$ has any probability less than 1, we cannot use (4.1) to draw any warranted conclusion from this high probability.

The difficulty can be traced to the assumption that F and G in (4.1) can be arbitrary formulas. Basically, we need a constraint that, when applied to the above argument, precludes applying (4.1) to the disjunctions $\ulcorner \sim Gc \ \vee \sim\beta_j t_1 ... t_n \urcorner$. It turns out that disjunctions create repeated difficulties throughout the theory of probabilistic reasoning. This is easily illustrated in the case of (4.1). For instance, it is a theorem of the probability calculus that $\text{prob}(F/G \vee H) \geq \text{prob}(F/G) \cdot \text{prob}(G/G \vee H)$. Consequently, if $\text{prob}(F/G)$ and $\text{prob}(G/G \vee H)$ are sufficiently large, it follows that $\text{prob}(F/G \vee H) \geq r$. For example, because the vast majority of birds can fly and because there are many more birds than giant sea tortoises, it follows that most things that are either birds or giant sea tortoises can fly. If Herman is a giant sea tortoise, (4.1) would give us a reason for thinking that Herman can fly, but notice that this is based simply on the fact that most birds can fly, which should be irrelevant to whether Herman can fly. This example indicates that arbitrary disjunctions cannot be substituted for G in (4.1).

Nor can arbitrary disjunctions be substituted for F in (4.1). By the probability calculus, $\text{prob}(F \vee G/H) \geq \text{prob}(F/H)$. Therefore, if $\text{prob}(F/H)$ is high, so is $\text{prob}(F \vee G/H)$. Thus, because most birds can fly, it is also true that most birds can either fly or swim the English Channel. By

(4.1), this should be a reason for thinking that a starling with a broken wing can swim the English Channel, but obviously it is not.

There must be restrictions on the properties F and G in (4.1). To have a convenient label, let us say that G is *projectible with respect to F* iff (4.1) holds. What we have seen is that projectibility is not closed under disjunction; neither of the following holds:

> If C is projectible with respect to both A and B, then C is projectible with respect to $(A \lor B)$.

> If A and B are both projectible with respect to C, then $(A \lor B)$ is projectible with respect to C.

On the other hand, it seems fairly clear that projectibility is closed under conjunction.

In formulating the principle of statistical syllogism, we must build in an explicit projectibility constraint:

(A1)   If G is projectible with respect to F and $r > 0.5$, then $\ulcorner Fc$ & $prob(G/F) \geq r \urcorner$ is a prima facie reason for believing $\ulcorner Gc \urcorner$, the strength of the reason depending upon the value of r.

Of course, if we define projectibility in terms of (4.1), (A1) becomes a tautology, but the intended interpretation of (A1) is that *there is* a relation of projectibility between properties, holding in important cases, such that $\ulcorner Fc$ & $prob(G/F) \geq r \urcorner$ is a prima facie reason for $\ulcorner Gc \urcorner$ when G is projectible with respect to F. To have a fully adequate theory we must augment (A1) with an account of projectibility, but that proves very difficult. (See my [1990] for further discussion of this.)

The term "projectible" comes from the literature on induction. Goodman [1955] was the first to observe that principles of induction require a projectibility constraint. I have deliberately chosen the term "projectible" in formulating the constraint on (A1), because in the theory of nomic probability, principles of induction become theorems rather than primitive postulates. The statistical syllogism provides the epistemological machinery that make the theory run, and the projectibility constraint on induction turns out to derive from the projectibility constraint on (A1). It is the same property of projectibility that is involved in both cases.

The reason provided by (A1) is only a prima facie reason, and as such it is defeasible. Like any other prima facie reason, it can be defeated by having a reason for denying the conclusion. The reason for denying the conclusion constitutes a rebutting defeater. But there are also important undercutting defeaters for (A1). In (A1), we infer the truth of $\ulcorner Gc \urcorner$ on the basis of probabilities conditional on a limited set of facts about c (the facts expressed by $\ulcorner Fc \urcorner$). But if we know additional facts about c that alter the probability, that defeats the prima facie reason:

(D1)   If G is projectible with respect to H then $\ulcorner Hc$ & $prob(G/F\&H) \neq prob(G/F) \urcorner$ is an undercutting defeater for (A1).

I will refer to these as *subproperty defeaters*. (D1) amounts to a kind of "total evidence requirement". It requires us to make our inference on the basis of the most comprehensive facts regarding which we know the requisite probabilities.[10]

5. Generalizations of the Statistical Syllogism

Most probabilistic reasoning proceeds in terms of (A1), which I claim is the rule underlying most work on default logic and defeasible inheritance hierarchies. However, (A1) is not the only defensible acceptance rule. There is another acceptance rule that is related to (A1), rather like *modus tollens* is related to *modus ponens*:

(5.1)   If G is projectible with respect to F and $r > 0.5$, then $\ulcorner \sim Gc$ & $prob(G/F) \geq r \urcorner$ is a prima facie reason for $\ulcorner \sim Fc \urcorner$, the strength of the reason depending upon the value of r.

For example, carbon 14 dating relies upon (5.1). The exponential law of radioactive decay enables us to compute the probability, given that something is a specified age, of the ratio of carbon 14 to carbon 13 lying in a certain envelope. When an anthropologist finds that the ratio of carbon 14 to carbon 13 in some artifact *does not* fall in the envelope, she concludes that it is not of the appropriate age. In this

---

[10] I first pointed out the need for subproperty defeaters in my [1983a]. Touretzky [1984] subsequently introduced similar defeaters for use in defeasible inheritance hierarchies.

way she rules out all but a certain range of ages and concludes that
the age of the artifact falls within the remaining ages. This reasoning
cannot be reconstructed in terms of (A1) because the exponential law
of radioactive decay does not provide any way of computing the probability of the age of an artifact lying in a certain envelope given that it
exhibits a specified ratio of carbon 14 to carbon 13.

It seems clear that (A1) and (5.1) are closely related. I suggest that
they are consequences of a single stronger principle:

(5.2)   If G is projectible with respect to F and $r > 0.5$, then $\ulcorner$prob(G/F)
         $\geq r\urcorner$ is a prima facie reason for the conditional $\ulcorner Fc \supset Gc\urcorner$, the
         strength of the reason depending upon the value of r.

(A1) can then be replaced by an instance of (5.2) and *modus ponens*,
and (5.1) by an instance of (5.2) and *modus tollens*.

Principle (5.2) itself can be illustrated by examples in which we do
not know whether either $\ulcorner Fc\urcorner$ or $\ulcorner \sim Gc\urcorner$ holds and hence cannot use
either (A1) or (5.1). For example, knowing something about the wiring
in the next room, but not knowing whether the lights are on, I can
know that the probability is high of the lights being on given that the
light switch is closed, and on that basis I can conclude in accordance
with (5.2) that *if* the switch is closed then the lights are on.

Although (5.1) and (5.2) appear to be correct as stated, there is a
somewhat more convenient way of formulating these acceptance rules.
In applying (5.2), $\ulcorner Fc\urcorner$ typically has two parts. It is equivalent to a
conjunction $\ulcorner Kc \& Uc\urcorner$, where $\ulcorner Kc\urcorner$ (the *known* part) formulates things
we already know about the situation, and $\ulcorner Uc\urcorner$ (the *unknown* part)
formulates additional "hypotheses" that are not known to be true.
Then the conditional we really want to infer is $\ulcorner(Uc \supset Fc)\urcorner$. We *could*
get this by inferring $\ulcorner((Kc \& Uc) \supset Fc)\urcorner$, and then doing something like
using exportation and *modus ponens*. However, this seems needlessly
complicated. We actually seem to make the inference directly, without
going through all of this. To capture this observation, I suggest refor-
mulating (5.2) as follows:

(A3)   If G is projectible with respect to both K and U and $r > 0.5$, then
        $\ulcorner Kc \,\&\, $prob$(G/K\&U) \geq r\urcorner$ is a prima facie reason for $\ulcorner(Uc \supset Gc)\urcorner$.

I propose to understand (A3) in such a way that (A1) is the limiting
case in which U is vacuous (i.e., tautologous). (5.1) can then be reformulated as follows:

(A2)   If G is projectible with respect to both K and U and $r > 0.5$, then
⌜$\sim Gc$ & Kc & prob$(B/K\&U) \geq r$⌝ is a prima facie reason for
⌜$\sim Uc$⌝.

I will refer to (A2) as *the inverse statistical syllogism* and (A3) as *the generalized statistical syllogism*. I will regard (A3) as the fundamental probabilistic acceptance rule. I take it that (A3) is actually quite an intuitive acceptance rule. It amounts to a rule saying that when F is projectible with respect to G, if we know that most G's are F, that gives us a reason for thinking of any particular object that it is an F if it is a G. The only surprising feature of this rule is the projectibility constraint. I have defended (A3) at book-length [1990], arguing that it forms the basis for all reasoning with probabilities (including inductive reasoning, which appears initially to go the other way, from non-probabilistic beliefs to probabilistic beliefs).

In describing a prima facie reason, it is as important to give an account of the defeaters as it is to give a formulation of the reason itself. Just as in the case of (A1), when we use (A3) we are making an inference on the basis of a limited set of facts about c. That inference should be defeated if the probability can be changed by taking more facts into account. This suggests that subproperty defeat for (A2) and (A3) should work in the same way as for (A1):

(5.3)   If G is projectible with respect to $(K\&U\&H)$ then ⌜Hc & prob$(G/K\&U\&H) \neq$ prob$(G/K\&U)$⌝ is an undercutting defeater for (A1), (A2), and (A3).

It turns out, however, that this account is inadequate.[11] There are simple counterexamples to (5.3). For instance, in an application of (A2), if ⌜Hc⌝ is our reason for believing ⌜$\sim Gc$⌝, it will typically be the case that prob$(G/K\&U\&H) <$ prob$(G/K\&U)$. To illustrate, in the example of the light switch and the light, observing that the light in the next

---

[11]   At this point I am correcting a deficiency in the account given in my [1990]. In that work I observed that there are apparent counterexamples to (5.3) as it applies to (A2) and (A3), and I made a proposal for handling them. However, I have since come to realize that my proposal does not work, so without discussing it further here, I will try again to solve the problem. For the interested reader, I note that the simplest counterexample to my earlier proposal is to observe that, according to that proposal, "The wire is broken" would be defeated as a defeater for (5.3) in the example of the light and the switch, because it is a reason for thinking that the light is not on.

room is off gives me a reason, in accordance with (A2), for believing that the switch is open. But if I subsequently learn that the wiring is broken, that lowers the probability of the light's being on given that the switch is closed, and hence defeats the inference, in accordance with (5.3). This is a correct instance of (5.3). Suppose, however, that my reason for believing that the light is off is that it looks that way to me. *The probability of the light's being on given that the switch is closed and the light looks as if it is off* is lower than *the probability of the light's being on given that the switch is closed*, so according to (5.3), observing that the light looks like it is off should also defeat the inference to the conclusion that the switch is open, but clearly it does not. This is a counterexample to (5.3).

There are similar counterexamples to the application of (5.3) to (A3). Suppose we know that the wiring from the switch to the light goes through a certain pipe, along with a lot of other wires, and we know that *some* of the wires in the pipe are broken. This lowers the probability that the light will be on if the switch is closed, and is intuitively a defeater. Principle (5.3) gets this one right. But now suppose instead that we know the light in question to be in the seminar room, along with lots of other lights, and we are told that *some* of the lights in the seminar room are not on. This also lowers the probability that the light is on if the switch is closed, and so it is an instance of (5.3), but it is not intuitively a defeater. This is equally a problem for (5.3) as applied to (A3). On the other hand, there do not appear to be any similar counterexamples to the application of (5.3) to (A1); there are no similar counterexamples to (D1).

What is the difference between the correct and incorrect instances of (5.3)? It seems that there are two ways H can lower the probability of G on $K\&U$: by interfering with the connection between G and $K\&U$, or by making G independently less probable without interfering with the connection. The former H's generate defeaters, and the latter do not. For example, knowing that the wire is broken interferes with the connection between the switch and the light, and so defeats an inference based on that connection. Being told by someone reliable that the light is off, on the other hand, does not interfere with the connection. It is an independent reason for thinking that the light is off, and leaves the connection intact, thus setting us up for a use of (A2) (which *assumes* the connection).

The cases in which H makes G independently less probable without interfering with the connection between ($K\&U$) and G are cases where (1) $\text{prob}(G/K\&U\&H) < \text{prob}(G/K\&U)$, and (2) because the connection remains intact, by making G less probable, it also makes ($K\&U$) less probable. The sense in which it makes ($K\&U$) less probable is that it makes the unknown part U less probable relative to the known part K. More precisely, what disqualifies an instance of (5.3) from being a defeater is that we know the following:

(DD) $\mathrm{prob}(U/K\&H) < \mathrm{prob}(U/K)$.

For example, in the application of (A2) to the switch and the light, the known part of F is a description of how they are supposed to be wired together, and the unknown part is that the switch is closed. Noting that the light is off gives us a reason for thinking that the switch is not closed. Learning that the wiring is broken constitutes a defeater for this inference, in accordance with (5.3). In this case, (DD) fails. That is, the probability of the switch's being closed given that the switch and light are supposed to be wired together but the wiring is now broken is no less than the probability of the switch's being closed given merely that the switch and light are supposed to be wired together. Knowing that the wiring is now broken is not negatively relevant to whether the switch is closed. On the other hand, according to (5.3), being told that the light is off should also be a defeater, but intuitively it is not. This is explained by noting that in this case (DD) holds. That is, the probability of the switch's being closed given that the switch and light are supposed to be wired together and I am told that the light is now off is less than the probability of the switch's being closed given merely that the switch and light are supposed to be wired together.

My suggestion is that the correct form of subproperty defeat for (A2) and (A3) results from adding the denial of (DD) as a qualification to (5.3):

(D)   If H is projectible with respect to both K and U, $\ulcorner Hc$ & $\mathrm{prob}(G/K\&U\&H) \neq \mathrm{prob}(G/K\&U)$ & $\mathrm{prob}(U/K\&H) \geq \mathrm{prob}(U/K)\urcorner$ is an undercutting defeater for (A1), (A2) and (A3).

The observation that the difficulties that arise for (5.3) when it is applied to (A2) and (A3) are not also difficulties for (D1) is now reflected in the fact that the condition (DD) can never hold in applications of (D1). (A1) corresponds to the case in which U is a tautology, but in that case it is impossible to have $\mathrm{prob}(U/K\&H) < \mathrm{prob}(U/K)$. Thus (D1) follows unchanged from (D).

This does not yet comprise a complete account of the defeaters for the statistical syllogism. I have argued [1990] that still more defeaters are required to characterize correctly our commonsense probabilistic reasoning. However, I will not pursue that here. The interested reader can consult the earlier work.

The statistical syllogism provides the most common example of defeasible reasoning in AI, but it is important to realize that not all defeasible reasoning can be subsumed under it. This is clearest in the case of perceptual knowledge, which proceeds in accordance with the prima facie reasons (2.2) and (2.3). It is certainly true that things are usually the way they appear. That is, perception is generally reliable. However, this is a contingent statistical truth that cannot be taken for granted in reasoning from images to judgments about physical objects, because we must be able to make such perceptual judgments before we can discover that perception is reliable. The reliability of perception can be ascertained only by comparing actual perceptual judgments with the state of the world, but our only ultimate access to the state of the world is via perception. Furthermore, although I have not discussed them here, there are numerous other examples of non-statistical prima facie reasons. [12]

6. Direct Inference and Definite Probabilities

Within probability theory, there is a distinction between two different kinds of probabilities, and this generates a distinction between two different kinds of expected situation-likings. *Indefinite probabilities* are general probabilities relating properties or concepts. They are about situation types rather than situation tokens. For example, we can talk about the probability of rain given that certain general meteorological conditions apply. This probability is not about its raining on any particular occasion, but about the general conditions under which rain is likely. By contrast, *definite probabilities* are what are often called "single-case probabilities" and are about situation tokens rather than situation types. For example, we can talk about the probability that it will rain tomorrow. In practical reasoning, plans are evaluated by appeal to definite probabilities rather than indefinite probabilities. For example, in deciding whether to carry an umbrella today, what interests me most is not the indefinite probability of its raining under some very general meteorological conditions but rather the definite proba-

---

[12] A number of these are discussed in Pollock [1974, chapters 5–7].

bility that it is going to rain today. On the other hand, it seems clear that the latter is somehow inferred from the former. The inference of definite probabilities from indefinite probabilities is called *classical direct inference*.[13]

It is useful to have a notational distinction between definite and indefinite probabilities. Accordingly, I will continue to symbolize indefinite probabilities using "prob", but will write definite probabilities using the uppercase "PROB". The basic idea behind classical direct inference was first articulated by Hans Reichenbach [1949]: in determining the probability that an individual c has a property F, we find the narrowest reference class X for which we have reliable statistics and then infer that PROB(Fc) = prob($Fx/x \in X$). For example, insurance rates are calculated in this way. There is almost universal agreement that direct inference is based upon some such principle as this, although there is little agreement about the precise form the theory should take. I have argued [1983, 1984], that classical direct inference should be regarded as proceeding in accordance with the following two epistemic rules (where ⌜Wφ⌝ abbreviates ⌜φ is warranted⌝):

(6.1) If F is projectible with respect to G then ⌜prob(F/G) = r & W(Gc) & W($P \equiv Fc$)⌝ is a prima facie reason for ⌜PROB(P) = r⌝.

(6.2) If F is projectible with respect to H then ⌜prob(F/H) ≠ prob(F/G) & W(Hc) & □($\forall x$)($Hx \supset Gx$)⌝ is an undercutting defeater for (6.1).

Principle (6.2) is called "the principle of subset defeat", because it says that probabilities based upon more specific information take precedence over those based upon less specific information. Note the projectibility constraint in these rules. That constraint is required to avoid various paradoxes of direct inference that turn in an essential way on disjunctions.

To illustrate this account of direct inference, suppose we know that Herman is a 40-year-old resident of the United States who smokes. Suppose we also know that the probability of a 40-year-old resident of the United States having lung cancer is 0.1, but the probability of a 40-year-old smoker who resides in the United States having lung cancer

---

[13] See chapter 2 and Pollock [1990] for a general account of this probabilistic reasoning. Other relevant work is by Kyburg [1974], Bacchus [1990], and Halpern [1990].

is 0.3. If we know nothing else that is relevant we will infer that the probability of Herman's having lung cancer is 0.3. Principle (6.1) provides us with one prima facie reason for inferring that the probability is 0.1 and a second prima facie reason for inferring that the probability is 0.3. However, the latter prima facie reason is based upon more specific information, and so by (6.2) it takes precedence, defeating the first prima facie reason and leaving us justified in inferring that the probability is 0.3.

I believe that (6.1) and (6.2) are correct rules of classical direct inference, but I also believe that the nature of direct inference has been fundamentally misunderstood. Direct inference is taken to govern inferences from indefinite probabilities to definite probabilities, but it is my contention that such "classical" direct inference rests upon parallel inferences from indefinite probabilities to indefinite probabilities. The basic rule of classical direct inference is that if F is projectible with respect to G and we know $\ulcorner\mathrm{prob}(F/G) = r \ \& \ \mathbf{W}(Gc)\urcorner$ but do not know anything else about c that is relevant, this gives us a reason to believe that $\mathrm{PROB}(Fc) = r$. Typically, we will know c to have other projectible properties H but not know anything about the value of $\mathrm{prob}(F/G\&H)$ and so be unable to use the latter in direct inference. But if the direct inference from $\ulcorner\mathrm{prob}(F/G) = r\urcorner$ to $\ulcorner\mathrm{PROB}(Fc) = r\urcorner$ is to be reasonable, there must be a presumption to the effect that $\mathrm{prob}(F/G\&H) = r$. If there were no such presumption then we would have to regard it as virtually certain that $\mathrm{prob}(F/G\&H) \neq r$ (after all, there are infinitely many possible values that $\mathrm{prob}(F/G\&H)$ could have), and so virtually certain that there is a true subset defeater for the direct inference. This would make the direct inference to $\ulcorner\mathrm{PROB}(Fc) = r\urcorner$ unreasonable. Thus classical direct inference presupposes the following principle regarding indefinite probabilities:

(6.3)   If F is projectible with respect to G then $\ulcorner\Box(\forall x)(Hx \supset Gx) \ \& \ \mathrm{prob}(F/G) = r\urcorner$ is a prima facie reason for $\ulcorner\mathrm{prob}(F/H) = r\urcorner$.

Inferences in accord with (6.3) comprise *non-classical direct inference*. Principle (6.3) amounts to a kind of principle of insufficient reason, telling us that if we have no reason to think otherwise, it is reasonable for us to anticipate that conjoining H to G will not affect the probability of F.

A common reaction to (6.3) is that it is absurd—perhaps trivially inconsistent. This reaction arises from the observation that in a large number of cases, (6.3) will provide prima facie reasons for conflicting inferences or even to logically impossible conclusions. For example, since in a standard deck of cards a spade is black and the probability of a black card's being a club is one half, (6.3) gives us a prima facie reason to conclude that the probability of a spade's being a club is one half, which is absurd. But this betrays an insensitivity to the functioning of prima facie reasons. A prima facie reason for an absurd conclusion is automatically defeated by the considerations that lead us to regard the conclusion as absurd. Similarly, prima facie reasons for conflicting conclusions defeat one another. If P is a prima facie reason for Q and R is a prima facie reason for $\sim Q$, then P and R rebut one another and both prima facie inferences are defeated. No inconsistency results. That this sort of case occurs with some frequency in non-classical direct inference should not be surprising, because it also occurs with some frequency in classical direct inference. In classical direct inference we often find ourselves in the position of knowing that c has two logically independent properties G and H, where $\text{prob}(F/G) \neq \text{prob}(F/H)$. When that happens, classical direct inferences from these two probabilities conflict with one another, and so each prima facie reason is a defeater for the other, with the result that we are left without an undefeated direct inference to make.

Although (6.3) is not trivially absurd, it is not self-evidently true either. The only defense I have given for it so far is that it is required for the legitimacy of inferences we commonly make. That is a reason for thinking that it is true, but we would like to know why it is true. Somewhat surprisingly, I was able to show [1990] that principle (6.3) can actually be derived from the acceptance rule (A3) and the calculus of nomic probabilities. Similar reasoning enables us to derive the following defeater for (6.3):

(6.4)   If F is projectible with respect to J then $\ulcorner\Box(\forall x)(Hx \supset Jx)$ & $\Box(\forall x)(Jx \supset Gx)$ & $\text{prob}(F/J) \neq \text{prob}(F/G)\urcorner$ is an undercutting defeater for (6.3).

I will refer to these as *subset defeaters* for nonclassical direct inference. Thus the theory of nonclassical direct inference can be derived from simpler principles, the most important of which is (A3).

We now have two kinds of direct inference—classical and non-classical. Direct inference has traditionally been identified with classical direct inference, but I believe that it is most fundamentally non-classical direct inference. The details of classical direct inference are all reflected in non-classical direct inference. If we could identify definite probabilities with certain indefinite probabilities, we could derive the theory of classical direct inference from the theory of non-classical direct inference. This can be done by noting that the following is a theorem of the calculus of nomic probabilities:

(6.5)   If $\Box(Q \equiv Sa_1...a_n)$ and $\Box(Q \equiv Bb_1...b_m)$ and $\Box[Q \supset (P \equiv Ra_1...a_n)]$
and $\Box[Q \supset (P \equiv Ab_1...b_m)]$, then
$\text{prob}(Rx_1...x_n \, / \, Sx_1...x_n \, \& \, x_1{=}a_1 \, \& \, ... \, \& \, x_n{=}a_n)$
$= \text{prob}(Ay_1...y_m \, / \, By_1...y_m \, \& \, y_1 = b_1 \, \& \, ... \, \& \, y_m = b_m)$.

This allows us to define a kind of definite probability as follows:

(6.6) $\text{prob}(P/Q) = r$ iff for some n, there are n-place properties R and S and objects $a_1,...,a_n$ such that $\Box(Q \equiv Sa_1...a_n)$ and $\Box[Q \supset (P \equiv Ra_1...a_n)]$ and $\text{prob}(Rx_1...x_n \, / \, Sx_1...x_n \, \& \, x_1 = a_1 \, \& \, ... \, \& \, x_n = a_n) = r$.

$\text{prob}(P/Q)$ is an *objective* definite probability. It reflects the state of the world, not the state of our knowledge. The definite probabilities at which we arrive by classical direct inference are not those defined by (6.6). We want classical direct inference to apprise us of probabilities that take account of everything we are warranted in believing about the current situation. This can be accomplished by taking $\mathbf{K}_\alpha$ to be the conjunction of all propositions warranted to degree α, and then defining a "mixed physical/epistemic" probability as follows:

(6.7) $\text{PROB}_\alpha(P) = \text{prob}(P/\mathbf{K}_\alpha)$

(6.8) $\text{PROB}_\alpha(P/Q) = \text{prob}(P/Q\&\mathbf{K}_\alpha)$.

Given this reduction of definite probabilities to indefinite probabilities, it becomes possible to *derive* principles (6.1) and (6.2) of classical direct inference from the principles of non-classical direct inference, and hence indirectly from (A3) and the calculus of nomic probabilities. The upshot of all this is that the theory of direct inference, both classical and nonclassical, consists of a sequence of *theorems* in the theory of nomic probability. We require no new assumptions in order to get direct inference. At the same time, we have made clear sense of the mixed physical/epistemic probabilities that are needed for practical reasoning.

The mixed physical/epistemic probabilities obtained in this way are relative to the index α that measures the degree of justification.

This relativization has a natural application in practical reasoning. We want to use these probabilities to compute expected values for plans. As we saw in chapter 1, we want these expected values to take account of everything we are justified in believing about the current situation. But what we are justified in believing is relative to the degree of justification. The degree of justification required in a particular context depends upon the importance of the reasoning, which is in turn determined by the strengths of the desires for the goals whose pursuit inspires the reasoning. Thus the values of the goals that a plan aims at satisfying will determine the value of α relative to which the definite probabilities are to be computed. This will be discussed further in subsequent chapters.

7. Induction

The simplest kind of induction is *enumerative induction*, which proceeds from the observation that all members of a sample X of A's are B's, and makes a defeasible inference to the conclusion that all A's are B's. This is what is known as the Nicod Principle. Goodman [1955] observed that the principle requires a projectibility constraint. With this constraint, it can be formulated as follows:

(7.1)   If B is projectible with respect to A, then $\ulcorner X$ is a sample of A's all of which are B's$\urcorner$ is a prima facie reason for $\ulcorner$All A's are B's$\urcorner$.

However, formulating the principle in this way merely scratches the surface of the logical complexities associated with enumerative induction. First, it is difficult to give a satisfactory account of the defeaters for this prima facie reason. Of course, counterexamples to the generalization are automatically rebutting defeaters, but the more interesting question is to ask what the undercutting defeaters look like. An important variety of undercutting defeater charges that X is not a "fair sample". This is easy to illustrate but hard to characterize in a general fashion. For example, suppose there is a random telephone poll of Tucson voters, and we discover to our amazement that everyone polled intends to vote for the Democratic candidate for mayor. By (7.1), this poll gives us a reason for believing that all Tucson voters will vote for the Democratic candidate. Now suppose it is subsequently ascertained that, purely by chance, everyone who was called in the survey was a registered Democrat, whereas only about half of the Tucson voters are Democrats. On this basis, we would reject the inductive inference, charging that the sample was not a fair one. There is no inclination to protest that the process of sampling was done incorrectly. It was, after all, a random telephone poll, and we would expect a random poll to choose an approximately equal number of Democrats and Republicans. However, upon discovering that this did not happen, it is no longer reasonable to accept the conclusion of the inductive inference. In other words, the discovery has given us a defeater for the inference. On the other hand, the discovery has not given us any reason (that we did not already have) for thinking that the conclusion is false. After all, it could happen that all of the Republicans are going to vote for the Democratic candidate. The defeater must be an undercutting defeater rather than a rebutting defeater. This much is clear, but how exactly to formulate the defeater is not at all clear.[14]

Another source of complexity concerns the strength of an inductive reason. As a general rule, the larger the sample, the stronger the reason. A separate factor concerns the diversity of the sample. For instance, if we are attempting to confirm a generalization about all mammals, our confirmation will be stronger if we sample wild animals in addition to domesticated animals.[15] It is not at all clear how to combine all of this into a precise principle telling us how strong the inductive reason is.

Enumerative induction has been a favorite topic of philosophers, but statistical induction is much more important for the construction of a rational agent. It is rare that we are in a position to confirm exceptionless universal generalizations. Induction usually leads us to statistical generalizations that either estimate the probability of an A being a B, or the proportion of actual A's that are B's, or more simply, may lead us to the conclusion that most A's are B's. Such statistical generalizations are still very useful, because the statistical syllogism enables a cognizer to make defeasible inferences from them to non-probabilistic conclusions.

A very rough formulation of a principle of statistical induction would proceed as follows:

---

[14] Fair sample defeaters are discussed at greater length in Pollock [1990], but no general account is given.

[15] Further discussion of this can be found in Pollock [1990, 315ff].

(7.2)   If B is projectible with respect to A, then $\ulcorner X$ is a sample of n A's r of which are B's$\urcorner$ is a prima facie reason for $\ulcorner \mathrm{prob}(B/A)$ is approximately equal to $r/n\urcorner$.

All of the problems that arise for a precise theory of enumerative induction arise again for statistical induction. In addition, there is a further problem connected with the fact that the conclusion of (7.2) is only that the probability is *approximately* equal to r/n. How good should we expect the approximation to be? There are obvious things to say, such as that the degree of approximation should improve as the size of the sample improves. I have argued [1990] that this can be made precise as follows. Abbreviating r/n as f, define:

(7.3) $L(n,r,p) = (p/f)^{rf}\cdot((1-p)/(1-f))^{n(1-f)}$.

$L(n,r,p)$ is the *likelihood ratio* of $\ulcorner\mathrm{prob}(A/B) = p\urcorner$ to $\ulcorner\mathrm{prob}(A/B) = f\urcorner$. I argued that each degree of justification corresponds to a minimal likelihood ratio, so we can take the likelihood ratio to be a measure of the degree of justification. For each likelihood ratio α we obtain the α-*rejection class* R_α and the α-*acceptance class* A_α:

(7.4) $R_\alpha = \{p \mid L(n,r,p) \le \alpha\}$

(7.5) $A_\alpha = \{p \mid L(n,r,p) > \alpha\}$.

We are justified to degree α in concluding that $\mathrm{prob}(A/B)$ is not a member of R_α, and hence we are justified to degree α in believing that $\mathrm{prob}(A/B)$ is a member of A_α. If we plot the likelihood ratios, we get a bell curve centered around r/n, with the result that A_α is an interval around r/n and R_α consists of the tails of the bell curve (figure 1). In interpreting this curve, remember that low likelihood ratios correspond to a high degree of justification for *rejecting* that value for $\mathrm{prob}(A/B)$, and so the region around r/n consists of those values we cannot reject, that is, it consists of those values that might be the actual value. This provides us with justification for believing that $\mathrm{prob}(A/B)$ lies in a precisely defined interval around the observed relative frequency, the width of the interval being a function of the degree of justification. For illustration, some typical values of the acceptance interval are listed in table 1. Reference to the acceptance level reflects the fact that attributions of warrant are relative to an index measuring the requisite degree of justification. Sometimes an acceptance level of .1 may be reasonable, at other times an acceptance level of .01 may be required, and so forth.

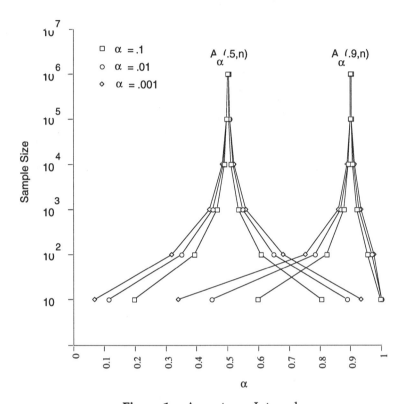

Figure 1. Acceptance Intervals

Table 1. Values of $A_\alpha(f,n)$.

$$A_\alpha(.5,n)$$
$$n$$

α	10	10^2	10^3	10^4	10^5	10^6
.1	[.196,.804]	[.393,.607]	[.466,.534]	[.489,.511]	[.496,.504]	[.498,.502]
.01	[.112,.888]	[.351,.649]	[.452,.548]	[.484,.516]	[.495,.505]	[.498,.502]
.001	[.068,.932]	[.320,.680]	[.441,.559]	[.481,.519]	[.494,.506]	[.498,.502]

$$A_\alpha(.9,n)$$
$$n$$

α	10	10^2	10^3	10^4	10^5	10^6
.1	[.596,.996]	[.823,.953]	[.878,.919]	[.893,.907]	[.897,.903]	[.899,.901]
.01	[.446,1.00]	[.785,.967]	[.868,.927]	[.890,.909]	[.897,.903]	[.899,.901]
.001	[.338,1.00]	[.754,.976]	[.861,.932]	[.888,.911]	[.897,.903]	[.899,.901]

The "justification" of principles of induction is one of the traditional problems of philosophy, but in an important sense, induction needs no justification. It represents an obviously rational way of reasoning. No one could reasonably doubt that an agent reasoning inductively is being rational. In another sense, however, there are important questions about induction. These concern not the general idea of inductive reasoning but the detailed specification of inductive principles, a formidable task. There is reason to hope that the task can be carried out, however. I have shown [1990] that principles of induction can be derived as theorems from the acceptance rule (A3) and the calculus of nomic probabilities.[16] This means that principles of induction like (7.1) and (7.2) should not be regarded as primitive epistemic principles. In fact, they are not even literally correct epistemic principles, because the "reasons" involved are not primitive reasons. The inferences leading

---

[16] Similar claims have been made in the past by those who believe in Bayesian inference. However, what they justify are not genuine principles of induction, but just forms of Bayes' theorem. The difference is important, because genuine principles of induction like the Nicod principle cannot be derived from Bayes' theorem.

to inductive conclusions turn out to be logically complex inferences. If (7.1) and (7.2) really described prima facie reasons, then a cognizer could make those inferences in a single step, without having to go through the complex reasoning described in their reconstruction [1990].

There is something initially puzzling about all of this. The theorems proved in my earlier work [1990] show that inductive reasoning is correct reasoning by showing that it can be justified by some complex arguments involving (A3) and the probability calculus. However, no one ever actually reasons that way. In fact, human beings make inductive inferences in a single bound. I suggest that human inductive reasoning is typically performed by Q&I modules rather than by ratiocination.

That we rely upon Q&I modules for much of our inductive reasoning is clear on grounds independent of the above. Even if (7.1) and (7.2) correctly described prima facie reasons, their application would require reasoners to do things they typically do not do. For instance, to use (7.2) to estimate a probability, a reasoner would have to collect a sample, compute the relative frequency in the sample, and then estimate the probability on that basis. When we are being careful, we do proceed in that way. But in ordinary everyday reasoning, there is no such thing as collecting a sample. To illustrate, I believe that there are more mountain bikes than road bikes on the streets of Tucson. If I believed this on the basis of (7.2), there would have to have been a time when I had compiled an explicit list of bicycles observed on the streets of Tucson, together with the information regarding which of them were mountain bikes and which were road bikes, and then only after compiling that list did I form the belief that there are more mountain bikes than road bikes on the streets of Tucson. But obviously I do not and never have had such a list. Instead, I rely upon my memory to keep rough track of proportions without remembering the individual instances that enter into the proportions. I remember that I have seen more mountain bikes than road bikes without remembering the individual sightings. As I make new sightings, my memory takes them into account in updating my estimate of the proportion of sightings that were mountain bikes and the proportion that were road bikes. Note that although we call this "memory", what we remember is not something we previously knew. Instead, our memory is summing up past observations.

It is a simple matter to describe an algorithm that will maintain a continually updated summary of our observations in this way. We need only keep track of the total number n of observations of A's and the current proportion p of them that have been B's. Then when we observe another A, we increment n by 1; and if the new A is a B, we set the new proportion to be $(np + 1)/(n+1)$, otherwise we set the new proportion to be $np/(n+1)$. Our memory need only record these two numbers, without keeping track of the individual observations.

Although this algorithm is efficient, it is not totally reliable because there is no way to check that we are not observing the same A over and over again and counting it repeatedly each time we observe it. If we do not recall the observations, there is no way to guarantee that this is not happening. Accordingly, there is no guarantee that the estimated proportion produced by the algorithm, and the corresponding estimate of the probability, is the same as what we would get if we kept track of the individual observations and made explicit use of (7.2).

In building an artilect, we must include the ability to perform both quick (but possibly inaccurate) inductive estimates of probabilities, and slower but more careful estimates. In each case, we must be able to measure the strength of the reason obtained, and we must have an account of the defeaters. I have already worked out some of this is worked [1990], but much remains to be done.

8. Other Topics

A complete epistemology includes much more than just perceptual knowledge and inductive reasoning. Some of the reasoning that will be of most direct relevance to AI concerns causal relations, temporal reasoning, spatial reasoning, reasoning about change and persistence, and reasoning about other rational agents. In addition, there are some general kinds of reasoning, such as abduction (inference to the best explanation) and reasoning by analogy, that must be incorporated into an artilect. No attempt will be made to address these topics here. The plan of the OSCAR project is to first produce a general architecture for rationality, and an inference engine for interest-driven defeasible reasoning, and then return to the analysis of more concrete epistemological problems once we have these tools in hand. Nevertheless, the brief epistemological sketch given in this chapter will provide some useful constraints on the structure of a reasoner, because a necessary condition for the adequacy of the design of a reasoner is that it be capable of performing the reasoning described.

Chapter 3
The Structure of
Defeasible Reasoning

1. Reasons and Defeaters

It was illustrated in chapter two that most rational thought involves reasoning that is *defeasible*, in the sense that the reasoning can lead not only to the adoption of new beliefs but also to the retraction of previously held beliefs. This chapter investigates the logical structure of defeasible epistemic reasoning. Defeasible practical reasoning will be investigated in chapter 7. The concern of this chapter is the semantics of defeasible reasoning (construed broadly, as in chapter one). Chapter 4 will turn to the procedural issue of how a rational agent can perform defeasible reasoning.

Reasoning proceeds by constructing arguments, where *reasons* provide the atomic links in arguments. *Conclusive reasons* are reasons that are not defeasible. Conclusive reasons logically entail their conclusions. Those that are not conclusive are *prima facie reasons*. Prima facie reasons create a presumption in favor of their conclusion, but it can be defeated. A reason will be encoded as an ordered pair $\langle \Gamma, p \rangle$, where Γ is the set of premises of the reason and p is the conclusion. Considerations that defeat prima facie reasons are *defeaters*. The simplest kind of defeater for a prima facie reason $\langle \Gamma, p \rangle$ is a reason for denying the conclusion. Let us define '$\neg$' as follows: if for some θ, $\varphi = \ulcorner \sim\theta \urcorner$, let $\neg\varphi = \theta$, and let $\neg\varphi = \ulcorner \sim\varphi \urcorner$ otherwise. Then we define:

If $\langle \Gamma, p \rangle$ is a prima facie reason, $\langle \Lambda, q \rangle$ is a *rebutting defeater* for $\langle \Gamma, p \rangle$ iff $\langle \Lambda, q \rangle$ is a reason and $q = \ulcorner \neg p \urcorner$.

Prima facie reasons for which the only defeaters are rebutting defeaters would be analogous to normal defaults in default logic [Reiter 1980]. Experience in using prima facie reasons in epistemology indicates that there are no such prima facie reasons. Every prima facie reason has associated undercutting defeaters, and these are the most important kinds of defeaters for understanding any complicated reasoning. This is illustrated in chapter 2, and more fully in Pollock [1974, 1986, and 1990]. Undercutting defeaters attack a prima facie reason without attacking its conclusion. They accomplish this by attacking the connection between the premises and the conclusion. For instance, ⌜x looks red to me⌝ is a prima facie reason for an agent to believe ⌜x is red⌝. But if I know not only that x looks red but also that x is illuminated by red lights and red lights can make things look red when they are not, then it is unreasonable for me to infer that x is red. Consequently, ⌜x is illuminated by red lights and red lights can make things look red when they are not⌝ is a defeater, but it is not a reason for thinking that x is not red, so it is not a rebutting defeater. Instead, it attacks the connection between ⌜x looks red to me⌝ and ⌜x is red⌝, giving us a reason for doubting that x wouldn't look red unless it were red. ⌜P wouldn't be true unless Q were true⌝ is some kind of conditional, and I will symbolize it as ⌜P » Q⌝. If ⟨Γ,p⟩ is a prima facie reason, then where ΠΓ is the conjunction of the members of Γ, any reason for denying ⌜ΠΓ » p⌝ is a defeater. Thus I propose to characterize undercutting defeaters as follows:

> If ⟨Γ,p⟩ is a prima facie reason, ⟨Λ,q⟩ is an *undercutting defeater* for ⟨Γ,p⟩ iff ⟨Λ,q⟩ is a reason and q = ⌜~(ΠΓ » p)⌝.

It will be convenient to abbreviate ⌜~(P » Q)⌝ as ⌜(P ⊗ Q)⌝. I will henceforth represent undercutting defeaters as reasons for ⌜(ΠΓ ⊗ p)⌝.

2. Arguments and Inference Graphs

Reasoning starts with premises that are input to the reasoner. (In human beings, they are provided by perception.) The input premises comprise the set *input*. The reasoner then makes inferences (some conclusive, some defeasible) from those premises using reason schemas. *Arguments* are structures recording the reasoning that is performed. It was urged in chapter two that reasoning begins with perceptual states rather than beliefs about perceptual states. Accordingly, the arguments that summarize our reasoning must be viewed as structures consisting of mental states, some of which are perceptual states but most of which are beliefs. This is a somewhat unusual construal of arguments, which are usually taken to be structures of propositions rather than structures of mental states, but this construal is forced upon us by the facts about perception. It is occasionally awkward to view arguments in this way, however. When the constituents of arguments are belief states, we can just as well represent the beliefs in terms of the propositions believed, and doing so makes the arguments look more familiar.

The simplest arguments are *linear*. These can be viewed as finite sequences of mental states or propositions, each of which is either a member of *input* or inferable from previous members of the sequence in accordance with some reason schema. The order in the sequence represents the order in which the inferences are made. Some aspects of that ordering may be inessential to the logical structure of the reasoning. Consider, for example, the following two arguments:

1. *(P&Q)*	1. *(P&Q)*
2. *P* from 1	2. *Q* from 1
3. *Q* from 1	3. *P* from 1
4. *(Q&P)* from 2 and 3.	4. *(Q&P)* from 2 and 3.

These represent different orders in which the inferences occur, but the dependency relations in the arguments are the same and could be represented more perspicuously as a graph:

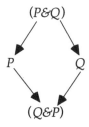

Which of these structures we regard as the argument depends upon what we take the argument to be encoding. If we interpret the argument as encoding an actual sequence of inferences, then it will have the first (sequential) form. If instead we take it as encoding the dependency relations, it will have the second (graphical) form. Both structures are useful for different purposes, so I propose to refer to the sequential structures as *arguments* and the graphical structures as *inference graphs*. We can think of reasoning as a process that builds inference graphs, and the process of construction is recorded (or displayed) in arguments. For many purposes, arguments and inference graphs are interchangeable.

When a reasoner reasons, it is natural to regard it as producing a number of different arguments aimed at supporting different conclusions. However, we can combine all of the reasoning into a single inference graph that records the overall state of the reasoner's inferences, showing precisely what inferences have been made and how inferences are based upon one another. This comprehensive inference graph will provide the central data structure used in evaluating a reasoner's beliefs. Accordingly, we can think of the function of reasoning to be that of building the inference graph. I will return to this point later.

Linear reasoning is a particularly simple form of reasoning in which each conclusion drawn is either given as a member of *input* or inferred from previous conclusions. Not all reasoning is linear. To see this, note that linear reasoning can only lead to conclusions that depend upon the members of *input*, but actual reasoning can lead to a priori conclusions like $(p \lor \sim p)$ or $((p \ \& \ q) \supset q)$ that do not depend upon anything. What makes this possible is *suppositional reasoning*. In suppositional reasoning we "suppose" something that we have not inferred from *input*, draw conclusions from the supposition, and then "discharge" the supposition to obtain a related conclusion that no longer depends upon the supposition. The simplest example of such suppositional reasoning is *conditionalization*. When using conditionalization to obtain a conditional $(p \supset q)$, we suppose the antecedent p, somehow infer the consequent q from it, and then discharge the supposition to infer $(p \supset q)$ independently of the supposition. Similarly, in *reductio ad absurdum* reasoning, to obtain $\neg p$ we may suppose p, somehow infer $\neg p$ on the basis of the supposition, and then discharge the supposition and conclude $\neg p$ independently of the supposition. Another variety of suppositional reasoning is *dilemma* (reasoning by cases).

If we are to encode suppositional reasoning in the inference graph, then the nodes of the inference graph must correspond to conclusions drawn *relative to particular suppositions*. To accomplish this, I will take the nodes of the inference graph to encode inferences to *sequents*, where a sequent is an ordered pair $\langle X, p \rangle$ consisting of a supposition (a set of propositions X) and a conclusion (a single proposition) p. If a node records the inference of a conclusion p relative to a supposition X, I will say that the node *supports p relative to the supposition X* or, alternatively, *supports the sequent* $\langle X, p \rangle$. If $X = \varnothing$, I will say simply that the node *supports p*. The inference relations between nodes are recorded in *inference links*. Where v and η are nodes, $\langle v, \eta \rangle$ is an inference link iff v was inferred from a set of nodes one of which was η. The *immediate inference ancestors* of a node are the nodes to which it is connected (from which it was inferred) by inference links. One complication calls for explicit mention. A reasoner might construct more than one argument supporting the same sequent. The nodes of the inference graph encode *inferences*, so there must be a separate node, each with its own inference links, for each argument supporting the sequent. This will allow us to associate unique strengths with nodes, regard different nodes as defeated by different defeaters, and so on. An *inference branch* is a finite sequence of nodes each of which is an immediate inference ancestor for the next. Let us say that η is an *inference ancestor* of ν iff there is an inference branch connecting ν to η. A node is a *pf-node* iff it represents a defeasible inference, in accordance with some prima facie reason. Let us say that μ is a *deductive ancestor* of ν iff μ is an inference ancestor of ν and the branch connecting them contains no pf-nodes. μ is a *nearest defeasible ancestor* of ν iff either (1) ν is a pf-node and $\mu = \nu$ or (2) μ is a deductive ancestor of ν and μ is a pf-node.

We normally talk about propositions being believed or disbelieved, but we need some similar terminology for talking about sequents in general, so I will apply the term "belief" to sequents. Belief in propositions corresponds to belief in sequents having empty suppositions. Belief in a sequent with a nonempty supposition might be called "conditional belief". An agent's beliefs constitute only a subset of the conclusions represented in the agent's inference graph, because when a conclusion is defeated by another conclusion, it is still represented in the inference graph, but it may not be believed. A rational agent's beliefs are its undefeated conclusions.

Rules of inference can be viewed as rules for adding nodes to the agent's inference graph. One way of conceptualizing this is to think of rules of inference as clauses in the recursive definition of "inference graph". On this conception, an inference graph is any set of inference nodes that can be constructed by starting from the set *input* and accumulating nodes in accordance with the rules of inference. Viewing rules of inference in this way, the following are some obvious inference rules:

Input

> If $p \in$ *input* and $\mathcal{G}$ is an inference graph, then for any supposition X, a new inference graph can be constructed by adding to $\mathcal{G}$ a node supporting $\langle X, p \rangle$ and letting the set of immediate inference ancestors of the new node be empty.

Supposition

> If $\mathcal{G}$ is an inference graph and X is any finite set of propositions, then if $p \in X$, a new inference graph can be constructed by adding to $\mathcal{G}$ a node supporting $\langle X, p \rangle$, and letting the set of immediate inference ancestors of the new node be empty.

Reason

If $\mathcal{G}$ is an inference graph containing nodes $\alpha_1,...,\alpha_n$ supporting each of $\langle X,p_1 \rangle,...,\langle X,p_n \rangle$, and $\langle \{p_1...,p_n\},q \rangle$ is a reason (either conclusive or prima facie), then a new inference graph can be constructed by adding to $\mathcal{G}$ a node supporting $\langle X,q \rangle$, and letting the set of immediate inference ancestors of the new node be $\{\alpha_1...,\alpha_n\}$.

Conditionalization

If $\mathcal{G}$ is an inference graph containing a node α supporting $\langle X \cup \{p\},q \rangle$ then a new inference graph can be constructed by adding to $\mathcal{G}$ a node supporting $\langle X,(p \supset q) \rangle$, and letting the set of immediate inference ancestors of the new node be $\{\alpha\}$.

Dilemma

If $\mathcal{G}$ is an inference graph containing a node α supporting $\langle X,(p \vee q) \rangle$, a node β supporting $\langle X \cup \{p\},r \rangle$, and a node γ supporting $\langle X \cup \{q\},r \rangle$, then a new inference graph can be constructed by adding to $\mathcal{G}$ a node supporting $\langle X,r \rangle$, and letting the set of immediate inference ancestors of the new node be $\{\alpha,\beta,\gamma\}$.

Other rules of inference graph formation could be included as well, but these will suffice for illustrative purposes.

A distinction must be made between two different kinds of suppositions and suppositional reasoning. In *factual* suppositional reasoning, we suppose that something *is* the case and then reason about what else is the case. In *counterfactual* suppositional reasoning, we make a supposition of the form, "Suppose it *were* true that *P*", and then reason about what *would* be the case. Both kinds of reasoning appear to support forms of conditionalization, but the inferred conditionals are different. Conditionalization from counterfactual suppositions yields counterfactual conditionals, whereas conditionalization from factual suppositions yields only material conditionals. These two kinds of suppositional reasoning work in importantly different ways. In factual suppositional reasoning, because we are supposing that something *is* the case, we should be able to combine the supposition with anything we have already concluded to be the case. Counterfactual suppositions, on the other hand, override earlier conclusions and may require their retraction within the supposition. Counterfactual suppositional reasoning is extremely interesting, but throughout this book, I will appeal only to factual suppositional reasoning. For such reasoning, the following inference rule is reasonable:

Foreign Adoptions
If $\mathcal{G}$ is an inference graph containing a node α supporting $\langle X,p \rangle$, and $X \subseteq Y$, then a new inference graph can be constructed by adding to $\mathcal{G}$ a node supporting $\langle Y,p \rangle$ and letting the immediate inference ancestors of the new node be the same as the immediate inference ancestors of α.

This rule is reasonable because in supposing that something is true, we should be able to combine it with anything else we are already justified in believing to be true. This rule would not be reasonable for counterfactual suppositional reasoning.

3. Defeat among Inferences—Uniform Reasons

The concept of epistemic justification that is of relevance to this investigation concerns belief updating. Justified beliefs are those mandated by the rules for belief updating. What an agent is justified in believing is a function of both what *input* premises have been supplied by the perceptual systems and how far the agent has gotten in its reasoning. A necessary condition for a belief to be jusitified is that the agent has engaged in reasoning that produced an argument supporting the belief, but that is not a sufficient condition because the agent may also have produced an argument that defeats the first argument.

The agent's reasoning is encoded in the inference graph, the nodes of which correspond to inferences. Defeat is both a relation between nodes of the inference graph and a monadic property of nodes. A node is defeated (has the monadic property) just in case it stands in appropriate defeat relations to other nodes. A justified belief is one supported by an undefeated node of the inference graph.

To complete this characterization of epistemic justification, we need an account of the defeat relations and a characterization of when those defeat relations render a node defeated. A general treatment of defeat relations requires us to take account of the fact that reasons differ in strength; some are better than others. If we have a reason for p and a reason for $\neg p$, but the latter is stronger than the former, then it wins the competition and we should believe $\neg p$. A general theory of reasoning requires us to talk about the strengths of reasons and how those strengths affect interactions between reasons. However, before addressing this complicated issue, consider how defeat between nodes could be analyzed if all reasons were of the same strength. This is *The Assumption of Uniform Reasons*.

One node of the inference graph defeats another by supporting a defeater for it. Recall, however, that in suppositional reasoning, different steps of reasoning may depend upon different suppositions. If a node η of the inference graph results from applying a prima facie reason ⟨Γ,p⟩, and a node σ supports a defeater for this prima facie reason, this does not automatically guarantee that σ defeats η because they may support their conclusions relative to different suppositions. Consider, for instance, the following pair of arguments, where P is a prima facie reason for Q, and D is a defeater for this prima facie reason:

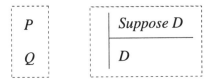

These could be represented by the inference graph diagrammed in figure 1. The defeater D is introduced as a mere supposition, and that supposition is not included in the suppositions made in η. Clearly we should not be able to defeat an inference just by *supposing* a defeater that has no independent justification. It seems that the support of a defeater by a node whose supposition is X should defeat only a defeasible

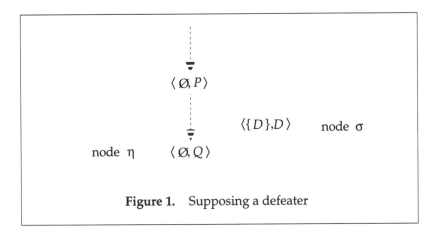

Figure 1.   Supposing a defeater

inference that is made relative to a supposition that includes X. Accordingly, on the assumption of uniform reasons we can define:

A node σ *rebuts* a node η iff:
(1) η is a pf-node supporting some proposition q relative to a supposition Y; and
(2) σ supports $\neg q$ relative to a supposition X, where $X \subseteq Y$.

A node σ *undercuts* a node η iff:
(1) η is a pf-node supporting some proposition q relative to a supposition Y; where $p_1,...,p_k$ are the propositions supported by its immediate ancestors; and
(2) σ supports $((p_1 \,\&\, ... \,\&\, p_k) \otimes q)$ relative to a supposition X where $X \subseteq Y$.

A node σ *defeats* a node η iff σ either rebuts or undercuts η.

Now let us consider how this account of defeat relations must be modified to accommodate reasons of varying strength.

4. Taking Strength Seriously

At this point, I will relax the simplifying assumption that all reasons are of the same strength.

Measuring Strength

If we are to take strength seriously, we must have some way of measuring it. One way is to compare reasons with a set of standard equally good reasons that have numerical values associated with them in some determinant way. I propose to do that by taking the set of standard reasons to consist of instances of the statistical syllogism. Recall from chapter two that this principle is formulated as follows:

The Statistical Syllogism:
> If $r > 0.5$ then $\ulcorner\mathrm{prob}(F/G) \geq r \,\&\, Gc\urcorner$ is a prima facie reason for $\ulcorner Fc\urcorner$, the strength of the reason being a monotonic increasing function of r.

Consequently, for any proposition p, we can construct a standardized argument for $\neg p$ on the basis of the pair of suppositions $\ulcorner\mathrm{prob}(F/G) \geq r \,\&\, Gc\urcorner$ and $\ulcorner(p \equiv \sim Fc)\urcorner$:

1. Suppose prob(F/G) ≥ r & Gc.
2. Suppose ($p \equiv \sim Fc$).
3. Fc from 1.
4. $\neg p$ from 2,3.

where the strength of the argument is a function of r. If X is a prima facie reason for p, we can measure the strength of this prima facie reason in terms of that value of r such that the conflicting argument from the suppositions ⌐prob(F/G) ≥ r & Gc⌐ and ⌐($p \equiv \sim Fc$)⌐ exactly counteracts it. We could take r itself to be the measure of the strength of the reason, but a somewhat more convenient measure is $2 \cdot (r - 0.5)$. This has the convenient consequence that the strength of an instance of statistical syllogism in which $r = 0.5$ is 0, and strengths are normalized to 1.0. So my proposal is:

If X is a prima facie reason for p, the strength of this reason is $2 \cdot (r - 0.5)$ where r is that real number such that an argument for $\neg p$ based upon the suppositions ⌐prob(F/G) ≥ r & Gc⌐ and ⌐($p \equiv \sim Fc$)⌐ and employing the statistical syllogism exactly counteracts the argument for p based upon the supposition X.

For instance, in a context in which a prima facie reason of minimal acceptable strength corresponds to an instance of the statistical syllogism in which $r = 0.95$, it follows that prima facie reasons must have a strength ≥ 0.9.

Conclusive reasons logically guarantee the truth of their conclusions given the truth of the premises, so there can be no accompanying attenuation in strength of justification. We can capture this by taking them to have strength 1.0.

I take it that this way of measuring the strengths of reasons is very natural. However, it has an important consequence that deserves emphasis. Instances of the statistical syllogism can be linearly ordered by strength, because that is a function of the real number r. Other reasons can be compared to instances of the statistical syllogism having the same strength, so it follows that all reasons can be linearly ordered by strength. Although this consequence is unsurprising, it does conflict with some recent proposals regarding nonmonotonic reasoning that assume the ordering of reasons by strength to be only a partial ordering.

Generic Bayesianism

Given a measure of the strengths of reasons, what are we to do with it? Strengths are important in deciding whether a reason is strong enough to justify a belief. It was indicated in chapter 1 that the strength of reason required to justify a conclusion is a function of our degree of interest in the conclusion. (This will be addressed further in chapter four.) However, there is a residual problem. Although individual reasons may be sufficiently strong to justify their conclusions in a one-step argument, how do we determine the degree of justification of the conclusion of a complex argument that combines inferences using a number of such reasons?

It is useful to distinguish between the degree of support of a conclusion and its degree of justification. Whether a conclusion is justified depends not just on how strong the arguments are that support it but also on whether those arguments are defeated. My present concern is with the strengths of arguments that combine inferences employing a number of reasons that are of less than unit strength. It is often supposed that, in such an argument, each inference attenuates the strength of the conclusion, and so, although each reason by itself is sufficiently strong, the degree of support of the ultimate conclusion may be too weak to justify believing it.

This supposition is usually coupled with a probabilistic model of reasoning according to which reasons make their conclusions probable to varying degrees, and the ultimate conclusion is justified only if it is made sufficiently probable by the cumulative reasoning. I will refer to this theory as *generic Bayesianism*.

According to generic Bayesianism, our epistemic attitudes towards a proposition should be determined by its probability. It will generally be necessary to compute such probabilities in order to determine the degree of justification of a belief. Some kinds of deductive inference can be applied "blindly" without going through such calculations, but only when the inferences are guaranteed to preserve probability. Let us say that an inference rule

$$\frac{P_1,...,P_n}{Q}$$

is *probabilistically valid* just in case it follows from the probability calculus that prob(Q) ≥ the minimum of the prob(P_i)'s. For the generic Bayesian, inference rules can be applied blindly, obviating the need for probability calculations, only if they are probabilistically valid.

If P logically entails Q, then it follows from the probability calculus that prob(Q) ≥ prob(P), and hence the generic Bayesian is able to conclude that the degree of justification for Q is as great as that for P. Thus deductive inferences from single premises can proceed blindly. However, this is not equally true for entailments requiring multiple premises. Specifically, it is not true in general that if $\{P,Q\}$ entails R, then prob(R) ≥ the minimum of prob(P) and prob(Q). For instance, $\{P,Q\}$ entails ($P\&Q$), but prob($P\&Q$) may be less than either prob(P) or prob(Q). Many of our most cherished inference rules, including *modus ponens*, *modus tollens*, and adjunction, turn out to be probabilistically invalid. No inference rule that proceeds from mutliple premises and uses them all essentially can be probabilistically valid. This is extremely counterintuitive. It means that a reasoner engaging in Bayesian updating is precluded from drawing deductive conclusions from its reasonably held beliefs. For instance, consider an engineer who is designing a bridge. She will combine a vast amount of information about material strength, weather conditions, maximum load, costs of various construction techniques, and so forth, to compute the size a particular girder must be. These various bits of information are, presumably, independent of one another, so if the engineer combines 100 pieces of information, each with a probability of 0.99, the conjunction of that information has a probability of only $.99^{100}$, which is approximately 0.366. According to generic Bayesianism, she would be precluded from using all of this information simultaneously in an inference—but then it would be impossible to build bridges.

As a description of human reasoning, this seems clearly wrong. Once one has arrived at a set of conclusions, one does not hesitate to make further deductive inferences from them. But an even more serious difficulty for generic Bayesianism is that the theory turns out to be self-defeating; if the theory were correct, it would be impossible to perform the very calculations required by the theory for determining whether a belief ought to be held. This arises from the fact that Bayesian updating requires a reasoner to decide what to believe by computing probabilities. The difficulty is that the probability calculations themselves cannot be performed by a Bayesian reasoner. To illustrate the difficulty, suppose the reasoner has the following beliefs:

(4.1) $\text{prob}(P \lor Q) = \text{prob}(P) + \text{prob}(Q) - \text{prob}(P \& Q)$
$\text{prob}(P) = 0.5$
$\text{prob}(Q) = 0.49$
$\text{prob}(P \& Q) = 0.$

From this we would like the reasoner to compute that $\text{prob}(P \lor Q) =$ 0.99, and perhaps go on to adopt $(P \lor Q)$ as one of its beliefs. However, generic Bayesianism cannot accommodate this. The difficulty is that the use of (4.1) in a computation is an example of a "blind use" of a deductive inference, and as such it is legitimate only if the inference is probabilistically valid. To determine the probabilistic validity of this inference, it must be treated on a par with all the other inferences performed by the reasoner. Although the premises are about probabilities, they must also be assigned probabilities ("higher-order probabilities") to be used in their manipulation. Viewing (4.1) in this way, we find that although the four premises do logically entail the conclusion, the inference is not probabilistically valid for the same reason that *modus ponens, modus tollens*, and adjunction fail to be probabilistically valid. It is an inference from a mutliple premise set, and despite the entailment, the conclusion can be less probable than any of the premises.

How serious this difficulty is depends upon the probabilities of the four probabilistic premises. The first premise is a necessary truth, so it must have probability 1. If the other premises also have probability 1, then it follows that the conclusion has probability 1 and so the inference is probabilistically valid after all. (Similarly, *modus ponens* is probabilistically valid for the special case in which the premises have probability 1.) Can we assume, however, that a belief like $\ulcorner \text{prob}(P) = 0.5 \urcorner$ automatically has probability either 1 or 0? Unless we are talking about Carnapian logical probability [Carnap 1950, 1952], that would seem totally unreasonable, and as such logical probabilities are insensitive to empirical facts, they are not appropriate for use in belief updating. The inescapable conclusion is that a Bayesian reasoner cannot perform the very calculations that are required for Bayesian reasoning.

It seems initially that there remains one possible avenue of escape for the generic Bayesian. If the set $\{P_1,...,P_n\}$ entails Q, the inference from $P_1,...,P_n$ to Q will not usually be probabilistically valid, but the inference from the *conjunction* $(P_1 \& ... \& P_n)$ to Q will be probabilistically valid. If in addition to believing each of the premises in (4.1), the reasoner also believes their conjunction, then it can validly infer that $\text{prob}(P \lor Q) = 0.99$. The reasoner cannot validly infer the conjunction of the premises from the individual premises, because adjunction is probabilistically invalid, but if in addition to knowing that the premises in (4.1) are highly probable, the reasoner also knows the conditional probabilities of each on conjunctions of the others, it can use those conditional probabilities to compute the probability of the conjunction of the premises by using the following principle:

(4.2) $\text{prob}(P \& Q) = \text{prob}(P/Q) \cdot \text{prob}(Q)$.

This is "the conditional probability strategy". Unfortunately, this strategy is subject to an overwhelming difficulty: even if the reasoner had the requisite conditional probabilities, it would be unable to use them to perform the computation in (4.2). That computation would involve reasoning as follows:

$$\text{prob}(P \& Q) = \text{prob}(P/Q) \cdot \text{prob}(Q).$$
$$\text{prob}(P/Q) = \alpha$$
$$\text{prob}(Q) = \beta$$
$$\overline{\text{prob}(P \& Q) = \alpha \cdot \beta}$$

The difficulty we encounter is precisely the same as the one we set out to solve in the first place: this is an inference from multiple premises, and as such is probabilistically invalid. To turn it into a valid inference, the reasoner would have to know the probability of the conjunction of the premises and make the inference from that conjunction instead. It was for this purpose that the conditional probability strategy was proposed initially. Thus rather than solving the problem, the strategy leads to an infinite regress.

The only conclusion that can be drawn from all of this is that generic Bayesianism is incoherent as a theory of belief updating. The probability calculations required of the reasoner proceed via deductive inferences that are not probabilistically valid, and hence the Bayesian reasoner is precluded from making the very calculations it needs to determine degrees of justification.

Generic Bayesianism is based upon the intuition that a proposition should be believed only if it is highly probable. If generic Bayesianism is logically incoherent, why is this intuition so compelling? The answer seems to be that the English word "probable" is ambiguous. We must distinguish between *statistical probability* and *epistemic probability*. Statistical probability is concerned with *chance*. We are using statistical probability when we talk about how likely it is to rain tomorrow, or about the probability of being dealt a royal flush in poker. Epistemic probability is concerned with the degree of justification of a belief. We are referring to epistemic probability when we conclude that the butler probably did it. All that means is that there is good reason to think the butler did it. It is certainly true that a belief is justified iff its epistemic probability is high; that is just what we mean by high epistemic probability. The lesson to be learned from the previous discussion is that rules like *modus ponens* and adjunction preserve high epistemic probability, and hence epistemic probability cannot be quantified in a way that conforms to the probability calculus. This should not be particularly surprising. There was never really any reason to expect epistemic probability to conform to the probability calculus. That is a calculus of statistical probabilities, and the only apparent connection between statistical and epistemic probability is that they share the same ambiguous name. It should have been obvious from the start that high epistemic probability is preserved by ordinary inference rules, and hence epistemic probability does not conform to the probability calculus.

The Weakest Link Principle

I have argued that generic Bayesianism must be rejected—belief updating cannot be performed by exclusively probabilistic methods. My proposal is that the degree of support for a conclusion should instead be computed in terms of the *Weakest Link Principle*, according to which a deductive argument is as good as its weakest link. More precisely:

> The degree of support of the conclusion of a deductive argument is the minimum of the degrees of support of its premises.

The simplest reason for favoring this principle is that it seems to be the only alternative to generic Bayesianism that is not completely ad hoc. Any other theory owes us an account of how the strength of an argument decreases as we add inferences from new premises. The only obvious account of that is the Bayesian account, but we have seen that it must be rejected.

There is also a strong argument in favor of the weakest link principle. This turns upon the fact that the objections to the Bayesian account can be applied more generally to any account that allows the strength of an argument to be less than its weakest link. On any such account, multi-premise inference rules like *modus ponens* and adjunction will turn out to be invalid, but then it seems unavoidable that the theory will be self-defeating in the same way as the Bayesian theory—by making it impossible for the reasoner to compute the degrees of support of its conclusions.

My defense of the weakest link principle has consisted of an attack on the alternatives, but there is also a very natural objection to the weakest link principle itself: faced with a long argument proceeding from multiple premises, we likely apt to view it with more suspicion than a simpler argument on the grounds that there is more that could go wrong with it. This sounds like a very Bayesian observation. However, its significance becomes less clear when we reflect that we are also inclined to regard complex, purely deductive arguments (proceeding from a priori premises) with suspicion, also on the grounds that there is more that could go wrong with them than with simple arguments. This certainly cannot be taken to show that the degree of support attaching to the conclusion of a deductive argument diminishes with the complexity of the argument (and correlatively that rules like *modus ponens* are invalid in purely deductive arguments), so it is doubtful that the analogous observation should have that consequence for arguments with contingent premises. I am inclined to think that what these observations really illustrate is the supervision of the reflexive reasoner rather than the built-in structure of the planar reasoner.

The above formulation of the weakest link principle applies only to deductive arguments, but we can use it to obtain an analogous principle for defeasible arguments. If P is a prima facie reason for Q, then we can use conditionalization to construct a simple defeasible argument for the conclusion $(P \supset Q)$, and this argument turns upon no premises:

> Suppose P
> ————————————
> Then (defeasibly) Q.
> Therefore, $(P \supset Q)$.

Because this argument has no premises, the degree of support of its conclusion should be a function of nothing but the strength of the prima facie reason. Next, notice that any defeasible argument can be reformulated so that prima facie reasons are used only in subarguments of this form, and then all subsequent steps of reasoning are deductive. The conclusion of the defeasible argument is thus a deductive consequence of members of *input* together with a number of conditionals justified in this way. By the weakest link principle for deductive arguments, the degree of support of the conclusion should then be the minimum of (1) the degrees of justification of the members of *input* used in the argument and (2) the strengths of the prima facie reasons.

Input consists of states like "That looks red to me", from which one can infer defeasibly, "That is red". Because something can look more or less clearly red, and that can affect the justification of the conclusion, we must assign differing "strengths" to the *input* states, depending upon how clearly the object looks red. These strengths must be factored into the computation of the degree of support for the conclusion of a defeasible argument. This yields *The Weakest Link Principle for Defeasible Arguments*:

> The degree of support of the conclusion of a defeasible argument is the minimum of the strengths of the prima facie reasons employed in it and the strengths of the *input* states to which it appeals.

The problem of computing degrees of support is thus computationally simple. Sometimes it will be convenient to talk about the *strength of the argument* as being the degree of support of its conclusion. Each node of the inference graph will be assigned a unique strength—the strength of the argument supporting it, computed in accordance with the weakest link principle.

The Accrual of Reasons

If we have two independent reasons for a conclusion, does that make the conclusion more justified than if we had just one? It is natural to suppose that it does, but upon closer inspection that becomes unclear. Cases that seem initially to illustrate such accrual of justification appear upon reflection to be better construed as cases of having a single reason that subsumes the two separate reasons. For instance, if Jones tells me that the president of Slobovia has been assassinated, that gives me a reason for believing it; and if Smith tells me that the president of Slobovia has been assassinated, that also gives me a reason for believing it. Surely, if they both tell me the same thing, that gives me a better reason for believing it. However, there are considerations indicating that my reason in the latter case is not simply the conjunction of the two reasons I have in the former cases. Reasoning based upon testimony is a straightforward instance of the statistical syllogism. We know that people tend to tell the truth, and so when someone tells us something, that gives us a prima facie reason for believing it. This turns upon the following probability being reasonably high:

(1)   prob(p is true / S asserts p).

When we have the concurring testimony of two people, our degree of justification is not somehow computed by applying a predetermined function to the latter probability. Instead, it is based upon the quite distinct probability

(2)   prob(p is true / S_1 asserts p and S_2 asserts p and $S_1 \neq S_2$).

The relationship between (1) and (2) depends upon contingent facts about the linguistic community. We might have one community in which speakers tend to make assertions completely independently of one another, in which case (2) > (1); and we might have another community in which speakers tend to confirm each other's statements only when they are fabrications, in which case (2) < (1). Clearly our degree of justification for believing p will be different in the two linguistic communities. It will depend upon the value of (2), rather than being some function of (1).

All examples I have considered that seem initially to illustrate the accrual of reasons turn out in the end to have this same form. They are all cases in which we can estimate probabilities analogous to (2) and make our inferences on the basis of the statistical syllogism rather than on the basis of the original reasons. Accordingly, I doubt that reasons do accrue. If we have two separate undefeated arguments for a conclusion, the degree of justification for the conclusion is simply the maximum of the strengths of the two arguments. This will be my assumption.

Defeat among Inferences
One of the most important roles of the strengths of reasons lies in deciding what to believe when one has conflicting arguments for q and $\neg q$. It is clear that if the argument for q is *much* stronger than the argument for $\neg q$, then p should be believed, but what if the argument for q is just slightly stronger than the argument for $\neg q$? It is tempting to suppose that the argument for $\neg q$ should at least attenuate our degree of confidence in q, in effect lowering its degree of justification. But upon further reflection, I am inclined to think that this is false.

Otherwise, if we acquired a second argument for $\neg q$, it would face off against a weaker argument for q and so be better able to defeat it. But that is tantamount to taking the two arguments for $\neg q$ to result in greater justification for that conclusion, and that is just the principle of accrual. So it seems that if we are to reject the latter principle, then we should also conclude that arguments that face weaker conflicting arguments are not thereby diminished in strength. There are cases that initially appear to be counterexamples to this. For instance, if Jones, whom I regard as highly reliable, tells me that the president of Slobovia has been assassinated, this may justify me in believing that the president of Slobovia has been assassinated. If Smith, whom I regard as signficantly less reliable, denies this, his denial may be insufficient to defeat my belief in the assassination, but surely Smith's denial should render me less confident of my belief. However, this example is analogous to those that appeared at first to illustrate the accrual of justification. What is happening is that contingent information is leading me to believe that the probability of an assertion's being true is lowered by its being denied by another at least somewhat reliable source, and this constitutes a subproperty defeater for the application of the statistical syllogism that is involved in my reasoning in this case. Accordingly, the original argument (based simply on Jones' assertion) is defeated outright, and I must instead base my belief in the assassination on the lower probability of its having happened given that Jones reported it and Smith denied it.

In the light of the preceding considerations, I think it should be concluded that an argument for $\neg q$ defeats an argument for q only if it is at least as strong as the argument for q. Accordingly, we can characterize rebutting defeat as follows:

A node α *rebuts* a node β iff:
  (1) β is a pf-node of some strength ξ supporting some proposition q relative to a supposition Y;
  (2) α is a node of strength η and supports $\neg q$ relative to a supposition X, where $X \subseteq Y$; and
  (3) $\eta \geq \xi$.

How does strength affect undercutting defeat? In previous publications, I have assumed that it does not—that all that is required for undercutting defeat is that the undercutting defeater be justified. But this view becomes incoherent when we take account of the fact that justification must always be relativized to a degree of justification.[1] It seems apparent that any adequate account of justification must have the consequence that if a belief is unjustified relative to a particular degree of justification, then it is unjustified relative to any higher degree of justification. However, this obvious constraint is violated by the principle that all that is required for undercutting defeat is that the undercutting defeater be justified. Suppose we have a strong reason P for some conclusion Q and a weaker reason for $(P \otimes Q)$. Relative to a low degree of justification, the undercutting defeater $(P \otimes Q)$ would be justified, and so Q would be unjustified. But relative to a higher degree of justification, $(P \otimes Q)$ would be unjustified, and so Q would turn out to be justified. This is perverse. It seems undeniable that degrees of justification must enter into undercutting defeat in the same way as for rebutting defeat:

A node α *undercuts* a node β iff:
(1) β is a pf-node of some strength ξ supporting some proposition q relative to a supposition Y; where $p_1,...,p_k$ are the propositions supported by its immediate ancestors; and
(2) α is a node of strength η and supports $((p_1 \And ... \And p_k) \otimes q)$ relative to a supposition X where $X \subseteq Y$; and
(3) $\eta \geq \xi$.

It will be convenient to encode defeat relations between nodes of the inference graph in a new set of links, called *defeat links*. Where μ and ν are nodes of the inference graph, $\langle \mu, \nu \rangle$ is a defeat link iff μ is a pf-node and ν defeats it relative to some degree of justification.

5. Other Nonmonotonic Formalisms

Although in general outline the theory of defeasible reasoning presented predates the most familiar theories of nonmonotonic reasoning in AI, it will seem unfamiliar to many researchers in AI because of the past isolation of philosophy and AI from one other. Accordingly, it will be useful to compare this theory to those more familiar in AI. The comparison will be scattered through the next several sections. Because

---

[1] I was led to see this as a result of discussions with Stewart Cohen.

the AI theories will be unfamiliar to most philosophers, I will give a brief account of each.

Argument-Based Approaches

The theory of defeasible reasoning adumbrated in this book is an "argument-based" theory, in the sense that it characterizes defeasible consequence in terms of the interactions between the inference steps of all possible arguments that can be constructed from the given set *input* using a fixed set of prima facie reasons and defeaters. Other argument-based approaches to defeasibility can be found in the work of Loui [1987], Simari and Loui [1992], and Lin and Shoham [1990]. The work of Horty, Thomason, and Touretzky [1990] and Horty and Thomason [1990] can also be viewed as an argument-based theory of defeasible reasoning, where the arguments have a rather restricted form. However, these theories are all based upon rather simple conceptions of argument, confining their attention to linear arguments. None of the AI theories of nonmonotonic reasoning appears to be sensitive to the importance of suppositional reasoning, but suppositional reasoning is essential in any reasoner that is capable of performing deductive and defeasible reasoning simultaneously. In addition, the systems of Horty, Thomason, and Touretzky [1990], Horty and Thomason [1990], and Simari and Loui [1992] accommodate only rebutting defeaters.

Much of the work that lies within the argument-based approach adds a form of "specificity defeat" that is not part of the theory adumbrated in this book. The details of specificity defeat have been worked out differently by different authors, but the basic idea is that when two arguments have conflicting conclusions, if one of the arguments is based upon a "more specific" set of premises, it should take precedence and the other argument should be regarded as defeated. Specificity defeat originated with Poole [1985, 1988], and represents a generalization of the subproperty defeaters that play so prominent a role in connection with the statistical syllogism. My own view is that the correctness of specificity defeat turns heavily upon the context in which it is being used. Horty, Thomason, and Touretzky [1990] apply it to defeasible inheritance hierarchies in which all nodes are logically simple. Such hierarchies can be viewed as networks of concepts related in the manner required for the application of the statistical syllogism, and the conclusions of such defeasible inheritance proceed in accordance with the statistical syllogism. So construed, specificity defeat amounts to subproperty defeat, and if it is formulated properly I have no objections to it. But in Horty and Thomason [1990] the defeasible inheritance hierarchies are extended so that the nodes can represent Boolean combinations of concepts (concepts constructed out of simple concepts using negation, conjunction, and disjunction). Here, there is a problem. As we saw in chapter 2, the principle of subproperty defeat must incorporate a projectibility constraint, and that has the effect of ruling out many disjunctions and negations. The result is that specificity defeat cannot be applied in general within such logically complex defeasible inheritance hierarchies. This difficulty has been completely overlooked in the literature.

Loui [1987] and Simari and Loui [1992] treat specificity defeat more generally, applying it to all defeasible reasoning, and not just defeasible reasoning in accordance with the statistical syllogism. This strikes me as entirely wrong. First, in cases in which the reasoning can be regarded as proceeding in accordance with the statistical syllogism, they will encounter the same projectibility problems as Horty and Thomason. Second, it was observed in chapter 2 that much defeasible reasoning cannot be regarded as proceeding in accordance with the statistical syllogism. For such reasoning, there is no reason to think that specificity defeat is a correct principle of reasoning. The only intuitive examples that have ever been given in support of it concern the statistical syllogism. The literature contains absolutely no examples illustrating its applicability elsewhere, and a conscientious effort on my part to construct such examples has ended in complete failure. It is for this reason that I reject specificity defeat as a general principle of defeasible reasoning.

Default Logic
In spirit, my own theory of defeasible reasoning seems close to Reiter's default logic [1980], with prima facie reasons and defeaters corresponding to Reiter's defaults. Defaults can be regarded as defeasible inference rules. Reiter writes defaults in the form $\ulcorner P{:}Q_1,...,Q_n/R\urcorner$, the interpretation being that P provides the premise for a default inference to the conclusion R, and any of $\sim Q_1,...,\sim Q_n$ will defeat the inference. Given a set D of defaults and a set W of premises, Reiter defines an *extension* of $\langle D,W\rangle$ to be a set E such that (1) $W \subseteq E$; (2) E is closed under deductive consequence; (3) for each default $\ulcorner P{:}Q_1,...,Q_n/R\urcorner$ in D, if $P \in E$ but none of the $\sim Q_i$ is in E, then R is in E; and (4) no proper subset E^* of E satisfies (1), (2), and the condition (3*) that for each default $\ulcorner P{:}Q_1,...,Q_n/R\urcorner$ in D, if $P \in E^*$ but none of the $\sim Q_i$ is in E, then R is in E^*. The extensions of pairs of defaults and premises are supposed

to represent the sets of rational belief sets one could have if one were given those defaults and premises as one's starting point. This is rationality in the sense of "rationality in the limit", that is, what one could reasonably believe if one had performed all relevant reasoning.

Although default logic is, in some ways, very similar to the theory of defeasible reasoning, there are also profound differences between the two theories. First, prima facie reasons are supposed to be logical relationships between concepts. It is a necessary feature of the concept *red* that something's looking red to me gives me a prima facie reason for thinking it is red. (To suppose we have to discover such connections inductively leads to an infinite regress, because we must rely upon perceptual judgments to collect the data for an inductive generalization.) By contrast, Reiter's defaults often represent contingent generalizations. If we know that most birds can fly, then the inference from being a bird to flying may be adopted as a default. In the theory of defeasible reasoning propounded in this book, the latter inference is instead handled in terms of the statistical syllogism, as discussed in chapter 2. A second contrast between the present theory of defeasible reasoning and Reiter's approach is that the latter is semantical (proceeding in terms of an unspecified deductive-consequence relation), whereas the former is argument-theoretic.

It is easily proven that if we identify prima facie reasons with defaults, confine our attention to linear arguments, consider only cases in which there is no collective defeat,[2] and identify the deductive-consequence relation with deductive provability in OSCAR, then the set of warranted conclusions generated by the present theory will be the same as the unique extension generated by Reiter's default logic. In situations in which collective defeat occurs, the two theories yield completely different results, because default logic is credulous and the present theory is skeptical. Recall that in cases of collective defeat, a skeptical theory dictates withholding belief, whereas a credulous theory dictates choosing one of the defeated conclusions at random and believing that. It was argued in chapter 2 that the standard defenses of credulous systems confuse epistemic and practical reasoning, and that credulous systems of epistemic reasoning are simply wrong. However, a skeptical version of default logic can be generated by requiring that default consequences be members of the intersection of all extensions, and this brings the two theories back into agreement on "simple"

---

[2] Collective defeat was introduced in chapter 2, and will be made precise in section 6 of this chapter.

cases,[3] provided we consider only linear arguments. Once we allow suppositional reasoning, the two theories diverge again. For instance, if we consider a default theory with the default $P:Q/Q$ and the corresponding defeasible theory in which P is a prima facie reason for Q and there are no undercutting defeaters, then from the empty set of premises the present theory of defeasible reasoning will generate the warranted conclusion $(P \supset Q)$, but skeptical default logic will not.

Circumscription

Circumscription was developed by McCarthy [1980, 1984]. The basic idea is that if we know that most A's are B's, then in reasoning about A's, we should assume that the set of exceptional A's that are not B's is *minimal*. In other words, we assume that the only exceptions are those forced upon us by other things we know. McCarthy captures this by adding second-order axioms to the theory. He begins by symbolizing ⌜most A's are B's⌝ as

$$(\forall x)\{[A(x) \ \& \sim ab(x)] \supset B(x)\}$$

where ⌜$ab(x)$⌝ symbolizes ⌜x *is abnormal (exceptional)*⌝. Letting $T(ab)$ be our initial theory about A's, B's, and abormality, the *circumscription of T* is the second-order principle:

$$T(ab) \ \& \ (\forall X)\{[T(X) \ \& \ (\forall x)(X(x) \supset ab(x))] \supset (\forall x)(ab(x) \supset X(x))\}.$$

This says that the theory holds for ab, and if the theory holds for any property X whose extension is a subset of the extension of ab, then the extension of ab is the same as the extension of X. In other words, the extension of ab is a minimal set sufficient to satisfy the theory T.

To illustrate, suppose our theory T is that most birds fly, and Tweety is a bird. We can express this as:

$$bird(Tweety)$$
$$(\forall x)\{[bird(x) \ \& \sim ab(x)] \supset fly(x)\}$$

We want to infer, defeasibly, that Tweety flies. The circumscription of this theory tells us that the set of nonflying birds is a minimal set satisfying this theory. The minimal set satisfying this theory is the empty set, so from the circumscription we can infer that Tweety flies.

---

[3] "Simple" cases are those that do not exhibit self-defeat, ancestor-defeat, or any of the other complexities discussed in sections 6–8.

Although circumscription captures some of the same inferences as my theory of defeasible reasoning, it also has some peculiar consequences, which, to my mind, show that it is not an adequate theory. To adapt an example from Etherington, Kraus, and Perlis [1991], consider a lottery that is held once a week. Each week, one ticket is drawn. Most tickets are not drawn so the ticket drawn is abnormal, in the technical sense employed in circumscription. Circumscribing abnormality, there will be one minimal extension of *ab* for each ticket, corresponding to that ticket's being drawn. A conclusion follows from the circumscription only if it is true in each minimal extension, so no conclusion follows to the effect that any particular ticket will not be drawn. So far, circumscription yields the right answer.[4] But now modify the example. Each week, instead of drawing just one ticket, from one to five tickets are drawn, the number being determined randomly. The minimal extensions of *ab* are still those in which just one ticket is drawn, so it is true in each minimal extension that only one ticket is drawn. Thus, each week, circumscription allows us to conclude that only one ticket will be drawn. But this conclusion is unreasonable. Neither default logic nor the theory of defeasible reasoning adumbrated in this book has this consequence. The undesirable conclusion is directly traceable to circumscription's minimization of abnormality, so it seems to show that this is not, after all, a satisfactory way of capturing the structure of defeasible reasoning.

In the following sections, circumscription and (skeptical) default logic will be compared with the theory of defeasible reasoning in their application to a number of problem cases. I will argue that, in at least some cases, the former theories give unsatisfactory results.

6. Computing Defeat Status

Justified beliefs are those supported by undefeated nodes of the inference graph. More precisely:

A belief is justified to degree δ iff it is supported by some undefeated node of the inference graph whose strength is $\geq \delta$.

---

[4] Etherington, Krause, and Perlis [1991] maintain that this is the wrong answer, and that it is reasonable to conclude of any given ticket that it will not be drawn. I disagree with them. See the discussion of the lottery paradox in chapter 2.

To complete this analysis, let us address the question of how the defeat status of a node of the inference graph is determined by its defeat relations to other nodes. It is initially plausible that there are just two ways a node can come to be defeated: (1) by its being defeated by some other node that is itself undefeated or (2) by its being inferred from a node that is defeated. Let us say that a node is *d-initial* iff neither it nor any of its inference ancestors are defeated by any nodes (that is, they are not the termini of any defeat links). D-initial nodes are guaranteed to be undefeated. Then we might try the following recursive definition:

(6.1)   1.   D-initial nodes are undefeated.
        2.   If the immediate ancestors of a node η are undefeated and all nodes defeating η are defeated, then η is undefeated.
        3.   If η has a defeated immediate ancestor, or there is an undefeated node that defeats η, then η is defeated.

To illustrate, suppose we have the inference graph diagrammed in figure 2, where defeasible inferences are indicated by dashed arrows, deductive inferences by solid arrows, and defeat links by arrows of the form "oooo⊶". α,β,ε,ν,μ,κ, and λ are d-initial nodes, so they are undefeated. By (6.1.3), ζ, ξ, and χ are then defeated. By (6.1.2), because β is undefeated and ξ is defeated, γ and δ are then undefeated.

In simple cases, all standard theories of defeasible reasoning and nonmonotonic logic will yield results that are in agreement with principle (6.1), but as we will see, the different theories diverge on some complicated cases.

I take it that principle (6.1) is an initially plausible proposal for computing defeat status. However, the operation of this recursive definition is not as simple as it might at first appear. In figure 2, principle (6.1) assigns "defeated" or "undefeated" to each node of the inference graph, but that will not always be the case. In particular, this will fail in cases of collective defeat, where we have a set of nodes, each of which is defeated by other members of the set and none of which is defeated by undefeated nodes outside the set. Consider the simple inference graph diagrammed in figure 3. In this case, α and ε are again d-initial nodes and hence undefeated. But neither β nor ζ will be assigned any status at all by principle (6.1), and then it follows that no status is assigned to any of γ,δ,ξ, or χ either.

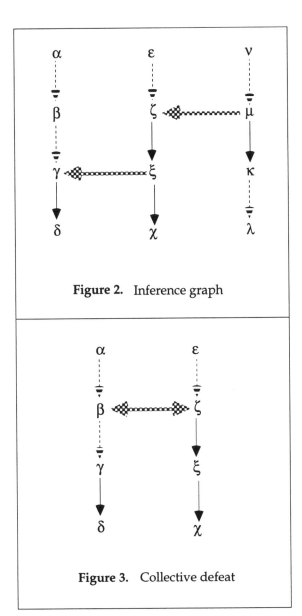

Figure 2. Inference graph

Figure 3. Collective defeat

Collective defeat was illustrated in chapter 2 by the lottery paradox. Suppose you hold one ticket in a fair lottery consisting of 1 million tickets, and suppose it is known that one and only one ticket will win. Observing that the probability is only .000001 of a ticket's being drawn given that it is a ticket in the lottery, it seems reasonable to accept the conclusion that your ticket will not win. The prima facie reason involved in this reasoning is the statistical syllogism. But by the same reasoning, it will be reasonable to believe, for each ticket, that it will not win. However, these conclusions conflict jointly with something else we are justified in believing: that some ticket will win. We cannot be justified in believing each member of an explicitly contradictory set of propositions, and we have no way to choose between them, so it follows intuitively that we are not justified in believing of any ticket that it will not win.[5] This is captured formally by the principle of collective defeat, which tells us that our prima facie reasons collectively defeat one another:

The Principle of Collective Defeat
If X is a set of nodes of the inference graph, each member of X is defeated by another member of X, and no member of X is defeated by an undefeated node that is not a member of X, then every node in X is defeated.

Collectively defeated inferences are defeated, in the sense that it is unreasonable to accept their conclusions.[6] But principle (6.1) does not rule them defeated. This may be less of a problem for principle (6.1) than it seems. We can regard the assignment of defeat statuses in figure 3 as correct, provided we go on to say that β and ζ should be assigned a third status distinct from both "defeated" and "undefeated". The need for a third defeat status is best illustrated by contrasting figure 2 with figure 4. In figure 2, ζ and hence ξ are defeated, and ξ thereby loses the ability to render γ defeated. In figure 4, both ζ and μ are defeated (it would not be reasonable to accept their conclusions), but ζ retains the ability to render β defeated, because it would not be

---

[5] Kyburg [1970] draws a different conclusion: we can be justified in holding inconsistent sets of beliefs, and it is not automatically reasonable to adopt the conjunction of beliefs one justifiably holds (i.e., adjunction fails). This was discussed in section 2.

[6] Not everyone accepts this diagnosis. For a defense of it, see my discussion of the lottery paradox in chapter 2.

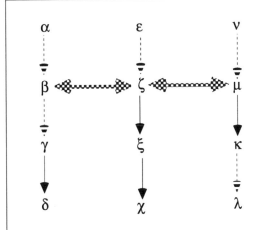

Figure 4. The propagation of provisional defeat

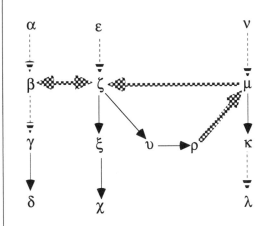

Figure 5. The extended propagation of provisional defeat

reasonable to accept the conclusion of β either. This is an unavoidable consequence of the symmetry of the inference graph. The relationship between β and ζ is precisely the same as that between ζ and μ. We must regard both as cases of collective defeat. The order in which the arguments are produced, or the nodes considered by the recursion, cannot affect their defeat status.

We can handle this by distinguishing between two kinds of defeat: *outright defeat* and *provisional defeat*. If a node undergoes outright defeat, it loses the ability to affect other nodes, but if a node undergoes provisional defeat, it can still render other nodes provisionally defeated. Provisionally defeated nodes are still "infectious". Provisional defeat can propagate, in two ways. First, as illustrated by figure 4, if a provisionally defeated node defeats a node that would not otherwise be defeated, this can render the latter node provisionally defeated. Second, if a node is inferred from a provisionally defeated node and its other immediate ancestors are undefeated, then that node may be provisionally defeated as well. That is, a node inferred from a provisionally defeated node is defeated but may still be infectious. This is illustrated by making structures like figure 4 more complicated so that the collective defeat of ζ and μ involves extended reasoning, as in figure 5. Here, υ and ρ are inferred from ζ, so they are defeated, but they must remain infectious in order to defeat μ and thus generate the provisional defeat of ζ and μ. If υ and ρ were defeated outright rather than provisionally, then μ would be undefeated, which would render ζ defeated outright, but that is intuitively wrong.

Outright defeat and provisional defeat are both defeat, in the sense that it is not reasonable to accept the conclusion of a node with either status. But the two defeat statuses are importantly different in that a node is rendered impotent if it is defeated outright, but if it is only provisionally defeated, it retains the ability to defeat other nodes.

The examples considered thus far can be handled by adding a fourth clause to principle (6.1):

(6.2)   1.   D-initial nodes are undefeated.
         2.   If the immediate ancestors of a node η are undefeated and all nodes defeating η are defeated outright, then η is undefeated.
         3.   If η has an immediate ancestor that is defeated outright, or there is an undefeated node that defeats η, then η is defeated outright.
         4.   Otherwise, η is provisionally defeated.

The automatic consequence is that otherwise undefeated nodes inferred from provisionally defeated nodes are provisionally defeated, and otherwise undefeated nodes defeated by provisionally defeated nodes are provisionally defeated. Principle (6.2) is equivalent to the analysis of defeat I have given elsewhere [1979, 1986, 1987]. However, I now believe that this account is inadequate, for the reasons that will be explored next.

7. Self-defeating Arguments

The inadequacy of principle (6.2) can be illustrated by a wide variety of examples. The simplest is the following. Suppose P is a prima facie reason for R, Q is a prima facie reason for $\sim R$, S is a prima facie reason for T, and we are given P, Q, and S. Then we can do the reasoning encoded in the inference graph diagrammed in figure 6. The nodes $\boxed{R}$ and $\boxed{\sim R}$ collectively defeat one another, but $\boxed{T}$ should be independent of either and undefeated. The difficulty is that we can extend the inference graph as in figure 7. Here I have used a standard strategy for deriving an arbitrary conclusion from a contradiction. Now the problem is that $\boxed{\sim T}$ rebuts $\boxed{T}$. According to principle (6.2), $\boxed{\sim R}$, and hence $\boxed{\sim T}$, are provisionally defeated, but then it follows that $\boxed{T}$ is also provisionally defeated. The latter must be wrong. There are no constraints on T, so it would have the consequence that all conclusions are defeated. This example shows that nodes inferred from provisionally defeated nodes are not always provisionally defeated. In figure 7, $\boxed{\sim T}$ must be defeated outright. There is no way to get this result from principle (6.2). My diagnosis of the difficulty is that the argument supporting $\boxed{\sim T}$ is "internally defective". It is *self-defeating* in the sense that some of its steps are defeaters for others. By principle (6.2), this means that those inferences enter into collective defeat with one another, and hence $\boxed{\sim T}$ is provisionally defeated, but my suggestion is that this should be regarded as a more serious defect—one that leaves $\boxed{\sim T}$ defeated outright and hence unable to defeat other inferences. Taking the *inclusive inference ancestors* of a node to be its inference ancestors together with itself, let us define:

A node η is *self-defeating* iff some of its inclusive inference ancestors defeat others.

Principle (6.2) should be modified so that self-defeating nodes are defeated outright rather than just provisionally.

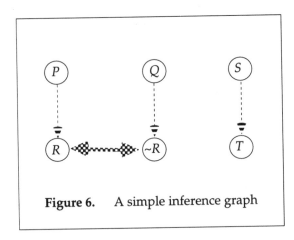

Figure 6.   A simple inference graph

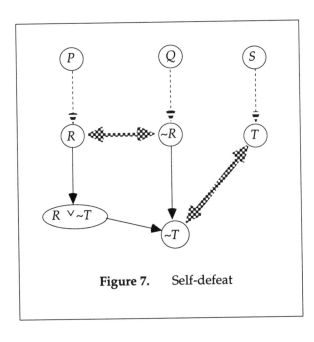

Figure 7.   Self-defeat

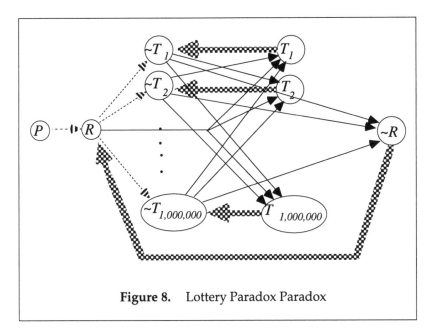

Figure 8.   Lottery Paradox Paradox

It is noteworthy that neither (skeptical) default logic nor circum-scription has any difficulty with the inference graph of figure 7. In default logic, there is one minimal extension containing R and another containing $\sim R$ but no minimal extension containing both and so none containing $\sim T$. Similarly, in circumscribing abnormality, either the inference to R or the inference to $\sim R$ will be blocked by abnormality, and in either case the inference to $\sim T$ will be blocked.

Circumscription does not fare so well when we turn to a second example of self-defeat that has a somewhat different structure. This concerns what appears to be a paradox of defeasible reasoning and involves the lottery paradox again. The lottery paradox is generated by supposing that a proposition R describing the lottery (it is a fair lottery, has 1 million tickets, and so on) is justified. Given that R is justified, we get collective defeat for the proposition that any given ticket will not be drawn. But principle (6.2) makes it problematic how R can be justified. Normally we will have only a defeasible reason for believing R. For instance, we may be told that it is true or read it in a newspaper. Let T_i be the proposition that ticket i will be drawn. In accordance with the standard reasoning involved in the lottery paradox, we can generate an argument supporting $\sim R$ by noting that the $\sim T_i$ jointly entail $\sim R$, because if none of the tickets is drawn, the lottery is not fair. This is diagrammed in figure 8. The difficulty is now that $\widehat{-R}$ rebuts $\widehat{R}$. Thus by principle (6.2), these nodes defeat one another, with the result that neither is defeated outright. In other words, the inference to R is provisionally defeated. Again, this result is intuitively wrong. Oviously, if we consider examples of real lotteries (e.g., this week's New York State Lottery), it is possible to become justified in believing R on the basis described. I propose once more that the solution to this problem lies in noting that the node $\widehat{-R}$ is self-defeating.

Default logic gets the example of figure 8 right, but circumscription gets it wrong. In circumscribing abnormality, all we can conclude is that one of the defeasible inferences is blocked by abnormality, but it could be the inference to R, so circumscription does not allow us to infer R.

On the argument-based approach, the difficulties diagrammed in figures 7 and 8 can be avoided by ruling that self-defeating nodes are defeated outright—not just provisionally. Because they are defeated outright, they cannot enter into collective defeat with other nodes, and so the nodes $\widehat{-R}$ and $\widehat{-T}$ in the preceding two examples are defeated outright, as they should be. This can be accomplished by revising principle (6.2) as follows:

(7.1)   1.   D-initial nodes are undefeated.
        2.   Self-defeating nodes are defeated outright.
        3.   If η is not self-defeating, its immediate ancestors are unde-
             feated, and all nodes defeating η are defeated outright,
             then η is undefeated.
        4.   If η has an immediate ancestor that is defeated outright, or
             there is an undefeated node that defeats η, then η is defeated
             outright.
        5.   Otherwise, η is provisionally defeated.

This is equivalent to one of the preliminary proposals made in my [1990]. However, it is still inadequate.

An interesting problem arises when the last step of an argument constitutes an undercutting defeater for an earlier step. Consider the inference graph diagrammed in figure 9. The node $\widehat{(P \otimes Q)}$ is self-defeating, because it defeats one of its own ancestors. Thus by principle (7.1), it is defeated outright. It then follows from principle (7.1) that the remaining nodes are undefeated. But this is most peculiar, because $\widehat{(P \otimes Q)}$ is a deductive consequence of $\widehat{R}$. If a node is undefeated, its deductive consequences should also be undefeated. Conversely, if

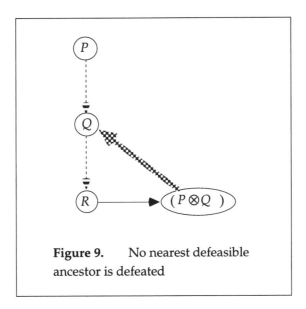

Figure 9.   No nearest defeasible
ancestor is defeated

a node is inferred deductively from a set of nodes (its *nearest defeasible ancestors*), then if the node is defeated, at least one of its nearest defeasible ancestors should also be defeated. It follows that at least (R) should be defeated. What about (Q)? Intuitions are unclear in such an abstract example, so let us turn to a concrete example.

Suppose we know (*i*) that people generally tell the truth, (*ii*) that Robert says that the elephant beside him looks pink, and (*iii*) that Robert becomes unreliable in the presence of pink elephants. $\ulcorner x$ looks pink$\urcorner$ is a prima facie reason for $\ulcorner x$ is pink$\urcorner$. Then Robert's statement gives us a prima facie reason for thinking that the elephant *does* look pink, which gives us a reason for thinking that it *is* pink, which, when combined with Robert's unreliability in the presence of pink elephants, gives us a defeater for our reason for thinking that the elephant looks pink. These relations can be diagrammed as in figure 10.   Node 7 is self-defeating, so one of its nearest defeasible ancestors ought to be defeated. These are nodes 5 and 6. Of these, it seems clear that node 6 should be defeated *by* having node 4 defeated. That is, in this example, it would not be reasonable to accept the conclusion that the elephant beside Robert looks pink. This strongly suggests that we should similarly regard (Q) as defeated in figure 9. Neither of these conclusions is forthcoming from principle (7.1). In earlier publications I tried to resolve these problems by generalizing the notion of self-defeat, but I no longer believe that those attempts were successful.

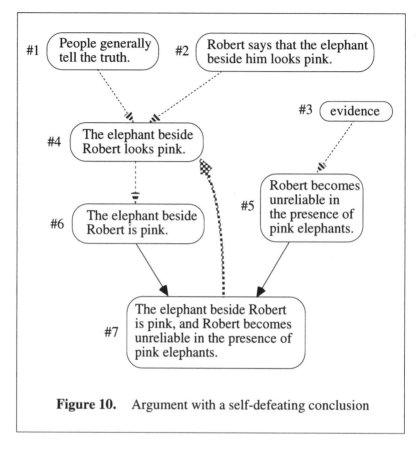

Figure 10.   Argument with a self-defeating conclusion

It turns out that circumscription gives the right result in figures 9 and 10. In figure 9, circumscribing abnormality has the consequence that either the inference to Q or the inference to R is blocked, and hence Q does not follow from the circumscription. On the other hand, default logic gives an outlandish result in figure 9. It turns out that there are *no* extensions in this case, and hence either nothing is justified (including the given premise P) or everything is justified, depending upon how we handle this case. This seems to be a fairly clear counter-example to default logic.

8. A New Approach

Default logic and circumscription handle some of the problem cases correctly and some incorrectly. The cases in which they fail tend to be ones in which they are not sufficiently sensitive to the structure of the arguments. For example, in figure 8, circumscription gets self-defeat wrong, and in figure 9, default logic gets self-defeat wrong. This suggests that the argument-based approach should be superior, but as we have seen, the formulations of the argument-based approach that are contained in principles (6.2) and (7.1) fail to deal adequately with at least one of the examples that default logic and circumscription get right. The attempts to salvage the argument-based approach by building in restrictions become increasingly ad hoc as the examples become more complex. I think it is time to abandon the search for such restrictions and look for another way of handling the problems. Here, I think that the argument-based approach has a lesson to learn from default logic and circumscription. Consider the first example of collective defeat—figure 7. Default logic and circumscription get this example right, but principle (6.2) gets it wrong, necessitating the explicit appeal to self-defeat in principle (7.1). It is illuminating to consider why default logic and circumscription have no difficulty with this example. This is because they take account of the relationship between the provisionally defeated conclusions R and $\sim R$ instead of just throwing them all into an unstructured pot of provisionally defeated conclusions. This allows us to observe that when R is "acceptable", $\sim R$ is not, and hence there are no circumstances under which $\sim T$ is "acceptable". Principle (6.2), on the other hand, washes these relationships out, assigning a blanket status of "provisionally defeated" to all provisionally defeated propositions.

The conclusion I want to draw is that the argument-based approach gets things partly right, and default logic and circumscription get things partly right. What is needed is a single theory that combines the insights of both. In order to take account of the structure of arguments, this will have to be an argument-based theory, but in assessing defeat statuses, it must take account of the interconnections between nodes and not just look at the defeat statuses of the nodes that are inference ancestors or defeaters of a given node. There is a way of taking account of such interconnections while remaining within the spirit of principles (6.1) and (6.2). Let us define a *status assignment* to be an assignment of defeat status that is consistent with the rules of principle (6.1). When nodes are either undefeated or defeated outright, then every status assignment will accord them that status, but when nodes are provisionally defeated, some status assignments will assign the status "defeated" and others the status "undefeated". Links between nodes will be reflected in the fact that, for example, every status assignment making one undefeated may make another defeated. This is made precise as follows:

> An assignment σ of "defeated" and "undefeated" to the nodes of an inference graph is a *status assignment* iff:
> 1. σ assigns "undefeated" to all d-initial nodes;
> 2. σ assigns "undefeated" to a node α iff σ assigns "undefeated" to all the immediate ancestors of α and all nodes defeating α are assigned "defeated"; and
> 3. σ assigns "defeated" to α iff either α has a immediate ancestor that is assigned "defeated", or there is a node β that defeats α and is assigned "undefeated".

The proposal is then:

(8.1)   A node is undefeated iff every status assignment assigns "undefeated" to it; otherwise it is defeated. Of the defeated nodes, a node is defeated outright iff no status assignment assigns "undefeated" to it; otherwise, it is provisionally defeated.

This simple proposal deals adequately with all but one of the examples we have considered. In figure 7, there is one status assignment assigning "defeated" to (R) and "undefeated" to $(\sim R)$, and another status assignment assigning the opposite statuses. On both assignments, $(\sim T)$ is assigned "defeated", so by principle (8.1), $(\sim T)$ is defeated outright. Figure 8 is analogous. In figure 8, for each i there is a status assignment assigning "defeated" to (T_i) but assigning "undefeated" to (R) and all the other (T_j)'s. Every such status assignment assigns "defeated" to $(\sim R)$. Thus by principle (8.1), (R) is undefeated and $(\sim R)$ is defeated outright, while all of the $(\sim T_i)$'s are provisionally defeated.

Of the above examples, principle (8.1) is able to handle all but that of figure 9. In figure 9, something unexpected happens. Any status assignment assigning "undefeated" to (Q) will also assign "undefeated" to (R) and to $(P \otimes Q)$, but then it must instead assign "defeated" to (Q). Thus no status assignment can assign "undefeated" to (Q). However, no status assignment can assign "defeated" to (Q) either, because then it would have to assign "defeated" to (R) and $(P \otimes Q)$ as well, from which it follows that it must instead assign "undefeated" to (Q). This shows that no status assignments are possible for the inference graph of figure 9. We can construct other examples of this same

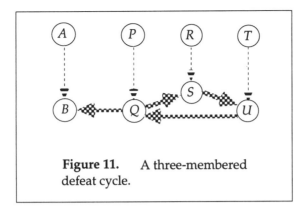

Figure 11.   A three-membered
defeat cycle.

phenomenon. The simplest involve odd-length defeat cycles. Consider
the inference graph diagrammed in figure 11. For example, we might
let *P* be "Jones says that Smith is unreliable", *Q* be "Smith is unreliable",
R be "Smith says that Robertson is unreliable", *S* be "Robertson is
unreliable", *T* be "Robertson says that Jones is unreliable", *U* be "Jones
is unreliable", and *A* be "Smith says that it is raining" and *B* be "It is
raining". Intuitively, Q, S, and U ought to defeat one another
collectively, and then because Q is provisionally defeated, B should
be provisionally defeated. That is precisely the result we get if we
expand the defeat cycle to four nodes. However, in the inference
graph containing the three-membered defeat cycle, there is no way to
assign defeat statuses consistent with principle (6.1). For example, if
Q is assigned "undefeated", S must be assigned "defeated", and
then U must be assigned "undefeated", with the result that Q
must be assigned "defeated"—a contradiction. Every other way of
trying to assign defeat statuses yields a similar contradiction. Consequently, there is no status assignment for the inference graph in figure
11. But surely, it should make no difference that the defeat cycle is of
odd length rather than even length. We should get the same result in
either case.

This difficulty can be rectified by allowing status assignments to be
partial assignments. They can leave gaps, but only when there is no
consistent way to avoid that. Accordingly, let us revise the earlier
definition as follows:

> An assignment σ of "defeated" and "undefeated" to a subset of
> the nodes of an inference graph is a *partial status assignment* iff:
> 1.   σ assigns "undefeated" to all d-initial nodes;

2. σ assigns "undefeated" to a node α iff σ assigns "undefeated" to all the immediate ancestors of α and all nodes defeating α are assigned "defeated"; and

3. σ assigns "defeated" to a node α iff either α has a immediate ancestor that is assigned "defeated", or there is a node β that defeats α and is assigned "undefeated".

Status assignments are then maximal partial status assignments:

σ is a *status assignment* iff σ is a partial status assignment and σ is not properly contained in any other partial status assignment.

With this modification, principle (8.1) handles the examples of figures 9 and 11 properly. In figure 9, nodes $\textcircled{Q}$, $\textcircled{R}$, and $\overline{\textcircled{(P \otimes Q)}}$ turn out to be (provisionally) defeated, and in figure 11, nodes $\textcircled{B}$, $\textcircled{Q}$, $\textcircled{Q}$, and $\textcircled{U}$ are (provisionally) defeated. This is my final proposal for the analysis of defeat for nodes of the inference graph.[7]

This analysis entails that defeat statuses satisfy a number of intuitively desirable conditions:

(8.2)   A node α is undefeated iff all immediate ancestors of α are undefeated and all nodes defeating α are defeated.

(8.3)   If some immediate ancestor of α is defeated outright then α is defeated outright.

(8.4)   If some immediate ancestor of α is provisionally defeated, then α is either provisionally defeated or defeated outright.

(8.5)   If some node defeating α is undefeated, then α is defeated outright.

(8.6)   If α is self-defeating then α is defeated outright.

---

[7] In a number of earlier publications [1979, 1986, 1987, 1990, 1990c, 1991, and 1992], I proposed that defeat could analyzed as defeat among *arguments* rather than inference nodes, and I proposed an analysis of that relation in terms of "levels of arguments". I now believe that obscured the proper treatment of self-defeat and ancestor defeat. I see no way to recast the present analysis in terms of a defeat relation between arguments (as opposed to nodes, which are argument steps rather than complete arguments).

9. The Paradox of the Preface

Much of my work on the analysis of defeat has been driven by an attempt to deal adequately with the lottery paradox and the paradox of the preface. The difficulty is that these two paradoxes seem superficially to have the same form, and yet they require different resolutions. I discussed the lottery paradox above, maintaining that it can be regarded as a straightforward case of collective defeat. Contrast that with the paradox of the preface [Makinson 1965], which can be presented as follows:

> There once was a man who wrote a book. He was very careful in his reasoning, and was confident of each claim that he made. With some display of pride, he showed the book to a friend (who happened to be a probability theorist). He was dismayed when the friend observed that any book that long and that interesting was almost certain to contain at least one falsehood. Thus it was not reasonable to believe that all of the claims made in the book were true. If it were reasonable to believe each claim then it would be reasonable to believe that the book contained no falsehoods, so it could not be reasonable to believe each claim. Furthermore, because there was no way to pick out some of the claims as being more problematic than others, there could be no reasonable way of withholding assent to some but not others. "Therefore," concluded his friend, "you are not justified in believing anything you asserted in the book." [Pollock 1991]

This is the paradox of the preface (so named because in the original version the author confesses in the preface that his book probably contains a falsehood). This paradox is made particularly difficult by its similarity to the lottery paradox. In both paradoxes, we have a set Γ of propositions, each of which is supported by a defeasible argument, and a reason for thinking that not all of the members of Γ are true. But in the lottery paradox we want to conclude that the members of Γ undergo collective defeat, and hence we are not justified in believing them, whereas in the paradox of the preface we want to insist that we are justified in believing the members of Γ. How can the difference be explained?

There is, perhaps, some temptation to acquiesce in the reasoning involved in the paradox of the preface and conclude that we are not justified in believing any of the claims in the book after all. That would surely be paradoxical, because a great deal of what we believe about the world is based upon books and other sources subject to the same argument. For instance, why do I believe that Alaska exists? I have never been there. I believe it only because I have read about it. If the reasoning behind the paradox of the preface were correct, I would not be justified in believing that Alaska exists. That cannot be right.

The paradox of the preface may seem like an esoteric paradox of little more than theoretical interest. However, the *form* of the paradox of the preface is of fundamental importance to defeasible reasoning. That form recurs throughout defeasible reasoning, with the result that if that form of argument were not defeated, virtually all beliefs based upon defeasible reasoning would be unjustified. This arises from the fact that we are typically able to set at least rough upper bounds on the reliability of our prima facie reasons. For example, color vision gives us prima facie reasons for judging the colors of objects around us. Color vision is pretty reliable, but surely it is not more than 99.9% reliable. Given that assumption, it follows that the probability that out of 10,000 randomly selected color judgments, at least one is incorrect, is 99.99%. By the statistical syllogism, that gives us a prima facie reason for thinking that at least one of them is false. By reasoning analogous to the paradox of the preface, it seems that none of those 10,000 judgments can be justified. And because every color judgment is a member of some such set of 10,000, it follows that all color judgments are unjustified. The same reasoning would serve to defeat any defeasible reasoning based upon a prima facie reason for which we can set at least a rough upper bound of reliability. Thus it becomes imperative to resolve the paradox of the preface.

The paradox of the preface can be resolved by appealing to the analysis of defeat proposed above.[8] The paradox has the following form. We begin with a set $\Gamma = \{p_1,...,p_N\}$ of propositions, where Γ has some property B (being the propositions asserted in a book of a certain sort, or being a set propositions supported by arguments employing a certain prima facie reason). We suppose we know that the probability of a member of such a set being true is high, but we also know that it is at least as probable that such a set of propositions contains at least one false member. Letting T be the property of being true, we can express these probabilities as:

$$\text{prob}(Tz \ / \ z{\in}X \ \& \ B(X)) = r$$
$$\text{prob}((\exists z)(z{\in}X \ \& \sim Tz) \ / \ B(X)) \geq r.$$

The latter high probability, combined with the premise $B(\Gamma)$, gives us

---

[8] This corrects my earlier discussion [1990, 1991].

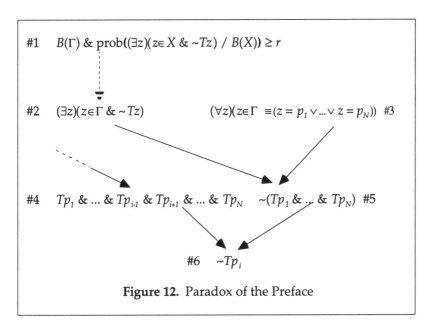

#1 $B(\Gamma)$ & $\text{prob}((\exists z)(z \in X \ \& \sim Tz) \ / \ B(X)) \geq r$

#2 $(\exists z)(z \in \Gamma \ \& \sim Tz)$ $(\forall z)(z \in \Gamma \ \equiv (z = p_1 \vee ... \vee z = p_N))$ #3

#4 $Tp_1 \ \& \ ... \ \& \ Tp_{i-1} \ \& \ Tp_{i+1} \ \& \ ... \ \& \ Tp_N$ $\sim(Tp_1 \ \& \ ... \ \& \ Tp_N)$ #5

#6 $\sim Tp_i$

Figure 12. Paradox of the Preface

a defeasible reason for $(\exists z)(z \in \Gamma \ \& \sim Tz)$. This, in turn, generates collective defeat for all the arguments supporting the members of Γ. The collective defeat is generated by constructing the argument scheme diagrammed in figure 12 for each $\sim Tp_i$.

A resolution of the paradox of the preface must consist of a demonstration that node 6 is defeated outright. A subproperty defeater for the reasoning from node 1 to node 2 arises from establishing anything of the following form (for any property C):

$$C(\Gamma) \ \& \ \text{prob}((\exists z)(z \in X \ \& \sim Tz) \ / \ B(X) \ \& \ C(X)) < r.^{[9]}$$

I have shown [1990, 251] that

$\text{prob}((\exists z)(z \in X \ \& \sim Tz) \ / \ B(X) \ \& \ X = \{x_1,...,x_N\} \ \& \ x_1,...,x_N$ are distinct$^{[10]}$ & $Tx_1 \ \& \ ... \ \& \ Tx_{i-1} \ \& \ Tx_{i+1} \ \& \ ... \ \& \ Tx_N)$

$= \text{prob}(\sim Tx_i \ / \ B(X) \ \& \ X = \{x_1,...,x_N\} \ \& \ x_1,...,x_N$ are distinct & $Tx_1 \ \& \ ... \ \& \ Tx_{i-1} \ \& \ Tx_{i+1} \ \& \ ... \ \& \ Tx_N)$.

---

[9] See section 6 of chapter 2 for more details on subproperty defeaters.

[10] "$x_1,...,x_n$ are distinct" means "$x_1,...,x_n$ are n different objects".

Now we come to the point at which the paradox of the preface differs from the lottery paradox. In the lottery paradox, knowing that none of the other tickets has been drawn makes it likely that the remaining ticket is drawn. By contrast, knowing that none of the other members of Γ is false does not make it likely that the remaining member of Γ is false. In other words,

$$\text{prob}(\sim Tx_i \ / \ B(X) \ \& \ X = \{x_1,...,x_N\} \ \& \ x_1,...,x_N \text{ are distinct } \&$$
$$Tx_1 \ \& \ ... \ \& \ Tx_{i-1} \ \& \ Tx_{i+1} \ \& \ ... \ \& \ Tx_N)$$

$$\leq \text{prob}(\sim Tx_i \ / \ B(X) \ \& \ X = \{x_1,...,x_N\} \ \& \ x_1,...,x_N \text{ are distinct}).$$

Equivalently, the different claims in Γ are not negatively relevant to one another. For example, the 10,000 color judgments were assumed to be independent of one another, so these two probabilities are equal in that case. In the case of the book, the various claims would normally be taken to support one another, if anything, and so be positively relevant rather than negatively relevant. There is no reason to believe that the condition $\ulcorner X = \{x_1,...,x_N\} \ \& \ x_1,...,x_N$ are distinct$\urcorner$ alters the probability, so it is reasonable to believe that the last-mentioned probability is just $1-r$, which, of course, is much smaller than r.[11] Thus we have

$$\text{prob}((\exists z)(z \in X \ \& \ \sim Tz) \ / \ B(X) \ \& \ X = \{x_1,...,x_N\} \ \& \ x_1,...,x_N \text{ are}$$
$$\text{distinct } \& Tx_1 \ \& \ ... \ \& \ Tx_{i-1} \ \& \ Tx_{i+1} \ \& \ ... \ \& \ Tx_N) < r.$$

Accordingly, the conjunction

$$\text{prob}((\exists z)(z \in X \ \& \ \sim Tz) \ / \ B(X) \ \& \ X = \{x_1,...,x_N\} \ \& \ x_1,...,x_N \text{ are}$$
$$\text{distinct } \& \ Tx_1 \ \& \ ... \ \& \ Tx_{i-1} \ \& \ Tx_{i+1} \ \& \ ... \ \& \ Tx_N) < r$$
$$\& \ p_1,...,p_N \text{ are distinct}$$

is warranted. Combining this with nodes 3 and 4 generates a subproperty defeater for the defeasible inference from node 1 to node 2, as diagrammed in figure 13. Consequently, node 8 defeats node 2.

---

[11] This inference proceeds by non-classical direct inference. See section 6 of chapter 2.

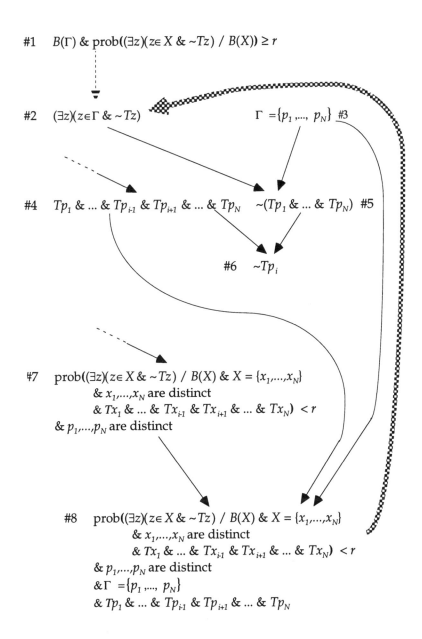

Figure 13. Resolution of the paradox of the preface

In computing defeat statuses, it is difficult to see the structure of this problem because there isn't room on a page to draw the entire inference graph. Figure 13 is only a partial diagram, because it does not take account of how the different Tp_i's are related to one another. The structure can be made clearer by considering a simpler problem having the same structure but with only three propositions playing the role of Tp_i's rather than a large number of them. Consider the inference graph diagrammed in figure 14. The pie-shaped regions are drawn in to emphasize the symmetry. The nodes supporting P_1, P_2, P_3, S, T and R are d-initial and hence undefeated. In evaluating the other nodes, note first that there is a status assignment assigning "undefeated" to the nodes supporting Q_1, Q, and Q_3. This assigns "undefeated" to the nodes supporting S_1, S_2, and S_3, and "defeated" to the nodes supporting $\sim Q_1$, $\sim Q_2$, $\sim Q_3$, and $\sim(Q_1 \ \& \ Q_2 \ \& \ Q_3)$. On the other hand, there can be no status assignment assigning "defeated" to the nodes supporting two different Q_i's, say Q_1 and Q_2, because if the latter were defeated, all nodes defeating the former would be defeated, and vice versa. (Note that this would still be true if there were more than three Q_i's.) Suppose instead that a status assignment assigns "defeated" to just one Q_i, and "undefeated" to the others. Then the node supporting S_i must be assigned "undefeated", and so the node supporting $\sim(Q_1 \ \& \ Q_2 \ \& \ Q_3)$ must be assigned "defeated". The result is that the node supporting $\sim Q_i$ must be assigned "defeated". That is the only node defeating that supporting Q_i, so the latter must be assigned "undefeated" after all. Hence there can be no node assigning "defeated" to a single Q_i. The result is that there is only one status assignment, and it assigns "undefeated" to the nodes supporting Q_1, Q_2, Q_3, S_1, S_2, and S_3, and "defeated" to the nodes supporting $\sim Q_1$, $\sim Q_2$, $\sim Q_3$, and $\sim(Q_1 \ \& \ Q_2 \ \& \ Q_3)$. Consequently, the former nodes are undefeated, and the latter are defeated outright.

This computation of defeat status can be applied to the paradox of the preface by taking the Q_i's to correspond to the nodes supporting each Tp_i. The nodes supporting the S_i's correspond to node 8 in figure 13. The nodes supporting the $\sim Q_i$'s correspond to note 6, the node supporting $\sim(Q_1 \ \& \ Q_2 \ \& \ Q_3)$ corresponds to nodes 2 and 5, and node supporting T corresponds to node 1, the node supporting R corresponds to node 7, and the nodes supporting the conjunctions of the form $(Q_i \ \& \ Q_j)$ correspond to node 4. Then a diagnosis analogous to that given for figure 14 yields the result that node 2, and hence node 6, are both defeated outright, while the nodes supporting the Tp_i's are undefeated. It follows that the conjunction $(Tp_1 \ \& \ ... \ \& \ Tp_N)$ is justified. In

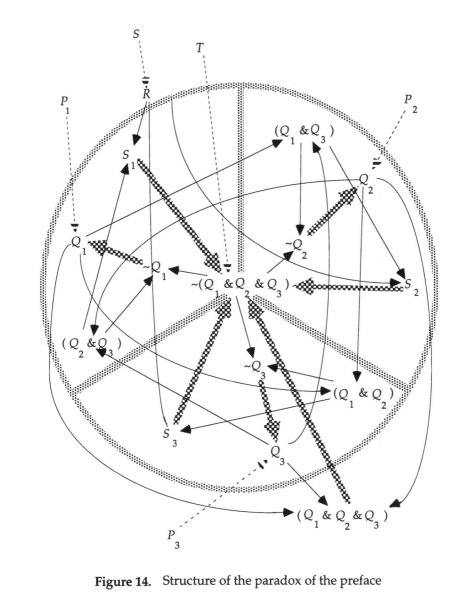

Figure 14. Structure of the paradox of the preface

other words, in the paradox of the preface, we are justified in believing that all the propositions asserted in that particular book are true, despite the fact that this is a book of a general type which usually contains some falsehoods.

If this still seems paradoxical, it is probably because one is over-looking the fact that "Books of this general sort usually contain false-hoods" formulates an *indefinite probability*, but "This book probably contains a falsehood" expresses a *definite* (single case) probability. The relationship between indefinite probabilities and definite probabilities is one of direct inference, which is a defeasible relation. In this case it is defeated by the fact that every proposition in the book is warranted, and hence the probability of *this* book's containing a falsehood is zero. (Warranted propositions automatically have probability one.) For more on direct inference, see section 6 of chapter 2.

This rather complex analysis shows that the difference between the paradox of the preface and the lottery paradox lies in the fact that the truth of the other propositions asserted in the book is not negatively relevant to the truth of the remaining proposition, but the other tickets in the lottery not being drawn *is* negatively relevant to the remaining ticket's not being drawn. This difference makes it reasonable to believe all the propositions asserted in the book but unreasonable to believe that none of the tickets will be drawn. This is also what makes it reasonable for us to believe our eyes when we make judgments about our surroundings. It is the analysis of defeat embodied in principle (8.1) that enables us to draw these congenial conclusions.

10. Justification and Warrant

A conclusion is justified if it is supported by an undefeated node of the inference graph. Reasoning starts with the set *input* and then pro-duces new nodes to be added to the inference graph. Given a fixed *input*, let $\alpha_1,...,\alpha_i,...$ be the nodes that would be constructed by the reasoner (if it had unlimited resources and could continue reasoning forever), in the order in which they would be produced, and let $\mathcal{G}_i$ be the set of the first i nodes, $\{\alpha_1,...,\alpha_i\}$. Conclusions justified at the ith stage of reasoning are just those supported by nodes in $\mathcal{G}_i$ that are undefeated relative to $\mathcal{G}_i$. Recall that the strength of a node is the minimum of the reason strengths of the reasons used in its inference ancestors and the strengths of the members of *input* that are inference ancestors of it. Epistemic justification is then made precise as follows:

A sequent S is *justified to degree* δ *at stage* i iff there is a node α of strength greater than or equal to δ such that (1) $\alpha \in \mathcal{G}_i$, (2) α is undefeated relative to $\mathcal{G}_i$, and (3) α supports S.

Epistemic justification has to do with the *current* status of a proposition. As reasoning progresses, a sequent can fluctuate repeatedly between being justified and being unjustified. For the purpose of evaluating a system of defeasible reasoning, it is useful to be able to talk about its behavior "in the limit". The notion of a sequent's being justified in the limit is what was called "warrant" in chapter 2. The definition of "warrant" given there can now be stated more precisely:

A sequent S is *warranted to degree* δ iff there is an i such that for every $j \geq i$, S is justified to degree δ at stage j.

Warrant, in this sense, characterizes the limit to which epistemic justification tends as reasoning proceeds.

Warrant is one way of understanding "justification in the limit". However, there is another obvious way of understanding this expression. Let $\mathcal{G}$ be the set of all nodes produced or producible by the reasoner, that is, $\bigcup_{i \in \omega} \mathcal{G}_i$. We can define a sequent to be *ideally warranted* iff it is justified relative to the whole set $\mathcal{G}$. More precisely:

A sequent S is *ideally warranted to degree* δ *(relative to input)* iff there is a node α (relative to *input*) of strength greater than or equal to δ such that (1) $\alpha \in \mathcal{G}$, (2) α is undefeated relative to $\mathcal{G}$, and (3) α supports S.

Ideal warrant has to do with what a reasoner should believe if it could produce all possible relevant arguments and then survey them. What is the relationship between warrant and ideal warrant? Interestingly, they need not be the same:

(10.1)   Warrant does not entail ideal warrant.
Proof: Suppose there is an infinite sequence $\alpha_1,...,\alpha_i,...$ of nodes such that for each i, α_{i+1} defeats α_i and for each odd i, α_{i+1} is produced by the reasoner before α_i. Then α_1 is undefeated relative to every $\mathcal{G}_i$ containing α_1, so its conclusion is warranted. But relative to $\mathcal{G}$, α_1 is provisionally defeated, and hence its conclusion is not ideally warranted. To illustrate the possibility of such an infinite sequence of nodes, we can postulate an infinite sequence of propositions Q_i all either in *input* or supported

by reasoning, and such that if we define D_i recursively by stipulating that $D_1 = (Q_0 \otimes P)$ and for $i > 1$, $D_{i+1} = (Q_i \otimes D_i)$, then (1) Q_0 is a prima facie reason for P, and (2) for each $i \geq 1$, Q_i is a prima facie reason for D_i.

(10.2) Ideal warrant does not entail warrant.

Proof: Suppose there is a node α and an infinite set of pairs of nodes $\langle \beta_i, \gamma_i \rangle$ such that for each i, β_i defeats α and γ_i defeats β_i. Suppose further that each β_i and γ_i is undefeated at the stage of reasoning at which it is first produced. Then α will cycle between being defeated outright relative to $\mathcal{G}_i$ and undefeated relative to $\mathcal{G}_i$ for progressively larger i, but α is defeated relative to $\mathcal{G}$. Thus the conclusion of α is ideally warranted but not warranted.

Warrant represents the "actual" behavior of the reasoner in the limit. We can think of ideal warrant as representing the set of conclusions we would "like" the reasoner to draw in the limit. Ideal warrant is a kind of ideal target. One kind of ideal adequacy condition for a defeasible reasoner is that these concepts should pick out the same conclusions. Let us define:

The sequence $\{\alpha_i\}_{i \in \omega}$ of nodes is *ideal* iff for every sequent S, S is warranted iff it is ideally warranted.

A defeasible reasoner is *ideal* iff the sequence of nodes it produces at progressively later stages of reasoning is ideal.

The preceding two theorems show that there can be argument sequences that are not ideal. Under what circumstances will a defeasible reasoner be ideal? In investigating this question, it is useful to think about defeat graphically, in terms of the defeat links that are represented in the inference graph. I will construe the directionality so that it is the parents of a node that defeat it. In diagraming defeat, I will write "$\alpha \, \triangleleft\!\!\infty\!\!\infty \, \beta$" when β is a parent of (defeats) α.

A *defeat branch* is any finite or infinite sequence $\{\xi_k\}$ such that for each i, $\langle \xi_i, \xi_{i+1} \rangle$ is a link. A *circular branch* is an infinite defeat-branch that repeats, i.e., there is a k such that for every $i \geq k$, there is a $j < k$ such that $\xi_i = \xi_j$. Collective defeat gives rise to circular branches. For example, the following collective defeat

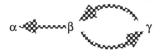

$\alpha \cdots\!\!\!\blacklozenge\!\!\sim\!\!\sim\!\!\beta \qquad \gamma$

gives rise to the circular branch $\langle \alpha,\beta,\gamma,\beta,\gamma,\beta,\gamma, ...\rangle$. Unless they are defeated by other nodes not on the branch, the nodes of a circular branch are all provisionally defeated relative to $\mathcal{G}$.

For $\{\alpha_i\}_{i\in\omega}$ to be ideal, it is sufficient that for each node β, the status of β eventually stabilizes. Define:

> The argument sequence $\{\alpha_i\}_{i\in\omega}$ is *stable in the limit* iff for every argument β in $\mathcal{G}$, β is undefeated (or defeated) relative to $\mathcal{G}$ iff there is a stage n such that for every $m \geq n$, β is undefeated (or defeated, respectively) relative to $\mathcal{G}_m$.

Clearly, if $\{\alpha_i\}_{i\in\omega}$ is stable in the limit then it is ideal. The only way stability in the limit can fail is for the status of some node β to cycle indefinitely at progressively later stages of reasoning. This can happen only if there is an infinite subsequence $\{\xi_k\}_{k\in\omega}$ of $\{\alpha_i\}_{i\in\omega}$ all of whose members are relevant to the defeat-status of β. Obviously there are only two ways to get infinitely many nodes connected to β: (1) either β or some node that is a defeat ancestor of β could be an infinite defeat-branch-point in $\mathcal{G}$; or (2) $\mathcal{G}$ could contain an infinite defeat-branch having β as its initial node. Let us consider these two possibilities separately.

Infinite defeat-branch-points (nodes defeated by infinitely many nodes) can lead to infinite cycling. This is illustrated by an example having the structure used in the proof of theorem (10.2). Suppose *input* = $\{P,R,S\}$, where P is a prima facie reason for Q, R is a prima facie reason for each of an infinite list of propositions D_i, each D_i is a prima facie reason for $(P \otimes Q)$, and S is a prima facie reason for each proposition $(D_i \otimes (P \otimes Q))$. With this set of prima facie reasons, if the ordering of the nodes is such that those supporting D_i and inferring $(P \otimes Q)$ from it alternate with those supporting $(D_i \otimes (P \otimes Q))$, then Q will alternate indefinitely between being justified and being unjustified at the different stages.

That the mere existence of infinite defeat-branch-points is insufficient to guarantee infinite cycling is obvious when we realize that, for many argument systems, it will be possible to construct infinitely many variants for any given argument. For example, we may be able to construct notational variants or add unnecessary steps. This can have the consequence that every defeat-branch-point will be an infinite defeat-branch-point. But this need not give rise to infinite cycling because the different defeat-branches are not independent; anything defeating a node on one will defeat the corresponding node on the other. Let us define:

> A node β is *subsumed by* a node γ iff any defeater for γ or one of its inference ancestors is also a defeater for β or one of its inference ancestors.

A necessary (but not sufficient) condition for infinite cycling to result from an infinite defeat-branch-point is that there is no finite set of parents of the branch point such that every other parent is subsumed by one of the parents in the finite set. I will call such a branch point *a non-redundantly infinite defeat-branch-point*. If a defeat-branch-point is not non-redundantly infinite, then defeating a finite set of its parents would defeat them all, and so only by having infinite cycling at one of the parents could we get infinite cycling at the branch point.

Noncircular infinite defeat-branches can also lead to infinite cycling. For example, as in theorem (10.1), infinite cycling would result if there were an infinite sequence of propositions Q_i all either in *input* or supported by reasoning, and such that if we define D_i recursively by stipulating that $D_1 = (Q_0 \otimes P)$ and for $i > 1$, $D_{i+1} = (Q_i \otimes D_i)$, then (1) Q_0 is a prima facie reason for P, and (2) for each $i \geq 1$, Q_i is a prima facie reason for D_i. On the other hand, circular branches cannot lead to infinite cycling. They contain only finitely many different nodes, so once those nodes are all generated by the reasoner, they will be marked as provisionally defeated and will stay that way unless one of the nodes is defeated by other nodes not on the branch. If one of the nodes of the circular branch is defeated by a node ν not on the branch, that will lead to infinite cycling only if ν cycles infinitely. ν itself could be on another circular branch, and so on. Thus we might get a sequence of interacting circular branches, as in figure 15. If the sequence is finite, there will still only be finitely nodes involved, and so infinite cycling will not result. Infinite cycling would be possible only if the sequence of interacting circular branches were infinite, but then we could construct a noncircular infinite defeat-branch by just combining the top parts of each loop.

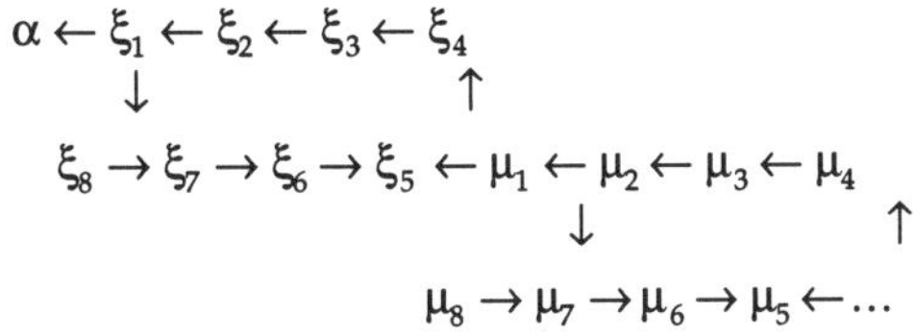

$$\alpha \leftarrow \xi_1 \leftarrow \xi_2 \leftarrow \xi_3 \leftarrow \xi_4$$
$$\downarrow \qquad\qquad \uparrow$$
$$\xi_8 \rightarrow \xi_7 \rightarrow \xi_6 \rightarrow \xi_5 \leftarrow \mu_1 \leftarrow \mu_2 \leftarrow \mu_3 \leftarrow \mu_4$$
$$\downarrow \qquad\qquad \uparrow$$
$$\mu_8 \rightarrow \mu_7 \rightarrow \mu_6 \rightarrow \mu_5 \leftarrow \dots$$

Figure 15. Interacting circular branches

Summarizing, we have the following simple lemma:

Lemma: If $\mathcal{G}$ contains no noncircular infinite defeat-branches and no non-redundantly infinite defeat-branch-points, then $\{\alpha_i\}_{i\in\omega}$ is stable in the limit, and hence ideal.

Although arrays of prima facie reasons and defeaters that will generate noncircular infinite defeat-branches and non-redundantly infinite defeat-branch-points are a formal possibility, I doubt that they are a real possibility. That is, we cannot find real examples of prima facie reasons having these structures. (My only reason for saying this is that I have tried and failed.) Accordingly, my strategy will be to adopt some realistic assumptions about the structure of the set of prima facie reasons that preclude these possibilities, and impose them as constraints on the design of a defeasible reasoner. It will then follow that the sequence of nodes produced by the reasoner is ideal.

Unless they are defeated by side branches, noncircular infinite defeat-branches lead to the provisional defeat of all of their nodes, but this defeat is peculiar because it does not arise from collective defeat. The only cases of provisional defeat that seem to arise in realistic systems of prima facie reasons and defeaters involve collective defeat. Accordingly, my first assumption will be that noncircular infinite defeat-branches are impossible:

Assumption 1: $\mathcal{G}$ contains no noncircular infinite defeat-branches.

The second assumption to be adopted is:

Assumption 2: For every proposition P and finite set X of propositions, there is a finite (possibly empty) set *nodes* of nodes in $\mathcal{G}$ supporting P relative to X such that any other node in $\mathcal{G}$ that supports P relative to X is subsumed by some member of *nodes*.

Both of these assumptions are finiteness assumptions. They tell us that for any finite *input* and finite supposition X, there is a limit to how much non-deductive reasoning we can do. Again, the only reason for making these assumptions is that I can think of no plausible counterexamples. Both assumptions ought to be provable for particular classes of arguments. Note, however, that their truth will depend essentially on what arrays of prima facie reasons and defeaters are supplied for the use of the defeasible reasoner.

Assumption 1 precludes infinite cycling resulting from infinite defeat-branches. The role of assumption 2 is to rule out non-redundantly infinite defeat-branch-points. To see that it does this, consider any node α in $\mathcal{G}$. α has only finitely many inference ancestors, and a node β can render α defeated only by defeating one of those ancestors. If a defeasible step infers P from Γ relative to a supposition X, then a node defeating this step must support either $\sim P$ or $(\Pi\Gamma \otimes P)$ relative to a subset of X. Accordingly, there are only finitely many conclusions that a defeating node can have, and hence by assumption 2, there is a finite set *nodes* of nodes in $\mathcal{G}$ supporting those conclusions and such that any other node in $\mathcal{G}$ that supports one of those conclusions is subsumed by some member of *nodes*. In other words, non-redundantly infinite defeat-branch-points are impossible.

We now have the following theorem:

(10.3) A defeasible reasoner is ideal if assumptions 1 and 2 hold.

This follows from the fact that if assumptions 1 and 2 hold then $\mathcal{G}$ contains no non-circular infinite defeat-branches and no non-redundantly infinite defeat-branch-points, and hence by the lemma, $\{\alpha_i\}_{i\in\omega}$ is ideal. Theorem (10.3) will be the fundamental theorem making possible the construction of the defeasible reasoner in chapter four.

11. Logical Properties of Ideal Warrant

It follows from the analysis of ideal warrant that it exhibits a number of simple formal properties. Let us introduce the following symbolization:

$\overset{\delta}{\underset{input}{\models}} P$ iff P is ideally warranted to degree δ (relative to *input*).

For some purposes, it is useful to be able to talk about the *defeasible consequences* of a set of assumptions. These are the propositions that can be inferred from those assumptions (relative to a fixed set *input*). Precisely:

$\Gamma \overset{\delta}{\underset{input}{\models}} P$ (*P is a defeasible consequence of Γ relative to input*, and Γ *defeasibly implies P*) iff there is a node α of strength greater than or equal to δ such that (1) $\alpha \in \mathcal{G}$, (2) α is undefeated relative to $\mathcal{G}$, and (3) α supports P relative to Γ.

Ideal warrant and defeasible implication have a number of obvious logical properties. Define:

$\Gamma \vdash P$ (*P is a deductive consequence of Γ, and Γ deductively implies P*) iff there is a node α such that (1) $\alpha \in \mathcal{G}$, (2) neither α nor any of its inference ancestors is a pf-node, (3) no member of *input* is an inference ancestor of α, and (4) α supports P relative to Γ.

P and *Q* are *deductively equivalent* iff $\{P\} \vdash Q$ and $\{Q\} \vdash P$.

Then we have:

$$\overset{\delta}{\underset{input}{\models}} P \text{ iff } \varnothing \overset{\delta}{\underset{input}{\models}} P.$$

If $\Gamma \vdash P$ then $\Gamma \overset{\delta}{\underset{input}{\models}} P.$

If $\Gamma \overset{\delta}{\underset{input}{\models}} P_1$ and ... and $\Gamma \overset{\delta}{\underset{input}{\models}} P_n$, and $\{P_1,...,P_n\} \vdash Q$, then $\Gamma \overset{\delta}{\underset{input}{\models}} Q.$

If $\Gamma \models^{\delta}_{input} P$ and $\Gamma \models^{\delta}_{input} Q$, then $\Gamma \models^{\delta}_{input} (P \& Q)$.

If P and Q are deductively equivalent then $\Gamma \cup \{P\} \models^{\delta}_{input} R$ iff $\Gamma \cup \{Q\} \models^{\delta}_{input} R$.

If $\Gamma \models^{\delta}_{input} P$ and $\Gamma \cup \{P\} \models^{\delta}_{input} Q$, then $\Gamma \models^{\delta}_{input} Q$.

If $\Gamma \models^{\delta}_{input} P$ and $\Gamma \models^{\delta}_{input} Q$ then $\Gamma \cup \{P\} \models^{\delta}_{input} Q$.[12]

If $\Gamma \cup \{P\} \models^{\delta}_{input} Q$, then $\Gamma \models^{\delta}_{input} (P \supset Q)$.[13]

12. Conclusions

This completes the semantical theory of defeasible epistemic reasoning. This chapter has developed the accounts of justification and warrant based upon the argument-based approach to defeasible reasoning in terms of prima facie reasons, rebutting defeaters, and undercutting defeaters. The next task will be to construct a procedural theory of defeasible reasoning based upon this semantical theory. The result will be the automated defeasible reasoner described in chapter 4.

---

[12] This is the principle Gabbay [1985] calls "restricted monotonicity".

[13] For further discussion of such logical principles, see [Gabbay 1985, 1991], Kraus, Lehmann, and Magidor [1990], and Makinson [1988].

Chapter 4
An Architecture for
Epistemic Cognition

Chapter 3 described the logical structure of defeasible epistemic reasoning. This chapter will propose an architecture for epistemic cognition capable of performing such defeasible reasoning. Such an architecture must integrate defeasible reasoning with Q&I modules and provide an interface with practical cognition. It turns out that the only difficult part of this task is describing the defeasible reasoner, and the bulk of this chapter will be devoted to that task.

1. Criteria of Adequacy for a Defeasible Reasoner

In designing a defeasible reasoner, one is faced with the problem of how to evaluate the reasoning that the reasoner performs. We want the reasoning to be "correct", but what is the criterion for correctness? The desideratum is not necessarily to build a reasoner that replicates human reasoning in all respects, because there may be more efficient ways of doing it. However, before we can decide whether a particular procedure is a more efficient way of doing it, we have to determine what the "it" is that we want the reasoner to do. I suggested in chapter 3 that *ideal warrant* is what a reasoner is ultimately striving for. A proposition is ideally warranted in a particular epistemic situation iff it is supported by an inference that is undefeated relative to the set of inferences comprising the set of all possible arguments that could be constructed starting from that epistemic situation.

Ideal warrant constitutes a kind of "ideal target" for a reasoner. But what exactly is the connection between ideal warrant and what we want a reasoner to accomplish? The simplest proposal would be that we want the reasoner to "compute ideal warrant". But if this is understood as requiring that the reasoner implement an effective procedure for deciding ideal warrant, then it is an impossible desideratum. All theorems of logic are automatically ideally warranted because the arguments supporting them are non-defeasible. This includes all theorems of the predicate calculus. If we give the system no non-logical reasons and no input premises, these are the only ideally warranted propositions. Thus a decision procedure for ideal warrant would give us a decision procedure for the predicate calculus. However, by Church's theorem, the set of theorems of the predicate calculus is not decidable. Thus *no* reasoner can compute ideal warrant in this sense.

A weaker proposal would be that we want the reasoner to systematically generate all ideally warranted propositions in some effective way, analogous to the manner in which a complete theorem prover generates all theorems of the predicate calculus. But this desideratum is also provably unsatisfiable, because the set of ideally warranted propositions can fail to be recursively enumerable (r.e.). This is because, as has been observed by numerous authors,[1] on any theory of defeasible reasoning, the ultimate correctness of a piece of defeasible reasoning (i.e., whether the conclusion of the reasoning will survive an indefinite amount of further reasoning and hence be ideally warranted) will always turn upon something else's *being unprovable*. Making this more precise, we have the following theorem:

> There are finite sets of input premises and finite sets of non-logical reasons such that the set of conclusions ideally warranted with respect to them is not r.e.

To prove this, suppose otherwise. Then for any finite set *input* and finite set of non-logical reasons, there is a way of mechanically generating the list of formulas ideally warranted relative to them. Given any first-order formula P, choose a sentence letter Q not occurring in P, let *input* = $\{Q\}$, and let the only non-logical reason be the prima facie reason $\langle\{Q\},P\rangle$. We have a prima facie reason for P, so P is ideally warranted iff there is no undefeated or provisionally defeated argument defeating this inference. Because Q is logically unrelated to P and there are no other prima facie reasons, the only possible defeating argument would be a deductive argument for $\sim P$. Thus in this situation, P is ideally warranted iff $\sim P$ is not a theorem of the predicate calculus. Consequently, the mechanical procedure for listing ideally warranted conclusions will list P iff $\sim P$ is not a theorem. This would generate a recursive enumeration of the non-theorems of the predicate calculus, but that is impossible by Church's theorem. It follows that the set of defeasible consequences of a set of premises may not be r.e., and there can be no effective procedure for generating the set of ideally warranted

---

[1] I think that the first were David Israel [1980] and Raymond Reiter [1980].

consequences of an arbitrary set of input premises and non-logical reasons.

If the desideratum for a defeasible reasoner is neither that of computing ideal warrant nor that of recursively enumerating the set of ideally warranted conclusions, what is it? We should take seriously the idea that defeasible reasoning is *defeasible*. That is, a defeasible reasoner may have to adopt a belief, retract it in the face of defeaters, and then reinstate the belief because the defeaters are themselves retracted. This cycle may be repeated an indefinite number of times. The most we can require of the reasoner is that its rules for reasoning guarantee that it will systematically modify its belief set so that it comes to approximate the set of ideally warranted propositions more and more closely. We want the set of beliefs to "approach the set of ideally warranted propositions in the limit". Ihave proposed [1989, 1991] that we understand this in the following sense:

> The rules for reasoning should be such that:
> (1) if a proposition p is ideally warranted then the reasoner will eventually reach a stage where p is justified and stays justified;
> (2) if p is ideally unwarranted then the reasoner will eventually reach a stage where p is unjustified and stays unjustified.

Thus the task of a reasoner is not to compute ideal warrant but to generate successive sets of beliefs that approximate ideal warrant more and more closely, in the above sense. We can make this mathematically precise as follows. Define:

> A set A is *defeasibly enumerable* iff there is an effectively computable function f such that for each n, $f(n)$ is a recursive set, and
> (1) $(\forall x)$ if $x \in A$ then $(\exists n)(\forall m > n)\ x \in f(m)$; and
> (2) $(\forall x)$ if $x \notin A$ then $(\exists n)(\forall m > n)\ x \notin f(m)$.

I will say that the sequence of recursive sets $f(n)$ is a *defeasible enumeration* of A. Defeasibly enumerable sets are the same as those Gold [1965] calls "limiting recursive" and Putnam [1965] calls "trial and error". Both authors establish that a set is of this type iff it is Δ_2 in the arithmetic hierarchy.

The intuitive difference between recursively enumerable sets and defeasibly enumerable sets is that recursively enumerable sets can be "systematically approximated from below", while defeasibly enumerable sets that are not recursively enumerable can only be systematically approximated from above and below simultaneously. More precisely, if A is r.e., then there is an effectively computable sequence of sets A_i such that

(1) $(\forall x)$ if $x \in A$ then $(\exists n)(\forall m > n)\ x \in A_m$;
(2) $(\forall x)$ if $x \notin A$ then $(\forall m)x \notin A_m$.

The sets A_i approximate A from below in the sense that they are all subsets of A and they grow monotonically, approaching A in the limit. If A is only defeasibly enumerable, however, the sets A_i need not be subsets of A. They may only approach A from above and below simultaneously, in the sense that they may contain elements not contained in A. Every such element must eventually be taken out of the A_i's, but there need not be any point at which they have *all* been removed. The process of defeasible enumeration can be pictured by thinking of A as a spherical region of space and the A_i's as representing successive stages of a reverberating elastic ball whose center coincides with the center of A. As the reverberations dampen out, the outer surface of the ball will come to approximate that of the spherical surface more and more closely, but there will never be a point at which the ball is contained entirely within the spherical surface.

The reverberating sphere metaphor can be used to give a precise mathematical characterization of the difference between A being r.e. (approximation from below) and d.e. (approximation from above and below simultaneously). If A is r.e. then

$$A = \bigcup_{n \in \omega} A_n.$$

On the other hand, if A is d.e. then what we have is:

$$A = \bigcap_{n \in \omega} \bigcup_{m \geq n} A_m = \bigcup_{n \in \omega} \bigcap_{m \geq n} A_m.$$

My initial proposal regarding reasoning and ideal warrant is that the set of ideally warranted propositions is defeasibly enumerable, and the rules for reasoning are rules for successively approximating ideal warrant in this way, that is, they are rules for constructing a defeasible enumeration. More accurately:

If $\mathcal{J}_\alpha(i)$ is the set of propositions justified to degree α after i applications of *update* to *input*, the reasoner is *d.e.-adequate* iff $\mathcal{J}_\alpha$ is a defeasible enumeration of the set of propositions ideally warranted to degree α.

At this point, I propose d.e.-adequacy as the primary criterion of adequacy for a reasoner. The objective of this chapter is to investigate how to construct a reasoner that is d.e.-adequate. The principal result of this chapter will be that if certain conditions are satisfied, then the set of ideally warranted conclusions is defeasibly enumerable and hence d.e.-adequate reasoners are possible. It will then be shown how to produce such a reasoner.

In actual practice, an automated reasoner does not strive to do all possible reasoning. Instead, it is constrained to construct arguments built using only limited resources for argument formation. For instance, it might construct only arguments that can be formulated within a certain system of first-order logic. These arguments will comprise a class $\mathcal{A}$. The inference graph relative to which we assess ideal warrant will consist only of inference nodes encoding inferences made within this class of arguments. The objective will then be to construct a reasoner that is d.e.-adequate relative to the class $\mathcal{A}$ of arguments.

The requirement that a reasoner provide a defeasible enumeration of ideal warrant is a *minimal* criterion of adequacy. Other criteria must also be involved in the choice of a reasoner. At the very least we must consider efficiency. But there is a different kind of adequacy condition that must also be met. If a reasoner is d.e.-adequate, there will be cases in which it will never stop reasoning. Any given proposition may be concluded, retracted, and reinstated many times. Every ideally warranted proposition will eventually reach a point where it is believed and is never subsequently retracted, and every ideally unwarranted proposition will eventually reach a point where it is not believed and never subsequently becomes believed, but the reasoner may never know that a given proposition has reached this stable state. It can inform us that "so far" a certain conclusion is justified, but it may have to continue forever in a possibly fruitless search for defeating arguments. This, of course, is just the way human beings work. This highlights a distinction between two concepts of defeasibility. The sense in which correct human reasoning is defeasible is that we regard such reasoning as "innocent until proven guilty". Once a conclusion becomes justified, it is reasonable to accept it provisionally and act upon it. By contrast, AI theories of nonmonotonic reasoning have usually focused on a stronger notion of defeasibility according to which a defeasible conclusion is acceptable only if it has been established that it is objectively devoid of faults. The latter amounts to *proving* that the conclusion is ideally warranted. This has made it seem mysterious how nonmonotonic reasoning can possibly function in a finite agent. The solution is to instead adopt the "innocent until proven guilty" construal of defeasibility, and allow a rational agent to act on its defeasible conclusions even though it has not conclusively established that there are no defeaters and even though, in the absence of more pressing tasks, it will continue to search for defeaters. The reasoning employed by such a rational agent must be *interruptible*,[2] in the sense that if at some point the agent must stop reasoning and act, it is reasonable to act on the conclusions drawn to that point. This is not ensured by d.e.-adequacy. For example, let R_1 be a reasoner that is both interruptible and d.e.-adequate. Let R_2 be just like R_1 except that for the first million steps it draws conclusions purely at random, and then after 1 million steps it withdraws all those randomly drawn conclusions and begins reasoning as in R_1. Clearly it would be unreasonable to make use of any of the conclusions drawn by R_2 during its first 1 million inference steps, so it is not interruptible. On the other hand, R_2 is still d.e.-adequate, because that concerns only its behavior in the limit, and its behavior in the limit is the same as that of R_1.

It is not clear how to construct a formal criterion of adequacy that will ensure interruptibility. It is tempting to require that the conditional probability that a conclusion is ideally warranted given that it is drawn at a certain stage of the reasoning is (1) high and (2) a monotonic increasing function of the number of the stage. But this is still insufficient to ensure interruptibility. For example, a reasoner satisfying this condition will continue to satisfy it if we modify it to initially draw conclusions at random when it is dealing with a certain isolated subject matter.

Because of the difficulty in formulating a mathematically precise characterization of interruptibility, I am going to ignore that condition here, but it is a topic that must eventually be addressed with care. My present objective will be merely to design a reasoner that is d.e.-adequate. I will return to interruptibility briefly in section six.[3]

---

[2] This point and the terminology are due to George Smith.

[3] Although I lack a formal characterization of interruptibility, the reasoning system implemented in OSCAR would seem, intuitively, to be interruptible.

2. Building a Defeasible Reasoner

The Monotonic Reasoner
In constructing a defeasible reasoner, we need rules governing the adoption of beliefs, the retraction of beliefs in response to the adoption of defeaters, and the reinstatement of beliefs in response to the retraction of defeaters. I propose to begin with the construction of a reasoner that ignores defeaters. This *monotonic reasoner* will be analogous to a deductive reasoner in that it constructs arguments and adopts as beliefs any conclusions supported by any of the arguments it constructs, but it will differ from a deductive reasoner in that it will use prima facie reasons as well as conclusive reasons as links in arguments. For the most part, it need not distinguish between prima facie and conclusive reasons. The monotonic reasoner will be investigated more fully in section 4.

Defeasible Reasoning without Collective Defeat or Self-Defeat
If we did not have to contend with collective defeat, self-defeat, and related phenomena, it would be quite easy to build a defeasible reasoner by modifying the monotonic reasoner. A defeasible reasoner must perform three kinds of operations: belief adoption, retraction, and reinstatement. These proceed as follows:

(1) The reasoner must adopt beliefs in response to constructing arguments, provided no defeaters have already been adopted for any step of the argument. This can be handled just as in the monotonic reasoner, except that when a defeasible inference occurs, there must be a check to ascertain whether a defeater for it has already been adopted as a belief.

(2) The reasoner must keep track of the bases upon which its beliefs are held. When a new belief is adopted that is a defeater for a previous inference step, then the reasoner must retract that inference step and all beliefs inferred from it.

(3) The reasoner must keep track of defeated inferences, and when a defeater is itself retracted (in accordance with (2)), this should reinstate the defeated inference. The reasoner can then either repeat the reasoning that followed from that defeated inference, or the reasoner can be constructed in such a way that it keeps track of that reasoning and reinstates it *en bloc*.

Flag-Based Reasoners

It is simple to build a reasoner that performs the functions just described. The first version of OSCAR was such a reasoner [Pollock, 1987]. One of the important characteristics of that reasoner is that once a defeasible inference step is defeated, the reasoner ceases exploring its consequences. The reasoner expends its resources investigating the consequences of a defeated inference only if the inference is reinstated. This seems like the only sensible way to proceed in defeasible reasoning. Why put effort into developing the consequences of an inference you already know to be defeated? However, this seemingly obvious design feature leads to apparently insuperable difficulties when we begin to worry about collective defeat.

Suppose α and β are long arguments each of which undercuts an early defeasible inference in the other:

$$\alpha: P \dashrightarrow Q \dashrightarrow \ldots \dashrightarrow {\sim}(A \gg B)$$

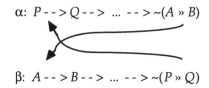

$$\beta: A \dashrightarrow B \dashrightarrow \ldots \dashrightarrow {\sim}(P \gg Q)$$

If the reasoner first discovers the defeat of β by α, it will stop reasoning from propositions supported by β and never discover the defeat of α by β. It appears that the only way to handle this correctly is to flag defeated beliefs as defeated, and have the reasoner continue to reason from them instead of simply discarding.

The preceding considerations seem to indicate that the production of arguments by the monotonic reasoner must be relatively insensitive to their defeat status, because the reasoner must continue reasoning from conclusions even when they are defeated. This suggests building a defeasible reasoner out of two largely autonomous modules. The first is the monotonic reasoner, which systematically makes inferences (generates arguments) and builds the inference graph without concern for the defeat status of the nodes of the graph. The second is a module that computes the defeat status of all the nodes that have been produced at each stage of reasoning relative to the set of all nodes so far produced. The reasoner will then be a simple loop:

```
(loop
    (MAKE-AN-INFERENCE)
    (RECOMPUTE-DEFEAT-STATUSES))
```

Each time the reasoner makes an inference, it thereby produces a new node. Let $\mathcal{G}_i$ be the set of nodes produced after i inferences. Each i represents a *stage of the monotonic reasoner*. The function RECOMPUTE-DEFEAT-STATUSES determines which of the nodes in $\mathcal{G}_i$ are defeated outright, which are undefeated, and which are provisionally defeated, at stage i, and hence determines which conclusions are justified at stage i. Let $\mathcal{J}_\alpha(i)$ be the set of all propositions justified to degree α at stage i of the monotonic reasoner. These will be taken to be the interim conclusions (the current beliefs) of the reasoner. I will call a reasoner of this sort a *flag-based reasoner*. The principal result of section 3 will be that if certain conditions are satisfied, then the sequence of justification-sets $\mathcal{J}_\alpha(i)$ will constitute a defeasible enumeration of the set of conclusions ideally warranted to degree α.

Flag-based reasoners mark a serious divergence from stage II reasoners. Flagging beliefs as provisionally defeated or defeated outright, and then continuing to reason with them, seems outrageously expensive. But there appears to be no alternative. It is worth at least noting that human reasoners are not totally insensitive to the consequences of defeated beliefs, even if they do not usually expend a large amount of effort in developing those consequences. In section 5, I will mention possibilities for minimizing this cost. But first, in section 3, I will address theoretical issues concerning the possibility of constructing a d.e.-adequate flag-based reasoner.

3. The Possibility of a D.E.-Adequate Reasoner

The results of chapter 3 make it quite easy to establish that, given certain reasonable assumptions, it is possible to construct a d.e.-adequate flag-based reasoner. Such a reasoner consists of a monotonic reasoner and an algorithm for computing defeat status. The only assumption that will be made about the monotonic reasoner is that it systematically generates every argument in $\mathcal{A}$. The definition given in chapter 3 of defeat-status relative to an inference graph provides an algorithm for computing defeat-status relative to $\mathcal{G}_i$.[4]

The objective is to show that the sequence of justification-sets $\mathcal{J}_\alpha(i)$ produced by the flag-based reasoner just described constitutes a defeasible enumeration of ideal warrant. This cannot be proven without

---

[4] This algorithm will be refined in chapter 9.

imposing further restrictions on the monotonic reasoner. What is automatic, however, is that the justification-sets constitute a defeasible enumeration of warrant. That is just the way warrant was defined. Thus if warrant and ideal warrant coincide, then the sequence of justification-sets also constitutes a defeasible enumeration of ideal warrant. The circumstances under which warrant and ideal warrant coincide were investigated in chapter 3, with the following result:

> If
> (1) $\mathcal{G}$ contains no noncircular infinite defeat-branches, and
> (2)   for every proposition P and finite set X of propositions, there is a finite (possibly empty) set $nodes$ of nodes in $\mathcal{G}$ supporting P relative to X such that any other node in $\mathcal{G}$ that supports P relative to X is subsumed by some member of $nodes$,
> then $\mathcal{J}_\alpha$ is a defeasible enumeration of ideal warrant.

As remarked in chapter 3, assumptions (1) and (2) are about the array of reasons available to the reasoner. Assumption (1) amounts to the assumption that all cases of provisional defeat arise out of collective defeat. Assumption (2) is a finiteness assumption. It tells us that for any finite *input* and finite supposition X, there is a limit to how much non-deductive reasoning can be done. Both assumptions ought to be provable for particular classes of arguments. Note, however, that we cannot expect to prove them as general theorems about the monotonic reasoner. Their truth will depend essentially on what arrays of prima facie reasons and defeaters are supplied for the use of the monotonic reasoner, and that will vary from application to application.

The flag-based defeasible reasoner should now work as follows. The monotonic reasoner builds the inference graph one node at a time. As each node is constructed, defeat links between it and pre-existing nodes are computed. Self-defeating nodes are detected and removed from the inference graph, because they can never be reinstated and hence there is no point in continuing to reason from them. Once these adjustments have been made to the inference graph, the defeat-statuses of the nodes are recomputed using the algorithm described in chapter 3. Rather than recomputing defeat-status from scratch each time a new node is added to the inference graph, it is sometimes possible to update the defeat-statuses by examining only those nodes whose status might be changed by the addition. This is at least true if the new node does not defeat any pre-existing node. In that case:

(1)   if every node defeating the new node η is defeated and all of
       η's immediate ancestors are undefeated, then η is undefeated;
(2)   if some node defeating η is undefeated or at least one of η's
       immediate ancestors is defeated, then η is defeated;
(3)   otherwise, η is provisionally defeated.

If the new node defeats some pre-existing node, then it can happen
that all the node statuses must be recomputed from scratch because
there may be defeat cycles that can be detected only by starting from
d-initial nodes.[5] This will be discussed further in chapter 9.

4. An Interest-Driven Monotonic Reasoner

The flag-based reasoner described in section 3 could actually be constructed, but it is impractical in one important respect: it operates by
having the monotonic reasoner systematically generate all possible
arguments in the class 𝒜. This is the so-called British museum algorithm.
Any automated reasoner that is practical employs a more efficient
control structure enabling it to focus its attention on arguments that
are more intimately connected with the conclusions it is trying to
establish. Earlier in the book, I expressed this point by saying that
reasoning is interest-driven. In this section, I will look more closely at
the structure of interest-driven monotonic reasoning, and then in the
next section I will apply the observations of this section to interest-driven
defeasible reasoning.

In an interest-driven reasoner, the reasoning done reflects in part
the conclusions the agent is trying to establish or the questions we are
trying to answer. Applying this observation to human beings, if we
are interested in knowing the value of 23 + 57, we reason differently
than if we are interested in knowing what time it is in Moscow. We
do not just reason randomly until we happen upon the answers to our
questions. This is related to a feature of rationality that has been
emphasized by Gilbert Harman [1986]: rationality does not mandate
the adoption of every belief for which we have good reasons. For

---

[5] More precisely, let us say that a node α *influences* a node β iff either (1) α
defeats β or a node influenced by β, or (2) α is an immediate inference ancestor of β
or a node influenced by β. Then when a node is added to the inference-graph, the
defeat statuses of all nodes influenced by it must be recomputed.

example, each belief P gives us a conclusive reason for any disjunction $(P \lor Q)$ containing P as a disjunct, but we do not arbitrarily infer such disjunctions. Our epistemic rules must honor the fact that we are information processors with a limited capacity for processing and storage. They do this in part by mandating inferences that are related, in specific ways, to our interests.

Let us consider more carefully how this is accomplished. Recall first that inferences are mediated by reasons—some conclusive and some defeasible. Of the conclusive reasons, some are part of logic itself, while the others can be regarded as "substantive", in the sense that they pertain to particular concepts. For instance, $\ulcorner x$ is a bachelor$\urcorner$ is a conclusive reason for $\ulcorner x$ is unmarried$\urcorner$, but this is not part of logic. This is a substantive reason pertaining specifically to the attributes of being a bachelor and being unmarried. By way of contrast, $\{P,Q\}$ is a conclusive reason for $\ulcorner (P \& Q) \urcorner$. This is the rule of adjunction, and it is generally regarded as part of logic. There may be no precise distinction to be made here, but I will follow the standard convention of referring to logical reasons as "logical inference rules". Thinking of these as rules for inferring sequents from sequents, some familiar inference rules can be formulated as follows:

adjunction

$$\frac{\langle \Gamma, p \rangle \; \langle \Lambda, q \rangle}{\langle \Gamma \cup \Lambda, (p \& q) \rangle}$$

simplification

$$\frac{\langle \Gamma, (p \& q) \rangle}{\langle \Gamma, p \rangle} \qquad \frac{\langle \Gamma, (p \& q) \rangle}{\langle \Gamma, q \rangle}$$

negation introduction

$$\frac{\langle \Gamma, p \rangle}{\langle \Gamma, \sim\sim p \rangle}$$

negation elimination

$$\frac{\langle \Gamma, \sim\sim p \rangle}{\langle \Gamma, p \rangle}$$

addition

$$\frac{\langle \Gamma, p \rangle}{\langle \Gamma, (p \lor q) \rangle} \qquad \frac{\langle \Gamma, p \rangle}{\langle \Gamma, (q \lor p) \rangle}$$

disjunctive syllogism

$$\frac{\langle \Gamma, \sim p \rangle \; \langle \Lambda, (p \lor q) \rangle}{\langle \Gamma \cup \Lambda, q \rangle} \qquad \frac{\langle \Gamma, \sim q \rangle \; \langle \Lambda, (p \lor q) \rangle}{\langle \Gamma \cup \Lambda, p \rangle}$$

conditionalization

$$\frac{\langle \Gamma \cup \{p\}, q \rangle}{\langle \Gamma, (p \supset q) \rangle}$$

modus ponens

$$\frac{\langle \Gamma, p \rangle \; \langle \Lambda, (p \supset q) \rangle}{\langle \Gamma \cup \Lambda, q \rangle}$$

modus tollens

$$\frac{\langle \Gamma, \sim q \rangle \; \langle \Lambda, (p \supset q) \rangle}{\langle \Gamma \cup \Lambda, \sim p \rangle}$$

reductio1   *reductio2*

$$\frac{\langle \Gamma \cup \{\sim p\}, p \rangle}{\langle \Gamma, p \rangle} \qquad\qquad \frac{\langle \Gamma \cup \{\sim p\}, (q \ \& \sim q) \rangle}{\langle \Gamma, p \rangle}$$

It is a familiar point in AI that we can think of reasoning as a search for appropriate paths through an "inference space", where the latter consists of sequents standing in inferrability relations to one another. Each sequent is related by inference links to sets of sequents from which it can be inferred. Reasoning from a set of premises to a conclusion consists of finding a path through the inference space from the premises to the conclusion. Searching for such a path can be done in either direction. We can work forwards from the premises ("forward chaining") or backwards from the conclusion ("backward chaining"). It seems clear that human beings do both. In trying to prove a theorem in mathematics or trying to construct a derivation in logic, we sometimes cast about more or less at random, drawing whatever conclusions we can until we eventually see some way to put them together to get to our desired conclusion. At other times we proceed in a much more deliberate fashion, in effect reasoning backwards from our desired conclusion. We can think of such backwards reasoning as deriving interests from interests. We begin by being interested in one sequent (our desired conclusion), and that leads us to become interested in other sequents from which the first could be inferred.

Backwards reasoning is sensitive to the desired conclusion but insensitive to the premises. Forwards reasoning is sensitive to the given premises but insensitive to the desired conclusion. Human reasoning combines both. In a finitely branching search space, combining search in both directions has the effect of narrowing the search space, as is indicated in figure 1.

It is natural to suppose that this is the entire explanation for the fact that humans engage in reasoning in both directions—it is just a matter of efficiency, aimed at narrowing the search space. On this view, backwards reasoning is just forwards reasoning done in reverse, and in any given instance we *could* (apart from efficiency) reason in just one direction or the other without combining the two. But it turns out that this view of reasoning is fundamentally mistaken. The problem is that, given natural selections of inference rules like those listed above, the inference space is infinitely branching in both directions. For instance, consider addition. Suppose we could use addition in forwards reasoning. Then if we inferred p, we would be led to infer

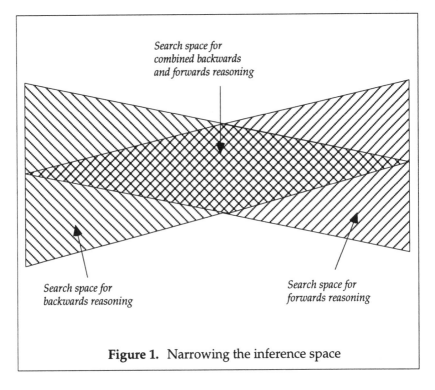

Search space for
combined backwards
and forwards reasoning

Search space for
backwards reasoning

Search space for
forwards reasoning

Figure 1. Narrowing the inference space

every disjunction containing p as a disjunct. But there are infinitely many such disjunctions, and most are useless in any given problem. In point of fact, we use addition only when we have some reason to be interested in the resulting disjunction. A related observation can be made about simplification. The use of simplification in backwards reasoning is also infinitely branching, and that would be even more catastrophic. Suppose we are interested in q. Backwards reasoning with simplification would lead us to adopt interest in $(p \& q)$, for *every* p, and then backwards reasoning with adjunction (which is presumably permissible) would lead us to adopt interest in p. Thus interest in anything would automatically lead to interest in everything, which would completely vitiate the interest restrictions in interest-driven reasoning.

Even rules that do not lead to infinite branching can create difficulties. For example, although adjunction does not lead to infinite branching, its use in forwards reasoning would be combinatorially explosive. Suppose we could use adjunction in forwards reasoning, and we inferred p and q. Then we would be led to infer $(p \& q)$. That does not seem so bad, but it would not stop there. We would go on to infer [(p & q) & p], (q & p), [(q & p) & (p & q)], [(q & p) & [(p & q) & p]], (p & [(q & p) & [(p & q) & p]]), and so on without limit. Obviously, we do not do that, and a reasoning system that performed in this way would be crippled. This largely useless reasoning would continually get in its way, taking up its resources and preventing it from making more useful inferences.

The somewhat surprising conclusion to be drawn from this is that some reasons are of use in backwards reasoning, and others are of use in forwards reasoning, and individual reasons are often precluded from playing both roles.[6] Accordingly, reasons can be classified as *forwards reasons* and *backwards reasons*. The following is a plausible classification of the inference rules (i.e., conclusive reasons) listed above:

Forwards reasons	Backwards reasons
simplification	adjunction
negation elimination	negation introduction
disjunctive syllogism	addition
modus ponens	conditionalization
modus tollens	reductio1

Note that reductio2 does not fit into either category. Used for forwards reasoning, it would have us derive infinitely many conclusions from a contradiction, and used for backwards reasoning it would have us adopt interest in infinitely many contradictions. I will return to this observation.

If a rule from either category is used for reasoning in the other direction, it is combinatorially explosive. It follows that there are profound differences in the structure of forwards reasoning and backwards reasoning, and neither is replaceable by the other. Both are indispensable for reasoning, and there is a definite logic governing when to use one and when to use the other. The choice is not just a matter of convenience. We literally could not arrive at our conclusions in any but the simplest cases without using both kinds of reasoning.

We can think of interest-driven reasoning as consisting of three operations: (1) we reason forwards from previously drawn conclusions to new conclusions; (2) we reason backwards from interests to interests; (3) when we have reasoned backwards to a set of sequents as interests and forwards to the same set of sequents as conclusions, then we

---

[6] A similar conclusion is advanced in Rips [1983, 1994].

discharge interest and conclude the sequent that led to those interests. For example, suppose we are given the premises $\{P, (P \supset Q)\}$ and are interested in the conclusion $(Q \lor R)$. From the latter, we could reason backwards to interest in Q and in R (using *addition* as our rule of inference). From the premises we could reason forwards to Q (using *modus ponens*). We then have Q as both a conclusion and an interest, so we can discharge interest. Our interest in Q derived from our interest in $(Q \lor R)$, so when we discharge interest, we conclude $(Q \lor R)$, and we are through.

This reasoning proceeds in accordance with three procedures:

REASON-FORWARDS

If a set of sequents X is a forwards reason for a sequent S, some member of X is newly concluded, and the other members of X have already been concluded, then conclude S.

REASON-BACKWARDS

If interest is adopted in a sequent S, and a set X of sequents is a backwards reason for S, then adopt interest in any members of X that have not already been concluded. If every member of X has been concluded, conclude S.

DISCHARGE-INTEREST

If interest was adopted in the members of X as a way of getting the sequent S, and some member of X is concluded and the other members of X have already been concluded, then conclude S.

However, as formulated, these procedures are inadequate for some interest-driven reasoning. To see why, first note that as a theoretical matter, there can be not only the forwards reasons and the "simple" backwards reasons discussed above, but also *generalized backwards reasons*. In a generalized backwards reason, the premises are segregated into two sets:

$$\frac{\langle \Gamma_1, p_1 \rangle, \dots, \langle \Gamma_n, p_n \rangle}{\langle \Gamma_{n+1}, q_1 \rangle, \dots, \langle \Gamma_{n+m}, q_m \rangle}$$
$$\langle \Gamma, r \rangle$$

where the premises in the first set (the *forwards premises*) function in a forwards direction and the premises in the second set (the *backwards premises*) function in a backwards direction. In other words, given interest in $\langle\Gamma,r\rangle$, the reasoner reasons backwards to interest in $\langle\Gamma_{n+1},q_1\rangle,...,\langle\Gamma_{n+m},q_m\rangle$, but only if the reasoner has already established $\langle\Gamma_1,p_1\rangle,...,\langle\Gamma_n,p_n\rangle$

A simple example of a generalized backwards reason would be the following:

$$\frac{\langle\Gamma,(\forall x)(Fx \supset Gx)\rangle}{\frac{\langle\Gamma,Fa\rangle}{\langle\Gamma,Ga\rangle}}$$

The effect of this reason will be that whenever the reasoner adopts interest in Ga, it will look at all universal generalizations $(\forall x)(Fx \supset Gx)$ that it has already concluded and adopt interest in their antecedents as a way of establishing Ga.

We can regard generalized backwards reasons as the most general form of backwards reasons, henceforth calling them simply "backwards reasons". The simple backwards reasons discussed earlier represent the special case in which the set of forwards premises is empty. To accommodate reasoning with these generalized backwards reasons, we can revise REASON-BACKWARDS and DISCHARGE-INTEREST as follows:

REASON-BACKWARDS
If interest is adopted in a sequent S, and a pair $\langle X,Y\rangle$ of sets of sequents is a backwards reason for S, where X is the set of forwards premises and Y is the set of backwards premises, then if every member of X has been concluded, adopt interest in any members of Y that have not already been concluded. If all members of both X and Y have been concluded, conclude S. If some members of X have not been concluded, then simply record $\langle X,Y\rangle$ as a potential reason for S, for use by DISCHARGE-INTEREST.

DISCHARGE-INTEREST
If interest was adopted in the members of Y as a way of getting the sequent S, and some member of Y is concluded and the other members of Y have already been concluded, then conclude S. If the pair $\langle X,Y\rangle$ has been recorded as a potential backwards reason for S, and some member of X is newly concluded and the other members of X have already been concluded, then

adopt interest in any members of Y that have not already been concluded. If all members of both X and Y have been concluded, conclude S.

To illustrate the importance of this generalization of interest-driven reasoning, let us return to the observation that reductio2 cannot be regarded as a simple backwards reason. This is of considerable significance, because there is reason to believe that the use of some form of this rule for backwards reasoning is essential in a deductive reasoner that is complete for first-order logic.[7] This problem can be solved by adopting the following variant of reductio2 as a generalized backwards reason:

$$\frac{\langle \Gamma \cup \{\sim p\}, q \rangle}{\langle \Gamma \cup \{\sim p\}, \sim q \rangle}$$
$$\frac{}{\langle \Gamma, p \rangle}$$

The effect of this is that, in trying to derive a contradiction from the supposition $\Gamma \cup \{\sim p\}$, the reasoner looks only for contradictions one of whose conjuncts have already been concluded. This avoids infinite branching, and when combined with reductio1, turns out to be sufficient to enable the construction of a complete deductive reasoner for first-order logic.

An interest-driven reasoner will work backwards from its existing interests, generating new interests, and forwards from its conclusions, generating new conclusions. The reasoner will then repeat the process recursively, working backwards from these new interests and forwards from the new conclusions. The strength of a new interest will be the strength of the interest from which it was derived, and the degree of justification of a conclusion will be the maximum of the degrees of justification of the conclusions from which it was inferred. At any given time, the reasoner may have drawn several new conclusions and acquired several new interests without yet having reasoned from them. It must choose one of them and reason from it, returning to the others later. Accordingly, new conclusions and new interests must be stored on a queue—the *inference-queue*—whose members are retrieved and processed one at a time. The *inference-queue* will be ordered in

---

[7] See my earlier discussion of this [1990a].

some fashion so that an attempt can be made to perform the most important or most useful inferences first. Strengths of interest and degrees of justification will play an important role in this ordering. When new conclusions are drawn, they will be added to the *inference-graph*. Similarly, the interests employed by backwards reasoning will be stored in a data-structure called the *interest-graph*, which records the interests and the purposes for which the interests arise. The general structure of the monotonic reasoner is diagrammed in figure 2.

An early stage in the construction of OSCAR consisted of the construction of an interest-driven deductive reason for the predicate calculus [Pollock 1990a], and the results were surprising. Consider, for example, the "Schubert steamroller problem":

$$(\forall x)(Wx \supset Ax) \qquad\qquad (\forall x)(\forall y)[(Cx \ \& \ By) \supset Mxy]$$
$$(\forall x)(Fx \supset Ax) \qquad\qquad (\forall x)(\forall y)[(Sx \ \& \ By) \supset Mxy]$$
$$(\forall x)(Bx \supset Ax) \qquad\qquad (\forall x)(\forall y)[(Bx \ \& \ Fy) \supset Mxy]$$
$$(\forall x)(Cx \supset Ax) \qquad\qquad (\forall x)(\forall y)[(Fx \ \& \ Wy) \supset Mxy]$$
$$(\forall x)(Sx \supset Ax) \qquad\qquad (\forall x)(\forall y)[(Wx \ \& \ Fy) \supset {\sim}Exy]$$
$$(\exists w)Ww \qquad\qquad\qquad (\forall x)(\forall y)[(Wx \ \& \ Gy) \supset {\sim}Exy]$$
$$(\exists f)Ff \qquad\qquad\qquad\quad (\forall x)(\forall y)[(Bx \ \& \ Cy) \supset Exy]$$
$$(\exists b)Bb \qquad\qquad\qquad\quad (\forall x)(\forall y)[(Bx \ \& \ Sy) \supset {\sim}Exy]$$
$$(\exists c)Cc \qquad\qquad\qquad\quad (\forall x)[Cx \supset (\exists y)(Py \ \& \ Exy)]$$
$$(\exists s)Ss \qquad\qquad\qquad\quad (\forall x)[Sx \supset (\exists y)(Py \ \& \ Exy)]$$
$$(\exists g)Gg \qquad\qquad\qquad\quad (\forall x)(Gx \supset Px)$$
$$(\forall x)[Ax \supset [(\forall w)(Pw \supset Exw) \supset$$
$$(\forall y)((Ay \ \& \ (Myx \ \& \ (\exists z)(Pz \ \& \ Eyz))) \supset Exy)]]$$

$$(\exists x)(\exists y)[(Ax \ \& \ Ay) \ \& \ (\exists z)[Exy \ \& \ (Gz \ \& \ Eyz)]]$$

This is a slightly whimsical symbolization of the following:

> Wolves, foxes, birds, caterpillars, and snails are animals, and there are some of each of them. Also, there are some grains, and grains are plants. Every animal either likes to eat all plants or all animals much smaller than itself that like to eat some plants. Caterpillars and snails are much smaller than birds, which are much smaller than foxes, which in turn are much smaller than wolves. Wolves do not like to eat foxes or grains, while birds like to eat caterpillars but not snails. Caterpillars and snails like to eat some plants. Therefore, there is an animal that likes to eat a grain-eating animal. [Pelletier 1986, 203]

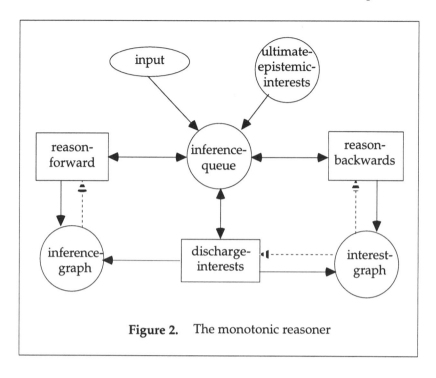

Figure 2. The monotonic reasoner

This problem has been attempted by a wide variety of theorem provers, and the fastest time reported is 6 seconds. That time is reported by Stickel [1985], running a connection-graph resolution theorem proving program on a Symbolics 3600 and applying it to the result of already transforming the problem into clausal form. In comparison, OSCAR did this problem in 13 seconds on a Symbolics 3600. It is also of interest to compare OSCAR with respected resolution theorem provers that are considered fast but do not do the Schubert steamroller problem as fast as Stickel's current system. An earlier theorem prover of Stickel was reported to do the problem in 2 hours 53 minutes, and the well-known ITP theorem prover was at one time reported to do it in 11 minutes [Cohn 1985].

Most theorem provers are designed to be used somewhat interactively, allowing the human operator to choose different proof strategies for different problems. That is desirable if they are to be used as tools, but it detracts from the theoretical significance of speed results. After all, given any valid formula P, we could introduce a rule saying "Infer P". Of course, no one would actually incorporate a rule like this into a theorem prover, but this just represents the extreme end of a continuum.

Fast times using strategies chosen especially for a particular problem may show little unless some theoretical rationale can be provided for the choice of strategy and the rationale built into the theorem prover itself so that it can choose its own strategies. In this connection it should be noted that OSCAR is a purely automatic theorem prover, using the same strategies on all problems. In contrast, Stickel's fast times are extremely impressive, but as he himself observes, they are very sensitive to how the set of support is chosen in his theorem prover. He first tried putting only the goal clause in the set of support, but that resulted in his theorem prover's taking 5,694 seconds. The 6 seconds time was achieved by eliminating the set of support restriction.

Even more interesting than the speed of the reasoner is its efficiency. Even on Stickel's fastest time, his theorem prover performed 479 inferences, and when his theorem prover was used non-interactively, it performed 245,820 inferences. Stickel also provides data on some other theorem provers doing the Schubert steamroller problem, according to which they performed between 1,106 and 26,190 inference steps. This means that between 91% and 99.98% of the inferences performed by these theorem provers were unnecessary. By contrast, OSCAR constructed a proof that was 42 lines long, and performed only 11 unnecessary steps. Of those 11 steps, 6 of them were among the given premises and were unnecessary for doing the problem. Omitting those, OSCAR performed only 5 unnecessary inferences, for a measure of 11%.

To take another example, a problem of moderate difficulty that has been run on a number of theorem provers is that of showing that a group is commutative if the square of every element is the identity element. This problem is from Chang and Lee [1973]. Letting $\ulcorner Pxyz \urcorner$ symbolize $\ulcorner x \cdot y = z \urcorner$, this problem can be formulated as follows:

$(\forall x)Pxex$
$(\forall x)Pexx$
$(\forall x)(\forall y)(\forall z)(\forall u)(\forall v)(\forall w)[(Pxyu \ \& \ (Pyzv \ \& \ Puzw)) \supset Pxvw]$
$(\forall x)(\forall y)(\forall z)(\forall u)(\forall v)(\forall w)[(Pxyu \ \& \ (Pyzv \ \& \ Pxvw)) \supset Puzw]$
$(\forall x)Pxxe$
$Pabc$

$Pbac$

OSCAR performed 19 inferences, 15 of which were used in the final proof. Thus 21% of OSCAR's inferences were unnecessary. By contrast,

Wilson and Minker [1976] give performance data for this problem on four theorem provers (this is the problem they call "Group2"). Where 21% of OSCAR's inferences were unnecessary, those theorem provers performed 79%, 87%, 96%, and 96% unnecessary inferences. Furthermore, these were presumably the results after tailoring the theorem provers to the problem to get the best performance. Stickel's PTTP (Prolog technology theorem prover) solves this problem in a startling .284 seconds (OSCAR required 8 seconds), but performs 1,136 inferences in the process. In terms of sheer speed, nothing can hold a candle to Stickel's PTTP on this problem, and I do not mean for these remarks to detract from its significance, but the percentage of unnecessary inferences is perhaps indicative of what can be expected from a resolution theorem prover that does not use strategies carefully tailored to the individual problem.

These redundancy figures hold up across a wide variety of problems. OSCAR was tested on Pelletier's problems for first-order logic [1986]. In solving Pelletier's propositional calculus problems (numbers 1-17), OSCAR's average percentage of unnecessary inferences was only 8%, and on the pure predicate calculus problems (numbers 18–47), the redundancy figure only went up to 26%. It appears that OSCAR's interest constraints are extremely effective in eliminating unnecessary inferences.

5. An Interest-Driven Defeasible Reasoner

A flag-based defeasible reasoner is built on top of a monotonic reasoner. If we start with an interest-driven monotonic reasoner, we can use that to generate an interest-driven defeasible reasoner. The desideratum for an interest-driven defeasible reasoner should no longer be d.e.-adequacy, because we only want to require the reasoner to discover the ideally warranted propositions we assign as interests. The obvious proposal is to relativize d.e.-adequacy to interests:

A reasoner is *i.d.e.-adequate relative to $\mathcal{A}$* iff, for any *input* and any proposition P in which the reasoner is interested: (1) if P is ideally warranted to degree α relative to $\mathcal{A}$, then there is some number n and node η of strength at least α that supports P and after n cycles of reasoning, η is undefeated and that defeat-status never subsequently changes; and (2) if P is not ideally warranted to degree α relative to $\mathcal{A}$, then there is some number n such that after n cycles of reasoning, every node of strength at least α that supports P is defeated (either provisionally or outright) and that defeat-status never subsequently changes.

An interest-driven defeasible reasoner makes no attempt to build the entire inference graph. It begins with the list of *ultimate-epistemic-interests*, supplied by practical cognition, and then it attempts to perform just those inferences that are relevant to those interests and build just that part of the inference graph that records the relationships between those inferences. The relevant inferences are those involved in constructing arguments supporting the propositions in *ultimate-epistemic-interests*, and all those arguments supporting defeaters for steps of those arguments, and defeaters for steps of the defeating arguments, and so on. This will automatically be achieved if (1) the monotonic reasoner is guaranteed to find all relevant arguments for anything in which it is interested, and (2) the reasoner automatically adopts interest in defeaters for each defeasible inference it performs. By virtue of these two conditions, if there is an argument supporting a desired conclusion, the reasoner will find it. If there is a directly defeating argument it will find that. Then it follows recursively that if there is a reinstating argument, the reasoner will find that, and so on.

However, condition (1) is not quite the condition that should be imposed on the monotonic reasoner. The difficulty is that every argument has infinitely many variants that result from adding redundant steps or from varying the way in which deductive inferences are made. It is not necessary for the monotonic reasoner to produce more than one of these variants. It will suffice to produce just one that "subsumes" all the others, where we define:

> An argument β *subsumes* an argument α iff (1) any defeasible inference occurring in β also occurs in α and does so relative to the same or a more inclusive supposition and (2) the strength of β is greater than or equal to the strength of α.

This has the result that β is "at least as resistant to defeat" as α, in the sense that any argument defeating β will also defeat α. Let us also define:

> A monotonic reasoner is *argument-complete relative to* $\mathcal{A}$ iff, for any *input* and any P and any argument α in $\mathcal{A}$ inferring P from *input* relative to a supposition X, if the reasoner is given *input* as

premises and adopts interest in P relative to X, then the reasoner will construct an argument β that subsumes α and infers P from *input* relative to X.

Then we have the following theorem, which is the justifying theorem for defeasible reasoning:

<u>Fundamental Theorem for Defeasible Reasoning</u>
  If $\mathcal{G}$ is the inference-graph generated by the set of arguments $\mathcal{A}$, and
(1) $\mathcal{G}$ contains no noncircular infinite defeat-branches, and
(2)   for every proposition P and finite set X of propositions, there is a finite (possibly empty) set *nodes* of nodes in $\mathcal{G}$ supporting P relative to X such that any other node in $\mathcal{G}$ that supports P relative to X is subsumed by some member of *nodes*,
  and a flag-based defeasible reasoner
(3)   is based upon an interest-driven monotonic reasoner that is argument-complete relative to $\mathcal{A}$,
(4)   adopts interest in defeaters for every defeasible inference it performs, and
(5)   computes defeat-status as in chapter 3,
  then it is i.d.e.-adequate relative to $\mathcal{A}$.

It was observed above that flagging beliefs as defeated and then continuing to reason with them seems unreasonably expensive. However, there is a way of alleviating this cost. The monotonic reasoner uses a scheme for prioritizing potential inferences and stores them on the *inference-queue*. Whatever prioritizing scheme is used, if it is modified in such a way that once beliefs are defeated, inferences involving them are given low priority, then the reasoner will pursue the consequences of defeated reasoning "only when it has time". This looks much like what human beings do. As long as the prioritizing is done in such a way that even low-priority inferences are eventually performed, the reasoner will remain i.d.e.-adequate.

The general structure of the flag-based defeasible reasoner involves only a slight modification to the monotonic reasoner. Specifically, a module for computing defeat statuses must be added, and a new database consisting of beliefs (justified conclusions) is constructed. This is diagrammed in figure 3.

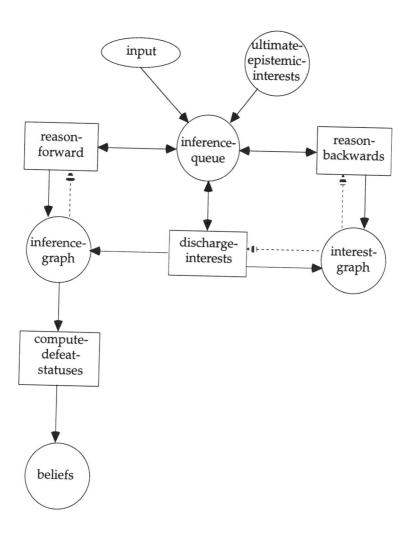

Figure 3. The defeasible reasoner

An interest-driven defeasible reasoner of the sort just described has been implemented. It is considered the latest version of OSCAR and is intended to provide the inference-engine for the OSCAR artilect.[8] It is described in more detail in chapter 9.

6. An Architecture for Epistemic Cognition

The defeasible reasoner just described represents the bulk of epistemic cognition, but not the whole of it. To obtain a general architecture for epistemic cognition, we must add two things: Q&I modules and an interface with practical cognition. Schematically, this is easy to do, and is diagramed in figure 4. Q&I modules represent an additional inference mechanism. We can regard them as driven by changes of belief (while drawing upon the set of beliefs), and like the other inference-mechanisms, their output goes into both the *inference-queue* and the *inference-graph*. It must be possible for explicit reasoning to override the conclusions drawn by Q&I modules. This can be done in two ways. First, conclusions drawn by Q&I modules can be assigned strengths (degrees of justification) when they are inserted into the *inference-graph*, and then if explicit reasoning provides a stronger reason for the negation of the conclusion, it will be rejected by rebutting defeat. It must also be possible to overturn a conclusion drawn by a Q&I module on the grounds that the module is unreliable under the present circumstances. Formally, this is analogous to having a reliability defeater for a prima facie reason.[9] This indicates that from a formal point of view, Q&I modules can be accommodated by treating them just like prima facie reasons for which the only undercutting defeaters are reliability defeaters.

Interfacing epistemic cognition with practical cognition involves four kinds of connections. First, practical cognition supplies the contents of *ultimate-epistemic-interests* by posing questions that arise in the course of practical reasoning. When practical cognition queries epistemic cognition by inserting an interest (encoded as a formula) into *ultimate-epistemic-interests*, the formula must be assigned a degree of interest,

---

[8] The first version of OSCAR was described in Pollock [1987]. That was followed by the interest-driven deductive reasoner described in Pollock [1990a], and then the interest-driven flag-based defeasible reasoner of Pollock [1992a].

[9] Reliability defeaters were discussed in section 2 of chapter 2.

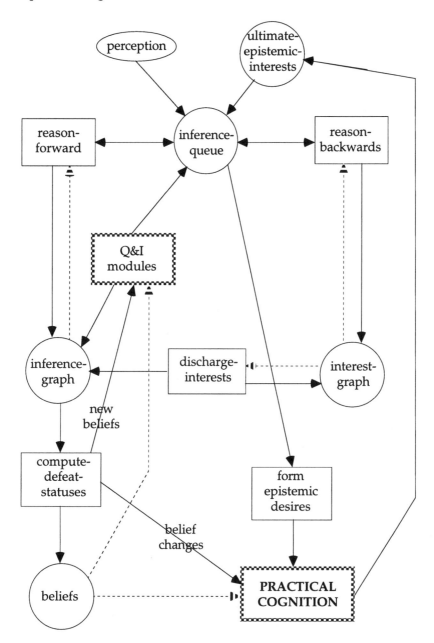

Figure 4. Epistemic cognition

and there must be some instruction for what to do with an answer once one is found. The latter will typically involve passing information back to practical cognition. (This will be illustrated in more detail in chapters 7 and 8.) These instructions constitute the second connection between epistemic cognition and practical cognition. Third, although most of the goals that drive practical cognition are produced by optative dispositions, we saw in chapter one that in a completely rational agent, beliefs about the expected likabilities of situation types must also have the power to produce goals. Fourth, as was observed in chapter 1, many questions posed for epistemic cognition cannot be answered purely by reasoning. Instead, they will require empirical investigation. Empirical investigation involves action, and that is driven by practical cognition. The mechanism for this is the formation of epistemic desires, which are desires to know the answers to questions that arise in the course of epistemic cognition. These epistemic desires are passed to practical cognition, which can then seek courses of action aimed at answering these questions.

The formation of epistemic desires is straightforward except for one problem that must be addressed. When are epistemic desires formed? Are they formed whenever interest is adopted in a new question, or is there some more restrictive mechanism that results in their being formed only with regard to selected interests? Introspection suggests that, at least in human beings, epistemic desires are formed in connection with every interest. After all, for any question at all, one way of answering it empirically may be to ask someone else, or to look it up in a book, or to consult your notes. This seems to create a problem, however. Each new desire leads, by way of practical cognition, to new ultimate-epistemic-interests. If these lead immediately to new epistemic desires, we have a loop, and it seems that epistemic cognition will be caught in an infinite regress. It appears to me that there is just one way to solve this problem, and that involves adjusting the degrees of interest. If the strength of an epistemic desire is always less than the strength of the interest from which it is obtained, then the reasoner will give priority to answering the question by reasoning rather than by empirical investigation. This will be an automatic consequence of using degrees of interest to prioritize reasoning, because the new epistemic interests that arise from practical cognition aimed at answering the question empirically will be placed later on the *inference-queue* than the interests derived from backwards reasoning. Consequently, the empirically driven interests will be retrieved from the *inference-queue* only after some attempt has been made to solve the problem by reasoning.

It should be observed that this general architecture accommodates reflexive cognition. Introspection is part of perception, and the judgments the reflexive cognizer makes about cognition are the product of either introspection itself or reasoning about information provided by introspection. The latter reasoning can proceed within the framework of reasoning described by this architecture. The reflexive cognizer can then alter the course of cognition by giving practical cognition the power to alter the contents of various data structures in various ways. For example, deciding to try one strategy for solving a problem before trying another amounts to reordering the *inference-queue*. Similarly, refraining from accepting a conclusion even when one has an apparently good reason for it amounts to deleting that conclusion from the *inference-queue*. The details of reflexive cognition may turn out to be very complicated, but however they go, it should be possible to fit them into the present architecture.

Several further observations about this architecture are in order. Etherington [1987] observed that for most nonmonotonic logics, little attention has been paid to the problem of updating beliefs (or extensions) in response to adding new premises (as opposed to simply starting over in the construction of the belief-set or the computation of the extension). If a defeasible reasoner is to be used as the inference engine in a rational agent, this is a serious problem. Such an agent is embedded in an environment that is continually feeding it more information, and it must repeatedly update its beliefs in response to such inputs. It is totally impractical to require such an agent to restart its reasoning from scratch every time it is given a new premise.

In OSCAR, there is no updating problem. If OSCAR is supplied a new premise after reasoning has already begun, OSCAR will quickly reach a point in its reasoning where its beliefs and arguments are the same as if that premise had been supplied at the beginning. This means that OSCAR can provide the inference engine for an interrupt-driven reasoner. Such a reasoner will receive additional premises from time to time after it has already begun reasoning. This will cause the reasoning to be interrupted at the end of a cycle, the new premises inserted into *input*, and then reasoning resumed.

There is another way in which an interrupt-driven reasoner is important. Most problems with which a reasoner is actually presented will be simple, and the reasoner will be able to perform all relevant reasoning and stop. It has been observed, however, that on problems of sufficient complexity, reasoning may never terminate. Note that this is equally true for human reasoners. Nevertheless, such a reasoner may have to take action at specific times, even though reasoning has not terminated. This is just the point made in section 1 that the reasoning must be interruptible. When the time comes to act, the reasoning will be interrupted and action taken based upon whatever the current set of beliefs is. It is always possible that if the reasoner had more time to reason, its beliefs would change in some crucial way, but the presumption behind defeasible reasoning is that at any stage of reasoning, if action must be taken, then it is reasonable to act on the basis of the current set of beliefs.

The upshot is that a real-time defeasible reasoner must be interrupt-driven in two respects: it must be continually receptive to new inputs, and it must be prepared to interrupt its reasoning and act on its current set of beliefs whenever action is required. The intention is that OSCAR will supply the inference engine for such a real-time reasoner.

7. Conclusions

The preliminary proposal made at the beginning of this chapter was that the appropriate criterion to apply in evaluating defeasible reasoners is that of d.e.-adequacy. This makes it possible for reasoners to be adequate despite the fact that the set of ideally warranted conclusions is not r.e. The chapter then investigated how to construct a d.e.-adequate reasoner. It was argued that such a reasoner cannot stop reasoning from a conclusion just because the arguments supporting it are defeated. Instead, it must flag conclusions as defeated but continue to reason from them. This suggests building the defeasible reasoner out of two largely autonomous modules: a monotonic reasoner that systematically produces arguments without worrying about their defeat status, and a module that computes defeat status relative to the arguments that have been produced at any given stage of reasoning. The main result of the chapter is that the sequence consisting of the sets of undefeated conclusions produced at each stage of operation of the monotonic reasoner constitutes a defeasible enumeration of ideal warrant provided the monotonic reasoner satisfies certain plausible constraints. This is not yet sufficient to produce a truly practical defeasible reasoner, however. The d.e.-adequacy of the reasoner constructed in this way requires the totally impractical assumption that the monotonic reasoner will systematically produce all possible arguments (the British Museum algorithm). This assumption can be replaced by the more reasonable assumption that the monotonic reasoner is interest-driven. This requires a change to the adequacy condition, replacing d.e.-adequacy by its interest-relative analogue, i.d.e.-adequacy. It was then shown that, subject to reasonable assumptions about the interest-driven monotonic reasoner, it can be used to generate an i.d.e.-adequate defeasible reasoner. This has been implemented in OSCAR.

There have been several earlier attempts to construct procedural theories of defeasible reasoning (misleadingly called "proof theories"), and there have been a few attempts to implement such theories in automated defeasible reasoners. The most noteworthy are those of Nute and Lewis [1986], Nute [1992], Levesque [1990], Ginsberg [1989], Baker and Ginsberg [1989], Geffner [1990], and Simari and Loui [1992]. There have also been some (generally unimplemented) special-purpose reasoners like that described by Horty, Thomason, and Touretzky [1990] and Horty and Thomason [1990] for reasoning within defeasible inheritance hierarchies. These reasoners are based upon a wide variety of approaches to defeasible reasoning. For example, the Ginsberg system is based upon circumscription, the Levesque theory on autoepistemic logic, and the Horty, Thomason, and Touretzky theory on defeasible inheritance. Despite their variety, it is very simple to compare all of these theories simultaneously to the present theory, because all of them attempt to build a reasoner that is analogous to a traditional theorem prover. Such reasoners produce r.e. sets of conclusions. Because that is possible only if the underlying logic is decidable, such defeasible reasoners have typically been restricted to the propositional calculus or some other very weak logic. By contrast, because OSCAR seeks to provide an i.d.e.-approximation to ideal warrant rather than a recursive enumeration of ideally warranted conclusions, it is applicable to the full predicate calculus, and indeed, OSCAR is deductively complete for the predicate calculus as well as being i.d.e.-adequate for defeasible reasoning.[10]

---

[10] OSCAR also stands in an interesting relationship to RMS's (reason maintenance systems). McDermott [1991] constructs a general framework for RMS's, and emphasizes the distinction between the application program and the RMS itself. That is parallel to the distinction in OSCAR between the monotonic reasoner and the module computing defeat status on the basis of the inference graph. The latter module by itself is quite similar to a "justification-based" RMS (of which the original example was Doyle's TMS [1979]). There are also some important differences, however. Standard justification-based RMS's have only one kind of link, corresponding to the inference links in the inference graph. They have no links corresponding to the defeat links, and correspondingly they are incapable of detecting undercutting defeat. They can only respond to inconsistencies, which is to say that they detect rebutting defeat. McDermott, however, constructs a more general kind of "nonmonotonic RMS" by adding dependencies between nodes that are formulated using a modal operator L, meaning "it is definitely true that". The idea comes from McDermott

In theory, OSCAR should provide a framework for the performance of all possible epistemic reasoning. In implementing any particular reasoning, three things must be done. First, we must specify a system of representation within which the inferences can be encoded. Second, we must supply a list of reasons, segregated into backwards and forwards reasons, and conclusive and defeasible reasons. This list of reasons will include the list of defeaters for the defeasible reasons. Third, we must specify the prioritizing scheme used in ordering potential inferences in the *inference-queue*. The last provides a fairly powerful tool for modifying the control structure of the reasoner. The theory is that any kind of epistemic reasoning can be implemented in OSCAR in this way. This may prove simplistic, but the only way to find out is to try to implement various important kinds of reasoning, and that will occur in the next stage of the OSCAR project.

The claim that all possible epistemic reasoning can be implemented in the framework provided by OSCAR may seem less pretentious if it is borne in mind that epistemic cognition consists of more than just reasoning. In any agent capable of quick responses to environmental inputs, reasoning must be augmented by a rich array of Q&I modules. Epistemic reasoning and epistemic Q&I modules jointly comprise epistemic cognition. Reasoning, by itself, is inherently slow. Human beings may well outperform OSCAR on many epistemic tasks, but

---

and Doyle [1980]. The result is not an RMS that computes defeat status in the same way OSCAR does, because McDermott explicitly opts for a credulous nonmonotonic logic. But it may be possible to use the same ideas to build a skeptical RMS that really does compute defeat statuses equivalently with OSCAR. In doing this, it should be noted that the literals upon which McDermott's RMS operates must be interpreted as expressing inferences (nodes of the inference graph) rather than propositions, but that seems to make no difference to the functionality. It can also be observed that the assumption-based aspect of McDermott's RMS is unnecessary for this application. In addition, the introduction of the modal operator L introduces more expressive power than is required for formulating prima facie reasons. All prima facie reasons can be expressed in a single form:

$$\neg P \ \lor \neg L \neg Q \ \lor \neg L(P \otimes Q) \lor Q \quad (P \text{ is a prima facie reason for } Q).$$

Accordingly, forms like $(LP \lor P)$ that give McDermott trouble ("odd loops") do not even arise in the formulation of prima facie reasons.

Although RMS's are quite close, at least in spirit, to OSCAR's defeat-status computation based on the inference graph, it is important to realize that the defeat-status computation is only part of OSCAR. RMS's are not themselves reasoners. The idea of building an i.d.e.-adequate reasoner by cycling between the monotonic reasoner and the defeat-status computation on the inference graph, and the proof that this will work, takes us far beyond an RMS.

that does not show that OSCAR is an inadequate epistemic reasoner. It may only reflect the fact that humans employ some powerful Q&I modules not available to OSCAR.

The framework provided by OSCAR does not commit us to much regarding the content of reasoning. In particular, we could augment OSCAR with a list of reasons that faithfully mimic the structure of human reasoning, but we could also supply lists of reasons that are quite foreign to human reasoning but are nevertheless sound schemas for reasoning. For instance, there is considerable psychological evidence to the effect that *modus tollens* is not a primitive inference rule in human beings,[11] but that does not make it unreasonable to incorporate *modus tollens* into an artilect. Similarly, most systems of automated deduction employ some form of unification, but it seems clear that this is not a primitive operation in human reasoning. In implementing special kinds of reasoning in OSCAR, we have a choice whether to attempt to mimic human reasoning or to try out ways of accomplishing the same ends more efficiently.

---

[11] See Smith, Langston, and Nisbett [1992] for a survey of some of the relevant literature.

Chapter 5
Plan-Based Practical Reasoning

1. Practical Cognition

A general account of the structure of rational cognition was proposed in chapter 1. According to that account, practical cognition is initiated by the formation of primitive desires, which are themselves either the product of optative dispositions or the result of epistemic cognition producing beliefs about the relative expected situation-likings of the desired states of affairs. Desires, in turn, encode goals, and the function of practical cognition is to design and execute courses of action aimed at the achievement of these goals. Epistemic cognition plays an essentially subservient role in this process. The function of epistemic cognition is to answer factual questions posed in the course of practical cognition. Chapters 2 through 4 investigated the structure of epistemic cognition, and paved the way for an investigation of practical cognition.

Practical cognition tries to find courses of action that will achieve goals. This kind of cognition has been a topic of interest in both philosophy and artificial intelligence. However, these two disciplines have tended to approach the topic in terms of very different models of practical cognition. The purpose of this chapter is to examine each model in light of the other and produce a unified model superior to both. Subsequent chapters will be devoted to working out the details of the model produced in this chapter.

The Philosophical Model
The philosophical model might equally be called the "economics model" or the "cognitive psychology model", because it is shared by all three fields. It is more commonly called simply the "decision-theoretic model".[1] On this model, a decision problem arises when we have a finite set $\mathcal{A}$ of alternative acts between which we must decide, a finite set $\mathcal{O}$ of exhaustive and exclusive possible outcomes, a function u assigning numerical utilities to the possible outcomes, and reasonable beliefs about (or assignments of) the values of the probabilities

---

[1] For examples of this literature, see DiFinetti [1975], Jeffrey [1983], Savage [1972], and Skyrms [1980].

prob(O/A) of each possible outcome on each act.[2] The *expected utility* of an act is defined:

$$EU(A) = \sum_{O \in \mathcal{O}} u(O) \cdot prob(O/A)$$

On the decision-theoretic model, rationality dictates choosing the act with the highest expected utility, if there is one. If there is a tie, then any of the acts of maximal utility is *rationally permissible*. An act is *rationally prescribed* iff it is rationally permissible and no alternative act is rationally permissible.

One of the main virtues of the decision-theoretic model is that it explicitly accommodates the possibility that the connection between acts and outcomes is only probabilistic. At the same time, it includes the deterministic case as the special case in which the connections are deterministic and hence the probabilities prob(O/A) are all 1 or 0. In this case, there will be a unique outcome resulting from each act, and comparing acts in terms of their expected utilities is equivalent to comparing them more simply in terms of the utilities of their outcomes.

Acts typically have *performance costs*, reflecting the amount of disutility incurred in their performance. The decision-theoretic model can, in principle, accommodate this by building performance costs into outcomes, but it can do that only by building into the outcomes a specification of the act performed. This has the effect of multiplying the number of possible outcomes. For some purposes, it is better to handle performance costs explicitly, subtracting them from the expected utility gains, thus redefining the expected utility of an act as follows:

$$EU(A) = \sum_{O \in \mathcal{O}} u(O) \cdot prob(O/A) - \text{expected-performance-cost}(A)$$

We subtract the *expected* performance cost rather than an *actual* performance cost because, at the time of decision, we may not know exactly what the performance cost will be.

It is typically assumed that we can infallibly perform the acts in the set $\mathcal{A}$, that is, the probability of our performing them if we try is 1.

---

[2] The decision-theoretic model is generally formulated using subjective probabilities, but that is an inessential feature of it. One could incorporate any kind of probability into this account. Because I have objections to subjective probability [Pollock 1986], I prefer to use some kind of partly objective probability. See Pollock [1990] for my preferred account of objective probability.

If that were not the case, then in deciding what act to try to perform, we would have to take account of the probability of being able to perform the act successfully. If an act had a high expected utility but it was unlikely we would be able to perform it, that would make it a correspondingly less desirable choice. An obvious ploy for avoiding this difficulty is to replace a fallibly performable act A by the (presumably) infallibly performable act *trying-to-A*. Then the probability of successfully performing A will automatically get factored into the probability of the various outcomes conditional on trying to A.

The AI Model

The standard model in AI is the *planning-theory model*.[3] On this model, the rational agent begins with certain goals it is trying to achieve, and then practical reasoning consists of designing a *plan* for achieving those goals. In the interest of making the problem more tractable it is generally pretended that the relationship between acts and outcomes is deterministic (although it is recognized that this is unrealistic).[4] In the simplest case, a plan for achieving a certain goal is just a sequence of acts that, when performed in that order, will result in that goal's being achieved. More generally, plans can involve conditional forks ("If the traffic is not too heavy, take Speedway; otherwise take Broadway."), loops ("Ring the bell repeatedly until someone answers the door."), and all of the other constructs of computer programs. A plan is much like a program that aims at achieving one or more goals. (The logical structure of plans will be discussed at length in chapter 6.) The current state of the art in AI focuses on finding even a single plan for achieving a goal. That turns out to be such a difficult computational problem that little attention has yet been paid to finding *optimal* plans, although it is generally recognized that must be the ultimate objective of a planning-theory.[5]

Plans have not gone totally unnoticed in philosophy. Bratman [1987] emphasizes the importance of plans in practical reasoning, and Harman [1986] makes some related observations. Bratman, Israel, and

---

[3] See Georgeff [1987] for a good summary of the current state of AI planning theory.

[4] One exception is Dean, Firby, and Miller [1988].

[5] Some work has been addressed at special cases of this problem. See particularly the work on NONLIN+ [Daniel 1983], Tate and Whiter [1984], and ISIS-II [Fox, Allen, and Strohm 1981].

Pollack [1991] attempt to build some bridges between philosophy and AI. But these are relatively rare exceptions. In philosophy, the decision-theoretic model has carried the day.

The Relationship between the Models

The function of practical cognition is to design and execute courses of action aimed at achieving the goals that are encoded in an agent's desires. The decision-theoretic model and the planning-theory model differ most significantly in their interpretation of "course of action". On the planning-theory model, a course of action is a plan of arbitrary complexity. On the decision-theoretic model, practical reasoning selects acts one at a time, and insofar as more complex courses of action result, this has to be the effect of selecting their component acts one at a time rather than selecting an entire sequence of acts as a single decision.

There are other less important differences between the two models. To many philosophers, the planning-theory model is likely to seem naive, particularly in its typical supposition that the act/outcome relation is deterministic (an assumption that will not be made in this book), and in its giving no explicit attention to the rational requirement that plans be, if not optimal, at least minimally good. But these shortcomings reflect the state of the art in planning theory more than the content of the theory. Furthermore, the planning-theory model seems to be talking about something important that the decision-theoretic model ignores: planning. It is undeniably true that a great deal of the practical reasoning in which human beings engage is concerned with the construction of plans. This plays no role at all in the decision-theoretic model. This suggests that the decision-theoretic model is overlooking some important aspects of practical reasoning and is accordingly incomplete, just as the planning-theory model is incomplete by (typically) ignoring probabilistic connections and comparisons of competing plans. What is puzzling is that, on the one hand, the decision-theoretic model is likely to seem intuitively right, but on the other hand it seems to leave no room for planning (or anything else) as a fundamental constituent of practical reasoning. On the decision-theoretic model, once we have talked about the expected utilities of acts, we have discussed everything of relevance to practical reasoning.

I will urge below that, contrary to initial appearances, the decision-theoretic model is inadequate. It gains its appearance of obvious correctness by focusing on what is actually just a special case of practical reasoning, and when put in a general context, the decision-theoretic

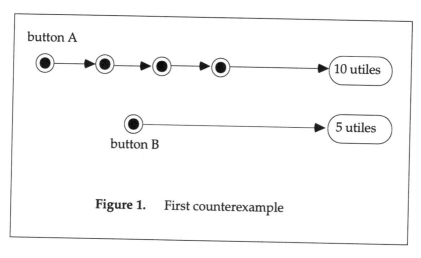

Figure 1.   First counterexample

model can produce intuitively incorrect prescriptions for action. This is a result of its ignoring the role of plans in practical reasoning. With its focus on plans, the planning-theory model is onto something important. It is, however, incomplete because it does not address the question of how plans are to be compared for purposes of choosing among them. What is needed is a theory of practical reasoning that takes plans seriously and generalizes the concepts of the decision-theoretic model to apply them to plans rather than acts.

2. The Inadequacy of the Decision-Theoretic Model

My claim is that in complex decision problems of the sort that require planning, the decision-theoretic model often prescribes what is intuitively the wrong action. This is most easily seen in an idealized problem of the sort addressed by standard planning-theory in which the act/outcome relation is deterministic. Take the simple case diagrammed in figure 1, in which I am presented with a panel on which there is a row of four buttons and below that a single button. Pushing the top four buttons in order from left to right will produce 10 utiles of utility, while pushing the bottom button (button B) will produce only 5 utiles. Obviously one ought to push the top four buttons. What does the decision-theoretic model tell us to do in this case? The decision-theoretic model applies to acts rather than plans, so in order to prescribe executing the *plan* of pushing button *A* and then each button following it in that row, the model would have to begin by prescribing pushing button *A*, then once that button has been pushed it would have to prescribe pushing the next button in the row, and so on. Does it do this? No. In evaluating *pushing button A*, we must compare the expected utility of that act with the expected utility of *pushing button B*. Because this is a deterministic case, the expected utility of *pushing button B* is simply 5 utiles. But the expected utility of *pushing button A* is not so easily calculated. *Pushing button A* does not by itself get us 10 utiles. It does that only when combined with the rest of the acts comprising the plan of *pushing all the buttons in the top row in order*. In computing the expected utility of the act of *pushing button A*, we must consider the probability that we will actually push the rest of the buttons in that row. Suppose the probability of pushing the remaining buttons given that we push button *A* is *r*. Then the expected utility of *pushing button A* is 10·*r*. The expected utility is 10 utiles only if *r* = 1. It might be urged that we are considering the actions of a rational agent, and a rational agent *will* push the remaining buttons, and hence *r* = 1. But this begs the question. The object of the exercise is to determine what a rational agent should do, so we are surely not entitled to assume an answer to this question in the course of computing the expected utilities that we will use in answering the question. However, without this assumption, we are not justified in supposing the probability is high that the rest of the buttons in the row will be pushed if button *A* is pushed. In fact, without begging the question and assuming the answer to the decision problem, it is hard to see how we could have any basis for supposing that the probability is higher than chance, and the probability of the buttons being pushed by chance is going to be *very low*—almost negligibly low. Accordingly, the decision-theoretic model prescribes pushing button *B* rather than button *A*, because that has a higher expected utility.[6]

In evaluating this counterexample, it is important to emphasize that the values of the probabilities employed in a decision problem must be the rational agent's *best estimates* of the probabilities, not the possibly unknown true values of the probabilities.[7] Because the correct

---

[6] This is a refinement of an argument given in Pollock [1983].

[7] This assumes that objective probabilities are being employed. If the decisions are being made in terms of subjective probabilities, it makes no apparent sense to talk about the "true values" of the probabilities, and hence this kind of problem cannot arise. I assume that even in the case of subjective probability, the values used must be in some sense "reasonable". Personalists sometimes talk as if the probabilities can just be pulled out of the air, and hence could be taken to be 1 in this

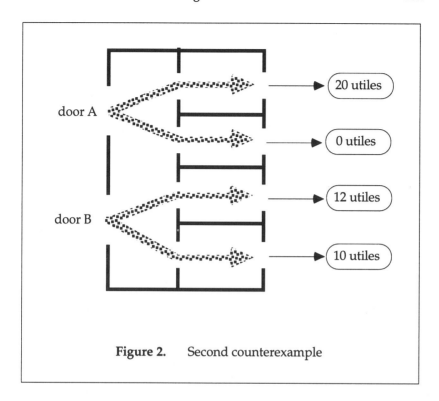

door A

door B

20 utiles

0 utiles

12 utiles

10 utiles

Figure 2.   Second counterexample

solution to the decision problem is to push the buttons in the top row in order, it may well be that the true value of the probability of the rest of the buttons in the row being pushed if button *A* is pushed is close to 1. But that is not something that the rational agent can use in solving the decision problem. He can only appeal to information available to him prior to solving the problem. And as we have seen, that yields an incorrect solution to the problem.

The temptation to suppose that the expected utility of pushing button *A* is 10 utiles derives from the fact that, in this example, it is obvious from the start what plan should be adopted, and it is the only plan whose first step consists of pushing button *A*. Consider a more complicated decision problem, diagrammed in figure 2, in which there is more than one candidate plan whose first step consists of performing the act being evaluated. Suppose we are faced with a simple maze.

---

case. But as a theory of practical *rationality*, I take that to be absurd. Rationality requires that the probabilities be assigned in some reasonable and non-arbitrary way.

There are two doors into the maze, and four paths through the maze. The top two paths begin at door A and lead to payoffs of 20 utiles and 0 utiles, respectively. The bottom two paths begin at door B, and lead to payoffs of 12 utiles and 10 utiles, respectively. Which door should we enter? Clearly, we should enter door A and traverse the upper path. Now let us apply the decision-theoretic model. We must compare the expected utility of entering door A with the expected utility of entering door B. But what are these expected utilities? The payoff resulting from entering door A depends upon which plan we adopt for traversing the maze after entering door A. If we take the upper path we will receive 20 utiles, and if we take the second path we will receive 0 utiles. So our choice of a plan determines the payoff. In computing the expected utility of entering door A, we can either assume that we will take the upper path or assume ignorance of which path we will take. If we assume ignorance, then it seems we should assign a probability of .5 to taking either path, and hence the expected utility of entering door A is 10 utiles and the expected utility of entering door B is 11 utiles. On this calculation, the decision-theoretic model prescribes entering door B, *but that is the wrong answer*! If we instead assume that if we enter door A we will take the upper path, and similarly if we enter door B, then we can compute the expected utilities to be 20 utiles and 12 utiles, respectively, and we get the correct prescription that we should enter door A. However, this assumes that we have some way of knowing that we will choose the upper path if we enter door A. This is typically something we do know about ourselves, but we are not entitled to use it here in computing the expected utility of entering door A because that would be circular. We believe that we will traverse the upper path only because we believe that is the rational thing to do. If we did not believe the latter then we would not normally believe that we will traverse the upper path. But the object of the exercise is to determine the rational thing to do, so we cannot just assume the solution to the decision problem in the course of computing the probabilities and utilities used in solving the problem.

The upshot of this is that the decision-theoretic calculation yields the right answer only if we have some way of choosing among different plans for traversing the maze prior to computing the expected utilities. If we have a way of choosing among different maze-traversal plans, then we can simply choose the best plan overall (not just the best plan that has us entering door A and the best plan that has us entering door B) and enter the door that plan prescribes. That is the solution to the decision problem. So to recapitulate, if we compute the expected utilities of entering the doors without first choosing which maze-traversal plan to adopt if we enter a given door, then the decision-theoretic model gives the wrong answer. But if we have a way of choosing among maze-traversal plans then there is no need to compute the expected utilities, because we should simply choose the best plan and execute it, and that will determine which door we enter.

The general difficulty is the following. On the decision-theoretic model, we choose among acts by computing their expected utilities. For acts that lead to a payoff only by being part of a multi-step plan, the decision-theoretic model would have to prescribe performing each step of the plan in sequence. However, if an act is the first step of more than one alternative plan (and in the real world, that will always be the case), there is no way to compute a meaningful expected utility for the act until we have decided which of the plans prescribing it we are going to execute if we perform the act. This requires us to have a way of choosing the best of several plans. But if we have a way of choosing the best plan from a set of alternative plans, then we should apply that to the set of *all* the alternative plans, choosing the best plan overall, and do what that plan prescribes. Once we have chosen the best plan, we have solved the decision problem. What we should do is whatever the best plan prescribes. In the above example, we choose to enter door *A* not because that has a higher expected utility than entering door *B* but because that is prescribed by the plan of traversing the top path, and that is the best of the four plans available to us.

This objection to the decision-theoretic model amounts to saying that it is either incorrect or redundant. It leads to incorrect prescriptions if we try to choose plans by applying the decision-theoretic model, one act at a time, to the acts comprising them, without making any assumptions about what plans will be adopted. On the other hand, if we have some other way of choosing among plans, so that in evaluating the expected utilities of acts we can assume what plans will be adopted, then the decision-theoretic model is redundant. If we have a way of choosing among plans, that in itself solves the decision problem and there is no need to decide among acts independently of deciding among the plans prescribing them.

None of this should be taken as implying that appeal to utilities and expected values plays no role in practical reasoning. It seems clear that the basis on which we choose among plans has to do with expected values. But I will postpone addressing this question until the next section. It proves to be more complicated than might be initially suspected. My point is simply that insofar as expected values are employed in decision theory, it cannot be the expected values of individual acts that are at issue. It should be plans that are compared in terms of their expected values, and then acts should be chosen because they are prescribed by the plans we have adopted.

At this point, a common response is that I am not really disagreeing with the classical decision-theorist, because what he means by "acts" is what I am calling "plans". Accordingly, evaluating plans in terms of their expected values is just what classical decision theory tells us to do. I think it is a bit perverse to call complicated plans replete with conditional forks, loops, etc., "acts", but if that is the way the decision-theorist wants his theory understood, we should evaluate it accordingly. I am, in fact, sympathetic to this kind of theory, and it will be discussed at length in the next section. It will turn out that this attempt to salvage the decision-theoretic model does not quite work. Because plans, unlike acts, are logically complex and can embed other plans, a more complex theory is required, but applying standard decision-theory to plans is a good first attempt at taking plans seriously.

3. Integrating Plans into the Decision-Theoretic Model

The examples employed in the last section are contrived ones. Let us run the argument again using a realistic example. Suppose I want to be in Los Angeles on Friday. To do this I may plan to fly on Thursday evening; to do that I may plan to buy a ticket from my travel agent today; to do that I may have to drive to the travel agent's office immediately (before it closes); and to do that I may have to get into my car now. Suppose I construct this plan as a way of getting to LA, and now I want to decide whether to execute the plan. On the decision-theoretic model, I have to decide what to do one act at a time. The first step consists of getting into my car now, so I have to decide whether to do that. The decision-theoretic model would have me decide whether to get into my car by evaluating the expected utility of this act and comparing that with the expected utilities of other acts I might perform instead. Suppose the alternative is sitting in the sun on my patio and listening to Mozart. Computing the expected utility of the latter act is, at least in principle, unproblematic. But it is senseless to ask about the expected utility of getting into my car as a way of evaluating that act in the context of my potential plan to go to LA. That would have me determine the probability of my being in LA on Friday conditional on my getting into my car now. Presumably *there is* such a probability, but what is at issue in a decision problem is not its (possibly unknown) true value but rather our best estimate of its value. We have to be careful about the context in which we evaluate the probability. We can evaluate it either (1) on the assumption that I have adopted the plan to get to LA in this way, or (2) without that assumption. What is at issue is whether to adopt the plan. If I have already adopted the plan, there is no decision problem left and nothing for the decision-theoretic model to do. However, if it is not assumed that I have adopted the plan, then the decision-theoretic model gives the wrong answer. Without the assumption that I have adopted the plan, it seems that the probability of my being in LA on Friday conditional on my getting into my car now is quite low, and so very little expected utility attaches to the latter, and the decision-theoretic model dictates that I should instead sit in the sun and listen to Mozart. Decision theory favors the grasshopper rather than the ant.

The decision-theoretic model must be deemed wrong as a general theory of practical rationality. Still, it seems that it is making an initially credible attempt to capture an important insight regarding how probabilities and utilities interact in practical reasoning. Where the model fails is in overlooking the role of plans in practical reasoning. Let us see if we can salvage the insights of the decision-theoretic model without giving plans short shrift.

A Two-Tiered Approach
The simplest proposal for integrating plans into the decision-theoretic model is to apply the model directly to plans rather than acts. In other words, (1) compute the expected values of plans rather than acts, (2) choose among alternative plans in terms of their expected values, and (3) choose acts on the basis of their being prescribed by plans chosen in terms of their expected values. This amounts to a *two-tiered* theory of decision making. It is ultimately acts we want to choose. For example, in trying to get to LA, I want to decide whether to get into my car now. But according to this theory, we decide in favor of getting into the car because it is part of a plan we have adopted, not because of its own expected utility. Acts must be chosen indirectly by applying decision-theoretic calculations to plans.

The Expected Value of a Plan
I think that this two-tiered model is on the right track, although difficulties arise when we try to articulate it precisely. The first difficulty lies in extending the concept of expected utility to plans. The simple

definition of expected utility for acts is inadequate when applied to plans for a number of reasons, including the following:

- The definition given for acts is applicable only to acts that can be performed infallibly, that is, to acts for which we can reasonably take the probability to be 1 that if we try to perform the act then we will succeed. This is certainly not true of plans. My plan to get to LA can go awry in many ways. My car may fail to start after I get into it with the intent of driving to my travel agent's office, I may have an auto accident en route, the flight may be sold out, I may get to the airport ticket-in-hand only to be bumped from the flight, the flight might be cancelled because of bad weather, and so forth. Clearly, in computing the expected value of a plan in a way that enables us to use that in deciding whether to adopt the plan, we must take account of how likely it is that we will be able to execute the plan successfully if we try.

- The simplest plans are sequences of acts arranged in temporal order, but plans can have very complicated logical structures. For example, plans can involve *conditional forks*. In making a plan, we may not know exactly what situation we will be in when it comes time to execute later stages of the plan, and so we may plan to do one thing if it is true that P and something else otherwise. For example, in planning how to get to my travel agent's office, I may plan to drive down Speedway if the traffic is not too heavy and otherwise to drive down Broadway. In evaluating the expected utility of a plan, we must take account of the probabilities of its being executed in different ways at conditional forks and the differing expected utilities of the different ways the plan may unfold. Plans can have logical structures that are complicated in other ways as well, so it is not just conditional forks that we must worry about. In general, plans can have all the logical structure exhibited by parallel computer programs (including iteration).[8]

---

[8] In AI planning theory, the use of conditionals in plans was first studied by Warren [1976] in WARPLAN-C. Iteration was investigated by Drummond [1985]. That the programs in question are parallel programs corresponds to the construction of non-linear plans, as in NOAH (Sacerdotti [1975, 1977]) and NONLIN [Tate 1977]. This will be discussed further in chapter 7.

- Just as the traditional model requires us to take account of the expected performance costs of an act, we must take account of the *expected execution cost* of a plan. This cost is not a fixed feature of the plan but may vary depending upon (1) the circumstances in which we are performing the acts prescribed by the plan and (2) exactly how we execute the plan (e.g., how it unfolds at conditional forks).

All of these difficulties can be finessed by following the suggestion of chapter 1 and defining the expected value EV(σ) of a plan σ to be the difference between the definite expected situation-liking of the situation type consisting of adopting σ and the definite expected situation-liking of the situation type consisting of not adopting σ, where *adopting* σ consists of forming the intention to execute σ.[9] The functional role of the mental state of adopting a plan will be discussed further in chapter 7. This definition of the expected value of a plan is, I believe, adequate for making sense of the notion, but it leaves unaddressed the quite difficult problem of computing or estimating such values. I will examine this problem more carefully in chapter 6.

Choosing Acts in Terms of Plans

It is ultimately *acts* that we must decide upon. Evaluating plans is of interest only as a way of choosing among the acts they prescribe. Choosing acts in terms of plans turns out to be a complicated matter. First, note that in decision problems we may have to compare individual acts with plans. For example, in deciding whether to sit in the sun or get into my car, I have to compare the act of sitting in the sun with the plan of which getting into my car is the first step. We can simplify the account by regarding individual acts as the limiting case of plans, so it

---

[9] Expected values are defined in terms of probabilities, but these probabilities could be either definite or indefinite. This gives rise to a distinction between definite and indefinite expected situation-likings. The indefinite probability of the agent's liking a situation given that it has certain features may be high, and yet because of the complexities of direct inference, the definite probability of the agent's liking the actual situation *if* it has those features could be low. This is because the actual situation will also have other features, and they can reverse the probabilities. Applying this distinction to the evaluation of plans, the expected value of a plan should be the difference between the definite expected situation-liking of the situation type consisting of adopting the plan and the definite expected situation-liking of the situation type consisting of not adopting the plan. In other words, in the language of chapter 1, the plan should be evaluated, not in the abstract, but in the present context.

is only plans that must be compared in decision problems. Traditional decision theory has focused exclusively on the degenerate case of one-step plans, and that is why it is inadequate.

An obvious difficulty for choosing among acts in terms of plans is that one and the same act may be prescribed by lots of different plans. Some of those plans may be good ones and others bad ones. In choosing an act, we have to worry about *all* the plans prescribing it. For instance, getting into my car may seem preferable to sitting in the sun if I just view the latter in terms of its pleasure value. But suppose it will also make me tan, and my boss likes tan employees and is likely to send me to LA on Friday if I get tan today and then go and show him my tan. Thus sitting in the sun is prescribed by an alternate plan for getting to LA on Friday. I will have to take this into account in deciding whether to sit in the sun or get into my car.

If an act is prescribed by two separate plans, it may contribute to achieving more than one goal and thereby become more valuable. Note, however, that in evaluating an act that is prescribed by two separate plans, we cannot just add the expected values of the two plans. We have to worry about how the two plans interact. There are different possibilities, among which are the following:

- The two plans may be independent of one another, in the sense that they share the same first step but then diverge in such a way that executing one does not interfere with executing the other, and they are plans for achieving unrelated goals so that successfully executing one does not affect the desirability of executing the other.
- The two plans may be independent in the sense that executing one does not interfere with executing the other, but they are plans for achieving the same goal, and hence if one plan is successful, the other loses its value.
- The plans may interfere with each other, in the sense that trying to execute one will make it more difficult to execute the other.

The only obvious way to evaluate an act that is prescribed by two or more plans is to combine them into a single plan and evaluate the composite plan in terms of the (yet to be determined) algorithm for computing the expected values of plans. We can then compare the individual plans with the composite plan and thereby decide either that we should adopt the composite plan or just one of the individual plans. This way of proceeding has the consequence that in evaluating an act, we can evaluate it in terms of *individual plans* prescribing it rather than in terms of collections of plans. This suggests that of the various plans prescribing an act, we consider the plan having the highest expected value and then evaluate the act in terms of that plan. That plan may or may not be a composite of several other simpler plans each prescribing the act.

Composites of plans will play an important role in the theory developed in this chapter, so it will be helpful to have a clear understanding of them. We can think of a plan as a set of plan-steps, where each plan-step encodes the operation to be performed, the conditions under which it is to be performed, and the dependency relations between this step and other steps (that is, which plan-steps are to be performed first). Plans must be "self-contained" in the sense that a necessary condition for a set σ of plan-steps to be a plan is that no plan-step in σ be explicitly dependent on any plan-steps not in σ. Accordingly, arbitrary subsets of plans will not usually be plans. We can turn them into plans, however, by removing the dependency relations to plan-steps not in the subset. Where η is a plan and σ^* is a subset of η, let us say that σ is the *purification* of σ^* iff σ results from deleting any dependency of plan-steps in σ^* on plan-steps not included in σ^*. Then we can define:

σ is a *subplan* of η, and η *contains* σ, iff η is a plan and σ is the purification of a subset of η.

$\sigma+\eta$ is a *composite* of σ and η iff $\sigma+\eta$ is a plan and there are sets σ^* and η^* such that $\sigma+\eta = \sigma^* \cup \eta^*$ and σ is the purification of σ^* and η is the purification of η^*.

In other words, a composite of two plans σ and η combines the plan-steps of both and orders them with respect to each other, thus producing σ^* and η^*, which differ from σ and η only in that they encode the additional ordering. Note that every plan is a subplan of itself. For technical reasons, it will be convenient to talk about the *null plan*, which is the empty set of plan-steps. The null plan is a subplan of every plan. A composite of a plan and the null plan is equal to the original plan.

In the interest of precision, let us define:

A plan *prescribes* an act α iff executing the plan under the present circumstances entails that α will be done.

Then the proposal under consideration is the following:

(1)   An act α is rationally permissible iff there is a rationally acceptable plan prescribing α.

There may be ties between plans so that more than one competing plan is rationally permissible. If all of the tied plans prescribe the same act, then it is rationally prescribed:

(2)   An act α is rationally prescribed iff there is a rationally acceptable plan σ prescribing α and every rationally acceptable plan competing with σ prescribes α as well.

This formulation takes account of the fact that there may be competing plans between which we cannot rationally choose and hence each of which is rationally acceptable. These are what Bratman [1987] calls *Buridan cases*. In Buridan cases we are free to adopt any of the rationally acceptable plans and hence it is rationally permissible to perform the acts prescribed by any of the rationally acceptable plans.

Choosing Plans
The two-tiered theory has us choose acts in terms of plans, in accordance with (1) and (2). In order to do this, we must know how to choose plans. Let us say that a plan σ is *superior* to a plan η iff $EV(\sigma) > EV(\eta)$. The simplest proposal for how to choose plans in terms of their expected values is the following, which is what we get by applying standard decision-theory to plans directly:

(3)   A plan σ is *rationally preferable* to a plan η iff σ and η are competitors and σ is superior to η.

(4)   A plan is *strongly acceptable* iff no other plan is rationally preferable.

(5)   A plan is *strongly prescribed* iff it is strongly acceptable and no competing plan is strongly acceptable.

It might then be proposed that it is rationally acceptable to adopt a plan (that is, the plan is rationally acceptable) iff it is strongly acceptable. Although strong acceptability would seem to be a sufficient condition for rational acceptability, it also seems plausible to propose that any subplan of a rationally acceptable plan is rationally acceptable. For example, because the plan of getting into my car now, driving to my travel agent's office, purchasing tickets to LA, and so forth, is rationally acceptable, so is the plan to get into my car now. This can be captured by the following analysis:

(6) A plan is rationally acceptable iff it is a subplan of a strongly acceptable plan.

Rational preferability is defined in terms of competition between plans. It is initially tempting to define:

Two plans *compete* iff the actual circumstances are such that it is impossible for both plans to be successfully executed.

However, this imposes too stringent a requirement for competition. For example, two plans σ and η could be so related that the probability of being able to execute either successfully is high, but if either is executed, then the probability of being able to execute the other successfully is low (but not zero). This is relevant to a decision regarding what plans to adopt. For instance, if the expected value of σ is significantly greater than that of η, it would be unreasonable to adopt η and then discover that you have thereby made it unlikely that you will be able to execute the more valuable plan σ successfully. This suggests that two plans should be regarded as competitors just in case it is less reasonable to adopt both than to adopt the better of the two by itself. It is reasonable (in the sense of rationally acceptable) to adopt *both* plans (individually) only if the two plans can be combined into a composite plan σ+η that has at least as high an expected value as either plan by itself. If this is not the case, then the plans should be regarded as in competition, and we should adopt only the superior one (the one having the higher expected value). Let us define:

Two plans σ and η *compete strictly* iff for every composite σ+η of σ and η, $EV(\sigma+\eta) < \max\{EV(\sigma), EV(\eta)\}$.[10]

For rather subtle reasons, this concept of competition is a bit too strict for any but one-step plans. If σ and η are multi-step plans, then there can be a plan ξ "in between" σ or η and σ+η, that is, either σ or η is a subplan of ξ and ξ is a subplan of σ+η. If such a plan were more valuable than any of σ, η, and σ+η, then it should be executed *in preference to* any of σ, η, or σ+η. This means that σ and η should not

---

[10] Where X is a finite set of real numbers, $\max(X)$ is the largest member of X.

both be executed, because that is the same thing as executing $\sigma+\eta$. Thus σ and η should be regarded as being in competition:

σ and η *compete* iff there is a composite $\sigma+\eta$ of σ and η and a subplan ξ of $\sigma+\eta$ such that (1) either σ or η is a subplan of ξ, (2) $EV(\xi) \geq \max\{EV(\sigma),EV(\eta)\}$, and (3) for every composite $(\sigma\blacklozenge\eta)$ of σ and η, $EV(\sigma\blacklozenge\eta) < EV(\xi)$.

There are two interestingly different cases of competition. In the more straightforward case, the plans "conflict" in the sense that executing one will make it more difficult to execute the other or will interfere with the other's accomplishing its goals. In the other case, the two plans aim at achieving the same goals, but the new plan is a better one for that purpose. In this case, adopting the new plan will make the old plan pointless. This is also a case of plan competition, because the composite of the two plans will have a lower expected value than the better of the two plans by itself.

The theory of practical reasoning now being considered consists of principles (1)–(6). Consider how this theory works in a particular decision problem. Suppose it is sunny today, but rain is predicted for the rest of the week. I would like to sit on my patio this afternoon and enjoy the sun, but I also have two errands to run. I must go to the bike shop and the bookstore. The bike shop is open today and tomorrow but closed the next day, and the bookstore is open today and the day after tomorrow, but closed tomorrow. One efficient plan for running the errands would be to go now and do them in a single trip. The alternative would be to have a separate plan for each errand, running one tomorrow and one the next day. Should I sit in the sun, or get into my car and run both errands in a single trip? Suppose that sitting in the sun is highly desirable but less desirable than achieving the ends of both errands. Suppose further, however, that it is not terribly onerous to make two separate trips. Adjust these values in such a way that the intuitively rational choice is to sit in the sun today and run the errands separately tomorrow and the next day. Can we get this result out of the above principle? It may seem that we cannot, on the grounds that getting into my car is prescribed by a plan that achieves the ends of both errands, and sitting in the sun has an expected utility less than the combined values of those ends. But this overlooks the fact that sitting in the sun is also prescribed by a more complicated composite plan that involves sitting in the sun today, going to the bike shop tomorrow, and going to the bookstore the next day. The expected value of this composite plan is higher than the expected value of the plan to run the errands today and forgo sitting in the sun, so it seems that sitting in the sun is to be preferred to running the errands today. That is the intuitively correct result.

This example illustrates the importance of being able to form composites of unrelated plans. Sitting in the sun becomes the preferred act only by being incorporated into a composite plan that combines it with separate plans for going to the bike shop tomorrow and the bookstore the day after tomorrow.

Coextendability
I believe that the account of plan acceptability embodied in principles (3) and (4) is on the right track. But as it stands, it is subject to a general logical difficulty having the consequence that under most circumstances, no plan will be rationally acceptable. We saw in the preceding example that we must sometimes construct composites of unrelated plans and compare them with other plans. The construction of such composites can be essential to getting the theory to prescribe the right acts. But the ability to construct such arbitrary composites also leads to the general difficulty. Given any plan, we can typically create another plan of higher value by combining the first plan with a plan that aims at realizing other unrelated goals. Suppose a plan σ is superior to a competing plan η. Let ν be a plan for achieving some other goals entirely unrelated to the goals at which σ and η aim. We can form a composite $\eta+\nu$ of η and ν, and $\eta+\nu$ may be superior to σ because of the spurious new sources of value acquired from the addition of ν. For example, in deciding whether to sit in the sun or run my errands today, I begin by comparing a plan σ prescribing sitting in the sun today and running the errands over the next two days with a plan η prescribing running both errands today. σ is superior to η. But now form a composite plan $\eta+\nu$ consisting of η together with the plan ν to have a sumptuous dinner at a good restaurant next week. According to (3), $\eta+\nu$ is preferable to σ, so sitting in the sun is not prescribed after all, or at least not on the basis of σ. Of course, we can also form a composite plan $\sigma+\nu$ by adding to σ the same plan to have a sumptuous dinner at a good restaurant next week. Then $\sigma+\nu$ will be preferable to $\eta+\nu$. But the process can be repeated by adding some other plan to $\eta+\nu$ to form $\eta+\nu+\mu$, and then adding it to $\sigma+\nu$ to form $\sigma+\nu+\mu$, and so on. The result is that every plan prescribing sitting in the sun is beaten by some plan prescribing running the errands today, and also every plan prescribing running the errands today is beaten by some

plan prescribing sitting in the sun. The upshot is that the account of plan preference contained in (3) leads to no plan's being acceptable.

An obvious suggestion is that although any finite composite containing one of σ and η can be beaten by a longer composite containing the other, we should take this process to the limit and consider the infinite composites that result from putting all of these plans together into a single plan. Then the infinite composite containing σ will have a higher expected value than the infinite composite containing η, and so it will be rationally acceptable.[11] There is, however, an overwhelming difficulty for this proposal. By their very nature, plans must be finite. Plans are schemes that we, as human beings, and other finite rational agents, design and execute. Thus there can be no infinite composites.

A resolution of this problem is suggested by the observation that beyond a certain point, constructing a composite plan of higher value is typically done by adding spurious additional elements that are unrelated to the original plan. Then, just as in the above example, we can add those same spurious elements to the competing plan, thus reversing the comparison again. This suggests that a plan σ is rationally preferable to a plan η if it is *coextendable* with η, in the sense that when more valuable competitors are constructed by adding unrelated sources of expected value to η, those same sources of expected value can be added to σ with the result that it stays ahead of its competition. This suggests defining:

A plan σ *is rationally preferable to* a plan η iff σ and η compete and there is a (possibly null) subplan μ of η and a composite σ+μ of σ and μ such that σ+μ is superior to η.

Thus, for example, the plan σ of staying home today and running my errands over the next two days is preferable to the plan η of running both errands today and having a sumptuous dinner at a good restaurant next week, because the subplan of having the dinner can be added to σ in such a way that the composite is superior to η.[12]

---

[11] These infinite composites are what I called "maximal strategies" in Pollock [1983].

[12] Philip Pettit has pointed out (in conversation) that there is an intuitive connection between the coextendability criterion and the Sure Thing Principle [Savage 1972]. According to the latter, one outcome is preferable to another if it is preferable given that some supposition P is true and also given that P is false. However, there does not appear to be any formal connection between the two principles.

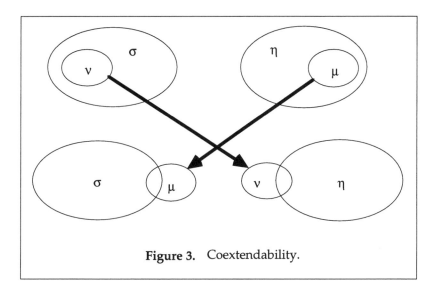

Figure 3. Coextendability.

However, this definition is not yet quite adequate. It could make two plans each rationally preferable to the other. The difficulty is that σ may also contain unrelated elements that could be added to η and might then reverse the comparison. This possibility can be factored in by revising the definition to read as follows:

A plan σ *is rationally preferable to* a plan η iff σ and η compete and there is a (possibly null) subplan μ of η and a composite σ+μ of σ and μ such that for every subplan ν of σ and a composite η+ν of η and ν, σ+μ is superior to η+ν.

It turns out that this definition can be simplified, because the second conjunct entails that σ and η compete:

Theorem 1: If there is a (possibly null) subplan μ of η and a composite σ+μ of σ and μ such that for every subplan ν of σ and composite η+ν of η and ν, σ+μ is superior to η+ν, then σ and η compete.

Proof: Assume the hypothesis. If $EV(\sigma) > EV(\sigma+\mu)$, redefine μ to be the null plan. Then we can assume that $EV(\sigma+\mu) \geq EV(\sigma)$, and it is still true that for every subplan ν of σ and a composite η+ν of η and ν, $EV(\sigma+\mu) > EV(\eta+\nu)$. It follows that $EV(\sigma+\mu) > EV(\sigma+\eta)$, and also that $EV(\sigma+\mu) > EV(\eta)$. Thus $EV(\sigma+\eta) < EV(\sigma+\mu) \geq \max\{EV(\sigma),EV(\eta)\}$. ■

Accordingly, we can define:

(3*) A plan σ *is rationally preferable to* a plan η iff there is a (possibly null) subplan μ of η and a composite σ+μ of σ and μ such that for every subplan ν of σ and a composite η+ν of η and ν, σ+μ is superior to η+ν.

This definition is illustrated by figure 3.

It is important to coextendability that the same thing is being added to both plans. Suppose we relaxed that requirement by defining either:

A plan σ *is preferable* to* a plan η iff there is a (possibly null) plan μ and a composite σ+μ of σ and μ such that σ+μ is superior to η.

or

A plan σ *is preferable** to* a plan η iff there is a (possibly null) plan μ and a composite σ+μ of σ and μ such that for every plan ν and a composite η+ν of η and ν, σ+μ is superior to η+ν.

These definitions would not work at all because under normal circumstances, they will have the consequence that any non-crazy plan σ is preferable* to *every* competing plan (we can always add *something* to σ to increase its expected value), and for the same reason no plan is preferable** to *any* non-crazy competing plan.

The very fact that coextendability requires adding the same thing to both plans, however, opens the way to some examples that appear at first to be potential counterexamples to (3*). Consider James, who is trying to decide between two career choices: physics and philosophy. There are two lectures on campus tonight at the same time, one in physics and the other in philosophy. James would find the physics lecture slightly more interesting than the philosophy lecture, which suggests that should be his choice. But he is teetering on the edge of deciding between careers in these two fields, and he knows that if he goes to the physics lecture that will decide him in favor of physics, and if he goes to the philosophy lecture that will decide him in favor of philosophy. Although the plan to attend the physics lecture has a higher expected value than the plan to attend the philosophy lecture, a composite of attending the philosophy lecture and later reading Keith Lehrer's book *Knowledge* has a higher expected value than attending the physics lecture. This is not a matter of coextendability, because if James goes to the physics lecture and becomes a physicist, he will get no particular value out of reading Lehrer's book. However, there is something *else* that can be added to the plan to attend the physics lecture—studying recent work on quantum electrodynamics—and this composite plan has a higher expected value than the plan to attend the philosophy lecture and later read Lehrer's book. Unfortunately, the comparison can again be reversed by adding something else of philosophical interest to the "philosophy plan", and then reversed again by adding something of interest to physicists to the "physics plan", and so on. This example differs from the preceding example in that what must be added to the physics plan and the philosophy plan to reverse the order of expected values are always different elements rather than the same element. The elements added to one plan would have no particular value when added to the other plan, because the first step of each plan affects a "change in life-style" that alters the subsequent value of related items.[13]

Because the simple plan of attending the physics lecture has a higher expected value than the simple plan of attending the philosophy lecture, there is some temptation to say that James should do that and go on to become a physicist. But upon further reflection, I find that unconvincing. Because those initial steps result in changed life-styles, they cannot be evaluated by themselves. Each creates opportunities for acquiring new sources of value not available on the other life-style. Furthermore, the opportunities resulting from the one choice do not outweigh those resulting from the other. Any finite set of opportunities available on the one life-style is matched by a finite set of opportunities available on the other. It seems to me that, under these circumstances, we should regard either life-style as rationally acceptable and hence should regard it as rationally permissible to attend either lecture. This is what (3*) tells us.

The Intransitivity of Plan-Preference

At this point I want to call attention to a peculiar feature of (3*). This definition of rational preference for plans does not make the relation transitive. Here is a simple example of the intransitivity. Suppose A at t_1, B at t_2, C at t_2, D at t_3, E at t_1, and F at t_2 are acts to be performed at the stated times. Two of these acts having the same time reference cannot both be performed, and suppose also that E at t_1 and B at t_2 interfere with each other so that they cannot both be performed successfully. Suppose that the acts are otherwise independent of one another, and the expected value of performing any sequence of them

---

[13] I am indebted to Patrick Fitzgerald for calling these examples to my attention.

is the sum of the expected values of the individual acts in the sequence. Suppose that the expected values of A at t_1, B at t_2, C at t_2, D at t_3, E at t_1, and F at t_2 are 1, 3, 2, 1, 4, and 1 utile, respectively. Now consider the following three plans:

$$\sigma \qquad A \text{ at } t_1 + B \text{ at } t_2$$
$$\eta \qquad\qquad C \text{ at } t_2 + D \text{ at } t_3$$
$$\mu \qquad E \text{ at } t_1 + F \text{ at } t_2$$

In order to compare these plans using coextendability, construct the following composites:

$$\sigma* \qquad A \text{ at } t_1 + B \text{ at } t_2 + D \text{ at } t_3$$
$$\eta* \qquad A \text{ at } t_1 + C \text{ at } t_2 + D \text{ at } t_3$$
$$\eta** \qquad E \text{ at } t_1 + C \text{ at } t_2 + D \text{ at } t_3$$
$$\mu* \qquad E \text{ at } t_1 + F \text{ at } t_2 + D \text{ at } t_3$$

Our independence assumptions imply that $EV(\sigma) = 4$, $EV(\mu) = 5$, $EV(\eta) = 3$, $EV(\sigma*) = 5$, $EV(\eta*) = 4$, $EV(\eta**) = 7$, and $EV(\mu*) = 6$. It follows that σ is rationally preferable to η, and η is rationally preferable to μ, but σ is not rationally preferable to μ. On the contrary, μ is rationally preferable to σ. This results from the fact that the part of μ that is added to η to yield a plan of higher value than μ (namely, E at t_1) cannot be added to σ with the same result because of a conflict with A at t_1. It follows that each of σ, η, and μ has a competitor that is preferable to it, and hence none is strongly acceptable.

It may seem that this result is a difficulty for (3*), because faced with these three plans, there has to be *something* that it is rationally acceptable to do. However, the fact that each of σ, η, and μ has a competitor that is preferable to it does not imply that there is *nothing* that it is rational to do—only that it is not rational to adopt any of *these* three plans. Using the same elements that were used in constructing these plans, we also constructed the plan $\eta**$ (E at t_1 + C at t_2 + D at t_3) and it has a higher expected value (7 utiles) than any of the other plans that can be constructed out of these elements. $\eta**$ is a competitor of every plan that can be built out of these elements and is not a subplan of $\eta**$, and $\eta**$ is rationally preferable to all such plans. So there is a plan that is rationally acceptable, namely $\eta**$. The failure of transitivity for plan preference does not create a difficulty in this case.

It takes little reflection to see that this same conclusion holds in general. Suppose we have any intransitive cycle of plans $\alpha_1, ..., \alpha_n$ where for each i, α_i is rationally preferable to α_{i+1}, and α_n is rationally preferable to α_1. I assume that each plan has only finitely many subplans. Consider all composites of the subplans of $\alpha_1,...,\alpha_n$. Of these, one or more will be *optimal*, having higher expected values than any of the non-optimal ones. η^{**} is optimal in the preceding example. It then follows that the optimal composites are rationally preferable to any of the non-optimal composites with which they compete, and so the optimal composites are all strongly acceptable (unless beaten by some other plans built out of other elements).

I take it then that the intransitivity of plan preference is not a problem for the theory. It is, however, an interesting result. I conjecture that because of the way plans are embedded in one another, there is no way to define plan preference so that it satisfies the axioms ordinarily assumed to hold for preference relations.

4. Warrant versus Reasoning

The preceding is still not plausible as a theory of practical reasoning. It would make practical reasoning too hard, because we would have to be able to survey all the infinitely many possible plans prescribing an act. At this point it is useful to recall the distinction between a theory of *reasoning* and a theory of *warrant*. A theory of reasoning describes how a rational agent should proceed in drawing conclusions at any given point. Reasoning is *defeasible* in the sense that it can lead to the adoption of a conclusion at one time and then mandate its retraction later, as a result of either additional reasoning or the acquisition of new information. If a rational agent has reasoned correctly up to the present time, then in one sense of "justified" its conclusions are justified. As a result of further reasoning, and without any new input, some of those conclusions may become unjustified and may subsequently become justified again, and so on. *Warranted conclusions* are conclusions that would be justified "in the long run". More precisely, a potential conclusion is *warranted* iff, if reasoning could proceed without limit, a point would be reached where the conclusion would become justified and would never subsequently become unjustified just as a result of further reasoning.[14]

---

[14] I am not distinguishing between warrant and ideal warrant here. In accordance with the results of section 10 of chapter 3, I assume that they coincide.

Warrant is an ideal notion. It is, in a certain sense, the target at which a reasoner aims. Just as we distinguish between epistemic and practical reasoning, we can distinguish between epistemic and practical warrant. My proposal is that although the preceding is not plausible as a theory of practical reasoning, it is plausible as a theory of practical warrant. That is:

(7)   The decision to adopt a plan σ is practically warranted iff σ is strongly acceptable.[15]

(8)   The decision to perform an act α is practically warranted iff there is a rationally acceptable plan prescribing α.

Together, (7) and (8) constitute a theory of practical warrant. That is, they describe what acts it would be rational to perform and what plans it would be rational to adopt if we could do all possible relevant reasoning.

My real interest is in a theory of practical reasoning, not a theory of practical warrant. I want to know how a rational agent should actually decide what to do, not what it would decide to do if, *per impossible*, it could do all relevant reasoning. Although a theory of practical warrant does not answer this question, it can be suggestive of the kinds of reasoning that are or ought to be involved in practical deliberation. It seems that practical deliberation ought to concern the construction and evaluation of plans. It seems clear that the kinds of reasoning involved in constructing plans and reasoning about their expected values concern factual questions and as such will fall within the purview of epistemic reasoning. A theory of epistemic reasoning will tell us when that reasoning is justified. In practical deliberation, the kind of reasoning that is uniquely practical rather than epistemic has to do with the adoption of plans. The reason the account of section 3 is not plausible as a theory of practical reasoning is that in order to use it to decide what plans to adopt, we would have to survey all logically possible plans. In practical deliberation, epistemic reasoning will produce candidate plans to be considered for adoption, and then a theory of practical reasoning should tell us what conclusions to draw on the basis of the consideration of a limited (usually very small) set of candidate plans. Given that we have tried to construct

---

[15] Although subplans of strongly acceptable plans are rationally acceptable, I take it that what we *adopt* are the strongly acceptable plans, and not the subplans.

relevant plans in a reasonable way and have reached justified conclusions about their expected values, how can we make a justified decision about what acts to perform? My suggestion is that a decision is justified at any given stage of reasoning iff it proceeds by applying (7) and (8) to the limited set of plans we have actually constructed and evaluated at that stage. As a first approximation we might try the following:

> The decision to adopt a plan σ is practically justified iff a rationally satisfactory search for plans has been conducted and it led to the discovery of no plan that we are justified in believing to be rationally preferable to σ.[16]

The main problem with this initial formulation turns upon the fact that we can have two competing plans neither of which is preferable to the other. In such a case, let us say that the two plans are *tied*. Following Bratman, I am calling such cases "Buridan cases". The preceding principle implies that in a Buridan case, we are justified in adopting both of the tied plans. This is clearly wrong. At best, we are justified in adopting *either* but not *both*. If there is no basis for choosing between the two plans, one should be chosen at random. A rational agent must have a way of making such random choices. My interim proposal is that the correct forms of the rules for justified plan adoption and justified action are as follows:

(9) The decision to adopt a plan σ is practically justified iff a rationally satisfactory search for plans has been conducted and either:
    (*i*)   for every plan μ discovered by the plan search, if we are justified in believing that μ competes with σ, then we are justified in believing that σ is preferable to μ; or
    (*ii*)   (*a*) the plan search has led to the discovery of no plan that we are justified in believing to be rationally preferable to σ, and (*b*) σ has been chosen randomly from the set of all competing plans discovered by the search which are justifiably believed to be tied with σ.

---

[16] Note that this is formulated as a theory about when the practical decision to *adopt a plan* is justified rather than when the epistemic conclusion that a plan is rationally permissible is justified. Taking rational permissibility to be defined by (1*), I see no plausibility in the view that this principle formulates a necessary and sufficient condition for the justification of the epistemic inference.

(10) The decision to perform an act is practically justified iff there is a plan whose adoption is practically justified and we are justified in believing that the act is prescribed by that plan.

This proposal will be further refined in chapters 7 and 8, but the present account will suffice for now.

Principles (9) and (10) appear to conflict with claims made by Bratman [1992]. Bratman urges that previously adopted plans constitute a "filter of admissibility" on what new plans can be reasonably considered:

> Consider my intention to fly back to SF on Sunday evening. As part of a partial plan it poses a problem for further deliberation: how am I to get to the airport from the hotel? One solution to this problem might be to take the afternoon limo to the airport. But this solution is inadmissible, given that I am also planning to meet an old friend in the afternoon. Other solutions include taking a cab and taking the bus, in either case after I meet my friend. Both are relevant and admissible options. But which is superior? Here I weigh relevant desire-belief reasons for and against these competing solutions; I weigh, for example, speed and convenience against cost, in order to reach a decision. This deliberation is framed by my prior, partial plan. My prior plan provides a background framework within which such weighing of desire-belief reasons is to be done.

I find this example unconvincing (and I know of no other examples that are more convincing). Suppose at the time I am making my plans, I know that there is no bus after noon, and a cab to the airport costs $150. Surely a rational person is going to at least consider forgoing the meeting with his friend and instead taking the (free) limo to the airport. What precludes that option under more normal circumstances is not that it conflicts with a plan already adopted but rather that it has a cost (not meeting one's friend) that is higher than the costs of other options, such as taking a bus or a cab. This reasoning can be handled straightforwardly by rules (9) and (10).

There is, however, a consideration that partially supports Bratman's claim. Adopting a new plan and retracting a previously adopted plan have computational costs for the agent. Because reasoning takes time and cognitive resources, it follows that even if the new plan is substantially better than a previously adopted plan with which it competes, it may not replace it. When a new plan is produced, its evaluation will be placed on a queue of cognitive tasks to be performed. But although the new plan is queued for evaluation, it may never actually be evaluated because more pressing matters may prevent its ever being retrieved from the queue. To take an extreme example, suppose you are a soldier who must run from one point to another under enemy fire. You carefully plot your course to take advantage of the available cover, and then you start running. Midway in your run you note some cover you previously overlooked, and it occurs to you that an alternative route might have been preferable. You are not, however, going to stop running at that point in order to evaluate the new plan. The plan may be queued for evaluation, but it will not actually be evaluated until you have completed your run, and at that point it is no longer of interest because the goal it aimed at achieving has already been achieved. The effect is that once a plan has been adopted, even if a better plan is subsequently discovered, the better plan will not immediately replace the original one. A rational agent will make the replacement only when she has time to do so. This is a sense in which adopted plans tend to be stable, but it does not reflect anything specifically about practical reasoning. Precisely analogous phenomena will occur in epistemic reasoning.[17]

I am reasonably confident that the preceding principles are on the right track. They do not, however, constitute a complete theory of practical reasoning. It will turn out that there are many additional complexities in practical reasoning that will become apparent only once we have a more detailed account of the nature of plans. Chapter 6 will be devoted to providing that account.

5. Resurrecting Classical Decision Theory

Neil Tennant (in conversation) has suggested a way of revising classical decision theory to avoid the objections formulated in section 2. It was observed that in both examples, classical decision theory yields the correct solution to the decision problem if our calculation of probabilities can be based on the assumption that we will continue to do what we (in fact) recognize as the rational thing. However, this is circular, because the objective of the theory is to determine the rational thing to do. Tennant observes that an alternative that also yields the correct

---

[17] This same point has been made by George Smith [1992] in his response to Bratman [1992].

solution is to compute the probabilities conditional on the assumption that we will continue to maximize expected utility (computed conditional on this same assumption). This amounts to a recursive definition of expected utility. We first compute the expected utilities of the final acts in the execution of a plan conditional on our having executed the first part of the plan, and determine what act maximizes expected utility on that assumption. Then we move back one step and determine what act maximizes expected utility conditional on the assumption that we will go on to perform the final act selected at the last step. And so on. In effect, expected utility is being defined by a kind of backwards induction on the plan-steps. When applied to the steps in a plan, this calculation should yield the expected value of the plan as the expected utility of the first step of a plan. Accordingly, selecting acts in this way appears to be equivalent to selecting plans in terms of their expected values and letting the plans selected determine what acts are to be performed.

There is, however, a problem with this proposal. Acts are *sui generis*. They are not inherently parts of plans. Or more accurately, every act is prescribed by infinitely many plans, and the different plans will have different expected values. Accordingly, the expected utility of an act cannot be identified with the expected value of an arbitrarily chosen plan that prescribes it. This amounts to observing that there is a problem in selecting the point at which we start the backwards induction in evaluating the expected utility of an act.

A natural suggestion is that we should identify the expected utility of an act with the expected value of the *best* plan prescribing it. But the fact that plans can be extended indefinitely by forming composites aimed at achieving additional goals indicates that there will not usually be any best plan. For every plan there will be a better plan. This is just the problem the coextendability criterion was designed to handle. The idea behind the coextendability criterion can be captured rather neatly in the context of evaluating acts by backwards induction. In comparing two acts, we should be able to start the backwards induction at any point where any further acts do not differentiate between the two acts being compared. For example, after running the maze we can expect to go to lunch. But that is true regardless of whether we enter door *A* or door *B*, and which door we enter will not affect the utility gained by going to lunch, so we can start the backwards induction at a point prior to the act of going to lunch.

Formulated precisely, this way of comparing two acts in terms of their expected utilities should be equivalent to choosing acts in terms of plans and choosing plans in terms of the coextendability criterion. However, this amounts to a greater divergence from classical decision theory than might at first be realized. In computing the expected utility of an act, the point at which we can start the backwards induction will depend upon what acts are being compared with the given act. For example, in deciding whether to enter door A or door B, we need not take account of the fact that either alternative allows us to go to lunch afterwards. But if we introduce a third option which precludes our going to lunch, then in deciding between that option and entering door A, we must take account of the fact that the latter allows us to go to lunch and so begin the backwards induction at a point after the act of going to lunch. In other words, an act will not have a single expected utility. It will only have expected utilities *relative to* other acts with which it is being compared.

A precise formulation of this modified version of classical decision theory should be equivalent to the plan-based decision theory proposed above. It should be emphasized, however, that this is at best a theory of warrant. Because there are limits to a rational agent's computational powers, he must plan ahead, deciding what to do tomorrow, and what to do after doing that, and so on. This amounts to constructing and adopting plans, so plans and their adoption must be essential ingredients in the intellectual repertoire of a rational agent, even if it is possible to formulate a theory of practical warrant that does not mention plans explicitly. A theory of practical *reasoning* must mention plans.

6. Simplifying the Decision Problem

I have urged that the decision-theoretic model should be replaced by what might be called *plan-based decision theory*. Unfortunately, plan-based decision theory makes practical reasoning much more complicated than it would be on the decision-theoretic model. It turns out, however, that in some commonly encountered special cases, the complexity of the decision problem can be substantially reduced. Pursuing this will also lead us to the characterization of a set of limiting cases in which the decision-theoretic model itself is provably correct.

In order to prove theorems about plan-acceptability, we must make some formal assumptions about plan composition, subplans, and expected values. The first six assumptions will become elementary theorems once the concept of a plan is made formally precise in the next chapter. The seventh assumption is a consequence of the analysis of the expected value of a plan proposed in the next chapter.

Assumption 1: A composite σ+(η+μ) of plans can be rewritten as a composite (σ+η)+μ. That is, if σ+(η+μ) is a composite of σ and η+μ, then there is a composite σ+η of σ and η such that σ+(η+μ) is also a composite of σ+η and μ.

Assumption 2: If σ and η are both subplans of μ, then there is a composite σ+η of σ and η that is a subplan of μ.

Assumption 3: If σ is a subplan of η and η is a subplan of μ, then σ is a subplan of μ.

Assumption 4: Given a composite σ+η of σ and η and a composite η+μ of η and μ, there is a composite having both the form (σ+η)+μ and the form σ+(η+μ) (that is, the composite preserves the dependency relations between members of σ and η and between members of η and μ).

Assumption 5: If a one-step plan ξ is a subplan of a composite μ+ν, then ξ is a subplan of either μ or ν.

Assumption 6: The only subplans of a one-step plan σ are σ itself and the null plan.

Assumption 7: If σ is a one-step plan prescribing the performance of an infallibly performable act α, then $EV(\sigma) = EU(\alpha)$.

Let us define:

A set $\mathcal{P}$ of plans is *closed under composition* iff for any plans σ and η in $\mathcal{P}$, every composite σ+η of σ and η is also in $\mathcal{P}$.

A set $\mathcal{P}$ of plans is *closed under subplans* iff for any plan σ in $\mathcal{P}$, if η is a subplan of σ then η is in $\mathcal{P}$.

If $\mathcal{P}$ is a set of plans and σ is a plan, σ is *$\mathcal{P}$-disjoint* iff σ contains no non-null subplan that is in $\mathcal{P}$.

The main problem in assessing the rational acceptability of a plan is that direct application of the definition would require us to compare the plan with all logically possible plans. The main way in which the problem can be simplified is by cutting down on the number of alternative plans that must be considered. This can be done if the plan being evaluated is a member of a set of plans that is appropriately "unrelated" to all plans outside the set. This is made precise by the concept of a linearly extendable set of plans[18]:

> A set $\mathcal{P}$ of plans is *linearly extendable to* a set $\mathcal{Q}$ of plans iff:
> (1) $\mathcal{P} \subseteq \mathcal{Q}$;
> (2) for every plan σ in $\mathcal{Q}$ that has a subplan in $\mathcal{P}$, there is a pair of plans σ^* and σ^{**} (the $\mathcal{P}$-core of σ and the $\mathcal{P}$-residue of σ, respectively) such that:
> (a) σ^* is a composite of plans in $\mathcal{P}$ and σ^{**} is in $\mathcal{Q}$ and is $\mathcal{P}$-disjoint; and
> (b) σ is a composite of σ^* and σ^{**}; and
> (3) for every plan μ that is a composite of plans in $\mathcal{P}$ and every plan v in $\mathcal{Q}$, if v is $\mathcal{P}$-disjoint then if $\mu+v$ is a composite of μ and v, $EV(\mu+v) = EV(\mu) + EV(v)$.

$\mathcal{P}$'s being linearly extendable to $\mathcal{Q}$ amounts to saying that any plan in $\mathcal{Q}$ can be divided into two component subplans, one (the $\mathcal{P}$-core) that is a composite of plans in $\mathcal{P}$ and the other (the $\mathcal{P}$-residue) "disjoint" from $\mathcal{P}$, in such a way that the $\mathcal{P}$-core and the $\mathcal{P}$-residue do not interact so as to add or detract from each other's expected values. Note that if $\mathcal{P}$ is closed under composition, then instead of talking about composites of plans in $\mathcal{P}$, we can simply talk about members of $\mathcal{P}$.

Let us also define:

> A set $\mathcal{P}$ of plans is *linearly extendable* iff it is linearly extendable to the set of all possible plans.

Lemma 1: If $\mathcal{P}$ is linearly extendable to $\mathcal{Q}$, $\mathcal{P}$ is closed under composition and subplans, σ is in $\mathcal{P}$, and a plan η in $\mathcal{Q}$ is rationally preferable to σ, then the $\mathcal{P}$-core of η is also rationally preferable to σ.

Proof: Suppose the hypothesis holds. As η is rationally preferable to

---

[18] The terminology derives from the "linearity assumption" in planning theory, which is the assumption that plans for achieving different goals do not interfere with one another.

σ, there is a subplan μ of σ and a composite $\eta+\mu$ of η and μ such that
(a) for every subplan ν of η and a composite $\sigma+\nu$ of σ and ν, $EV(\eta+\mu) > EV(\sigma+\nu)$.

Let η^* be the $\mathcal{P}$-core of η and η^{**} be the $\mathcal{P}$-residue. As μ is a subplan of σ, $\mu\in\mathcal{P}$, and then as $\eta^*\in\mathcal{P}$, any composite $\mu+\eta^*$ of μ and η^* is in $\mathcal{P}$. Let ξ be any subplan of η^* and $\sigma+\xi$ any composite of σ and ξ. By assumptions 2 and 3, there is a composite $\xi+\eta^{**}$ of σ and η^{**} that is a subplan of η. By assumption 4, there is a composite $\sigma+(\xi+\eta^{**})$ of σ and $\xi+\eta^{**}$ that is also a composite $(\sigma+\xi)+\eta^{**}$ of $\sigma+\xi$ and η^{**}. By (a):

(b) $EV(\eta+\mu) > EV(\sigma+(\xi+\eta^{**})) = EV((\sigma+\xi)+\eta^{**})$.

By assumption 1, $\mu+(\eta^*+\eta^{**})$ can be rewritten as $(\mu+\eta^*)+\eta^{**}$. By hypothesis, $EV(\eta+\mu) = EV(\mu+(\eta^*+\eta^{**})) = EV((\mu+\eta^*)+\eta^{**}) = EV(\mu+\eta^*)+EV(\eta^{**})$. As ξ is a subplan of η^*, $\xi\in\mathcal{P}$, so $\sigma+\xi\in\mathcal{P}$, and hence $EV((\sigma+\xi)+\eta^{**}) = EV(\sigma+\xi)+EV(\eta^{**})$. Hence by (b), $EV(\mu+\eta^*)+EV(\eta^{**}) > EV(\sigma+\xi)+EV(\eta^{**})$, and so $EV(\mu+\eta^*) > EV(\sigma+\xi)$. We have shown that for every subplan ξ of η^*, $EV(\mu+\eta^*) > EV(\sigma+\xi)$, so η^* is rationally preferable to σ. ∎

Our main theorem is an immediate corollary of lemma 1:

Theorem 2: If $\mathcal{P}$ is linearly extendable to $\mathcal{Q}$ and $\mathcal{P}$ is closed under composition and subplans, then for any plan σ in $\mathcal{P}$, there is a plan in $\mathcal{Q}$ that is rationally preferable to σ iff there is a plan in $\mathcal{P}$ that is rationally preferable to σ.

Let us define:

A set $\mathcal{P}$ of plans is *isolated* iff $\mathcal{P}$ is linearly extendable and closed under composition and subplans.

According to principle (7), the decision to adopt a plan σ is practically warranted iff σ is strongly acceptable, that is, no plan is rationally preferable to σ. It follows immediately from theorem 2 that:

Theorem 3: If $\mathcal{P}$ is an isolated set of plans, then the decision to adopt a plan σ in $\mathcal{P}$ is practically warranted iff there is no plan in $\mathcal{P}$ that is rationally preferable to σ.

It would seem that we frequently deal with isolated sets of plans, in which case theorem 3 constitutes a considerable simplification of the problem of determining which plans we are warranted in adopting.

Perhaps more important, theorem 2 also generates a simplification of the problem of determining what plans we are practically justified in adopting. Define:

A set $\mathcal{P}$ of plans is *dynamically isolated* iff $\mathcal{P}$ is linearly extendable to the set of all plans resulting from a rationally satisfactory search for plans, and $\mathcal{P}$ is closed under composition and subplans.

According to principle (9), the decision to adopt a plan σ is practically justified iff a rationally satisfactory search for plans has led to the discovery of no plan that we are justified in believing rationally preferable to σ. It follows immediately from theorem 2 that if $\mathcal{P}$ is a dynamically isolated set of plans, then in deciding whether to adopt a plan in $\mathcal{P}$, we can confine our search for rationally preferable plans to plans that are also in $\mathcal{P}$.

Traditional decision theory confined its attention to acts, which can be regarded as one-step plans. The decision problem can be simplified still further for one-step plans. First we prove:

Lemma 2: If σ and η are one-step plans, then η is rationally preferable to σ iff (1) $EV(\eta) > EV(\sigma)$ and (2) for every composite $\sigma+\eta$ of σ and η, $EV(\sigma+\eta) < EV(\eta)$ (that is, σ and η compete strictly).

Proof: Assume that σ and η are one-step plans. η is rationally preferable to σ iff there is a subplan μ of σ and a composite $\eta+\mu$ such that for any subplan ν of η and composite $\sigma+\nu$, $EV(\eta+\mu) > EV(\sigma+\nu)$. Because σ and η are one-step plans, their only subplans are themselves and the null plan, so this is equivalent to:

Either
(a) $EV(\eta) > EV(\sigma)$ and for every composite $\sigma+\eta$ of σ and η, $EV(\eta) > EV(\sigma+\eta)$
or
(b) there is a composite $\eta+\sigma$ of σ and η such that $EV(\eta+\sigma) > EV(\sigma)$ and for every composite $\sigma+\eta$ of σ and η, $EV(\eta+\sigma) > EV(\sigma+\eta)$.

But (b) is impossible, so η is rationally preferable to σ iff (a) holds. ■

It is in principle possible to have one-step plans σ, η, and μ, any two of which are strictly competing but the competition is "cancelled" by combining all three plans, in the sense that the expected value of a composite of all three is at least as great as the expected value of any of the plans individually. Let us define:

> $\mathcal{P}$ is a *strongly competing* set of plans iff for any finite subset X of $\mathcal{P}$, the expected value of some member of X is at least as great as the expected value of any composite of members of X.

With the help of lemma 2 we prove another lemma about one-step plans:

Lemma 3: If $\mathcal{P}$ is a strongly competing set of one-step plans and $\mathcal{P}$ is linearly extendable to $\mathcal{Q}$, then if $\sigma \in \mathcal{P}$, $\eta \in \mathcal{Q}$, and η is rationally preferable to σ, then some member of $\mathcal{P}$ is also rationally preferable to σ.

Proof: Assume the hypothesis. As η is rationally preferable to σ, there is a subplan μ of σ and a composite $\eta+\mu$ such that for every subplan v of η and composite $\sigma+v$, $EV(\eta+\mu) > EV(\sigma+v)$. In particular, μ and $\eta+\mu$ must be such that for every composite $\sigma+\eta$ of σ and η, $EV(\eta+\mu) > EV(\sigma+\eta)$. As σ is a one-step plan, μ must be either σ or the null plan. If $\mu = \sigma$ then there is a composite $\eta+\sigma$ of σ and η such that for every composite $\sigma+\eta$ of σ and η, $EV(\eta+\sigma) > EV(\sigma+\eta)$, which is impossible, so μ must be the null plan. Therefore, for every subplan v of η and composite $\sigma+v$, $EV(\eta) > EV(\sigma+v)$. Let η^* be the $\mathcal{P}$-core of η and η^{**} its $\mathcal{P}$-residue. η is a composite $\eta^*+\eta^{**}$, and η^{**} is a subplan of η, so $EV(\eta^*) + EV(\eta^{**}) = EV(\eta+\eta^{**}) = EV(\eta) > EV(\sigma+\eta^{**}) = EV(\sigma) + EV(\eta^{**})$. Consequently, $EV(\eta^*) > EV(\sigma)$. By hypothesis, $\mathcal{P}$ is a strongly competing set of plans, and η^* is a composite of members of $\mathcal{P}$, so at least one of the plans ξ in the composite is such that $EV(\xi) \geq EV(\eta^*)$. Thus $EV(\xi) > EV(\sigma)$. Because $\mathcal{P}$ is a strongly competing set of plans, ξ and σ are strictly competing. Thus by lemma 2, η^* is rationally preferable to σ. ∎

Our main theorem about one-step plans is now:

Theorem 4: If $\mathcal{P}$ is a strongly competing set of one-step plans and $\mathcal{P}$ is linearly extendable to $\mathcal{Q}$, then for any plan σ in $\mathcal{P}$, there is a plan in $\mathcal{Q}$ that is rationally preferable to σ iff there is a plan in $\mathcal{P}$ having a higher expected value than σ.

A simple account of warranted adoption for one-step plans is an immediate corollary of theorem 4:

Theorem 5: If $\mathcal{P}$ is a linearly extendable set of strongly competing one-step plans, then the decision to adopt a plan σ in $\mathcal{P}$ is practically warranted iff there is no plan η in $\mathcal{P}$ such that $EV(\eta) > EV(\sigma)$.

We get a similar simplification to the theory of practical justification. If we have conducted a rationally satisfactory search for plans, $\mathcal{P}$ is a set of strongly competing one-step plans, and $\mathcal{P}$ is linearly extendable to the set of plans resulting from the search, then in deciding whether to adopt a plan σ in $\mathcal{P}$, we need merely look at the other members of $\mathcal{P}$ and ask whether any of them has a higher expected value.

Finally, if we make one further assumption, the theory of warranted plan adoption reduces exactly to traditional decision theory. This is the assumption that the one-step plans in $\mathcal{P}$ prescribe acts that are infallibly performable. In that case, by assumption 7, we get:

Theorem 6: If $\mathcal{A}$ is a set of infallibly performable acts, $\mathcal{P}$ is the set of one-step plans prescribing the members of $\mathcal{A}$, and $\mathcal{P}$ is linearly extendable and strongly competing, then for any act α in $\mathcal{A}$, the decision to perform α is practically warranted iff there is no act β in A such that $EU(\beta) > EU(\alpha)$.

This theorem is important because it spells out precisely the limits of traditional decision theory.[19] It is also important because it seems clear that the assumptions of theorem 6 are often satisfied, and are normally satisfied in those cases to which traditional decision theory is applied. Thus although the decision-theoretic model fails as a general theory of practical rationality, the intuitions underlying it are correct for the special case that drives them.

---

[19] Classical decision theory is formulated in terms of acts being *alternatives* to one another. In Pollock [1983], I argued that it is very difficult to make sense of that notion. Theorem 6 resolves this problem by reducing the alternativeness relation on acts to the competition relation on plans. We can say that two acts are alternatives iff the one-step plans prescribing them are competitors. Equivalently, two acts are alternatives iff performing both has a lower expected value than performing the more valuable of the two.

7. Conclusions

The decision-theoretic model directs activity by evaluating acts one at a time in terms of their expected utilities. I have argued that except in certain special cases, this constitutes an inadequate theory of practical reasoning. In the general case, acts must be viewed as parts of plans and the plans evaluated as coherent units rather than piecemeal in terms of the acts comprising them. Rationality dictates choosing acts by first choosing the plans prescribing them. Plans, in turn, are compared by looking at their expected values. However, because plans can be embedded in one another, a rational agent cannot select plans just by maximizing expected values. Instead, an agent must employ the more complex coextendability criterion. It does turn out, however, that in one precisely defined limiting case, the traditional decision-theoretic model is provably correct.

The next several chapters will be devoted to working out the details of the plan-based theory of practical reasoning that has been sketched in this chapter. Chapter 6 will investigate the logical structure of plans. Chapters 7 and 8 will consider the way in which plans are constructed and adopted and the way in which the activity of a rational agent is directed by the plans it has adopted.

Chapter 6
The Logical Structure of Plans

In the last chapter, it was argued that practical reasoning must proceed by constructing and adopting plans, and actions should be chosen because they are prescribed by the plans the agent has adopted. Plans thus become a central element in the theory of practical reasoning, and to make further progress in understanding the nature of that reasoning, we must have a clear understanding of plans. That is the objective of this chapter.

Plans are, by definition, what we construct when we plan. Accordingly, we cannot make much progress discussing plans in isolation from planning. My strategy will be to make some general observations about how we construct and use plans and derive conclusions about the structure of plans from those observations.

There is a large body of literature on planning, but it is noteworthy that this literature has focused on the operation of planning, with little attempt to give a general account of the logical structure of plans.[1] Each planning theory has, for the most part, dealt with particular kinds of plans, without attempting to say what plans in general should be like. This chapter attempts to rectify this oversight.

1. Plans, Desires, and Operations

Primitive and Instrumental Desires

We engage in planning about how to satisfy desires. Sometimes we know how to satisfy our desires without having to engage in any further planning. (If I form the desire to open the door, I know how to do that.) In such a case we are appealing to *procedural knowledge* ("knowing how") which consists of (usually simple) plan schemas that are either hardwired in the agent or have been previously constructed and can be reused in similar circumstances. To avoid an infinite regress, there must be some "basic acts" that an agent knows how to perform without having to plan. In human beings, these may

---

[1] Georgeff and Lansky [1986] and Allen, Hendler, and Tate [1990] are good collections of important papers from the planning-theory literature.

be limited to elementary motor skills. Often we have to engage in at least rudimentary planning, and sometimes we have to engage in quite complex planning.

As a result of planning, I may form the new desire to do something *in order to* satisfy the initial desire. For example, if I feel sleepy and desire not to sleep, I may adopt the plan to go into the kitchen and fix a cup of coffee. This produces in me the *desire* to go into the kitchen and fix a cup of coffee—it becomes something I "want to do". This is an *instrumental desire*. Instrumental desires correspond to plans or plan-steps. Instrumental desires may give rise to further planning for how to fulfill them.

Operations
For the sake of uniform terminology, I will take *acts* to be physically specifiable action-types and *actions* to be particular instances of acts. So *raising my arm* is an act, and a particular instance of raising my arm is an action. It is tempting to think of plans as prescribing the performance of acts, but that is simplistic. *Going into the kitchen and fixing a cup of coffee* is not, in the present sense, an act. It is something I *do*, and I do it by performing a sequence of actions, but it is not itself an act. Let us call it an *operation*. This operation cannot even be identified with a sequence of acts, because there are many different ways of going into the kitchen and fixing a cup of coffee, and each of these corresponds to a different sequence of acts.

Operations may be characterized in part by what they accomplish rather than just how they are done. Roughly, I perform the operation of *going into the kitchen and fixing a cup of coffee* iff I perform a sequence of actions that gets me into the kitchen and results in a cup of coffee being prepared by me while I am there. There can be other constraints in the specification of an operation as well, including constraints (of varying degrees of specificity) on the time the operation is to be performed and constraints on how it is to be done. For example, *painting my garage*, *painting my garage next week*, and *painting my garage with my left hand* are all operations. We can regard acts (physically specifiable action-types) as the limiting case of operations. Instrumental desires are desires to perform operations.

Most operations are performed by performing a finite sequence of actions. There are, however, exceptions. Suppose Jones and I are building a shed. We plan to construct the first wall while it is lying on the ground. We will then raise it up, and I will lean against it, holding it in place until Jones gets some braces attached. Consider the plan-step that consists of my leaning against the wall until Jones gets it braced. *Leaning against the wall until Jones gets it braced* must be viewed as an operation, but it is a complex kind of operation. It takes place over an extended time interval and cannot be broken into simpler constituents except in an arbitrary way. It involves doing something continuously, over the performance interval. Other examples of such operations would be *Follow the yellow brick road until you get to the first fork*, or *Keep working on this problem until it is time to go to class*. These "continuous operations" have the form *Keep doing A until P*, where *doing A* cannot be broken into simpler constituents. This is more like *engaging in a process* than performing an action.

Hierarchical Planning and Scheduling
It is striking how schematic our plans often are. For example, I may plan to paint my garage next week without at this point being any more specific about just when next week I will paint it. I leave that undecided for now and decide later when exactly to do the work. That later decision is postponed in order to take account of the additional information I will acquire as the time for painting approaches. I will decide to paint my garage *when it is most convenient*, and convenience is a matter of what else is happening and what else I have to do—matters that I cannot reliably predict at this time. For precisely the same reason, I may leave unspecified precisely how I intend to perform an operation. As the time for painting approaches, I may form more detailed plans. For instance, I may plan to paint the south side of the garage in the morning so the sun will not be too hot, I may plan to go to the paint store today in order to get supplies, and so forth. But some details are typically left undecided right up until the time they must be executed. For example, I do not decide precisely where to position the ladder until I do it, and I do not decide whether to step onto the ladder first with my right foot or my left foot until it is time to climb the ladder.[2]

These examples illustrate that plans are schematic in two different ways. They may leave unspecified (to varying degrees) both *when* to perform an operation and *how* to perform it. These matters must often be decided before the plan can be executed, however, so this will

---

[2] This is a familiar point in AI planning theory, where such plans are said to be *partial*. [Sacerdotti 1975, 1977].

require further planning. In this sense, planning is *hierarchical*.[3] This further planning is of two sorts. Sometimes it is concerned exclusively with when to perform operations already planned. I will refer to such planning as *scheduling*. At other times, the additional planning concerns how to perform an operation. In this connection, recall that operations are often characterized, in part, by what they are intended to accomplish (e.g., *fix a cup of coffee*). As such, the planning required for their operation is of the same "problem-solving" variety as the original planning that led to the plan prescribing the operation. I will refer to planning that is not simply scheduling as *teleological planning*. Teleological planning concerns how to do things or how to accomplish certain goals.

The distinction between scheduling and teleological planning will turn out to be an important one, and I will say much more about it later. It cannot, however, be made precise as a distinction between two kinds of plans differentiated by their content. Teleological plans can also include prescriptions about the absolute or relative times of the performance of the plan-steps, but in that case the temporal specifications are chosen simultaneously with the plan and are part of the package. The distinction must be drawn in terms of the way the two kinds of planning proceed, and this will be discussed in chapter 7. The importance of the distinction lies in part in the fact that by leaving times as unspecified as possible, we facilitate the coordination of different plans. Even within a single plan, the ability to decide later the exact time to perform the plan-steps enables us to minimize execution costs by taking advantage of unpredictable features of the circumstances in which we will find ourselves at execution time.

When we engage in further planning for how to execute a previously adopted plan, regardless of whether the further planning is scheduling or of the teleological variety, we are engaged in *subsidiary planning*. In chapter 7, I will discuss what effect scheduling has on a previously adopted plan. Leaving that aside for now, consider what happens when we engage in teleological planning for how to perform an operation prescribed by a previously adopted plan. The result is sometimes to transform an old plan into a new, more specific plan. But usually the old plan and the new *execution plan* are kept separate. The execution plan is not literally part of the old plan. It is "called by" the old plan, in precisely the sense that programs may call one another. There are obvious advantages to this in cases where we later have to change our

---

[3] This is again a familiar point in AI. [Sacerdotti 1975, 1977].

plans. (Note the similarity to conventional programming wisdom.) If we run into difficulty, we can change an execution plan without having to reconsider the plan that calls it. Of course, sometimes difficulties with execution plans will result in reconsideration of the plans calling them. This happens, at least, when we encounter difficulty constructing a good execution plan.

2. Plans as Programs

The simplest plans are linear sequences of operations. But plans often have more complicated structures. For example, my garage-painting plan may be the following: First, get the paint. Then someday next week when the weather is good, begin by painting the south side of the garage, then paint the west side, then the north side, and then if there is still time, paint the east side. If there isn't enough time to finish the east side, postpone that until the next day. This plan involves steps that are conditional in two ways. First, some steps have *preconditions*. For example, the actual painting is to begin only if the time is sometime next week and the weather is good. Second, the last step involves a *conditional fork*. Because I am uncertain whether I can finish the job in one day, I plan for that eventuality: I plan to paint the east side *if there is time*, and otherwise to do it the next day.

The use of conditional steps enables us to make plans in the face of partial ignorance about the circumstances that will be encountered during execution of the plan. The use of partial (schematic) plans is another mechanism that accomplishes the same thing. Sometimes we do not know precisely what will happen, but we can be confident that what actually occurs will fall within a narrow range of alternatives, and then it may be convenient to plan ahead for each alternative. This is particularly true if the planning for each alternative is fairly complex (and so could not be done during execution) and we will have very little advance warning of which alternative we will face. But at other times the set of possible alternatives may be too large to plan ahead for each possibility and the decisions we will have to make when faced with the actual alternative are expected to be easy to make. In that case it is better to keep the plans schematic and fill in the details on the fly.

Let us say that a plan-step is *called* when all of the plan-steps leading up to it have been executed. Plan-steps can be conditional in two different ways, represented by the following plan for riding an elevator:

1. *Position yourself in front of the elevator door.*
2. *If the door is closed, push the button.*
3. *When the door is open, walk through it into the elevator.*
4. *Ride the elevator to the desired floor.*

The second step contains a condition that is checked immediately upon that plan-step being called. If the condition is satisfied, the step is executed; if it is not satisfied, then no operation is performed. Nonsatisfaction of this condition does not have the consequence that the plan has not been executed. The third step is conditional in a different way. If, at the time that step is called, the door is not open, we do not ignore the step and proceed with the rest of the plan. Instead, we wait for the condition to become satisfied. If it does not become satisfied, the step has not been executed and we have failed to execute the plan. I will call these *if-conditions* and *when-conditions*, respectively. If-conditions are useful because the agent may not know what conditions it will encounter when the plan is executed. When-conditions reflect ignorance of timing. The agent may not know just when a plan-step should be executed, and so it inserts a when-condition to determine that. Both are often formulated in English using "if", but they function differently in plans and must be clearly distinguished.

Both if- and when-conditions are situation-types.[4] That they may be satisfied at one time but not at another time sets them apart from what, in philosophical logic, are often called "states of affairs". The latter either obtain or fail to obtain *simpliciter*. They cannot obtain at one time and fail to obtain at another.[5]

If-conditions are evaluated at the time a plan-step is called. If the if-condition is not satisfied at that time, the operation prescribed by the plan-step need not be performed. By contrast, when-conditions prescribe waiting until something happens and then performing the operation prescribed by a plan-step. The when-condition typically refers to something repeatable, and the intent is for the agent to wait until it happens *subsequent to the plan-step's being called*. For example, if I am trying to meet someone at the airport, but am unsure what flight she will be on, I may plan to wait until the noon shuttle arrives, and if she has not arrived by then, I will go back to my office. But the

---

[4] They are what are called "fluents" in the situation calculus [McCarthy and Hayes 1969].

[5] See Pollock [1984].

noon shuttle arrives every day, so in formulating the plan we need some way of referring to the first arrival to occur subsequent to that plan-step's being called. As a general mechanism for this, I will allow when-conditions to use a dedicated variable *call-time* in their formulation, where this variable is always bound to the time the plan-step is called. Thus the when-condition *the noon shuttle has arrived* can be formulated more accurately as *the noon shuttle has arrived at a time subsequent to *call-time**.

Conditionals are programming constructs. Plans can also involve other standard programming constructs. For example, a plan can contain loops. The plan for getting into an elevator might be made more complicated by containing a contingency plan regarding what to do if you do not succeed in entering in while the door is open:

1. *Position yourself in front of the elevator door.*
2. *If the door is closed, push the button.*
3. *When the door is open, try to walk through it into the elevator.*
4. *If you fail, push the button and try again.*
5. *Once you have succeeded, ride the elevator to the desired floor.*

Executing the fourth step of this plan involves returning to the second step and looping.[6]

Plans can also involve something like variable-binding. For instance, I may plan to stop in the doorway of the meeting room, look around until I locate Stephen, and then walk over and greet him. Consider the relationship between the steps of *looking around until I locate Stephen* and *walking over and greeting him*. The function of the first step is to determine his location, and then the next step uses that location. In order to do that it must have some way of accessing the location just found, which means that the location must be stored somehow for later retrieval. The standard way of representing this is with variable-binding. We can think of the operation of *looking around until I locate Stephen* as returning the location as a value, and then the actual plan-step has the form

bind-variable *x* value-of (*looking around until I locate Stephen*)

---

[6] There has been some related work on recursion and iteration in plans. See Manna and Waldinger [1987] and Strong [1971].

and the next plan-step has the form

walk to location x and greet Stephen.

Given that plans can incorporate conditionals, loops, and variable-binding, it follows that all standard programming constructs can be incorporated into plans (because others can be defined in terms of these primitive constructs). In other words, we can think of plans as programs for accomplishing various ends. When-conditions are not standard programming constructs in serial computing, but they may become such in parallel computing where the order of execution of program steps cannot be predicted beforehand. Although there is a formal parallel between plans and computer programs, there is an important conceptual difference in that we think of each step of a computer program as having a determinate outcome, but the results of performing plan-steps can generally be predicted only with varying degrees of probability.

Another important difference between plans and programs as generally conceived is that plans must be taken to have the form of parallel programs rather than serial programs. This is not because plan-steps must be performed simultaneously (although that is sometimes true), but because the exact order in which plan-steps are performed is frequently left unspecified in a plan. Some must precede others, but often it will not make any difference in which order the steps are performed, and that can be left up to matters of convenience, or can be determined later in light of the need to coordinate with other plans.[7] For example, let us embellish the elevator-plan and turn it into a plan for riding the elevator to Jones' floor:

1. *Position yourself in front of the elevator door.*
2. *Check the number of Jones' floor on the directory next to the elevator.*
3. *If the door is closed, push the button.*
4. *When the door is open, walk through it into the elevator.*
5. *If you fail, push the button and try again.*
6. *If you succeed, push the button for Jones' floor.*
7. *Ride the elevator to that floor.*[8]

---

[7] Tate, Hendler, and Drummond [1990] refer to such plans as *partial order plans*. The first planner capable of generating partial-order plans was NOAH [Sacerdotti 1975].

[8] Note that an explicit representation of the structure of this plan would

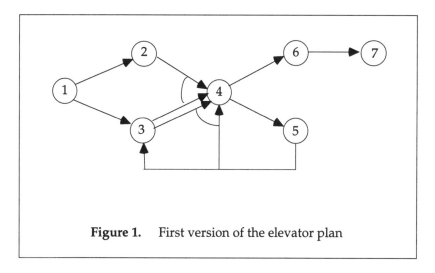

Figure 1. First version of the elevator plan

The plan need not specify the order in which steps 2 and 3 are performed. All that it should require is that both are performed after step 1 and before step 4. The order of dependency can be graphed as in figure 1. Note the difference between step 3 and step 4. Both are linked to pairs of preceding steps, but in different ways. Either both step 2 and step 3 or both step 3 and step 5 must be executed before step 4 is executed. This is indicated by linking the arrows together. Step 3, on the other hand, is to be executed when *either* step 5 or step 1 is executed. The notation used is the familiar notation from and/or graphs.

3. Plans as Graphs

I find the graphical representation of plans to be the most general and most useful. It can be made explicit by *defining* plans to be sets of plan-nodes, where the plan-nodes are data structures encoding the links in the graph and the condition/operator structure of the plan-steps. This can be done as follows:

A *plan-node* is a data structure having slots for the following:
- *Call sets.* This is a set of sets of plan-nodes. Successful "non-vacuous" execution (that is, execution in which the if-conditions

---

involve binding a variable to the number found for Jones' floor in step 2 and then using that in steps 6 and 7.

are satisfied) of all the nodes in any of these sets "calls" the
current node. Different sets represent different paths to the
current node. For example, the call-sets for node 3 above will
be {{node 1} {node 5}}, while the call-sets for node 4 will be
{{node 2, node 3} {node 3, node 5}}. The difference reflects the
difference between *or*-links and *and*-links.

- *If-condition*. If this condition is satisfied at the time the node is
  called, then successful non-vacuous execution of the node requires that the node-operation be performed at a time beginning
  with a time at which the when-condition is satisfied. If this
  condition is not satisfied, the node is executed vacuously without
  anything being done.

- *When-condition*. Performance of the operation is to begin at a
  time when this condition is satisfied. It need not begin immediately upon the when-condition's becoming satisfied, but it
  must begin while the when-condition is satisfied. The variable
  call-time is bound to the time a node is called.

- *Operation*. This is the operation to be performed. Among the
  possibilities are *nulop* (the null operation, whose performance
  requires nothing) and *bind-variable*. I will refer to this operation
  as the operation *prescribed* by the node.

- *Subplan*. This is a plan for how to perform the operation. Like
  any other plan, it is a set of plan-nodes, and it may be empty.

- *Goals*. It will be convenient to keep track of which nodes of a
  plan aim at the "direct" satisfaction of goals without any further
  action on the part of the agent. This slot lists the goals (if any)
  that the present node aims to satisfy directly. A node is *goal-laden*
  iff this list is nonempty.

These six slots will suffice for the current investigation of the logical
structure of plans. For actually building a planning system that constructs plans with this structure, it may be useful to add some slots to
hold further information. For example, the following may prove useful:

- *Expectations*. This keeps track of what we expect to be the case
  when this node is called. It will be used for monitoring plan-
  execution. If expectations are not satisfied, plans must be re-
  evaluated and possibly aborted.

For now, however, I will take a plan-node to have only the first six
slots.

To explain the precise meaning of the slots of a plan-node, we must define what it is for a plan consisting of such plan-nodes to be executed. We begin by defining the following concepts:

If n and m are plan-nodes, n is an *immediate-ancestor* of m iff n is a member of some member of the call-sets of m.

m is an *immediate descendant* of n iff n is an immediate-ancestor of m.

n is an *ancestor* of m iff n is an immediate-ancestor of m or n is an immediate-ancestor of an ancestor of m.

m is a *descendant* of n iff n is an ancestor of m.

A *plan* is a finite set of plan-nodes, closed under the ancestor-relation (that is, if n is in the plan and m is an ancestor of n, then m is also in the plan).

Initial nodes are those with which plan execution begins, and terminal nodes are those with which plan execution ends:

n is an *initial node* iff $\varnothing \in$ (call-sets n).

n is a *terminal node* of a plan σ iff there is no node m in σ that is a descendant of n.

A plan is executed by a finite sequence of operation-performances, where an operation-performance is a concrete event. An operation-performance has associated with it a time interval over which it occurs, which I will call the *performance interval* of the performance. Suppose σ is a plan all of whose nodes have empty subplans. To say that σ is executed by a sequence of operation-performances relative to a time t_0 is to say that plan execution began at t_0 (so that is the time at which the initial nodes were called), and the operation-performances represent the performance of the operations of nodes that were executed non-vacuously in executing the plan. More generally, plans can call other plans that are subplans for their nodes. In that case, what is required is that the subplan (rather than the operation) be executed at the appropriate time.

To make this precise, let us begin by defining a *flat plan* to be one all of whose nodes have empty subplans. A *hierarchical plan* is any plan that is not a flat plan. For every hierarchical plan there is an "executionally equivalent" flat plan that results from recursively replacing nodes having nonempty subplans by their subplans (adjusting the call-sets in the obvious way, that is, the initial nodes of a subplan are called by the nodes that originally called the node for which that is a subplan, and nodes called in part by that node are instead called by the terminal nodes of the subplan). I will call this the *flattening* of the hierarchical plan. A hierarchical plan is executed by a sequence of operation-performances iff its flattening is. What remains is to define execution for flat plans. That is done as follows:

If σ is a flat plan and μ is a set of pairs $\langle op,n \rangle$ where op is an operation-performance and $n \in \sigma$, then μ *satisfies* σ relative to a starting time t_0 iff:

(1)   the operation-performances in distinct members of μ are distinct;

(2)   each non-initial node is called by previous performances, that is, for each $\langle op,n \rangle \in \mu$:

    (a) op is the performance of an operation of the type prescribed by n;

    (b)   there is a set $\{n_1,...,n_k\}$ that is a call-set of n (k possibly 0) such that for some $op_1,...,op_k$, $\langle op_1,n_1 \rangle,...,\langle op_k,n_k \rangle \in \mu$ and if the performance intervals of $op_1,...,op_k$ are $[_1t_1,_1t_2],...,[_kt_1,_kt_2]$ respectively, then the if-condition of n is satisfied at the time t^*, which is the latest time of $_1t_2,...,_kt_2$ (or at t_0 if $k = 0$);

    (c)   if $[t_1,t_2]$ is the performance interval of op, then $t_0 \leq t_1$, and the when-condition of n is satisfied at t_1. If the when-condition is formulated using the variable *calltime*, this is taken to denote t^*, defined as in (b);

(3)   if a plan-step is called by some of the performances, then it is performed, that is, for each $n \in \sigma$, if

    (a)   there is a set $\{n_1,...,n_k\}$ that is a call-set of n (k possibly 0), and

    (b)   there are $op_1,...,op_k$ such that $\langle op_1,n_1 \rangle,...,\langle op_k,n_k \rangle \in \mu$, and if the performance intervals of $op_1,...,op_k$ are $[_1t_1,_1t_2],...,[_kt_1,_kt_2]$ respectively then the if-condition of n is satisfied at the latest time of $_1t_2,...,_kt_2$ (or at t_0 if $k = 0$),

    then there is an op such that $\langle op,n \rangle \in \mu$.

In clauses (2c) and (3), the case where $k = 0$ is the case where n is an initial node. Then we define:

A sequence $\langle op_1,...,op_k \rangle$ of distinct operation-performances *executes a flat plan* σ relative to a starting time t_0 iff there is a mapping η from $\{op_1,...,op_k\}$ to σ such that the set of pairs $\{\langle op_1,\eta(op_1)\rangle,...,\langle op_k,\eta(op_k)\rangle\}$ satisfies σ relative to the starting time t_0.

A plan is *executed* iff it is executed by some sequence of operation-performances.

The preceding definitions give precise content to the slots of a plan-node. I will refer to this as the *OSCAR plan representation framework*. It can be illustrated by considering the plan to ride the elevator to Jones' floor. We can diagram it as a graph of plan-nodes as in figure 2. The "naked" arrow pointing to node 1 indicates that it is an initial node.

Note the addition of node 3a to the diagram. This is required by the precise semantics that has now been provided for the if-condition. The if-condition plays two separate roles: (1) it determines whether the operation is to performed, and (2) it directs the flow of execution through the plan. If the if-condition is not satisfied, then the node is executed vacuously, and its execution does not contribute to the calling of its immediate descendants.[9] This has the consequence that if node 2 has been executed but the door is open when node 3 is called, then nodes 2 and 3 together will not call node 4. To get node 4 called under these circumstances, we must add node 3a.

We can distinguish six different kinds of conditional-dependency that we may want to build into plans:

1. A conditional can determine whether an operation is to be performed and direct the flow of execution by determining whether descendant nodes are to be called. This is the standard case expressed by the if-condition in plan-nodes.

2. A conditional can direct the flow of execution without specifying any operation to be performed. This is accomplished in the OSCAR plan formalism by employing nodes prescribing the null operation, as in node 5.

---

[9] This allows us to chain a number of plan-nodes together, all conditional on the if-condition of the first node.

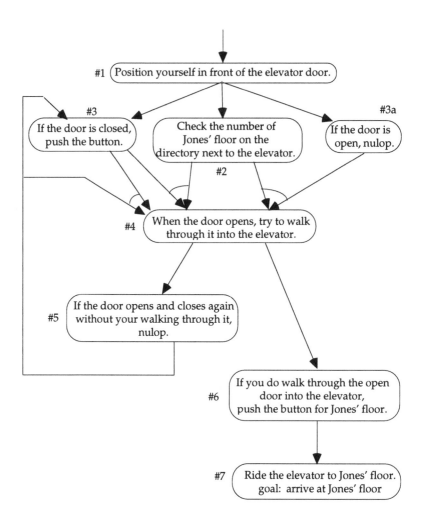

Figure 2. The elevator plan

3. A conditional can determine whether an operation is to be performed, without affecting the flow of execution. This was the intent of step 2 in the informal description of the elevator plan. This can be captured (as in the example) in the OSCAR plan formalism by a pair of nodes having the same immediate descendants, where one of the nodes specifies that if the condition is satisfied then the operation is to be performed, and the other specifies that if the condition is not performed then the null operation is to be performed. The function of the second node is just to direct the flow of execution, as in case (2) above.

4. It is often desirable to list several exclusive cases and specify what operation is to be performed and how the flow of execution is to go as a function of which case is satisfied. That is readily accommodated in the OSCAR plan formalism by having a separate node for each case.

5. We frequently want to list several exclusive cases and specify what operation is to be performed, without affecting the flow of control. This can be accomplished just as above by using separate nodes for each condition but giving them all the same immediate descendants.

6. We may want to list several exclusive cases and have them determine the flow of execution without specifying any operation to be performed. Again, this can be done by having different nodes for each case, each node prescribing the null operation.

If-conditions determine *whether* an operation is to be performed. When-conditions impose constraints on *when* an operation is to be performed. The when-condition of a node does not indicate that the operation should be performed immediately upon the condition's being satisfied. Rather, the operation is to be performed beginning at *some time* at which the condition is satisfied. A when-condition "opens a window of opportunity". Sometimes we also want to specify when the window of opportunity closes by using a condition we would formulate in English as, "When Q and before R". For instance, in constructing a plan for getting into a car, we might include a plan-step of the form "When you get into the car and before you start driving, fasten your seatbelt". It might seem initially that this kind of when/before locution can be expressed by using a when-condition of the form *you are in the car and have not yet started driving*. This is inadequate, however. The second part of the condition is to be understood as requiring that you have not yet started driving *since getting into the car,* not that you have not yet *ever* started driving. However, in the expression *"you are in the car and have not yet started driving"*, there is no way to refer to the time of getting into the car, so there is no way to give this the intended meaning. What we want to require is that you have not yet started driving *since* the first time you got into the car *since* the time the node was called. This cannot be expressed using a single plan-node, but we can express it using a pair of nodes. Recall that the variable *call-time* is bound to the time a node is called. In general, a node of the form

If P,
when Q,
before R,
op.

can be regarded as an abbreviation for the following pair of nodes:

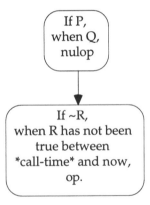

In this construction, the first node is automatically executed as soon as Q becomes true, so that is the *call-time* for the second node. The second node is then successfully executed if R is not true at call time and does not become true before *op* is performed.

I believe that this formalism will prove generally adequate for the formulation of plans. This assumption provides the basis for the design of the PLAN-EXECUTOR, discussed in chapter 8.

4. The Expected Value of a Plan

In chapter 5, an account was proposed for how to choose between competing plans in terms of their expected values. The expected value of a plan σ was defined to be the difference between the definite expected situation-liking of the situation type consisting of adopting the plan and the definite expected situation-liking of the situation type consisting of not adopting the plan. This suffices to render the concept well-defined, but a rational agent engaged in plan-based practical reasoning is still faced with the formidable task of computing or estimating the expected values of plans. This task is complicated by the fact that the way in which a plan is executed may depend upon contingent facts governing how the plan unfolds at conditional forks, which can in turn affect the expected execution costs and the likelihood of being able to perform the prescribed operations. We can deal with this by defining the notion of an *execution path* through a plan. Intuitively, an execution path is an ordering of plan nodes that describes a way a plan may be executed. Which execution path will actually occur can be predicted only with probability. We can, however, compute the probability of each execution path, and the expected value of each execution path, and then we can evaluate the entire plan as a weighted average of the expected values of the execution paths. More precisely, where σ is a plan and Ω is the set of all possible execution paths for σ, we can calculate the expected value of σ as follows:

(4.1) $$EV_\alpha(\sigma) = \sum_{\rho \in \Omega} EV(\rho) \cdot PROB_\alpha(\rho/\sigma)$$

where $PROB_\alpha(\rho/\sigma)$ is the probability of ρ being the actual execution path given that σ is adopted.[10] The index α is the degree of justification relative to which the probabilities are being computed. This will be determined by the degree of interest in the plan.

We must understand execution paths in a way that accommodates the fact that we may try to execute a plan and fail. Failures of execution can contribute significantly to the value of the plan. Failed attempts at execution produce *truncated execution paths*. Such truncations can result from either failed when-conditions or failures to perform operations

---

[10] Note that the execution of a plan begins at the time it is adopted. Its initial nodes are called at that time. Of course, if they involve when-conditions, nothing may actually happen for some time afterwards (sometimes years).

during when-conditions. Execution paths that are not truncated are *complete*.

Obviously, failures of execution can contribute negatively to the value of a plan. For example, if a plan involves jumping over a crevasse and we try and fail, the results may be catastrophic. At a more mundane level, executing the first part of a plan may involve significant execution costs, which will be recouped by achieving the goals of the plan only if the plan is successfully executed. On the other hand, it must not be overlooked that a single plan may aim at achieving several goals (e.g., a plan to run several errands on one trip), and some of the goals may be achieved even if we fail to execute the entire plan. Thus truncations can have positive values as well as negative values.

In using (4.1) to compute expected values, a complication arises from the fact that plans containing loops may have infinitely many (progressively less probable) execution paths, in which case the sum becomes an infinite sum. Although this is not a difficulty for the theoretical correctness of (4.1), it creates a major practical problem for an agent that must actually compute the sum. This must be addressed by any attempt to implement plan-based practical reasoning, but it will not be addressed here.

For some looping plans, where we plan to keep doing something until we fail, there will be no finite complete execution paths. All finite paths represent execution failure at some point, and an infinite path will have zero probability. The plan is adopted with the assumption that execution will eventually fail, and it gets its entire value from truncated execution paths.

To complete this account, we must give a precise definition of "execution path". Because of parallelism, execution paths are best conceived as graphs charting the course of execution of a plan, with the links recording which nodes are called by which. Precisely, define:

A *(possibly truncated) execution path through a plan* σ is a finite graph ξ whose nodes are labeled by plan-nodes of the flattening of σ and is such that for each node η of ξ, if η is labeled by the plan-node n of the flattening of σ, and X is the set of immediate-ancestors of η in ξ, then the set of plan-nodes of the flattening of σ labeling the members of X is a member of the call-set of n.

ξ is a *truncated* execution path through a plan σ iff ξ is an execution path through σ and there is a plan-node n of the flattening of σ such that some call-set of n consists of plan-nodes that label nodes of ξ, but n does not label any node of ξ.

ξ is a *complete* execution path through σ iff ξ is an execution path through σ and ξ is not truncated.

The intent of this definition is that the execution path represents the nodes that were non-vacuously executed and their calling history. If a set of plan-nodes labeling nodes in the execution graph is a member of the call set of a plan-node not labeling a node in the execution graph, then the latter plan-node was not non-vacuously executed. That is, either its when-condition was never satisfied, or the operation was not successfully performed when the when-condition was satisfied. Accordingly, the execution path is a truncated execution path.

To incorporate (4.1) into an artilect, we must supply algorithms for computing the probabilities and expected values of execution paths. The probability $PROB_\alpha(\rho/\sigma)$ is the probability of ρ's being the execution path given that σ is adopted. The general flavor of how this probability is computed can be gleaned from the following special case. A *linear execution path* is one such that given any two nodes, one is an ancestor of the other. (This precludes the parallel execution of nodes.) Such an execution path is a linear sequence $\rho_1,...,\rho_k$ of nodes. The probability of the execution path is the probability of the conjunction of those nodes being executed in that order. If ρ is a complete execution path, that probability is the product

$$PROB_\alpha(\rho_1/\sigma)\cdot PROB_\alpha(\rho_2/\rho_1\&\sigma)\cdot...\cdot PROB_\alpha(\rho_k/\rho_1\&...\&\rho_{k-1}\&\sigma).$$

If ρ is a truncated execution path, then the product must contain one more term representing the probability of execution being truncated at ρ_k. For execution paths involving the parallel execution of different nodes, things are somewhat more complicated, but the general idea is the same. The difference is that we must consider sets of nodes rather than individual nodes. The probability of the execution path is the probability of executing all initial nodes times the probability of executing all nodes called by the initial nodes given that they are called, and so forth.

The expected value of an execution path can be regarded as having two constituents. First, in constructing a plan, the assumption is that the only sources of positive value are the goal-laden nodes. This may seem an unreasonable assumption, because the goals of a plan are the situation-types that initiated the planning, but once a plan is discovered it may be apparent that it has beneficial side effects that were not among the original goals of the plan. However, this can be handled by adding such side effects to the list of goals as they are discovered. Each goal has an expected value, which is stored as the strength of the desire encoding it,[11] and each goal-laden node has a certain propensity to achieve the goal and realize that expected value. It must be borne in mind, however, that the expected value of a goal may be affected by its being embedded in the context of the execution path. Different goals achieved by an execution path may either interfere with or reinforce each other, and other aspects of the execution path can also affect the value of a goal. Accordingly, we must look at the expected value of the goal *in the context of the execution path*. This is the difference between the expected situation-liking of the goal, in that context, and the expected situation-liking of the goal's not being achieved, in that context. The probability that the goal will be achieved by execution of the goal-laden node may also be a function of the actual execution path in which the goal-laden node occurs. Thus the positive value of a goal-laden node is the product of the expected value of the goal in the context of that execution path and the probability of the goal's being achieved by the execution of the goal-laden node in the context of that execution path, less the expectation of achieving the goals anyway, without executing the plan. The positive constituent of the expected value of the overall execution path is the sum of these values for all the goal-laden nodes occurring in it. The second constituent of the value of an execution path is its execution cost. That is the sum of the expected costs of performing each operation in the execution path in the context of that path. These costs must include any known adverse side effects of executing the operation in the context of the execution path.

We must be careful to avoid a simplistic view of goals. It is tempting to regard goals as fixed situation-types. But as Georgeff [1987] points out, there can also be goals of maintaining a current state or of preventing a certain state. Even more problematic is the fact that we may have the goal to achieve as much of something as we can. For instance, having spilled water on the kitchen floor shortly before I must leave for school, I may adopt the plan of mopping the floor until I must leave, with the goal of getting it as dry as I can in the time I have. Such a goal can be viewed as a variable situation-type, with a variable parameter. The value of a situation of this type is a function of the value of the parameter. Such a goal is not achieved *simpliciter*. It is achieved with a certain parameter value. Accordingly, the expected

---

[11] See the discussion of this in chapter 1.

value of such a goal is the expected value computed on the basis of a probability distribution of the values of the parameter.

Top-level plans are plans that are not subsidiary to other plans. The preceding account of expected values was designed with top-level plans in mind, but it also works for subsidiary plans if we treat their goals properly. The goal of a subsidiary plan is the execution of some operation prescribed by a node of a higher-level plan. This goal is encoded in an instrumental desire. In an ideally rational agent, the strength of a desire is the difference between the expected situation-liking of the desire's being satisfied and the expected situation-liking of its not being satisfied, and this can be taken as a measure of the expected value of the instrumental goal.[12] Suppose we have two instrumental desires and plans for their satisfaction, but the plans compete. In deciding which plan to adopt, an agent should look at which desire is stronger and at the execution costs of the plans, so this suggests that instrumental desires work just like primitive desires in contributing value to a plan. Of course, for primitive desires, the "raw desire strength" may differ from the value of the goal in the context of the plan, and in that case it is the latter that must be employed in computing expected values. But the same is true of instrumental desires. To illustrate, suppose an instrumental desire arises from a plan to achieve a certain goal G. Suppose a subsidiary plan is constructed for satisfying the instrumental desire, and it turns out fortuitously that it will also achieve G independently and prior to satisfying the instrumental desire. It was urged above that in order to get the computation of expected value to come out right, when it is discovered that a plan contributes to the situation-liking in a previously unanticipated way, that must be added to the list of goals for the plan. Accordingly, in the case envisaged, G must be added to the list of goals for the subsidiary plan. This will have the result that G and the instrumental desire will each contribute value to the plan. This, however, seems wrong. Once G is achieved, the satisfaction of the instrumental desire becomes worthless. This problem is resolved by noting that just as primitive goals must be assessed in the context of the plan, the same is true of instrumental goals. The instrumental goal must be evaluated in terms of the difference between the expected situation-liking of the desire's being

---

[12] There is a further complication, which will be ignored for the time being: instrumental desires and instrumental goals are conditional on the node of the higher-level plan from which they are derived being called. The proper treatment of such conditional goals will be discussed in chapter 7.

satisfied *in the context of the plan* and the expected situation-liking of its not being satisfied *in the context of the plan*. In the context of an execution path in which *G* is achieved first, subsequent satisfaction of the instrumental desire will receive a value of zero.

To recapitulate, the expected value of a plan was defined to be the difference between the definite expected situation-liking of the situation type consisting of adopting the plan and the definite expected situation-liking of the situation type consisting of not adopting the plan. The problem then arose how to compute these expected values. I have described a solution to this problem, and it might be possible to build an agent that actually performs the calculations described in an explicit manner. It should be emphasized, however, that I am not claiming that human beings proceed in this way. At least at the level of explicit reasoning, it is clear that human beings do not normally perform such complex calculations in the course of their planning. I conjecture, however, that human beings emply Q&I modules that approximate these calculations to some degree. In this connection it should be observed that although human estimates of probabilities do not produce precise numerical values, they do produce more than ordinal comparisons. We are able to estimate not just that one outcome is more likely than another but also that it is *a lot* more likely, or just *a little* more likely, and so forth. Human neural hardware seems to lend itself to analogue computations yielding such estimates rather than to precise digital calculations. I conjecture that similar Q&I modules perform analogue computations yielding at least rough approximations of the calculations of expected values described above.

Chapter 7
An Architecture for Planning

1. Practical Reasoning

I have argued that a rational agent directs its activity by adopting plans and acting upon them. I have given a general account of the logical structure of plans and a preliminary account of the criteria that a rational agent uses in choosing among plans. The objective of this chapter is to complete the latter account and describe the architecture of a rational agent capable of plan-based practical reasoning. The architecture determines the control structure that governs the way in which the rational agent uses the logical rules of plan-based reasoning to arrive at practical conclusions. The ultimate objective is to produce an account of sufficient precision to provide the basis for an artilect—OSCAR.

A rational agent begins with primitive desires about the future produced by epistemic cognition and optative dispositions and then deliberates about how to satisfy those desires. The agent adopts plans on the basis of that deliberation. We can distinguish two central tasks within practical reasoning: (1) constructing and adopting plans; and (2) directing activity given our desires and plans. We can think of (1) as being performed by a functional module called the PLANNER, and (2) by a functional module called the PLAN-EXECUTOR. The flow of data through these modules is depicted in figure 1, which is a slight embellishment of figure 3 of chapter 1. Circles represent databases and rectangles represent data-processing modules. Solid arrows indicate the flow of new data that drives the operation of the modules, and dashed arrows indicate the retrieval of previously stored data. One possibly misleading feature of this diagram is that it might be read as depicting epistemic cognition as separate from the PLANNER and PLAN-EXECUTOR. That is not the intent of the diagram. It will become apparent that large parts of planning and plan execution are carried out by epistemic cognition.

This chapter will investigate the PLANNER and the next chapter will investigate the PLAN-EXECUTOR.

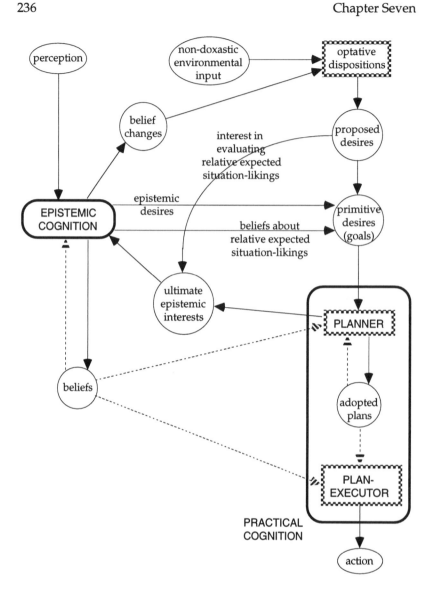

Figure 1. Flow of data in practical reasoning

2. Planning

We can usefully distinguish three levels of planning: we plan for *how to satisfy* a primitive desire, for *how to perform* the operations prescribed by other plans, and for *when to perform* them. I will refer to the first of these three kinds of plans as *top-level plans* and the others as *subsidiary plans*. Planning for how to do something is *teleological planning*. This consists of means-end reasoning and general problem solving. Planning for when to do something is *scheduling*. Teleological planning and scheduling proceed in importantly different ways. When a teleological subsidiary plan is adopted, it is not integrated into the original plan. It is a separate plan that is called by the original plan. The original plan remains intact. But scheduling proceeds by modifying the original plan, adding timing instructions. (Of course, timing instructions can also be incorporated into a plan when it is first constructed. They need not be the result of subsequent scheduling.) The nature of these timing instructions will be discussed in the next section.

The initial planning that transpires in response to the acquisition of primitive desires is top-level teleological planning. It has already been observed that such planning tends to be rather schematic. Suppose I form the desire for my garage to look better. In response to that desire, I may adopt the top-level plan to paint it. Notice just how schematic this plan is. It contains no specification at all of how I will go about painting it or when I will do it. Having adopted this simple top-level plan, I must plan further. The adoption of this plan must somehow initiate subsidiary planning for how to paint the garage. The resulting subsidiary plan might take the following form:

1. Buy the paint.
2. Make sure the ladder is in good condition.
3. When the weather is good, paint each wall of the garage.

The structure of this plan can be represented more accurately by the following graph:

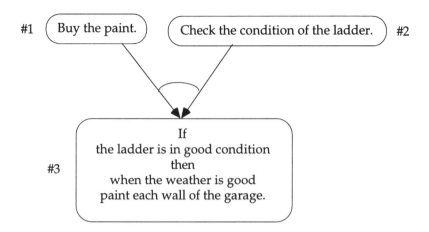

Consider each plan-node. Node 1 is going to require further subsidiary planning. I must plan how to buy the paint: what kind of paint, what color, at what store I should buy it, how I will pay for it, and so forth. Node 2 illustrates something that will be of considerable importance. Although checking the condition of the ladder is a rather complicated procedure, I need not plan for how to do it, because I "know how to do it". Such knowledge consists of a stored plan schema that I am able to retrieve and act upon whenever I want to check the condition of a ladder. I will call such stored plan schemas *standing plans* and will discuss them at greater length later. Node 3 is similar because I know how to paint the wall of a garage.

Having constructed this subsidiary plan for how to paint my garage, and perhaps a further subsidiary plan for node 1, I am still not ready to paint my garage, because nothing in this plan tells me when to do anything. Node 3 does contain a when-condition, but it is a very indefinite one. As it stands, I can execute this plan at any future time as long as the weather is good when I do the actual painting. This plan cries out for scheduling. I must decide when to buy the paint, when to check the ladder, and when to do the actual painting. This requires further subsidiary planning. It must eventually be determined *exactly* when operations are to be performed, but my initial scheduling may be much more indefinite than that. For example, I may decide to buy the paint tomorrow. That leaves undetermined just when tomorrow I will do it. When tomorrow rolls around, I must do some more specific scheduling. At that point I may decide to buy the paint in the afternoon, but that is still pretty indefinite. As the day progresses and

I get a better picture of what I must do during the day, I will be in a position to decide more precisely just when I will buy the paint. Knowing that I am going to the grocery store after lunch, I may decide to pick up the paint on my way to the grocery store. Notice that I may also wait until making this decision to decide just where to buy the paint. Because I am going to buy it while on my way to the grocery store, it may be more convenient to buy it at one paint store (*The Flaming Rainbow*) rather than another, and so I choose my paint store on that basis.

Let me summarize my conclusions so far. First, our top-level plans tend to be very schematic. Adopting a schematic plan must lead to the initiation of further subsidiary planning. Second, our teleological planning typically leaves the scheduling of nodes quite indefinite. At some point, further scheduling must occur. Third, some aspects of teleological planning may depend upon decisions regarding scheduling, so scheduling and teleological planning must be interleaved.

The PLANNER can be viewed as having three components: (1) a component that initiates planning when new primitive desires are acquired; (2) a component that actually does the planning, constructing new plans that thereby become candidates for adoption; and (3) a component that determines whether to adopt a candidate plan. These are the PLANNING-INITIATOR, the PLAN-SYNTHESIZER, and the PLAN-UPDATER, respectively. As I conceive it, the PLANNING-INITIATOR responds to the acquisition of new desires. It is the trigger that begins the process of planning. As such, it can initiate the operation of the PLAN-SYNTHESIZER, which produces new plans that are put in a database of *candidate-plans*. The PLAN-SYNTHESIZER is responsible for both teleological planning and scheduling. The PLAN-UPDATER is responsible for all changes in what plans are adopted. Such a change can consist of either the adoption of a new candidate plan or the withdrawal of a previously adopted plan. This encompasses the modification of previous plans, because that consists of withdrawing the original plan and adopting the modified plan. This somewhat more detailed understanding of the PLANNER allows us to diagram it as in figure 2.

The next task is to give more precise descriptions of each of the modules in this diagram. Before doing that, however, contrast this architecture with the architecture implicit in some of the early AI planning literature. That architecture has a simple form. *All* of the agent's desires are presented to the PLAN-SYNTHESIZER simultaneously, in one package, and then the PLAN-SYNTHESIZER is expected to fabricate a plan for this combination. If an agent's desires change—for example, as a

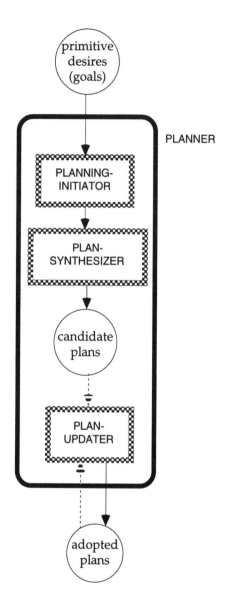

Figure 2.   Architecture of the PLANNER

result of acquiring a new desire—then the planning must be redone. The obvious objection to this architecture is that it could work only for artificially circumscribed problems. First, a real agent embedded in the real world has a huge number of desires. No planning algorithm could actually produce a single plan for the simultaneous satisfaction of all these desires. Second, new desires are added with great rapidity. It is totally impractical to replan from scratch whenever a new desire is acquired. Third, this architecture completely overlooks the need to choose between competing plans. It cannot be assumed that the PLAN-SYNTHESIZER will produce only optimal plans. That is an impossible desideratum. The first two of these considerations indicate that any rational agent able to function in the real world must be able to plan incrementally for the satisfaction of different desires and then work at combining the plans.[1] The task of combination requires evaluating plans in the context of other plans and rejecting plans that would be good by themselves but are not good plans when combined with other good plans.

3. Scheduling

To get a better grasp on how scheduling works, let us think some more about the example of painting my garage and deciding when to buy the paint. This example of scheduling illustrates several things. First, scheduling need not specify times very exactly. Initially, I decided to buy the paint tomorrow, then tomorrow afternoon, and finally on my way to the grocery store. I may never explicitly make a more precise decision regarding when to buy the paint, because having decided to buy it on the way to the grocery store, I let the exact timing be determined by the process of executing the plan. I will say more about this when I talk about plan execution in the next chapter. The second point illustrated by this example is that scheduling can determine times in different ways. We can schedule a plan-node to be executed at an absolute time (e.g., 3 P.M.) or during an absolute time interval (e.g., this afternoon), or we can schedule it relative to the execution of other plan-nodes (e.g., on my way to the store).

---

[1] For some attempts to deal with this problem, see Sussman [1973], Tate [1974], Waldinger [1977], and Pednault [1986].

The logical structure of scheduling is fairly simple. Whenever a new plan is adopted, its nodes become candidates for scheduling. The original teleological planning proceeds by constructing the bare bones of a plan that will, with a certain probability, result in the satisfaction of a desire. Scheduling proceeds by looking for occurrences to which nodes of the plan can be linked with the result that the embellished plan becomes preferable to its ancestor. Scheduling often accomplishes this by coordinating steps from different plans (e.g., buying the paint on the way to the grocery store) or taking account of circumstances external to the plan that affect either execution costs or the probability of successfully executing the plan (e.g., taking account of the fact that the paint store is closed from noon to 1 P.M. for lunch). Scheduling constrains the times at which nodes are called (their call-times) with two mechanisms. First, it establishes additional *scheduling links* between nodes. The addition of such links imposes new constraints on the order in which nodes are executed. The links that are imposed by the initial teleological planning will henceforth be called *teleological links*. The scheduling links and the teleological links together will comprise the call-sets for a node. Scheduling links can occur between members of a single plan or members of different plans, and can link nodes of subsidiary plans and higher-level plans. The result of adding such links is to create new plans that combine previously separate plans. Scheduling may have the effect of explicitly incorporating subsidiary plans into their containing plans.

Scheduling links between pre-existing nodes constrain the call times of nodes *relative to each other*. Scheduling can also fix call times absolutely, stipulating either that a node is to be called at a certain time, or when some particular event occurs. Such absolute scheduling can be achieved by introducing *timing nodes* into a plan. These are nodes that are automatically "executed" at a certain time or when a certain event occurs (without the agent's having to do anything). They can be represented in the OSCAR planning formalism as nodes in which everything but the when-condition is vacuous: *when P, nulop*. We can then set the absolute call time of a node by taking the unit set of a timing node to be one of the call-sets of the given node. For example if we want node *n* to be called at 3 P.M., we can construct a timing node *m* having the form *when it is 3 P.M., nulop*. Then if we insert {*m*} into (call-sets *n*), this has the result that *n* is automatically called at 3 P.M.. This can be represented graphically as follows:

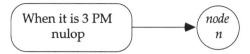

Scheduling imposes timing constraints on previously adopted plans. It is important to realize, however, that timing constraints can also be part of the original teleological plan (in which case they are included in the teleological links). For instance, I may decide to go to a concert that has performances only on Saturday and Sunday evenings. My only way to get to the concert is to go with Joe, who has a car, and he is going on Sunday. Thus my teleological planning leads me to plan to go with Joe on Sunday. Although teleological considerations may, in this manner, impose timing constraints, they usually leave many scheduling questions unanswered. For example, although teleological considerations determine that I will go to the concert on Sunday, they do not determine that I will leave the house at 7:18 P.M.. We rarely decide *precisely* when we are going to do something until we actually do it.

The distinction between scheduling and teleological planning does not lie in the content of the plans produced but in the nature of the planning operation itself. Scheduling can be defined as the ordering of pre-existing nodes with respect to each other or with respect to new timing nodes. Teleological planning is any other planning.

Although scheduling is a different operation from teleological planning, it is not independent of it. Difficulties in scheduling can lead to changes in teleological planning. For example, suppose I need an ingredient for a meal I am cooking, and to get it I must hurry to the grocery store. This may leave me without time to stop at the paint store, so I alter that part of my schedule. But having altered that part of my schedule, there is no longer any reason to buy the paint from *The Flaming Rainbow* rather than another paint store, so I may alter that part of my subsidiary plan regarding how to buy the paint.

We often make schedules *before* adopting a plan for how to perform an operation and then fine-tune them later as we refine our teleological plans. For example, I may decide to go to the store after lunch and before going to school without deciding on a precise route. In making such a schedule, I am relying upon general knowledge about how long it will take to go to the store and knowledge to the effect that my precise route will not make much difference to the time required. There is usually no need to make schedules very precise, so such rough general knowledge is normally quite adequate.

4. The PLANNING-INITIATOR

The PLANNING-INITIATOR initiates both teleological planning and scheduling for the satisfaction of newly acquired goals (encoded as primitive desires) and newly planned operations (encoded as instrumental desires). A superficial examination of the circumstances in which plans actually get constructed suggests that the structure of the PLANNING-INITIATOR must be rather complicated. For example, upon acquiring a new desire, we sometimes produce a plan for its satisfaction immediately. But on other occasions, we seem to postpone planning until we have more time to think about it or more information at our disposal. I suggest, however, that the structure of the PLANNING-INITIATOR is actually quite simple and that all of this apparent complexity can be accommodated by a simple architecture. When we acquire a new desire, it is immediately sent to the PLAN-SYNTHESIZER, along with a measure of the strength of the desire. The latter is used for prioritizing the reasoning tasks involved in constructing plans. In particular, it determines the degree of interest assigned the queries sent to the interest-driven epistemic reasoner. The PLAN-SYNTHESIZER then processes the new desires in the order determined by their degrees of interest. While they are awaiting processing, the desires will be stored on a queue, ordered according to priority, and the PLAN-SYNTHESIZER will retrieve them one at a time. I will refer to this queue as the *desire-queue*. My suggestion is that such a prioritized *desire-queue* represents the main structure of the PLANNING-INITIATOR. Items are retrieved from the *desire-queue* in order of strength, and when an item is retrieved, it is passed to the PLAN-SYNTHESIZER.

Delayed Planning
This simple architecture may seem too simple to accommodate the facts about how planning actually transpires. The first difficulty is that planning often seems to be postponed. Rather than planning for the satisfaction of a desire as soon as we acquire it, we may wait until we have more time or more information. However, such delayed planning can be explained by several different general facts about cognition, without complicating the PLANNING-INITIATOR. The most important point is that thinking takes time and resources. We almost always have more cognitive operations to perform than we can perform at any given instant. Accordingly, they must be put on a queue and await their turn. The order in which they are prioritized on the queue reflects some rough measure of importance. In the case of planning

for the satisfaction of desires, strong desires are queued in front of weak desires and so will receive priority in planning. For example, if I am put in a room with a tiger, I will most likely begin planning immediately for how to get away from the tiger because that is something I desire very strongly. If at the same time I become mildly curious about the identity of the composer of the background music that I hear, that too will go on my *desire-queue*, but the desire will be sufficiently weak that I may never get around to planning for its satisfaction because I may always have more pressing things to think about.

A second general feature of cognition that leads to delayed planning is that the construction of plans is carried out by the epistemic reasoner, and epistemic reasoning is interest-driven. This has two important consequences for planning. First, interests come in varying strengths. When the practical reasoner poses a question for the epistemic reasoner, the strength of the interest that attaches to the question is determined by the strengths of the desires leading the practical reasoner to pose that question. The point of assigning strengths to interests is that they govern the priorities that the epistemic reasoner assigns to trying to answer the questions. To illustrate this point with the preceding example, suppose I become interested in the identity of the composer before noticing the presence of the tiger. The practical reasoner will pass to the epistemic reasoner the task of planning how to discover the identity of the composer, and the epistemic reasoner may begin thinking about that. But then when I notice the tiger, questions of much greater urgency are passed to the epistemic reasoner, with the result that although the questions about the composer remain of interest, no further reasoning about them will occur until the more pressing questions about the tiger are answered.

Furthermore, even if a question of great interest is passed to the epistemic reasoner, this does not guarantee that much of anything is going to happen. Only if the reasoner has beliefs at its disposal from which it can make progress in answering the question will the reasoner engage in active reasoning to that end. If a rational agent does not have appropriate information at its disposal for answering a question, then even though it retains strong interest in the answer, it may not *do* anything at all in connection with the question. It may just record the interest and wait for some relevant new information to come along. Consequently, although the planning for the satisfaction of strong desires may be initiated before the planning for the satisfaction of weak desires, there may be nothing the reasoner can do immediately in planning for the strong desires, and so plans for satisfying the weak desires may be produced before plans for satisfying the strong desires.

A final observation is that ordering by strength is only the default ordering of the *desire-queue*. A reflexive reasoner can engage in practical reasoning *about* how best to order planning, and override the default ordering. For instance, a reflexive reasoner can observe that planning for a lesser desire must be done immediately if the desire is to be achieved, while planning for a greater desire can be safely postponed, and on that basis reorder the *desire-queue*.

Opportunistic Planning

Another kind of phenomenon also seems initially to require the PLANNING-INITIATOR to have more structure than I have given it. This is what might be called *opportunistic planning*. For example, when I hear about a new book and form the desire to read it, I do not immediately plan a trip to the bookstore. But when I am in the bookstore or know that I am going to be there or in the vicinity, that may inspire me to form a plan to look for the book and buy it if it is in stock. In such opportunistic planning, I acquire a new desire, but instead of immediately planning for its satisfaction, I *seem* to store it and keep my eyes open for opportunities to satisfy it. I think that this is a misdescription of what is going on, however. Planning is not really being delayed. Rather, I believe I will be in the vicinity of the bookstore sometime soon. Given that belief, a plan to buy the book when I am in the vicinity of the bookstore has a higher expected value than a plan to make a special trip to buy the book, and so I adopt the former plan. All that is happening in such opportunistic planning is that I am making use of beliefs about forthcoming opportunities. These beliefs make it feasible to formulate plans with when-conditions that will latch onto such opportunities. This does not require any additional complications in the architecture of the PLANNING-INITIATOR.

Somewhat the same phenomenon is illustrated by the earlier example of painting my garage. I may not decide from which paint store I will buy the paint until I schedule the plan-step of buying the paint. Once I decided to buy the paint on my way to the grocery store, that led me to decide to buy the paint from *The Flaming Rainbow*, because it was on the way to the grocery store. What may have happened here is that when first planning to buy the paint, I had the belief that I would probably be in the vicinity of some suitable paint store sometime in the near future, and so I adopted the plan of buying the paint when presented with such an opportunity. When I planned my trip to the grocery store, I realized that would put me in the vicinity of *The Flaming Rainbow*, and so I decided to buy the paint there.

Subsidiary Teleological Planning

Both of these examples of opportunistic planning illustrate a further phenomenon. Initially, we plan to do something (buy the paint or the book) when some particular kind of opportunity presents itself. Later, when we acquire the belief that we are about to be presented with such an opportunity, we adopt the more specific plan to perform the operation on that occasion. This involves further planning. This further planning is a special case of subsidiary planning. Having decided to do something when a particular kind of opportunity presents itself, we must then plan for how to do it. That involves planning to do it on a particular occasion. Such planning must be initiated by the PLANNING-INITIATOR. The same point applies to all subsidiary planning. When subsidiary planning is required, it must be the PLANNING-INITIATOR that initiates it. The mechanism for this is the production of *instrumental desires*.[2] It is a familiar point that once I plan to do something in order to satisfy a desire, I acquire the new desire to do that. This is an instrumental desire. It might seem puzzling that we have instrumental desires. Why not just have primitive desires? There is a simple computational answer to this question. Instrumental desires provide a mechanism for making planning recursive. Initially, a primitive desire is placed on the *desire-queue*. When it is retrieved from the queue, planning for its satisfaction is initiated. If that produces a plan, the adoption of the plan produces new instrumental desires in us to execute the plan steps. These instrumental desires go on the *desire-queue* right along with primitive desires, and when they are retrieved from the *desire-queue*, that initiates subsidiary planning for their satisfaction.

Applying this model to the paint store example, I first plan to go the paint store sometime when I am in the vicinity. That produces in me the instrumental desire to go to the paint store sometime when I am in the vicinity, and that desire initiates planning for doing that. However, this is a case of delayed planning; although interest in constructing such a plan is passed to the epistemic reasoner, it does not at first have sufficient information at its disposal to allow it to construct a plan. Only when I decide to go to the grocery store do I acquire beliefs that enable a subsidiary plan to be constructed. The subsidiary plan that is constructed is the plan to stop at *The Flaming Rainbow* on the way to the grocery store.

---

[2] See the discussion of instrumental desires in chapter 1.

Procedural Knowledge
This picture of recursive plan initiation via instrumental desires must be modified in one respect. Not all desires require planning. If they did we would have an infinite regress. There must be some desires an agent knows how to satisfy without further planning. These are of two kinds. First, there must be some basic desires for whose satisfaction the agent has built-in procedures. This is most obviously the case for simple motor skills. If I desire to raise my arm, I have a built-in procedure for doing that. Of course, that procedure can be disrupted by injury, exhaustion, or physical constraint, but as long as it is not, it is unnecessary for me to plan how to raise my arm.

It is rare for me to form the desire to raise my arm, because when I do raise my arm, that is generally part of a more complex routine that constitutes procedural knowledge for how to do something of a higher level. For example, if I form the desire to turn on the ceiling light, I know how to do that by raising my arm and activating the wall switch. This procedural knowledge constitutes a plan schema. I previously referred to such plan schemas as *standing plans*, and we can regard them as stored in a *library-of-standing-plans*. My standing plan for turning on the light is activated by the desire to turn on the light. The presence of the standing plan in my *library-of-standing-plans* makes it unnecessary for me to plan how to turn on the light.

Standing plans are plan schemas (as opposed to individual plans) for how to do various things. When a standing plan is retrieved and instantiated, the result is a plan for achieving some goal. In human beings, an important feature of standing plans is that, having produced such an instantiation, we need not make an explicit decision to adopt the standing plan. Its adoption is automatic unless something leads us to override it. On the other hand, it can be overridden in particular cases. For example, if I suspect that I will get a shock from touching the light switch, I could turn on the light by pushing the switch with a stick. This indicates that standing plans are *default plan schemas* for achieving specifiable goals under some specifiable general circumstances.

We can distinguish between two ways in which standing plans can be default governors of behavior. The simpler is that instantiating a plan schema for a particular task can automatically provide us with a defeasible reason for adopting that plan. (The nature of such defeasible reasons will be discussed further when we talk about the PLAN-UPDATER.) However, merely having a reason for adopting a plan requires us to think about whether to adopt it and then make a decision to do so. At least in human beings, our procedural knowledge often shortcuts such decision making, leading us to adopt instances of standing plans automatically and without reflection unless something forces us to think about them. This distinction can be marked as the distinction between standing plans as *weak defaults* and standing plans as *strong defaults*.

A feature of standing plans that goes hand in hand with their role as strong defaults is that although such standing plans can readily be retrieved for the purpose of directing activity, they cannot easily be retrieved for inspection by epistemic cognition. When we use them for directing activity, we seem to retrieve them one step at a time (as each step is called) rather than as a complete plan. If the standing plan is sufficiently simple, we may be able to reconstruct it by imagining its execution and keeping track of what we would do at each stage, but for complex standing plans (like that involved in our procedural knowledge for how to walk down a hall or how to swing a tennis racket), the plan is often too complex for that to be feasible. This observation is much like saying that such standing plans are "compiled in".

Human beings employ both kinds of standing plans—compiled and uncompiled. Some standing plans are constructed by explicit planning and when their instances are retrieved they are treated like any other plans. For example, whenever we acquire a new skill from a book or by figuring it out in a theoretical way, we begin with an explicitly formulated plan for how to do it. Then for a while, whenever we want to exercise that skill, we make explicit appeal to that uncompiled standing plan, which at that point is functioning as a weak default. As time passes and we become more expert at the skill, the originally explicit plan tends to become more sophisticated and gets compiled in so that we are no longer able to retrieve it for theoretical inspection. Consider learning to ride a bicycle. Initially you learn rules like, "If you feel yourself leaning to the left, turn the handlebars counterclockwise", but in time you acquire much more sophisticated rules for steering a bicycle, and at that point you are generally unable to articulate them explicitly.

Another kind of standing plan is what Bratman [1987, 1989] has called *personal policies*. An example of a personal policy is, "Fasten your seatbelt when you get into the car." The personal policy is a kind of plan schema that is retrieved whenever you are in the appropriate kind of situation. Because the plan itself is readily retrieved by epistemic cognition, it is functioning only as a weak default rather than a strong default.

Standing plans are extremely important in any rational agent embedded in a rapidly changing environment. Plan synthesis is slow. If an agent always had to construct plans anew before undertaking action, it would not be able to interact with its environment in an effective way. It is the employment of standing plans that enables human beings to function in real time. My suspicion is that the vast majority of actions taken by adult human beings are directed by standing plans rather than by explicit new planning. Planning is the exception rather than the rule. Furthermore, the use of standing plans as strong defaults is faster than their use as weak defaults, so this is also of extreme importance in a rational agent. The use of standing plans as strong defaults must, however, be viewed as a practical Q&I module rather than as a part of practical reasoning itself. Such strong defaults are not, strictly speaking, *reasoning*. They supplement practical reasoning rather than being a part of it. Only the use of standing plans as weak defaults is properly part of practical reasoning. Saying this is not in any way to denigrate the importance of strong defaults, however.

The storage of standing plans involves storing at least three items: (1) a specification of the type of desire to be satisfied, (2) a specification of the circumstances under which the plan is to be activated to satisfy that desire, and (3) the plan schema itself. When the PLANNING-INITIATOR retrieves a desire from the *desire-queue*, it matches it against the desire-types in its *library-of-standing-plans*, and if an entry has a matching desire-type, it then checks to see whether the circumstances are believed to be of the appropriate type. If they are, it uses the match to set the values of the variables used to instantiate the plan, and then the plan is passed to the PLAN-UPDATER, which decides whether to adopt it. At this point a weak default standing plan is treated just like any other plan. When I discuss the PLAN-UPDATER, I will argue, however, that we automatically have a defeasible reason for adopting the instantiation of the standing plan. I will also make some suggestions about how strong default standing plans might be integrated into the picture. If the PLAN-UPDATER adopts some standing plan for the satisfaction of the triggering desire, then the adopted plan is sent on to the PLAN-EXECUTOR, but if no standing plan is adopted, then the PLANNING-INITIATOR activates the PLAN-SYNTHESIZER in order to plan explicitly for the satisfaction of the triggering desire.

Basic actions are actions for which we have built-in procedural knowledge of how to perform them. However, there can be special circumstances in which we are unable to perform a basic action. For example, I will not be able to raise my arm if my hands are tied behind my back. This suggests that basic actions should be regarded as the limiting case of standing plans and processed in the same way.

Scheduling
On the present model of planning initiation, subsidiary teleological planning is mediated by the production of instrumental desires. The same mechanism can be used for scheduling. Whenever a desire (either primitive or instrumental) to do something is retrieved from the *desire-queue*, it is automatically passed to the PLAN-SYNTHESIZER for scheduling. On the present model, the PLAN-SYNTHESIZER handles both scheduling and teleological planning.

An Architecture for Planning Initiation
The picture of the PLANNING-INITIATOR that emerges from this is the following. Primitive desires are placed on the *desire-queue* as they are acquired, and ordered according to the strength of the desire. When a desire is retrieved from the *desire-queue*, a check is run to see whether the agent has built-in procedural knowledge of how to satisfy it or possesses acquired procedural knowledge in the form of a standing plan for its satisfaction stored in its *library-of-standing-plans*. If the agent has either kind of procedural knowledge, it is retrieved and passed to the PLAN-UPDATER, which determines whether to adopt it. If it is adopted, it is passed to the PLAN-EXECUTOR without producing any new instrumental desires.[3] If no standing plan is adopted, the PLANNING-INITIATOR passes the desire to the PLAN-SYNTHESIZER for explicit planning. When the PLAN-SYNTHESIZER produces a candidate plan for the satisfaction of the desire, that plan is passed to the PLAN-UPDATER, which decides whether to adopt it. If the plan is adopted, that produces instrumental desires for the execution of its nodes, and these desires are placed back on the *desire-queue*, to start the whole process over again. The resulting architecture of plan initiation is diagrammed in figure 3.

5. Complex Desires

The architecture for planning initiation makes fundamental appeal to desires, both primitive and instrumental. But there are some details concerning desires that remain to be worked out in order for this architecture to work.

---

[3] This will be qualified a bit in the discussion of the PLAN-SYNTHESIZER.

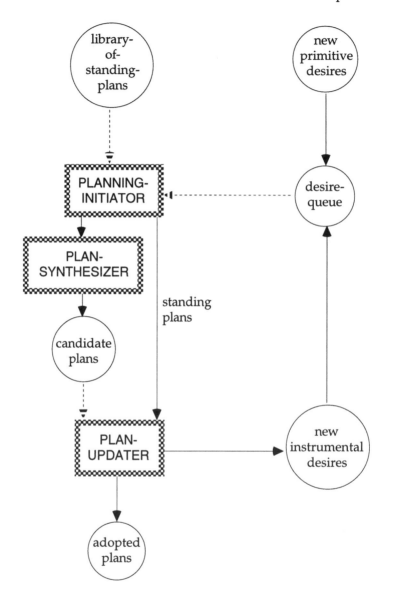

Figure 3. Planning initiation

Conditional Primitive Desires
Some optative dispositions are built-in. An example is the disposition to get hungry under certain physiological circumstances. But most of our optative dispositions are learned. For example, a miser was not born with the desire for money or a book lover with the desire to read. Some of these optative dispositions produce logically simple desires, that is, desires that certain states of affairs come to obtain. However, many optative dispositions produce conditional desires instead. For instance, suppose my favorite author writes two kinds of novels: detective stories, which I love, and romance novels, which I despise. Upon hearing that she has written a new book, I may form the desire to read it *if* it is a detective story.

How exactly do these conditional desires interact with the *desire-queue* and the PLANNING-INITIATOR initiator? Typically, the strength of a conditional desire is attenuated in proportion to the believed probability of its antecedent. For example, if I think it is unlikely that the new book is a detective story, I will not expend much effort pursuing it. This affects the position of the desire on the *desire-queue*. Conditionality also affects the retrieval of standing plans. Standing plans are retrieved on the basis of a match with the consequent of the conditional desire. Similarly, the PLAN-SYNTHESIZER formulates plans conditional on the supposition that the antecedent of the desire is satisfied. The PLAN-UPDATER should evaluate the expected values of the candidate plans using the strength of the conditional desire rather than the (estimated) strength the unconditional desire will have if the antecedent turns out to be true.

If the antecedent of a conditional desire is subsequently judged to be true, that will have an effect on any planning or queueing done with respect to the conditional desire. If the conditional desire is still on the *desire-queue*, it must be deleted and the unconditional desire inserted into the *desire-queue* instead. The expected values of any plans produced for the conditional satisfaction of the conditional desire will have to be re-evaluated in light of the (presumably) increased strength of the unconditional desire. This updating of plan evaluations will be a standard feature of the PLAN-UPDATER, which must be prepared to do such re-evaluation whenever relevant beliefs change.

Instead of discovering that the antecedent of the desire is true, we may discover that it is false. That should have the effect of cancelling all planning for the desire. The desire should be deleted from the *desire-queue* if it is still there, and if any planning for its conditional satisfaction has already occurred, that should be cancelled.

Maximizing Desires

Thus far I have been talking about desires to the effect that some specifiable state of affairs obtain. As was observed in chapter 6, a different kind of desire is for as much of something as possible. For instance, having spilled water on the kitchen floor shortly before I must leave for school, I may adopt the plan of mopping the floor until I must leave, with the goal of getting it as dry as I can in the time I have. Such a goal can be viewed as a state *type*, with a variable parameter. The strength of the desire for a state of this type is a function of the value of the parameter. Such a desire is not satisfied *simpliciter*. It is satisfied to a certain degree,6 or with a certain parameter value. Accordingly, the expected value of a plan aimed at the satisfaction of such a maximizing desire must be computed on the basis of a probability distribution of the values of the parameter.

For placement on the *desire-queue*, the maximum strength of the desire is used. For instance, in the case of the spilled water, what I "really would like" is to get the floor completely dry, so it is the strength of the desire for that optimal state that determines where it is placed on the *desire-queue*.[4]

Conditional Instrumental Desires

There are also some questions about instrumental desires that must be resolved. First, we must consider exactly what instrumental desires should be produced in response to the adoption of a plan. Two obvious possibilities suggest themselves. The first is that an agent should only form instrumental desires to execute nodes when they are called. When a plan is first adopted, only the initial nodes are called, so on this view, an agent should have instrumental desires to execute only the initial nodes. However, consideration of examples makes it apparent that this is not correct. For example, I may plan a business trip to LA. My plan may be to arrange with certain individuals to meet with them at a particular time; then after making those arrangements, to fly to LA in time for the meeting; and then to hold the meeting. If I do not form instrumental desires to execute nodes until the nodes are called, then I would not form the instrumental desire to fly to LA until I have completed the arrangements for the meeting. But in that case, I would not do any subsidiary planning for flying to LA until I have completed the arrangements. However, if I am confident that I can

---

[4] Having this kind of desire will make a difference to what problem the PLAN-SYNTHESIZER poses for the theoretical reasoner.

make the arrangements for the meeting, then I may well start planning for the flight before I have completed the arrangements and I may even begin executing my subsidiary plan. For instance, I may make my flight reservations. This seems clearly rational and indicates that the formation of instrumental desires should not wait until a node is called.

On the other hand, if a node is not yet called, and it is uncertain whether it will be called (e.g., it is on one execution path stemming from a conditional fork), then a rational individual does not automatically form the desire to execute it come what may. For instance, suppose once more that I want to buy paint on my way to the grocery store. There are two routes to the grocery store, and I plan to choose between them on the basis of how heavy the traffic is when I am driving. If I take one route, I will stop at *The Flaming Rainbow* to buy paint, and if I take the other route I will instead stop at *The Chartreuse Flamingo* to buy paint. Having adopted this plan, I do not form the instrumental desire to buy paint at *The Flaming Rainbow*. What I do is form the *conditional desire* to buy paint at *The Flaming Rainbow* if I go that way. This amounts to forming the desire to execute the plan-node *if it is called*. I suggest that this is true in general. When a plan is adopted, we form conditional instrumental desires to execute each plan-node if it is called. As the initial nodes are already called, we form unconditional instrumental desires to execute them. These conditional and unconditional instrumental desires are placed on the *desire-queue*, and when they are retrieved, they are passed to the PLAN-SYNTHESIZER for planning for their satisfaction. In the case of conditional desires, we plan for their conditional satisfaction, that is, we seek a plan for satisfying them if the antecedent turns out to be true. In general, the handling of conditional instrumental desires in planning is the same as the handling of conditional primitive desires.

Avoidance Desires

Georgeff [1987] notes that among our goals are sometimes *goals of maintenance*, that is, we desire to prevent certain things from changing. This is a special case of a more general kind of desire, which is a desire to avoid something. In the case of maintenance desires, we desire to avoid something's changing. More generally, we may want to avoid something's happening. A soldier moving through enemy territory may want to avoid being seen, a crook may want to avoid being caught, a driver may want to avoid becoming enmeshed in five o'clock traffic, a professor may want to avoid being assigned to university committees, and so forth. Such avoidance desires raise interesting problems for planning, because it is not clear that we actually plan for their satisfaction. It is often more accurate to say that we remain alert for situations in which the contra-desired states of affairs may happen and *then* engage in practical reasoning for their avoidance. For example, when the soldier who wants to avoid being seen comes to a clearing, he will at that point engage in practical reasoning about how to get around it without being seen. Similarly, when the driver who wants to avoid five o'clock traffic notes that it is getting close to five o'clock, she will at that point begin to think about how to avoid it (e.g., by leaving work early, by taking an alternate route, or by doing something else that does not require her to drive during the busy period).

On the other hand, we sometimes adopt plans aimed at the general avoidance of contra-desired states of affairs. A police officer who wants to avoid being shot may take to wearing a bulletproof vest at all times, and a driver who wants to avoid five o'clock traffic may adopt a general work schedule that allows her to leave for home at four o'clock. There seems to be nothing special about this kind of planning. It is just like the planning for the satisfaction of any other desire.

How then do we accommodate the kind of avoidance desires for which we do not adopt general plans but instead simply remain alert for the possible occurrences and then plan for their avoidance? We can fruitfully distinguish between individual desires and desire-types here. The police officer who wears a bulletproof vest is *trying to avoid ever getting shot*, and the driver who adjusts her work schedule is *trying to avoid driving in five o'clock traffic as much as possible*. The former is just an ordinary desire of the sort for which we plan all the time, and the latter is a maximizing desire. On the other hand, the soldier who wants to avoid being seen can be regarded as being subject to repeated desires not to be seen. This requires having some mechanism for producing in him repeated desires not to be seen whenever the circumstances are such as to suggest that he may be seen. The advantage of viewing the situation in this way is that it explains why he plans for the individual instances of the desire-type rather than adopting a general plan for the satisfaction of a single desire not to be seen ever or to be seen as infrequently as possible. However, to make this work we need an account of the mechanism that produces these repeated desires. I will now suggest that one such mechanism has to do with the structure of plans.

In constructing plans, we sometimes take note of the most obvious things that could go wrong, keep them in mind, and try to avoid their happening as we execute other plans. One way to do that is to build their avoidance into the plan, thus increasing its expected value and placing their avoidance on our list of desires. This is to treat their general avoidance as a single thing that we desire rather than as a *type* of thing that we desire. But I am inclined to think that we often proceed in another way. When we construct a plan, along with the various nodes we store information about possible causes of plan-misfire. Then when it is time to execute a node, we check to see whether the source of misfire is at all likely, and if it is, we form the desire to avoid it. The strength of the desire is presumably proportional to the probability of the contra-desired state of affairs occurring. An elegant way of achieving all of this within the OSCAR plan formalism is to build the *non-occurrence* of the contra-desired states of affairs into the plan-nodes as part of the specification of the operation prescribed by that node. It is important that what is being built in is the *non-occurrence* rather than the *avoidance* of the contra-desired states of affairs. The difference is that if we make *avoiding P* part of the specification of the operation, that requires us to *do something* to avoid P. If we merely include the non-occurrence of P as part of the operation and it is likely that P will not occur even if we take no active steps to avoid it, that is sufficient to make it likely that that part of the operation will be successfully performed and hence will allow the plan to have a high expected value without our automatically having to take action to avoid the contra-desired states of affairs. On the other hand, if at some point during the plan execution it becomes likely that P will occur, then the general mechanisms of planning initiation that are responsible for subsidiary planning will have the effect that a strong desire for the non-occurrence of P will go on the *desire-queue*, and the account of the PLAN-SYNTHESIZER given below will have the effect that we will engage in active planning for its avoidance.

Desire Strengths
Instrumental desires are conditional desires for the execution of plan-nodes if they are called. The mechanism that initiates subsidiary planning involves placing instrumental desires on the *desire-queue*. But there is a technical problem that must be solved in order to do this. The placement of desires on the *desire-queue* is a function of their strength, so if instrumental desires are going to be placed on the *desire-*

queue, they must have associated strengths. We need an account of how these strengths are determined. It seems clear that the strength of an instrumental desire should be related to the expected value of that plan from which it originates. The obvious proposal is to identify the strength of the desire with the expected value of the plan. There are complications, however. A single plan can aim at achieving several different goals, while a node of that plan may be involved in seeking only one of those goals. All of the goals will contribute jointly to the expected value of the plan, but goals unrelated to a node should not affect the strength of the instrumental desire for the execution of that node.

There are two ways in which a node of a plan may be unrelated to some of the goals at which the plan aims. First, note that if one plan aims at the satisfaction of a desire, so does its composite with any other plan. But we do not want the strength of a desire increased by the composition of the first plan with an unrelated plan. Second, a plan can aim at the achievement of several different goals sequentially. For example, we might have a plan to run several errands on a single trip. A node of this plan may be called only after the initial goals have already been achieved, so their values should not contribute to the strength of the desire to execute the remainder of the plan. Let us define the *tail* of a plan, *relative to one of its nodes*, to be the set of nodes that are descendants of that node. This subplan will make the node in question an initial node and will strip off all nodes calling that node (and their calling ancestors) except insofar as they are called by loops originating with the given node. The tail of a plan relative to a node is the smallest subplan containing that node essentially. Then the strength of the instrumental desire for the execution of a node should be equal to the expected value of the tail relative to that node.

The expected values of plans may have to be updated as we acquire new information. (This will be discussed further in section 6). As the strengths of instrumental desires are determined by the expected values of plans, these strengths may have to be updated as well and their positions on the *desire-queue* modified accordingly. This requires some mechanism for keeping track of the sources of the desire-strengths. That is not problematic, however, because the PLANNER must keep track of the sources of instrumental desires anyway in order to link the subsidiary plans that are produced for their satisfaction to the plans to which they are subsidiary.

6. The PLAN-SYNTHESIZER

Although the construction of plans is computationally difficult, the architecture of the PLAN-SYNTHESIZER need not be complex. In general outline, the operation of the PLAN-SYNTHESIZER is as follows. The PLAN-SYNTHESIZER is activated by the PLANNING-INITIATOR, which sends it the specification of a desire for whose satisfaction a teleological plan is required or for which scheduling is required. The function of the PLAN-SYNTHESIZER is then to arrange for the construction of such a plan and send it on to the PLAN-UPDATER. It does this by passing two tasks to epistemic cognition. The *teleological task* is the task of constructing a plan for the satisfaction of that desire which is minimally good.[5] (The concept of a minimally good plan will be given a technical definition in section 7. In the meantime it should be understood intuitively.) If the desire is an instrumental desire, the *scheduling task* is the task of looking for ways of improving the plan that generated the desire by inserting scheduling links and timing nodes. In both cases, the actual plan construction is carried out by epistemic cognition. It is important to realize that these are tasks of epistemic reasoning, and not tasks of practical reasoning. That a particular plan satisfies one of these specifications is an objective matter of fact. I will return to a discussion of this epistemic reasoning later, but for now, suppose epistemic cognition constructs such a plan. It is then passed to the PLAN-UPDATER, which decides whether to adopt it. If the PLAN-UPDATER adopts the plan, this fact is signaled to the PLAN-SYNTHESIZER, which adjusts its search for new plans in light of this.

To make this account more precise, consider how the PLAN-SYNTHESIZER passes its problem to epistemic cognition. Epistemic cognition is interest-driven. It has two kinds of interests: determining whether certain formulas are true ("whether" questions), and finding bindings for variables that make certain open formulas true ("which" questions). Interests are passed to epistemic cognition by putting them in the list of *ultimate-epistemic-interests*. The interests on this list are prioritized by assigning numerical degrees to them. These numerical degrees reflect the importance of the practical problems that give rise to the epistemic problems. As a first try, we might let the degree of interest be the same as the strength of the triggering desire. However,

---

[5] Instead of constructing a new plan from scratch, the construction of a plan for a new desire may involve modifying a previous plan so that it aims at satisfying the new desire as well as achieving its original goals.

this is inadequate in cases in which the triggering desire will almost certainly be satisfied without the agent's doing anything about it. If something is very likely to happen on its own, then even if we desire it, we probably could not construct a better plan for its satisfaction than the null plan. In such a case, we do not want to put a lot of effort into trying. This suggests that the strength of our epistemic interest should be the product of the strength of the triggering desire and our estimate of the probability of its not occurring on its own. This constitutes a general solution to the problem of assigning degrees to members of *ultimate-epistemic-interests*, because such interests always arise from practical problems. The operation of the epistemic reasoner is such that these practically motivated epistemic interests can give rise to further epistemic interests connected with them only indirectly, but at every point, when the epistemic reasoner becomes interested in a formula as a way of inferring another formula in which it is already interested, the degree of interest in the new formula is simply the maximum of the degrees of interest in all formulas from which interest in it is derived. Recall that these degrees of interest are used by the interest-driven reasoner to prioritize its reasoning. It pursues questions of greater interest first.

Degrees of justification are assigned to the conclusions drawn by the epistemic reasoner. One of the functions of degrees of justification is that the more important a question, the more justified a rational agent must be before it can confidently accept an answer to the question. Thus degrees of justification and degrees of interest go hand in hand.[6]

When the task set for epistemic cognition is that of finding variable-bindings that will satisfy an open formula, it is not automatically finished when it is adequately justified in believing it has found one such binding. There may be many, in fact infinitely many, and in general we may want epistemic cognition to go on searching. Applying this to the search for plans, suppose epistemic cognition concludes that a certain plan is a minimally good one for satisfying some desire. This conclusion is passed to the PLAN-UPDATER. Suppose the PLAN-UPDATER adopts the plan. It is natural to suppose that this should lead to a cancellation of the search for plans aimed at satisfying that desire.

---

[6] A useful interest rule is the following. If we have a reason for P, but it is not strong enough, adopt interest in the reason at the higher interest level. This will trickle back down the argument recursively and lead us to look for better reasons for the weak links in the arguments.

However, adopting a plan for the satisfaction of a desire should not make us totally oblivious to better plans if they come along. For example, suppose I need something at the grocery store, and the only way to get there is to walk, so despite the fact that it is raining, I adopt the plan to walk. Then a friend offers me a lift. I am, and should be, able to appreciate the fact that this enables me to construct a better plan for getting to the grocery store and making my purchase. However, if I had no interest at all in finding plans for getting to the grocery store, I would be unable to draw that conclusion. Adopting one plan for getting to the grocery store certainly relieves some of the urgency in looking for other plans, but it should not cancel interest in them altogether. What it must do is simply lower the degree of interest in finding such plans, thus making the search for such plans a matter of lower priority.

At this point it becomes useful to separate subsidiary teleological planning and scheduling and look at each by itself, because the differences between them become important.

Subsidiary Teleological Planning
If (1) a plan for the satisfaction of a desire were "perfect", in the sense that it is certain to result in the satisfaction of the desire without attenuating its value, (2) the probability of its successful execution were 1, and (3) its execution were costless, then there could never be a better plan, and so there would no reason to continue searching. But of course no plan can ever be perfect in this sense. As long as a plan is less than certain to succeed and has some execution cost, there is always the possibility of finding a better plan. The expected value of a perfect plan for satisfying a desire is simply the product of the strength of the desire and the estimated probability of the desire's not being satisfied without our doing anything. The expected value of a plan aimed at satisfying several desires is the sum of these products for the different desires. Let the *degree of imperfection* of a plan be the difference between this figure and its expected value. When the PLAN-UPDATER adopts a plan for the satisfaction of a desire or set of desires, the degree of interest that epistemic cognition should retain in finding additional plans for the satisfaction of that desire or set of desires should be determined by the degree of imperfection of the adopted plan. Notice, however, that the remaining interest should be changed to an interest in finding plans rationally preferable to the one already found.

Scheduling

Similar observations can be made about scheduling. However, we must be more careful than we have been in formulating the scheduling task the PLAN-SYNTHESIZER passes to epistemic cognition. Let us call the node from which an instrumental desire is derived its *parent node* and the plan of which it is a node its *parent plan*. As a first approximation, the scheduling task is that of adding scheduling links to the parent node (and possibly also timing nodes to which to connect the scheduling links) in such a way that the resulting plan is rationally preferable to the original parent plan. This account of the scheduling task is a bit simplistic, however. Scheduling usually consists of coordinating steps from different plans, in which case the scheduling links tie together steps from the different plans. In this case the objective should be to produce a composite plan rationally preferable to the union of the originally separate subplans.

Given this understanding of the scheduling task, suppose epistemic cognition produces such a composite plan and the PLAN-UPDATER adopts it. A rational agent will still be sensitive to the discovery of better ways of scheduling the node in question, so adopting this schedule should not result in a complete cancellation of interest in other schedules, but as in the case of subsidiary teleological planning, it should result in diminished interest in such schedules. This degree of interest should be determined by the degree of imperfection of the adopted schedule. It should also change our interest from scheduling the node to scheduling it in a way rationally preferable to the adopted plan.

Scheduling tends to be unstable, for two reasons. First, as time passes, an agent acquires new desires. For example, suppose I plan to sit at my desk writing all morning, but then I develop a craving for a cup of coffee. To accommodate this desire, I may change my plan and decide to get up and fix a cup of coffee as soon as I come to a convenient break in my work. This decision can also lead to reversing previous scheduling decisions. For instance, I might also have planned to make a phone call when I break for lunch, but it may occur to me that I can do that while I am waiting for the coffee to brew, and so I rearrange my schedule accordingly. It is to accommodate new desires that we leave schedules as indefinite as possible and do not choose arbitrarily between tied schedules.[7]

Another way in which scheduling tends to change over time is that it tends to get more precise as I acquire more information. For instance,

---

[7] See section 8.

in planning to paint my garage, I initially planned to buy paint sometime today. Then when I acquired the belief that I would be passing close to the paint store on the way to the grocery store, I planned more precisely to buy paint on my way to the grocery store. As the time for action approaches, we tend to learn more and more about what else will be happening, and we can use that information to refine our schedule.

Both of these kinds of changes will occur automatically as long as epistemic cognition retains interest in finding preferable schedules. When the information becomes available that makes it possible to construct preferable schedules, epistemic cognition will do so as long as it does not have to do more important reasoning that interferes.

The Architecture of the PLAN-SYNTHESIZER
This is all that needs to be said about the PLAN-SYNTHESIZER. Its architecture is basically simple. It is diagrammed in figure 4. This does not mean, however, that plan synthesis is simple. The hard part of plan synthesis lies in the work done by epistemic cognition when it searches for plans that aim at the satisfaction of a specified desire and are at least minimally good. This reasoning is very complex, and no automated reasoner currently in existence is able to do this kind of reasoning satisfactorily. The various planning algorithms of AI planning theory aim at producing such plans. Thus they are really aimed at a problem of epistemic reasoning, not one of practical reasoning. The limitations encountered by these planning algorithms are invariably tied to their inability to handle certain kinds of sophisticated epistemic reasoning.

Consider the kinds of epistemic reasoning required for plan synthesis. First, plans are sets of nodes, and nodes are probably best represented set-theoretically as well. The epistemic reasoner must be able to reason *about* plans, comparing them and drawing conclusions about them, and hence must be able to deal with them as objects. This suggests that it must at least be able to handle finite set theory. That is already a very difficult problem given the current state of automated reasoning. No extant automated reasoner can handle more than rather trivial bits of set theory. In addition, the reasoner must be able to assess the expected values of plans in order to determine whether they are minimally good and whether one is rationally preferable to another, and for that it must be able to reason about probabilities. That is also a formidable task. Finally, the reasoner must be able to reason about causal and temporal relations between events in the

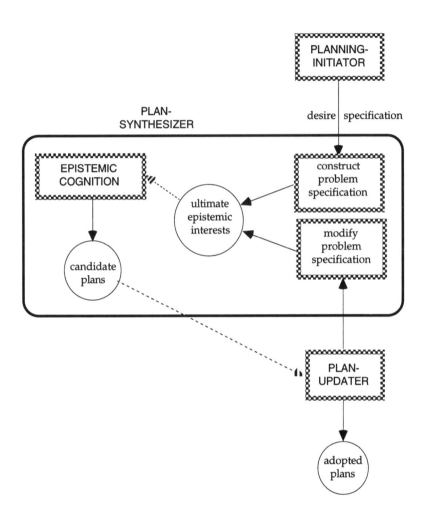

Figure 4. Architecture of the PLAN-SYNTHESIZER

physical world. There is a large literature in AI about such reasoning, most of it spawned by planning theory, but the problems involved in such reasoning are far from solved. It seems likely that much of the reasoning involved in plan synthesis is analogical, and explanation-based learning may play an important role. Of course, none of this should be surprising. Epistemic reasoning has no point in a rational agent other than to serve practical reasoning. Thus *all* of epistemic reasoning should be of at least indirect relevance to plan synthesis.[8]

The upshot is that the epistemic reasoning required by practical reasoning is probably much more complicated than the structure of the practical reasoning itself. My purpose here is to describe the architecture of the practical reasoner, and I have every expectation that can be done without solving all the problems of epistemic reasoning that are required to build a rational agent. Such epistemic reasoning will have to be the target of much more research.

It is noteworthy that many standard AI planning algorithms look more like Q&I modules than implementations of planning within a system of epistemic reasoning. It is unclear whether human beings employ Q&I modules for planning, but it is clear that such modules could be a useful addition to an artilect. In particular, incorporating such modules into an implementation of the architecture described here will allow a test of the architecture without first solving all of the problems of epistemic reasoning enumerated above.

7. The PLAN-UPDATER

Adopting Plans
The PLAN-UPDATER is responsible for the adoption and retraction of plans. The fundamental principles underlying plan adoption are those

---

[8] In deciding whether to perform an action or adopt a plan, we often consider hypothetically what would happen if we were to do it. There is an obvious limit to how much of this hypothetical reflection we can do, and there is no limit to how much of it there is to do. We "reflect" on it, imagining what would be likely to happen if we were to perform the act. (Note that this is a probability judgment.) We often overlook things when we do this. That is a common source of plan misfire. Some people are better than others at foreseeing consequences. The amount of reflection we perform is affected by how much time we have. If things are developing rapidly, we may not reflect at all, but just immediately execute a standing plan when its preconditions become satisfied.

For human beings, it is possible that dreaming and daydreaming play an important role in planning. They enable the agent to run through scenarios "off line", and consider what would be likely to happen if various actions were performed.

emerging from chapter 5. At that point I proposed the following rule of plan adoption provisionally:

(PA)   The decision to adopt a plan σ is practically justified iff a rationally satisfactory search for plans has been conducted and either:

(i)   for every plan μ discovered by the plan search, if we are justified in believing that μ competes with σ, then we are justified in believing that σ is preferable to μ; or

(ii)   (a) the plan search has led to the discovery of no plan that we are justified in believing to be rationally preferable to σ, and

         (b) σ has been chosen randomly from the set of all competing plans discovered by the search which are justifiably believed to be tied with σ.

Thus far, the discussion of the PLANNER has focused on the concept of a rationally satisfactory search and has tried to make certain aspects of that concept precise. In light of that account, let us reconsider the rule for choosing between the plans revealed by a rationally satisfactory search. We are now in a position to see that (PA) gives a misleading description of Buridan cases.

Buridan Cases

Buridan cases are those in which competing plans are tied. The basic observation about Buridan cases is that in deciding what actions to perform, a rational agent chooses at random between the tied plans. However, this is a remark only about the actions performed as a result of the planning, and not directly about the plans themselves. At some point a random choice must be made, but that could be either (1) a random choice between competing plans, resulting in one of the tied plans' being adopted at random, or (2) a random choice between the actions dictated by the tied plans, without either of the tied plans' ever being adopted in its own right. This is really a question about the control structure of the rational agent. At what point in the architecture is the random choice made? The simplest suggestion would be that a random choice between plans is made immediately upon producing the competing plans. However, it takes little reflection to see that, in human beings, things are more complicated than that. Returning to the example of painting my garage, a decision had to be made about where to buy the paint. Suppose there were two paint stores between which I could not initially decide. Eventually I decided on *The Flaming Rainbow*, because it was on my route to the grocery store. That decision made the plan to buy the paint there preferable to the plan to buy it at the other store. But what happened prior to my deciding to go to the grocery store? I did not initially decide at random to buy the paint at one of the stores, and then later change my mind because I had a better reason to buy it at the other store. What I did was decide to buy the paint *either* at *The Flaming Rainbow* or at *The Chartreuse Flamingo*, but I did not at that point decide arbitrarily to adopt one plan rather than the other. Instead, I stored the set consisting of the two competing plans and waited until I had some basis for choosing between them.

Consider another example. Suppose I am undecided whether to go to a movie tonight or stay home and watch TV. At this point I do not arbitrarily decide to adopt one of these plans rather than the other. I decide to do one or the other but leave open which I will do until either some new consideration gives me a reason to choose one or until I *have to* choose. In this example, when it comes time to get ready to go to the movie, I must make a choice, but there is no reason to make a choice before that, and a rational agent will not make a choice. That would amount to prematurely closing off options that could later turn out to be the best options.

If an agent has a set Σ of plans that are tied and between which it cannot decide, the rational decision is the disjunctive decision to execute *one* of these plans. Eventually the agent must decide between the plans, and if there is still no objective basis for doing so then the decision must be made at random. The time at which a decision must finally be made is the time at which one of the plans in Σ first requires something to be done. More accurately, it is the last time at which the when-condition of one of the initial nodes of one of the plans in Σ is satisfied in conjunction with the if-condition's having been satisfied. So in Buridan cases, the PLANNER must store sets of plans adopted disjunctively. These are stored as intentions, and in such cases our intentions are disjunctive. For instance, I may intend to either go to the movie or stay home and watch TV. In the general case, intentions encode disjunctively adopted sets of plans rather than individual plans. Later, when a choice is forced upon the agent, a plan chosen at random is adopted. But notice that this is done at execution time and not in advance. In other words, such random choices are made by the PLAN-EXECUTOR rather than the PLANNER.

The preceding remarks apply to teleological planning, but much the same is true of scheduling. Scheduling tends to be a matter of continually refining previous schedules as the agent acquires new information or adopts new plans to be fitted into the schedule. For example, in deciding when to buy the paint for my garage, I schedule the purchase more and more precisely as time passes. First, I planned (yesterday) to buy the paint today. Then I planned to buy it this afternoon. Then I planned to buy it on my way to the grocery store. In this way I generate increasingly precise schedules. But it is important to realize that I may never generate an absolutely precise schedule. As a consequence, at any given time it will typically be the case that nodes from many different plans have been called, their when-conditions are satisfied, and they are waiting to be executed by having their operations performed. For instance, I plan to call my travel agent sometime this afternoon to check on my car rental in New Zealand, I plan to start the barbecue grill pretty soon to fix dinner, I plan to run out to the mailbox and retrieve my mail before it gets dark, and so forth. All three of these plans have nodes that have been called and are awaiting execution. The when-conditions are sufficiently broad that I can successfully execute them any time during the next several hours. I *might* engage in further planning and refine my schedule for when to do them, but more likely a time will come when I just decide to do one of them, and then later I will decide to do another, and so on. These decisions are the work of the PLAN-EXECUTOR, not the PLANNER.

The fact that schedules are left flexible until we acquire a good reason for refining them in some way indicates that, like teleological planning, we do not choose arbitrarily between tied schedules until we have to. When we have several competing candidate schedules, we normally select one only if it is preferable to all the others. There is, however, one important difference between tied schedules and tied teleological plans. Usually, tied schedules differ only in their scheduling of some particular node (or nodes) within a continuous temporal interval. For example, I may have good reason to buy the paint between 2 P.M. and 3 P.M., but not have any reason to prefer one time in that interval to any other time. Rather than choosing randomly to buy the paint at some particular instant, I leave unspecified when exactly to buy the paint, deciding merely to buy it sometime between 2 P.M. and 3 P.M.. The times between 2 P.M. and 3 P.M. are preferable to other times, but tied among each other. In effect, I am undecided between infinitely many absolutely precise schedules, but I can represent that whole set of schedules with one imprecise schedule which can be adopted as a single plan rather than disjunctively adopting the infinite set of more precise plans. This will not always be the case, but it is frequently so. This is an important difference between tied schedules and tied teleological plans.

There are some examples in which, contrary to what I have just urged, we do seem to choose schedules at random. Suppose I must fly to either Boston or New York for a business meeting on a certain date (I can choose either city), and then whichever city I choose, I must fly to the other city for a business meeting a week later. There are two possible schedules here. It seems that if there is nothing to favor one schedule over the other, I will choose one at random. I do not leave the matter undecided until I get to the airport and then decide on the spur of the moment to fly to New York. However, this example is like the teleological example of deciding whether to go to the movie or stay home and watch TV. If nothing favors one destination rather than the other for my first trip, I do not decide on a destination until I have to. But eventually I will have to. I must buy my ticket and arrange the business meeting. So when one of the competing schedules mandates doing something, *then* I will have to decide randomly between the two schedules. Just as in the case of teleological planning, if there is nothing to favor the one schedule over the other, there is no reason to make up my mind beforehand. There is nothing irrational about leaving the schedule indeterminate until the last minute, deciding only when I finally have to take action. Once again, in order to act we must eventually make a random choice between competing schedules, or a random choice regarding when to act within the constraints of a single imprecise schedule, but that is no longer a matter of planning. That decision is made when it is time to act, so it is made by the PLAN-EXECUTOR rather than the PLANNER.

Perhaps in most cases the PLAN-SYNTHESIZER produces only a single adoptable plan, and so we adopt it outright. But what this discussion of Buridan cases shows is that sometimes the rational decision will be a disjunctive one deciding on a set of plans without deciding on a particular member of the set. This requires some small changes in the architecture of the PLANNER as it has so far been described. Specifically, the list of *adopted-plans* must either be replaced or augmented by a list of *disjunctively-adopted-plan-sets*. From a logical point of view, we need only the latter. Adopted plans can be identified with plan-sets having single members. But for computational reasons, it may be more convenient to keep these two lists separate, so I will take the *disjunctively-adopted-plan-sets* to include only plan-sets with multiple members, and when ties are resolved in Buridan cases I wil take the randomly chosen plan to be moved into the list of *adopted-plans*.

In Buridan cases, subsidiary planning cannot await a decision between the members of a disjunctively adopted plan-set, because that decision may not occur until it is time to act on the chosen plan. Thus each member of such a plan-set must generate new instrumental desires that are placed on the *desire-queue* and passed to the PLANNING-INITIATOR. I suggest that the strength of these instrumental desires should be attenuated in proportion to the number of plans in the plan-set, just as the desires corresponding to non-initial nodes are attenuated in proportion to the probability of their being called.

The preceding remarks apply only to Buridan cases, but it may seem that Buridan cases, in which plans are *exactly* tied, will be unusual. In human beings, they are not so unusual because our estimates of probabilities tend to be very inexact. As a result, plans are often tied *insofar as we can tell*. This suggests that even in agents producing more precise estimates, if plans are *almost* tied, it might be useful to treat them as a Buridan case simply because a slight bias in favor of one of them has a high probability of being reversed as we acquire more relevant information. This suggests treating them as tied until action must be taken, and then choosing the plan with the higher value. But I will not pursue this line of inquiry further at this time. It will be investigated during implementation.

Choosing Plans
The preceding understanding of Buridan cases forces us to take a second look at rule (PA). That rule has us randomly choosing between tied plans in Buridan cases. That is not so much incorrect as misleading. We make the random choice only when we have to start taking action on one of the plans if it is to be the one chosen for execution. We can clarify this by rewriting (PA) as a rule for "disjunctively adopting" sets of tied plans:

(PA*) The decision to disjunctively adopt a set of plans Σ is practically justified iff (1) if Σ has more than one member then any two members of Σ are justifiably believed to compete, (2) a rationally satisfactory search for plans has been conducted, and (3) either:
  (*i*) Σ has a single member σ, and for every plan μ discovered by the plan search, if we are justified in believing that μ competes with σ, then we are justified in believing that σ is preferable to μ (in this case, σ is adopted outright); or
  (*ii*) (*a*) Σ has more than one member,
          (*b*) the plan search has led to the discovery of no plan that

we are justified in believing to be rationally preferable to any member of Σ, and

(c) for every plan μ not in Σ, if μ is justifiably believed to compete with every member of Σ, then some member of Σ is justifiably believed to be preferable to μ.

On this account, adopting a plan σ amounts to disjunctively adopting its unit set $\{\sigma\}$. Notice that $(PA^*)(ii)(b)$ has the consequence that if a plan μ is known to compete pairwise with the members of Σ but we are in ignorance about how it compares (in terms of rational preferability) with the members of Σ, then μ is treated as if it is tied with them.

Rationally Satisfactory Searches
Rationally satisfactory searches for plans must be organized in certain ways in order for (PA^*) to work properly. Suppose the plan search produces the tied plans μ and σ, and so the agent disjunctively adopts the set $\{\mu,\sigma\}$. Then a new plan ν is produced, and it is tied with both μ and σ. At this point, (PA^*) has the consequence that the decision to disjunctively adopt $\{\mu,\sigma\}$ is no longer practically justified. That disjunctive adoption should be withdrawn and the agent should instead disjunctively adopt $\{\mu,\sigma,\nu\}$. This illustrates the rather obvious point that reasoning underlying plan adoption must be defeasible. But now suppose that instead of the new plan ν being tied with both μ and σ, ν is tied only with μ and does not compete with σ. (PA^*) has the consequence that, given only this information, the original set $\{\mu,\sigma\}$ should still be disjunctively adopted. That seems unreasonable. What should actually happen is that the agent should note that because ν does not compete with σ, a composite $\nu+\sigma$ is preferable to both μ and σ and should be adopted in their place. (PA^*) has precisely this consequence provided the plan search produces the composite $\nu+\sigma$. This indicates that a rationally satisfactory plan search must be organized in such a way that it systematically examines composites of plans already produced.

A bit more can be said about the nature of rationally satisfactory searches. Plan synthesis is a task of epistemic reasoning. Thus, that an agent has (up to the present time) behaved rationally in its search for candidate plans is a matter of epistemic rationality. What is the connection between the epistemic rationality of the search and the practical justification of adopting a plan produced by the search? Suppose that an agent has behaved rationally in its search for plans up to the present time. Does it follow that the agent is practically justified in adopting one of these plans if it judges that plan to be preferable to all of the competing plans it has discovered? It might be supposed that this is false on the grounds that a rationally adequate search must at least produce all of the "most obvious" candidate plans before the agent is justified in adopting the best candidate plan.

This qualification should be rejected. A crucial feature of reasoning is that it must be "interruptible". In general, there will always be more reasoning that could be done, but the agent may have to take action before it can do more reasoning. Rational thought must be such that when the agent has to act, it is reasonable to act on the basis of its current justified conclusions, even if there always remains the possibility of those conclusions' being retracted at a later time. This is an essential characteristic of justification, either epistemic or practical. Indeed, this is virtually a definition of justification—justified conclusions are those it is reasonable to act upon at the present time.

Defeasible Reasons for Plan Adoption
A noteworthy fact about human beings is that in many (perhaps most) cases of routine planning, no more than a single plan for achieving a particular goal is ever produced. We do not generate a large number of different candidate plans and then choose among them. We produce a single plan, and if it is "sufficiently good", we are willing to act upon it without engaging in further search. This is essentially Herbert Simon's [1977] observation that we often satisfice rather than maximize. One plan that is always available to us is the null plan, which has an expected value of zero. For any other plan to be such that it is reasonable to act upon it, the agent must reasonably believe that it is better than null plan, that is, that it has a positive expected value. Let us take this to be our official definition of a plan's being *minimally good*. My suggestion is that if, at the time an agent must act, only a single new plan has been uncovered, and to the best of the agent's knowledge it does not compete with any of the previously adopted plans, then it is reasonable to act upon that plan iff the agent justifiably believes that it is a minimally good plan. This suggests in turn that as soon as a plan is discovered and evaluated as minimally good, it becomes defeasibly reasonable to adopt that plan. This practical decision must be defeasible, however, because if another plan is subsequently produced and judged

to be preferable to the first, then the adoption of the first plan should be retracted and the new plan adopted in its place.[9]

Given the right structure for rationally satisfactory searches, the following principle captures the preceding observations and can be regarded as a corollary of (PA*):

(P1) $\ulcorner \sigma$ is a minimally good plan$\urcorner$ is a defeasible reason for adopting σ.

Principle (P1) formulates only a defeasible reason for adopting σ. To get a grasp of what the defeaters for (P1) should be, suppose the plan search produces a new candidate plan σ, and the agent must decide whether to adopt it. There are four possibilities: (a) the agent might simply adopt σ; (b) the agent might adopt σ while retracting the adoption of some previously adopted plans or disjunctive set of plans to which σ is rationally preferable; (c) the agent might decline to adopt σ on the grounds that it competes with another plan that is rationally preferable to it; (d) the agent might incorporate σ into a disjunctive set of tied plans and disjunctively adopt the set.

In deciding whether to adopt σ, the agent should first check to see whether σ is minimally good. If it is, then the agent has a defeasible reason for adopting it. If the agent is unaware of any conflicts with previously adopted plans, then σ should be adopted. In other words, the agent is in situation (a). But if the agent notes that a plan α that competes with σ has also been adopted, the agent must investigate whether σ is preferable to α. If σ is judged to be preferable to α, then the agent has a defeasible reason for adopting σ and retracting α. This is situation (b). If the agent judges α to be preferable to σ, then it should decline to adopt σ but retain α. This is situation (c). Situations (b) and (c) could be handled with the help of a single defeater for (P1):

$\ulcorner \alpha$ is justifiably believed to be rationally preferable to $\sigma \urcorner$ is a defeater for (P1).

However, this defeater need not be adopted as a separate principle because it is a consequence of a more general defeater that is needed to handle situation (d):

(P2) $\ulcorner \alpha$ is justifiably believed to compete with σ and σ is not justifiably believed to be preferable to $\alpha \urcorner$ is a defeater for (P1).

---

[9] Simon's official definition of satisficing [1977, 173] does not incorporate defeasibility.

When applied to the case of ties, (P2) defeats the adoption of the individual members of the tied plan-sets. In this case, we need a principle supplementing (P1) that governs disjunctive adoption:

(P3) $\ulcorner \alpha_1,...,\alpha_n$ are justifiably believed to compete pairwise, each is justifiably believed to be minimally good, and none is justifiably believed to be preferable to another $\urcorner$ is a prima facie reason for disjunctively adopting $\{\alpha_1,...,\alpha_n\}$.

Note that (P1) is a special case of (P3). Furthermore, the defeater formulated by (P2) should also be a defeater for (P3):

(P4) $\ulcorner \alpha$ is justifiably believed to compete with each of $\alpha_1,...,\alpha_n$ and no α_i is justifiably believed to be preferable to $\alpha \urcorner$ is a defeater for (P3).

Reasoning with principles (P1)–(P4) should lead to the same disjunctive adoptions as reasoning with principle (PA*).

In light of these rules, plan adoption can occur in two ways. The most straightforward occurs when new plans are produced by the PLAN-SYNTHESIZER and put into the set of *candidate-plans*. These are produced either in response to epistemic interest in plans that are aimed at satisfying a specified desire and are minimally good, or in response to epistemic interest in a plan aimed at satisfying that desire and preferable to some already adopted plan that is aimed at the satisfaction of that desire and is minimally good. When epistemic cognition produces a plan and puts it on the list of *candidate-plans*, it also produces a belief to the effect that the plan in question is either minimally good or preferable to other plans aimed at satisfying the same desire. This provides a defeasible reason for adopting the new plan, in accordance with (P1), and a reason for retracting any plans to which it is rationally preferable, in accordance with (P2).

A second way in which plan adoption can occur is when an already adopted plan μ is retracted. When that happens, the PLAN-UPDATER signals the PLAN-SYNTHESIZER to reinitiate planning, which happens by interesting epistemic cognition in finding an appropriate plan. It may turn out, however, that an appropriate plan σ has already been constructed. σ may have been constructed but not adopted because μ was judged preferable, but if that latter judgment is subsequently retracted, then σ may be adopted after all. The logical mechanics of this consist of first having a defeasible reason of the form of (P1) for adopting σ but also having a defeater of the form of (P2). When μ is retracted, the defeater is retracted, thus reinstating the reason for adopting σ, and so the latter is adopted.

Two kinds of considerations can lead to the retraction of plans. Just as in the case of epistemic reasoning, plans are retracted as a result of either retracting their bases (this consists of either retracting beliefs or retracting desires) or acquiring a defeater for the defeasible basis upon which they were adopted. The latter proceeds in terms of (P2) or (P4).

8. An Architecture for Planning

It is useful to combine our conclusions about the architecture of plan-based practical reasoning into a single diagram. This is done in figure 5. To get an overview of the theory, consider the dynamics of planning and plan adoption that results from this architecture. The basic idea is that the rational agent is looking for minimally good plans, and it keeps its eyes open for better plans without devoting too much cognitive effort to finding them. Because planning is hierarchical, plans can be adopted without working out all of the details. Plans are adopted on the basis of judgements about their expected values, so the adoption of partial plans requires the agent to employ general information about the likelihood of being able to perform non-basic operations and the expected execution costs and consequences of such performances. The reasoning involved in adopting a partial plan on this basis proceeds by direct inference.

Many of the complications of practical deliberation arise from discovering conflicts among plans. Epistemic cognition must have some interest in discovering such conflicts but not an overwhelming interest that would occupy all of its time. In the "doxastic" implementation described in the next section, this is handled by the same mechanism that leads the epistemic reasoner to become interested in defeaters for its defeasible reasoning. Again, epistemic cognition must have some interest in finding defeaters but not so strong an interest that it spends all of its time looking for defeaters.

Conflicts among plans can arise from either scheduling problems or interactions that change the expected value of a plan from that estimated by the initial direct inference. When such conflicts are found and lead to the plan's no longer being judged minimally good, the defeasible epistemic reasoner will automatically reopen interest in

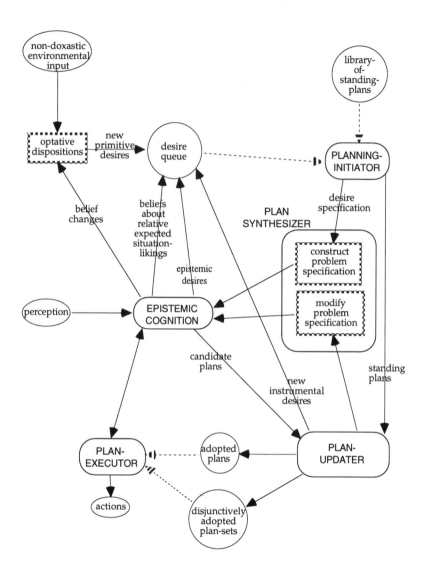

Figure 5. Architecture for plan-based practical reasoning

finding a minimally good plan for achieving the goals of the original plan. This will often lead to repairs in the original plan rather than replanning from scratch. In hierarchical planning, this will be automatic if the discovered conflict concerns only subsidiary plans and does not lead the agent to retract the belief that the higher-order plan is minimally good. In that case, only the subsidiary plan needs to be replaced, which amounts to saying that the overall plan is "repaired" rather than replaced. Of course, the conclusion that a subsidiary plan is not minimally good can also lead to a reassessment of the expected value of the higher-order plan and will sometimes lead to its rejection as well.

It was noted above that scheduling tends to be unstable, in two ways. First, as time passes, we tend to acquire new information that allows us to refine schedules. The new information breaks ties, leading to the adoption of more precise schedules that are preferable to the original ones. But scheduling is also unstable in another respect. The acquisition of new information often leads us to retract earlier scheduling decisions and adopt different schedules. Just as in the case of teleological planning, the agent retains an interest in finding better schedules, and when it finds one, that defeats the adoption of the earlier schedule. But if new information later changes the evaluation of the refined schedule in such a way that it is no longer judged preferable to the earlier schedule, the PLAN-UPDATER will automatically withdraw the refined schedule from the list of *adopted-plans* and reinstate the original schedule. It may then be moved to refine the original schedule in a different way.

9. The Doxastification of Planning

Plan Updating

For two different reasons, practical reasoning is defeasible. First, practical decisions are based upon beliefs supplied by epistemic cognition. If those beliefs are retracted, the practical decisions based upon them must also be retracted. Second, plan adoption proceeds in accordance with principles (P1)–(P4) of section 7, and those are themselves principles of defeasible practical reasoning. Defeasibility introduces an important complication into the theory of practical rationality. It is insufficient to state just the defeasible reasons and defeaters for practical reasoning. We must also describe the structure of the reasoning itself. This is no simple task. We have already seen how complex defeasible epistemic reasoning is. Defeasible practical reasoning promises to be equally complex. Must we construct an entire inference engine for defeasible practical reasoning? Reflection on human thought suggests an intriguing way of handling this. Rather than requiring separate computational modules for defeasible epistemic reasoning and defeasible practical reasoning, human cognition makes do with a single module dedicated to epistemic reasoning and then integrates practical reasoning into that module using a technical trick. The trick involves "doxastifying" normative judgments. Corresponding to the adoption of a plan is the "epistemic judgment" (that is, belief) that *it should be an adopted plan*. This judgment is epistemic in name only. It requires no "objective fact" to anchor it or give it truth conditions. It is merely a computational device whose sole purpose is to allow us to use defeasible epistemic reasoning to accomplish defeasible practical reasoning. Let us abbreviate $\ulcorner \sigma$ should be an adopted plan$\urcorner$ (where this is a practical "should", not a moral "should") as $\ulcorner \sigma$ is *adoptable*$\urcorner$. Similarly, let us say that a set of plans is *disjunctively-adoptable* iff it should be disjunctively adopted. A plan is adoptable iff its unit set is disjunctively-adoptable. Then principles (P1)–(P4) can be rewritten as rules for epistemic reasoning about plans being adoptable and sets of plans being disjunctively-adoptable. Recall that (P1)–(P4) are as follows:

(P1) $\ulcorner \sigma$ is a minimally good plan$\urcorner$ is a defeasible reason for adopting σ.

(P2) $\ulcorner \alpha$ is justifiably believed to compete with σ and σ is not justifiably believed to be preferable to α $\urcorner$ is a defeater for (P1).

(P3) $\ulcorner \alpha_1,...,\alpha_n$ are justifiably believed to compete pairwise, each is justifiably believed to be minimally good, and none is justifiably believed to be preferable to another $\urcorner$ is a prima facie reason for disjunctively adopting $\{\alpha_1,...,\alpha_n\}$.

(P4) $\ulcorner \alpha$ is justifiably believed to compete with each of $\alpha_1,...,\alpha_n$ and no α_i is justifiably believed to be preferable to α $\urcorner$ is a defeater for (P3).

Now consider the following array of epistemic prima facie reasons and defeaters:

(E1) $\ulcorner \sigma$ is a minimally good plan$\urcorner$ is a defeasible reason for $\ulcorner \sigma$ is adoptable $\urcorner$.

(E2a) $\ulcorner \alpha$ competes with σ and α is minimally good $\urcorner$ is a defeasible undercutting defeater for (E1).

(E2b) $\ulcorner \sigma$ is preferable to $\alpha \urcorner$ is a conclusive undercutting defeater for (E2a).

(E3) $\ulcorner \alpha_1,...,\alpha_n$ compete pairwise and each is minimally good $\urcorner$ is a prima facie reason for $\ulcorner \{\alpha_1,...,\alpha_n\}$ is disjunctively-adoptable $\urcorner$.

(E4a) $\ulcorner$ One of $\alpha_1,...,\alpha_n$ preferable to another $\urcorner$ is a conclusive undercutting defeater for (E3).

(E4b) $\ulcorner \alpha$ is minimally good and competes with each of $\alpha_1,...,\alpha_n \urcorner$ is a defeasible undercutting defeater for (E3).

(E4c) $\ulcorner$ some α_i is preferable to $\alpha \urcorner$ is a conclusive undercutting defeater for (E4b).

With this array of prima facie reasons and defeaters, the epistemic reasoner will conclude that a plan is adoptable iff a properly constructed defeasible practical reasoner would adopt the plan, and it will conclude that a set of plans is disjunctively-adoptable iff a properly constructed defeasible practical reasoner would disjunctively adopt the set of plans.[10] To illustrate, suppose we have a prima facie reason of the form (P1) for adopting σ, but we also have a defeater of the form (P2). Then we will have a prima facie reason of the form (E1) for concluding that σ is adoptable, and a defeater of the form (E2a) for this prima facie reason, and we will lack a defeater-defeater of the form (E2b). The upshot is that the same practical reasoning can be accomplished by coupling the defeasible epistemic reasoner with a much simpler practical reasoner that adopts or retracts plans on the basis of epistemic judgments to the effect that they are or are not adoptable.

It is important to realize that the terms "adoptable" (or "should be adopted") and "disjunctively-adoptable" are not given definitions in

---

[10] The defeasible theoretical reasoner works by adopting interest in defeaters whenever it makes a defeasible inference. Preference between plans results from relations between composites of subplans of those plans. For rules (E1)-(E4c) to work properly, the reasoner must consider those composite plans that generate preference relations and consider whether they should be adopted in place of the plans that are first proposed. This examination of composite plans must be built into the interest rules governing the evaluation of plans.

this account. They are just placeholders in epistemic reasoning. Their purpose is to give the reasoning the right structure to implement the planning architecture. I will refer to this reduction of defeasible practical reasoning to defeasible epistemic reasoning as *the doxastification of practical reasoning*, because it reduces defeasible practical reasoning to epistemic reasoning about beliefs. This turns out to be immensely important for the structure of practical reasoning and may be one of the most important ideas in the theory of rationality propounded in this book.[11]

The doxastification of practical reasoning has the result that most of the work of plan updating is done by the epistemic reasoner rather than by the PLAN-UPDATER itself. Doxastification is an extremely powerful device, and it has the consequence that the PLAN-UPDATER can be quite simple. The PLAN-SYNTHESIZER poses questions for epistemic cognition regarding the adoptability of plans satisfying certain constraints, and then epistemic cognition goes its merry way. In particular, it will adopt, and sometimes withdraw, beliefs to the effect that various plans are adoptable. All the PLAN-UPDATER must do is respond to *changes* in beliefs of the form ⌜σ is adoptable⌝. When such a belief is adopted, the PLAN-UPDATER adopts σ, and when such a belief is withdrawn, the PLAN-UPDATER retracts the adoption of σ. It was observed earlier that when the adoption of a plan is retracted, this must reinitiate planning for the satisfaction of the desires the retracted plan aimed at satisfying. But this is now automatic. Whenever the epistemic reasoner retracts a belief in which it was originally interested, that has the effect of re-awakening interest in it. Similarly, if the epistemic reasoner is looking for a variable binding that satisfies a certain formula, and it acquires an appropriate belief (a belief in an instance of the formula), then if it subsequently retracts that belief, that will automatically lead it to reopen the search for variable bindings. That latter is what is involved in the search for plans, so the search for plans will automatically be reopened without any new instructions having to be passed to the epistemic reasoner.

---

[11] I conjecture that something similar may be true of moral judgments. Presumably morality arises only in a "community of rational agents". However that goes, moral judgments are going to be analogous to practical judgments in affecting agents' behavior, and like any other complex reasoning, moral reasoning must be defeasible. The "doxastifying" of moral reasoning could be nothing but a computational device to enable us to employ the defeasible theoretical reasoner in moral reasoning, without having to build an entirely new inference engine for that purpose.

Adopting Standing Plans

Thus far I have discussed only explicit planning, where epistemic cognition constructs the plan in response to the PLAN-SYNTHESIZER's initiating a plan search. But the PLAN-UPDATER must also handle the case in which the plan search is short-circuited by the retrieval of a standing plan. In that case, the PLAN-SYNTHESIZER forwards the standing plan to the PLAN-UPDATER, where it must be decided whether the standing plan should be adopted. If the standing plan is adopted, that is the end of the matter (although the reasoning here is defeasible, so the standing plan might later be retracted), but if the standing plan is not adopted, then the PLAN-SYNTHESIZER must initiate a plan search. How does the PLAN-UPDATER decide whether to adopt a standing plan?

If standing plans are to serve as defaults, there must be some kind of prima facie reason for adopting an instance of a standing plan when it is retrieved. This prima facie reason for adopting instances of standing plans need not be postulated as a new primitive rule for practical reasoning. It can instead be derived from the rules already enumerated. This can be accomplished by noting that the account of standing plans as defaults must be augmented with an account of the conditions under which it is rational to adopt a plan schema as a standing plan. An obvious proposal is that this is based upon the belief that plans of this form will usually be minimally good plans. This automatically gives us a prima facie reason (in the form of the statistical syllogism) for thinking that a particular instance of the plan schema is a minimally good plan. Rule (E1) then gives us a prima facie reason for concluding that the instance of the plan schema is adoptable. This proposal also clarifies how standing plans can be overridden. They will automatically be overridden if, in a particular case, the agent has reason to believe that the instantiation of the standing plan is not a minimally good plan after all, or the agent has another plan that is believed to be preferable.

The preceding seems unproblematic for weak default standing plans, but there are interesting problems involved in incorporating strong default standing plans into this picture. If we cannot retrieve strong default standing plans for epistemic inspection, how can we decide that a particular instance of a standing plan is not a minimally good plan, and how can we compare it with possibly competing plans to see whether it should be overridden? Consider a concrete example. Most adult human beings know how to walk down a sidewalk. They have a compiled-in standing plan for this operation and use it without further thought under most circumstances. However, faced with a ledge jutting out from a cliff and a thousand-foot drop on one side, even if the ledge is as wide and flat as a sidewalk, most people will proceed very cautiously and think about every step. This is reasonable, because although one is no more likely to fall off the ledge than to fall off the sidewalk, the results of a fall would be much more serious and hence the plan that was a minimally good one for walking along the sidewalk may not be a minimally good one for walking along the ledge. That is, when applied to the ledge, even though the probability of falling is very low, the results of falling are so serious that the plan may have a negative expected value. To accommodate such reasoning in a rational agent, the agent must have some information about the probabilities of various outcomes of attempts to execute standing plans. This information must be stored with the plans and retrieved by PLAN-UPDATER, which uses it in deciding whether to adopt the standing plan. This information could be stored either in the form of beliefs or in a more encapsulated form that would be accessible only for a background computation of expected value (one not carried out by explicit reasoning). The doxastification of practical reasoning suggests that this information must be stored in the form of beliefs, but the possibility remains that it is stored both ways in order to facilitate efficient computation, because calculation carried out by explicit reasoning is comparatively slow.

The probability beliefs that make standing plans defeasibly reasonable pertain to the probabilities of outcomes resulting from the execution of the standing plan under very general circumstances. There may be features of the present circumstances that alter those probabilities. For example, I have a standing plan for walking down a sidewalk, and stored with that plan is the information that the probability of its successful execution is extremely high. That makes it defeasibly reasonable for me to adopt that standing plan if I want to get to the other end of the sidewalk. But in extraordinary circumstances, this defeasible reason may be defeated. For example, suppose I am a soldier under enemy fire, and I would be fully exposed if I walked down the sidewalk, but there is a low wall bordering it so that I could crawl down the sidewalk with impunity. Then a rational agent will elect to crawl rather than walk. This is because I have specific information about the current situation that leads to a different probability estimate from the general one stored with the standing plan. This leads to a different assessment of the expected value of the standing plan, and in this case the conclusion is that it is not a minimally good plan.

The natural way to handle this reasoning is in terms of epistemic reasoning involving direct inference. The stored probability is an indefinite probability conditional upon very general circumstances. It supports a direct inference to the conclusion that the probability of the plan's being successfully executed is high. But our more specific information about the enemy fire includes beliefs about the indefinite probability of successfully executing the plan under more specific circumstances, and we believe that those circumstances actually obtain. Accordingly, this probability takes precedence, defeating the direct inference from the more general probability and supporting instead a direct inference to the conclusion that the plan is not likely to be successfully executed.

This reasoning is straightforward provided the relevant probabilities are all encoded in beliefs. Given that the rational agent possesses all of these beliefs, the reasoning underlying the adoption or rejection of the standing plan can proceed in terms of principles (E1)–(E4c). No new principles are required to enable epistemic cognition to make all of the requisite judgments.

A Doxastic Implementation

The doxastification of plan adoption has implications for the rest of the planning architecture. The lists of *adopted-plans* and *disjunctively-adopted-plan-sets* are encoded as beliefs about adoptability and disjunctive-adoptability. For the rest of the PLANNER to make use of these beliefs, it must either respond to the beliefs directly or use the beliefs to construct the associated lists and then perform computations on the lists. Reflection upon the latter alternative indicates that it would introduce serious complications into the architecture, because if the adoptability-beliefs are subsequently withdrawn, the lists must be adjusted accordingly, and computations based upon them must also be adjusted. In other words, the rest of the practical reasoner must also operate defeasibly. This suggests a thorough-going doxastification of the entire architecture. The trick to achieving this consists of making use of the full structure of *ultimate-epistemic-interests*.

First, I have talked about practical cognition sending queries to epistemic cognition by placing the queries in *ultimate-epistemic-interests*, but that need not be the only source of ultimate epistemic interests. It is compatible with the architecture for there to be a list of *permanent-ultimate-epistemic-interests* that are in *ultimate-epistemic-interests* from the start, without having to be placed there by practical cognition. Second, recall that an ultimate epistemic interest encodes a query, together with a degree of interest and an instruction for what to do with an answer. The latter instruction can be of any kind. In particular, it can tell the reasoner to insert another query into *ultimate-epistemic-interests*. With these observations, suppose we supply epistemic cognition with the following *permanent-ultimate-epistemic-interests* and supplement (E1)–(E4c) with the following prima facie reasons and defeaters:

permanent-ultimate-epistemic-interests:
(U1)   Find a w such that w is a suitable goal.
       When the belief that w is a suitable goal is produced:
            insert ⌜find an x such that x is a minimally good plan for achieving w⌝ into *ultimate-epistemic-interests*.
(U2)   Find an x such that x is an adoptable plan.
       When this belief is acquired:
            insert ⌜find a y such that y is a plan for achieving the same goals as x and y is rationally preferable to x⌝ into *ultimate-epistemic-interests*.
(U3)   Find an x such that x is a disjunctively-adoptable plan-set.
       When the belief that x is a disjunctively-adoptable plan-set is produced, for each initial node z of a member of x:
            insert ⌜z's if-condition was satisfied when z was first called, and its when-condition is satisfied but soon to become un-satisfiable⌝ into *ultimate-epistemic-interests*.
       When this belief is acquired, choose some x in y at random, and have introspection supply the belief that x was randomly chosen for adoption.

forwards directed prima facie reasons:
(E5)   Desiring w is a prima facie reason for believing ⌜w is a suitable goal⌝.
(E6)   ⌜x is an adoptable plan and w is a situation-type consisting of executing a non-basic node of x if it is called⌝ is a prima facie reason for ⌜w is a suitable goal⌝. (A non-basic node is one whose operation is not a basic act.)

forwards directed conclusive reasons:
(E7)   ⌜w is a situation-type having positive relative expected situation-liking⌝ is a conclusive reason for ⌜w is a suitable goal⌝.
(E8)   ⌜y is a disjunctively-adoptable plan-set, and x was chosen randomly from the members of y⌝ is a conclusive reason for ⌜x is an adoptable plan⌝.

backwards directed conclusive reasons:

(E9) $\ulcorner x$ is a situation-type having a non-positive relative expected situation-liking $\urcorner$ is a conclusive reason for $\ulcorner x$ is not a suitable goal $\urcorner$.

(E10) $\ulcorner x$ is a situation-type having a non-positive relative expected situation-liking $\urcorner$ is a conclusive undercutting defeater for (E5).

These will combine to give us the reasoning diagrammed in figure 6. The arrows of the form "▪▪▪▪▪(||)▪·" signify that finding an instance of one member of *ultimate-epistemic-interests* leads to the insertion of a new query. My claim is that this constitutes a doxastic implementation of the planning architecture diagrammed in figure 5.

To see how this works, let us step through the operation of a reasoner supplied with these *permanent-ultimate-epistemic-interests* and reasons. The reasoner begins with a permanent interest in finding suitable goals. "Suitable goal" is now treated as an undefined place-holder, just like "adoptable plan" or "disjunctively-adoptable plan-set". It is a paraphrase of "goal that should (from a practical point of view) be adopted". The reasoner has three ways of finding suitable goals. If optative dispositions produce the desire for w, by (E5), this constitutes a prima facie reason for concluding that w is a suitable goal. This corresponds, in figure 5, to sending the desire to the PLANNING- INITIATOR provisionally but querying epistemic cognition about whether w is a situation-type having positive relative expected situation-liking. The latter query is now automatic, because the defeasible epistemic reasoner always adopts interest in defeaters for its inferences, and (E10) formu-lates a defeater for (E5). (E7) formulates the "direct epistemic reason" for adopting goals. I will discuss (E6) below.

Once the reasoner concludes that w is a suitable goal, in accordance with (U1), it sends an interest in finding minimally good plans for achieving w to *ultimate-epistemic-interests*. This leads to the epistemic reasoning that constitutes plan synthesis. The reasoning leading to the search for plans will be prioritized by epistemic cognition according to the degree of interest attached to finding the plan, and that will be determined by the importance of the goal. This prioritization im-plements the prioritizing of the *desire-queue* in figure 5.

When the reasoner draws the conclusion that a plan is minimally good, this leads, via (E1) or (E3), to the conclusion that it is adoptable or a member of a disjunctively-adoptable plan-set. In the latter case, in accordance with (U3), a query is sent to *ultimate-epistemic-interests*

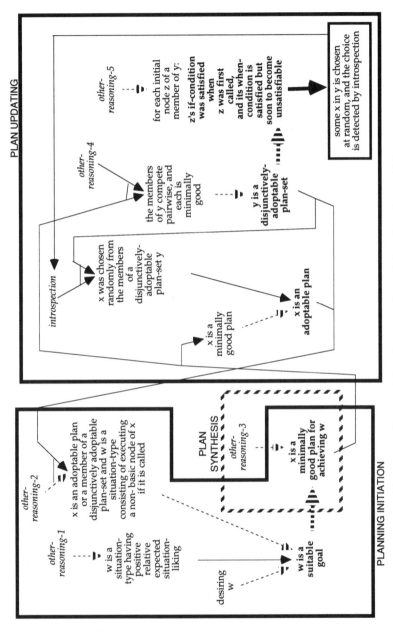

Figure 6. Doxastic implementation of the planning architecture

leading the reasoner to attend to the conditions under which a choice must be made between the members of the plan-set. When the reasoner concludes that a choice must be made, that is done and the information that it was done is supplied via introspection (still in accordance with (U3)) and constitutes a reason (by (E8)) for concluding that the randomly selected plan is adoptable.

When it is concluded that a plan is adoptable, (E6) provides a reason for thinking that executing its nodes if they are called constitutes a suitable goal. This corresponds to the production of instrumental desires in figure 5.

The upshot is that the apparently complex dynamics of plan adoption and modification, and of scheduling, need not be handled in an ad hoc way in a rational agent in which practical reasoning is doxastified. These complex dynamics result in a natural way from the functioning of defeasible epistemic reasoning and its employment in the practical reasoner. Note, however, that a good deal of the reasoning required is left unspecified in figure 6. The reasoning included in *other-reasoning-1* concerns the computation of expected situation-likings. *Other-reasoning-2*, *other-reasoning-4*, and *other-reasoning-5* are reasoning about the structure of plans. *Other-reasoning-3* is the hardest reasoning. This is the reasoning involved in finding plans. As indicated in section six, this reasoning will be of the same general sort that is involved in constructive existence proofs in mathematics. Enabling the epistemic reasoner to perform such reasoning is a difficult task, but not one unique to planning.

An obvious consequence of doxastification of planning is that the PLAN-EXECUTOR must also be doxastified, because it must direct action in terms of defeasible plan-adoptability beliefs. That will be discussed in the next chapter.

Chapter 8
Acting

1. Reactive Agents and Planning Agents

In a rational agent, most acting is the result of plan execution. The PLAN-EXECUTOR is the module that executes plans. One of the principal goals of this chapter is to describe the architecture of the PLAN-EXECUTOR. However, this by itself would not be a complete picture. It was observed in chapter 1 that optative dispositions produce two kinds of desires: desires for the future and desires for the present. Only the former can be the subject of planning. The agent cannot plan for the present. Planning takes time, and it is impossible to plan ahead for a situation that is already here. Desires for the present are typically, but not always, desires *to do* something. Those that are not can play no role in directing action (e.g., I hope that my daughter is home safely by now, but if she isn't, there is nothing I can do about it).

As described in chapter 1, a *reactive agent* would guide its actions solely on the basis of its desires for present action (what I called "present-tense action desires"). For example, in response to a pain in its hand, it would form the desire to withdraw its hand, and it would do so forthwith. Present-tense action desires can compete. A reactive agent might have several present-tense action desires, only one of which can be satisfied. In such a case, the best the reactive agent can do is act on the desire that is strongest, that is, do what it most wants to do.[1]

An agent capable of planning can do better. One way to build a planning agent is to give it the ability to predict what its present-tense desires are going to be and plan ahead for their satisfaction. Alternatively (or in addition), a planning agent can have dispositions to form desires for the future and then plan for their satisfaction. Ideally, desires for the future should satisfy a coherence condition: the agent now desires X for future time t iff at t the agent will then have a present-tense desire for X. Desires for the future need no longer be desires to do something. They can be desires for arbitrary states of affairs to obtain. Either of these mechanisms gives a point to present-

---

[1] An interesting implementation of reactive agents can be found in Agre and Chapman [1987].

tense desires that are not desires to do something, because the agent can plan ahead for them before they come into existence. The coherence condition just formulated is too strong to be perfectly implementable, because what is desired for a future time can change unpredictably as time passes, both as a result of acquiring additional information and as a result of changes in character. But at least the coherence condition should hold most of the time. Otherwise planning is not going to be an improvement over reacting.

Planning can supplement but not replace reacting to present-tense action desires. Agents will still be subject to some unpredictable present-tense action desires and those cannot be handled by planning. So in designing a rational agent, we must, in effect, begin with a reactive agent and then incorporate planning on top of that. To see how these two sources of action initiation are integrated, we must first understand how plan execution works. That is the topic of the next section.

2. The PLAN-EXECUTOR

The PLAN-EXECUTOR is the module that executes plans. It will proceed roughly as follows:

(1)   Call initial nodes and execute them.
(2)   Recursively execute nodes called by nodes that have already been executed.

Several complications must be addressed. First, the epistemic reasoning presupposed by plan execution is defeasible, and the PLAN-EXECUTOR must accommodate that. The way to do that is, once more, through the doxastification of practical reasoning. As in the PLANNER, doxastification will allow the bulk of the reasoning involved in plan execution to be done by epistemic cognition. Second, having adopted a plan and begun its execution, a rational agent does not proceed blindly, come what may. A rational agent monitors the course of plan execution. If things do not go as anticipated, the execution of the plan may be aborted. This monitoring consists of keeping a continual check on whether the part of the plan remaining to be executed (the *tail* of the plan) is, under the present circumstances, an adoptable plan in its own right. The computational module that does this will be called the *TAIL-MONITOR*. As long as the TAIL-MONITOR does not abort plan execution, the PLAN-EXECUTOR will proceed recursively to execute nodes as they are called. A common phenomenon will be that the tail of the plan is modified by further scheduling as plan execution proceeds. Typically, as we see how the execution of a complex plan develops and what is true of our current situation, we will acquire reasons for scheduling the remaining nodes more precisely than we did before plan execution began. This has the effect, via the TAIL-MONITOR, of replacing the tail of the plan by a modification of it that involves further scheduling, adopting that modification, and then beginning its execution. Of course, it too may be modified as execution progresses.

Schematically, the PLAN-EXECUTOR can be regarded, as in figure 1, as consisting of a loop. The loop begins by retrieving a node from a list of *called-nodes* (originally the initial nodes of top-level adopted plans). It checks to see whether the if-conditions are satisfied. It does this by passing that question to epistemic cognition. If it is determined that the if-condition is not satisfied, execution of that node terminates. If it is determined that the if-condition is satisfied, the PLAN-EXECUTOR instructs epistemic cognition to become interested (and remain interested) in whether the when-condition is satisfied. If at some point epistemic cognition produces the belief that the when-condition is satisfied, it passes this information back to the PLAN-EXECUTOR. The PLAN-EXECUTOR then passes the operation of the node to the ACTION-INITIATOR, along with the subsidiary plan for its execution if there is one. (The ACTION-INITIATOR will be discussed further below.) Among other things, it resolves last-minute scheduling questions. When it chooses an operation for execution, it checks to see whether it is accompanied by an execution plan. If it is not, the operation is assumed to be a basic act, for the performance of which the agent has hardwired routines. Those routines are then executed mechanically. If instead there is an execution plan, its initial nodes are inserted into the list of called-nodes, and its execution begins. If a time comes when the TAIL-MONITOR decides the plan is no longer executable even if a subsidiary plan is adopted, then execution will be aborted. The ACTION-INITIATOR must monitor the execution of an operation to ensure that it is successful. It does this by querying epistemic cognition. If epistemic cognition concludes that the operation was successfully executed, the PLAN-EXECUTOR concludes that the node was executed and updates the list of *called-nodes* and inserts the new tails that begin with each newly called node into the set of *adopted-plans*. Then the whole routine begins again.

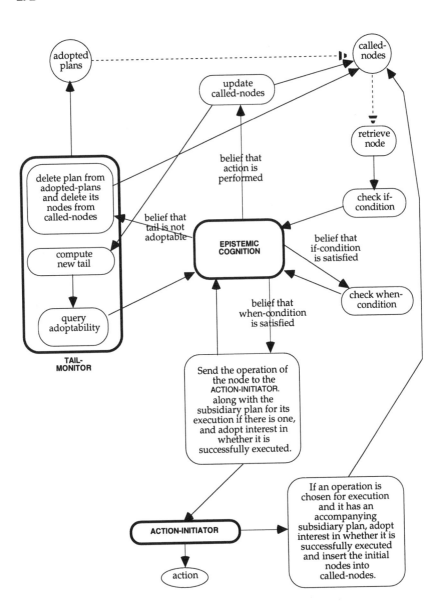

Figure 1. The PLAN-EXECUTOR

Running in parallel with this is the TAIL-MONITOR. As soon as a node is called, the TAIL-MONITOR instructs epistemic cognition to be continually interested in whether the tail of the plan is adoptable. If at any point epistemic cognition concludes that it is not, the TAIL-MONITOR aborts the plan execution. The epistemic conclusion that the tail is not adoptable may be accompanied by another epistemic conclusion to the effect that a modification of it is adoptable, and then the PLAN-EXECUTOR will automatically begin executing the modification just as it executes other adopted plans.

It would be straightforward to write a program to perform these operations mechanically, but that would not accommodate the defeasability of the agent's access to whether if- and when-conditions are satisfied, operations have been successfully executed, and so forth. If the agent's beliefs about these matters change, this must alter the course of plan execution. It seems that the best way to handle this is by doxastifying plan execution. In other words, implement the PLAN-EXECUTOR in terms of epistemic reasoning by making one addition to the *permanent-ultimate-epistemic-interests* and adding the following reason schemas:

permanent-ultimate-epistemic-interests:
(U2*) Find an x such that x is an adoptable plan.
When the belief that x is an adoptable plan is acquired:
 insert ⌜find a y such that y is a plan for achieving the same goals as x and y is rationally preferable to x⌝ into *ultimate-epistemic-interests*;
 for each initial node z of x: insert ⌜z is executable⌝ into *ultimate-epistemic-interests*.
(U4) Find a v such that v is an executable operation.
When the belief that v is an executable operation is acquired, send v to the ACTION-INITIATOR. (The ACTION-INITIATOR will insert ⌜v has been executed⌝ into *ultimate-epistemic-interests* when it tries to execute v.)

forwards directed prima facie reasons:
(E11) ⌜x is the tail of y with respect to z and z was an executable node and z has been executed⌝ is a prima facie reason for ⌜x is an adoptable plan⌝.
(E12) ⌜z is an executable plan-node of expected-value δ, and x is the (nonempty) subsidiary plan of z⌝ is a prima facie reason for x⌜ is an adoptable plan⌝.

forwards directed conclusive reasons:

(E12) $\ulcorner y$ is the subsidiary plan for z, and z is an executable node, and y has been fully executed $\urcorner$ is a conclusive reason for $\ulcorner$node z has been executed $\urcorner$.

(E13) $\ulcorner$Node z was executable, v is the operation prescribed by node z, and v was executed during the time z was executable $\urcorner$ is a conclusive reason for $\ulcorner z$ was executed $\urcorner$.

(E14) $\ulcorner x$ is an adoptable plan and z is an initial node of $x\urcorner$ is a conclusive reason for $\ulcorner z$ is called $\urcorner$.

(E15) $\ulcorner x$ was an executable node of plan y and x has been executed $\urcorner$ is a conclusive reason for $\ulcorner x$ is no longer executable $\urcorner$.

backwards directed conclusive reasons:

(E16) $\ulcorner z$ is called, its if-condition was satisfied when it was first called, and its when-condition is satisfied $\urcorner$ is a conclusive reason for $\ulcorner z$ is an executable plan-node $\urcorner$.

(E17) $\ulcorner v$ is the operation prescribed by an executable plan-node z of expected-value $\delta\urcorner$ is a conclusive reason for $\ulcorner v$ is an executable operation of strength $\delta\urcorner$.

(E18) $\ulcorner x$ is not prescribed by any executable plan-node of expected-value $\delta\urcorner$ is a conclusive reason for $\ulcorner x$ is not an executable operation of strength $\delta\urcorner$.

These combine to give us the reasoning diagrammed in figure 2. This constitutes a doxastic implementation of the plan execution architecture diagrammed in figure 1. To verify this, let us step through the operation of a reasoner supplied with these *permanent-ultimate-epistemic-interests* and reason schemas. We begin with beliefs of the form $\ulcorner x$ is adoptable $\urcorner$, supplied by the planning architecture of chapter 9. The pursuit of such beliefs was already among the *permanent-ultimate-epistemic-interests*, but (U2*) adds an instruction to the effect that whenever such a belief is acquired, queries about whether the initial nodes of x are executable should be inserted into *ultimate-epistemic-interests*. These queries are answered in terms of (E16) and (E17). If the reasoner concludes that an initial node z is executable and it also concludes that z prescribes an operation v, then it concludes, by (E18), that v is an executable operation, and by (U4), it sends v to the ACTION-INITIATOR and that initiates interest in whether v has been executed. Information to the effect that various operations have been executed is used to conclude that nodes prescribing them have been executed (by

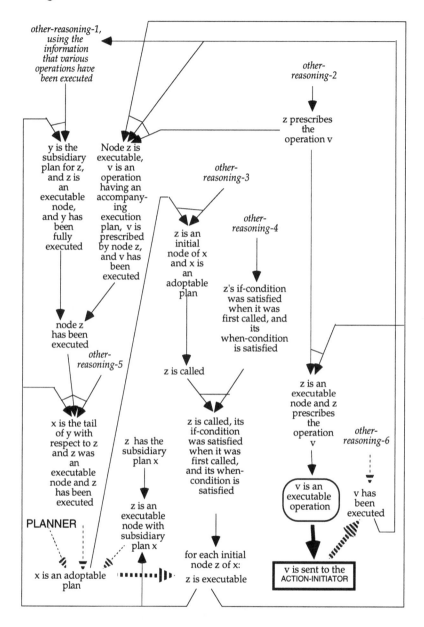

Figure 2. Doxastic implementation of the plan execution architecture

(E13)) and that plans have been fully executed. When it is concluded that an initial node z has been executed, it is inferred by (E11) that the tail of x with respect to z is an adoptable plan, and the loop begins again. Thus we have a doxastic implementation of the PLAN-EXECUTOR.

3. The ACTION-INITIATOR

The PLAN-EXECUTOR places operations awaiting execution in a list of *executable-operations*. In addition, the agent may have primitive present-tense desires to perform some operation, and these are also placed on the list of *executable-operations*. The task of the ACTION-INITIATOR is to decide which of these operations to execute at any given time. When it decides to execute one of these operations, it monitors the attempted execution and when it is ascertained that the operation has been successfully executed, that operation is deleted from the list of *executable-operations*.

The fundamental question about the ACTION-INITIATOR is, how does it decide what to do when? The main difficulty in answering this question arises from the fact that the planning architecture adumbrated in chapter 7 leaves an important gap between planning and acting. This is due, in part, to the fact that scheduling is rarely very precise. Rationality dictates leaving schedules as flexible as possible to accommodate new plans as they are adopted and to enable the agent to make use of new information that may lower execution costs if plan execution is scheduled in light of it. Return to the example of painting my garage. As the time for buying the paint approaches, I schedule the purchase more and more precisely. First, I planned (yesterday) to buy the paint today. Then I planned to buy it this afternoon. Then I planned to buy it on my way to the grocery store. In this way I generate more and more precise schedules. But I may never generate an absolutely precise schedule. When I actually get into the paint store and stand at the counter, there has to be something that makes me decide to buy the paint *now* (rather than 30 seconds from now, or 5 minutes from now). At any given time, it will typically be the case that nodes from many different plans have been called, their when-conditions are satisfied, and they are waiting to be executed by having their operations executed. For instance, I plan to call my travel agent sometime this afternoon to check on my car rental in New Zealand, I plan to start the barbecue grill pretty soon to fix dinner, I plan to run out to the mailbox and retrieve my mail before it gets dark, and so forth. All three of these plans have nodes that have been called and are awaiting execution. The when-conditions are sufficiently broad that I can successfully execute the nodes any time during the next several hours. I might engage in further planning and refine my schedule for when to do them, but more likely a time will come when I just decide to do one of them, and then later I will decide to do another, and so on. These decisions are the work of the ACTION-INITIATOR rather than the PLANNER. To complete the theory of rational plan execution, we need an account of how the ACTION-INITIATOR decides what to do at any given time.

It was proposed in chapter 1 that the best that can be done without further planning is to marshal the machinery of the reactive agent and "do what the agent most wants to do." Plan-nodes correspond to instrumental desires, and instrumental desires have strengths associated with them. This strength is inherited by the mandated operation when it is passed to the ACTION-INITIATOR. The executable operations are things the agent "wants to do", and the strength is a measure of how badly the agent wants to do it. The ACTION-INITIATOR selects the one the agent wants most to do (if there is a tie it randomly selects one of the most preferred operations) and then initiates the execution of that operation, deleting it from the list of *executable-operations*. At the same time it queries epistemic cognition about whether the operation is executed successfully. If the belief is adopted that the operation was not executed successfully, then it is reinserted into the list of *executable-operations* so that the agent can try again.

The ACTION-INITIATOR has the hardwired ability to initiate basic acts (basic motor skills). If an executable operation is a basic act and it is not accompanied by an execution plan, then when it is selected for execution, the built-in routines are executed automatically. The built-in routines can be overridden by accompanying the act with an execution plan. For instance, I can normally raise my arm automatically by executing built-in routines for that purpose. But if my arm is anesthetized, I may instead raise it by lifting it with my other arm. Operations that are not basic acts *must* be accompanied by execution plans. Whenever an operation is accompanied by an execution plan and the operation is selected for execution, that subsidiary execution plan is judged adoptable and its initial nodes are judged to be called. The execution of the subsidiary plan is then carried out by the PLAN-EXECUTOR.

This simple model of action initiation explains a great deal. There is a temptation in the theory of practical reasoning to think of the adoption of a plan as beginning a process that grinds inexorably to the execution of the plan unless it is subsequently retracted (that is, unless the agent changes its mind). But that is inaccurate. Adopting a plan is not like setting a train moving on rigid rails. Although I plan to do something and never explicitly change my mind, the plan may never be executed just because I never feel like executing it. There may always be other things I want to do more. This can include doing nothing. For example, I might adopt the plan to go to the grocery store this afternoon. As the afternoon progresses, it occurs to me at various times that I planned to go to the grocery store, but each time my reaction is, "Oh, I don't feel like going just now. I will do it later." Finally, the afternoon is over and I have not gone, but there was never a point at which I explicitly retracted my plan to go. I just didn't do it.

It is not only lethargy that can keep plans from being executed. I may have planned to go to the grocery store but I became engrossed in writing this chapter, and every time I thought about going to the store I decided that I would rather keep writing and go later. Eventually the afternoon was over and I had not gone.

Notice that lethargy and wanting to continue writing are present-tense action desires rather than operations prescribed by plans. That is, they are primitive desires produced by optative dispositions and concern our present behavior rather than our future behavior. Presumably lethargy is the result of a built-in optative disposition, whereas wanting to continue writing is almost certainly the result of an acquired optative disposition. These examples illustrate the importance of the mechanisms of the reactive agent even in a sophisticated planning agent. Such mechanisms play an extremely important role in "modulating" the behavior of the planning agent.

Chapter 9
OSCAR

1. Constructing an Artilect

The previous chapters described the architecture of an artilect in sufficient detail that it is now possible to build systems having that architecture. The most natural way to do that is to write a computer program to implement the architecture, but it it is important to realize that the design of the artilect is a more general enterprise. I have proposed a functional description of how a system of rational cognition can work. This enterprise is not different in kind from giving a functional description of the steering mechanism of a car or the wiring diagram of a television set. In each case, the functional description is describing how something works.[1] Something can conform to the functional description, and hence work that way, while being built in many different ways and out of many different materials. What is perhaps unique about cognition is that only the input and output are directly constrained by the physical world. What goes on in the middle can proceed in any way compatible with the functional description. The same system of cognition could be realized biologically, on a microchip, or with a system of water hoses and valves. Implementing it by writing a computer program is just a way of realizing it in electronic circuitry. Programming a computer is not different in principle from wiring a circuit using a soldering iron. Loading the program closes gates in the computer's circuitry, and one could do the same thing on a larger-scale circuit with a soldering iron. There is nothing magical about implementing cognition in a program. That is just one of many ways to build a physical system that satisfies the functional description. However, given the current state of the art, it is certainly the most convenient way of building such a system, so that is how I will proceed. This in no way commits us to the view that the mind is much like a digital computer. The use of a digital computer is just one way to implement the functional description. There may be many other kinds of hardware in which the same functional description can be implemented (perhaps more efficiently but probably not so easily). Bi-

---

[1] For an extended discussion of functional descriptions, see my [1989].

ological hardware is certainly one way of doing this, and connectionist networks might be another.

It is to be emphasized that this book has proposed an *architecture* for a rational agent, not a complete functional description of a rational agent. The difference is an important one. An architecture is a framework within which cognition operates. Different parts of the framework can be filled out in various ways, resulting in somewhat different rational agents that still have the same architecture. The architecture itself can be viewed as a programmable computational device. It is programmed by providing computational modules and data structures for the varous functional constituents. To explain this more fully, let us look at the details of the architecture. The architecture I have proposed is summarized in three crucial diagrams: figure 4 of chapter 4, figure 6 of chapter 7, and figure 2 of chapter 8. For convenience, these diagrams are repeated here, with new numbers. The doxastification of practical cognition has the effect of collapsing much of it into epistemic cognition, with the result that we can summarize the architecture with a single more general diagram that omits the details of the doxastification (presented in figure 4). A striking feature of this diagram is the way it makes it clear that although epistemic cognition is subservient to practical cognition, almost all of the work of cognition is done by epistemic cognition. The objective of cognition is to produce actions that are conducive to the agent's "living the good life", but (with the help of doxastification) the mechanisms for selecting such actions are almost entirely epistemic.

Different parts of the OSCAR architecture have different motivations. In some cases, I have argued that there is only one way rational cognition can work, and that has generated some of the more general features of the architecture. In other cases, there may be many ways to achieve a design goal, where the design goal is dictated by more abstract features of the architecture. In such cases, the design proposed has often been influenced by rather general features of human cognition. But no claim is made that this is an entirely accurate model of human cognition, and in some respects it clearly is not.

We can regard the OSCAR architecture as a programmable computational device. Programming it consists of specifying the contents of some databases that the rest of the architecture accesses. These databases constitute the list of *permanent-ultimate-epistemic-interests*, the lists of prima facie and conclusive reasons, the relation used for prioritizing the *inference-queue*, and a list of Q&I modules. It is not far fetched to regard this as a matter of programming a general computational device.

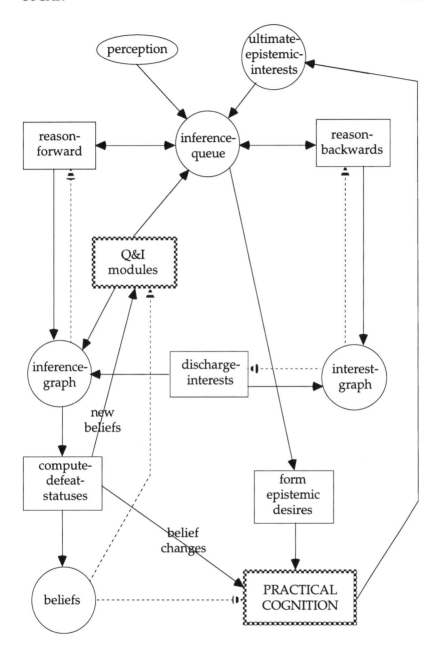

Figure 1.   Epistemic cognition

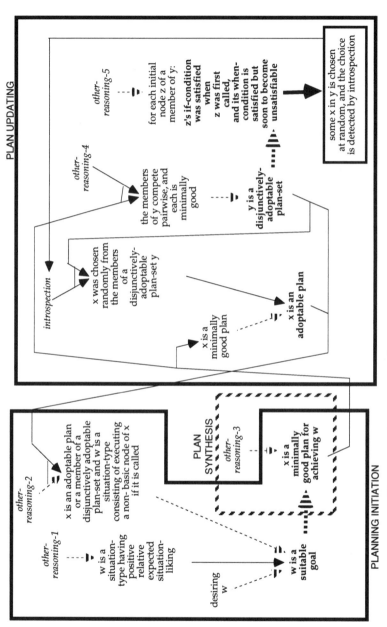

Figure 2. Doxastic implementation of the planning architecture

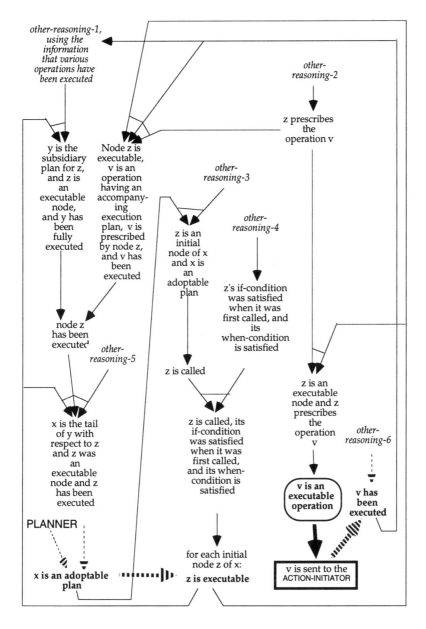

Figure 3. Doxastic implementation of the plan execution architecture

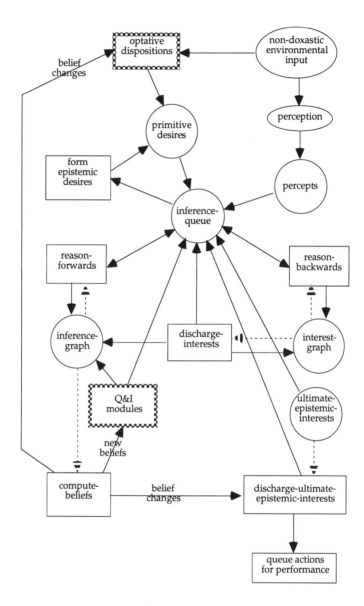

Figure 4. An architecture for rational cognition

Furthermore, it would be unreasonable to stipulate the contents of these databases as a fixed part of the OSCAR architecture, because it is unlikely that there is just one good way of constructing such databases. In human beings, it is done one way, but there may be other ways of doing it that are, for some purposes, preferable. In particular, the best choices for these databases may depend heavily on the hardware used for implementing the architecture. Different hardware may be better suited to different kinds of computations. For instance, human beings are very good at pattern matching but seem to find unification (two-way pattern matching) unnatural. On the other hand, unification plays an important role in most contemporary systems of automated reasoning, and it is easily computed on a digital computer. This suggests that a system of reason-schemas employing unification might be better suited for an implementation of the OSCAR architecture on a digital computer than it is for certain kinds of biological implementations.

Thus far, the OSCAR architecture has been described in rather loose prose, the thrust of the book being to defend the general ideas constituting the architecture rather than laying them down in a form that makes them easily implementable. The next section gives a more precise description of the architecture.

2. The General Architecture

The OSCAR architecture begins with a *situation-evaluator*, which produces a (real-measurable) degree of liking for the agent's current situation. This is presumed to be sensitive to the agent's beliefs about its situation. The *likability* of a situation is the degree the agent would like it if it had true beliefs about all relevant aspects of the situation. The objective of the agent's reasoning is to put itself in situations that are more likable than the situations in which it would find itself if it did not take action.

Ideally, plans are evaluated in terms of the *expected likability* of their being adopted. This involves reasoning about both likabilities and probabilities. Such reasoning is computationally difficult, so the OSCAR architecture also allows the use of shortcut procedures for producing approximate evaluations of plans. Such shortcut procedures are called *Q&I modules* ("quick and inflexible"). Q&I modules occur throughout rational cognition. A mark of rationality, however, is that when the output of Q&I modules conflicts with the output of explicit reasoning, the agent overrides the Q&I modules and adopts the conclusion of the reasoning.

Goals are judged suitable or unsuitable on the basis of their expected likability. The function of goals is to direct the course of planning. The use of goals constitutes a control structure for planning, in accordance with figure 2. Shortcut procedures for the choice of goals are indispensable in any realistic agent, because the agent must be able to live in the world before it acquires the general knowledge required for evaluating the suitability of goals. These take the form of Q&I modules called *optative dispositions*, which are dispositions to adopt goals.

In OSCAR, the bulk of the computational work involved in practical cognition is relegated to epistemic cognition. Accordingly, the core of OSCAR is a sophisticated system of epistemic cognition, based upon a general-purpose defeasible reasoner. Practical cognition functions by passing queries to epistemic cognition. These queries comprise the list of *ultimate-epistemic-interests*. The introduction of a query initiates epistemic cognition aimed at answering it, and queries are stored along with instructions for what to do with an answer. OSCAR begins with an interest in finding suitable goals. This is encoded as a permanent member of *ultimate-epistemic-interests*. When such a goal is found, the corresponding instruction is to insert a new query into *ultimate-epistemic-interests* regarding the discovery of adoptable plans aimed at achieving the goal. When such a plan is found, a query is inserted regarding the satisfaction of the preconditions of its plan-steps. When that query is answered affirmatively, the corresponding instruction is to pass the prescribed action to the ACTION-INITIATOR. Thus most of the work of practical cognition is performed by passing queries to *ultimate-epistemic-interests* with appropriate instructions for what to do with answers to the queries. In many cases, those instructions take the form of inserting new queries into *ultimate-epistemic-interests*.

In OSCAR epistemic cognition is performed jointly by a general-purpose defeasible reasoner and an array of special-purpose Q&I modules. Although an interface to the Q&I modules has been provided, no Q&I modules have been incorporated into the present implementation.

This general architecture is encoded as follows:

OSCAR:

- Insert the members of *permanent-ultimate-epistemic-interests* into *ultimate-epistemic-interests,* and insert them into the *inference-queue*.
- Insert the members of *premises* into the *inference-queue,* adopting

interest in rebutting defeaters for those that are not necessary truths.

- Initialize *global-assignment-tree*.
- Do the following repeatedly and in parallel:
  - Run environmental input through the optative dispositions, insert the resulting desires into the *inference-queue*, and encode this input in nodes of the *inference-graph*. Update the desire-strengths of desires already on the *inference-queue*, and adjust their priorities in light of changes in desire-strength.
  - Insert new perceptual states into the *inference-queue* and encode this input in nodes of the *inference-graph*. Update the saliences of percepts already on the *inference-queue* and adjust their priorities in light of changes in salience.
  - THINK
  - INITIATE-ACTIONS

Epistemic cognition is performed by THINK, whose principal function is to engage in defeasible and deductive reasoning. OSCAR's defeasible reasoner is based upon seven fundamental ideas: (1) an argument-based account of defeasible reasoning (formulated in chapter 3), (2) an analysis of defeat-status given a set of interrelated arguments (defended in chapter 3), (3) a general adequacy criterion for automated defeasible reasoners, called "i.d.e.-adequacy" (defended in chapter 4), (4) the claim that a general-purpose defeasible reasoner must have the kind of structure I have called "flag-based" (defended in chapter 4), (5) an algorithm for computing defeat-status, (6) an interest-driven monotonic reasoner (presented briefly in chapter 4), and (7) an account of degrees of justification, degrees of interest, and their interactions (discussed in chapter 3). I will give a brief summary of each of these ideas.

Argument-Based Defeasible Reasoning
In OSCAR, reasoning consists of the construction of arguments, where reasons are the atomic links in arguments. Defeasibility arises from the fact that some reasons are subject to defeat. Arguments are encoded as *inference-graphs*. The nodes of an inference-graph represent premises and conclusions, and the links between the nodes represent dependency relations. All of OSCAR's reasoning is combined into a global inference graph—the *inference-graph*. In the interest of theoretical clarity, I defined inference-graphs in such a way that different arguments for the same conclusion are represented by different nodes. This made it clearer

how the algorithm for computing defeat-status works. That algorithm proceeded in terms of "status assignments", which are defined as follows. We first define:

A node of the *inference-graph* is *initial* iff its node-basis and list of node-defeaters is empty.

σ is a *partial status assignment* iff σ is a function assigning "defeated" and "undefeated" to a subset of the nodes of an inference-graph in such a way that:

1. σ assigns "undefeated" to all initial nodes;
2. σ assigns "undefeated" to a node α iff σ assigns "undefeated" to all the members of the node-basis of α and σ assigns "defeated" to all node-defeaters of α; and
3. σ assigns "defeated" to a node α iff either some member of the node-basis of α is assigned "defeated", or some node-defeaters of α and is assigned "undefeated".

σ is a *status assignment* iff σ is a partial status assignment and σ is not properly contained in any other partial status assignment

A node is undefeated iff every status assignment assigns "undefeated" to it; otherwise it is defeated.

However, for the purpose of implementing defeasible reasoning, using different nodes to represent different arguments for the same conclusion is an inefficient representation, because it leads to needless duplication. If we have two arguments supporting a single conclusion, then any further reasoning from that conclusion will generate two different nodes. If we have two arguments for each of two conclusions, and another inference proceeds from those two conclusions, the latter will have to be represented by four different nodes in the inference-graph, and so on. This is illustrated in figure 5, where P and Q are each inferred in two separate ways, and then R is inferred from P and Q.

A more efficient representation of reasoning would take the inference-graph to be an and/or graph rather than a standard graph. In an and/or graph, nodes are linked to *sets* of nodes rather than individual nodes. This is represented diagramatically by connecting the links with arcs. In an and/or inference-graph, when we have multiple arguments for a conclusion, the single node representing that conclusion will be tied to different bases by separate groups of links. This is illustrated in figure 6 by an and/or inference-graph encoding the same reasoning as the standard inference-graph in figure 5. In an and/or inference-graph, a *support-link* will be a *set* of supporting-arrows connected with an arc.

Although and/or graphs provide an efficient representation of reasoning, they complicate the computation of defeat-status. Using simple inference-graphs, we can use the defeat-status computation of chapter 2 to compute defeat-statuses, and then use the computed defeat-statuses to compute the degrees-of-justification for the nodes in the inference-

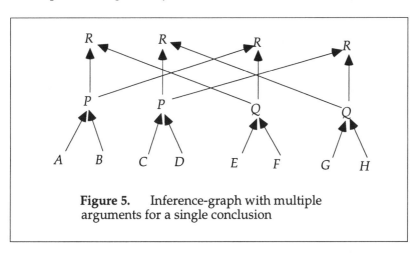

Figure 5. Inference-graph with multiple arguments for a single conclusion

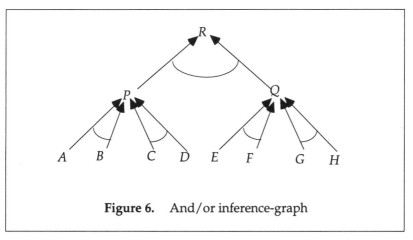

Figure 6. And/or inference-graph

graph. The degree-of-justification for a node is zero if it is defeated, and it is its degree-of-support otherwise.

With and/or inference-graphs, we can no longer separate the computation of defeat-statuses and degrees-of-justification. To illustrate, consider the two inference-graphs in figures 7 and 8. They could arise from different degrees of justification for the two nodes supporting R. In figure 7, only the rightmost node is strong enough to defeat S, whereas in figure 8, only the leftmost node is strong enough to defeat S. The difference has repurcusions, because in figure 7, S is provisionally defeated, and hence T is also provisionally defeated, but in figure 8, S is defeated outright, and hence T is undefeated. The difficulty is now that if we try to represent these as and/or graphs, we get the same graph, drawn in figure 9. This representation cannot distinguish between the situation diagrammed in figure 7 and that diagrammed in figure 8, and accordingly leaves the defeat-status of T indeterminate.

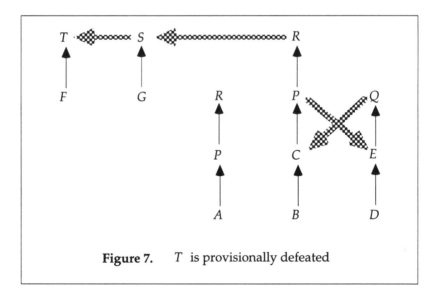

Figure 7. T is provisionally defeated

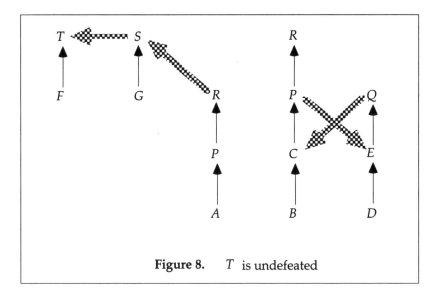

Figure 8. *T* is undefeated

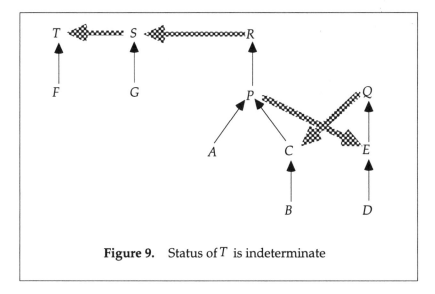

Figure 9. Status of *T* is indeterminate

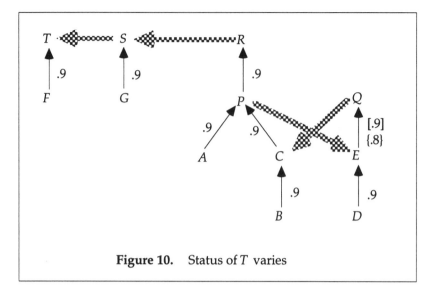

Figure 10.   Status of T varies

This difficulty can be avoided by attaching strengths to the support-arrows. In figure 10, if we attach the strengths in brackets, we get a representation of figure 6, and if we attach the strenghts in braces, we get a representation of figure 7.

With this modification, we can construct a defeat-status computation that is equivalent to that for simple inference-graphs. The trick is to take the defeat-status of a node to be its undefeated-degree-of-justification rather than just "defeated" or "undefeated". If all arguments supporting a node are defeated, then the undefeated-degree-of-justification is 0. Otherwise, it is the maximum of the strengths of the undefeated arguments. We can then modify the definition given in chapter 2 as follows:

A node of the *inference-graph* is *initial* iff its node-basis and list of node-defeaters is empty.

σ is a *partial status assignment* iff σ is a function assigning real numbers between 0 and 1 to a subset of the nodes of an inference-graph and to the support-links of those nodes in such a way that:
1. σ assigns its degree of justification to any initial node;
2. If σ assigns a value α to a defeat-node for a support-link and assigns a value less than or equal to α to some member of the link-basis, then σ assigns 0 to the link;

3. Otherwise, if σ assigns values to every member of the link-basis of a link and every link-defeater for the link, σ assigns to the link the minimum of the strength of the link-rule and the number σ assigns to the members of the link-basis.
4. If every support-link of a node is assigned 0, the node is assigned 0;
5. If some support-link of a node is assigned a value greater than 0, the node is assigned the maximum of the values assigned to its support-links.
6. If every support-link of a node that is assigned a value is assigned 0, but some support-link of the node is not assigned a value, then the node is not assigned a value.

σ is a *status assignment* iff σ is a partial status assignment and σ is not properly contained in any other partial status assignment

The analysis of defeat-status in terms of status assignments is now more complicated than it was for simple inference-graphs. We want the analysis to be equivalent to the analysis given in terms of simple inference-graphs. To accomplish this, we begin by noting that each simple inference-graph can be rewritten as an and/or graph, and then each node of the and/or graph corresponds to a set of nodes of the simple graph. A node of the simple inference-graph, on the other hand, corresponds to an *argument* in the and/or graph. An argument is a kind of connected sub-tree of the graph. More precisely:

An *argument from* an and/or inference-graph $\mathcal{G}$ *for* a node N is a subset $\mathcal{A}$ of the nodes and support-links of the graph such that (1) if a node in $\mathcal{A}$ has any support-links in $\mathcal{G}$, exactly one of them is in $\mathcal{A}$, (2) if a support-link is in $\mathcal{A}$ then the nodes in its support-link-basis are also in $\mathcal{A}$, and (3) N is in $\mathcal{A}$.

Nodes in the simple inference-graph correspond one-one to arguments in the and/or inference-graph. The definition of a partial status-assignment for and/or graphs just amounts to saying that a node is assigned "undefeated" iff it is either an initial node or some argument for it consists of nodes and links that are assigned "undefeated".

The result we want to ensure is the following *Correspondence Theorem*:

A node of the and/or inference-graph is undefeated iff one of the corresponding nodes of the simple inference-graph is undefeated.

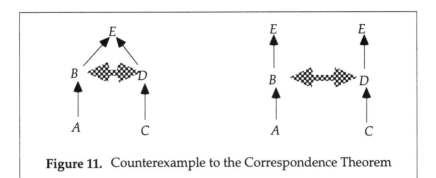

Figure 11. Counterexample to the Correspondence Theorem

The computation of defeat-statuses for and/or inference-graphs must be done in such a way as to make the preceding true. To this end, it is tempting to define:

A node of the and/or inference-graph is undefeated iff every status assignment assigns a non-zero value to it; otherwise it is defeated.

However, this does not make the Correspondence Theorem true. Figure 11 is a simple counterexample, with the simple inference-graph on the right and the corresponding and/or graph on the left. In the simple graph, there are two status-assignments, and one assigns "undefeated" to the left "*E*" and the other assigns "undefeated to the right "*E*", but neither "*E*" is assigned "undefeated" by both status-assignments, so both are defeated. In the and/or graph, there are also two status-assignments, and each assigns "undefeated" to "*E*" (by making a different argument undefeated). Thus on the above proposal, "*E*" would be undefeated in the and/or inference-graph, but defeated in the simple inference-graph.

This example makes it clear that the difficulty lies in the fact that, in the and/or graph, there is no argument that comes out undefeated on both assignments. This suggests that the correct analysis of defeat-status for and/or inference-graphs is:

A node of the and/or inference-graph is undefeated iff the graph contains an argument for the node which is such that every status assignment assigns a non-zero value to all nodes and links in the argument; otherwise it is defeated.

With this definition it becomes simple to prove the Correspondence Theorem by induction on the length of the arguments. Note that this would make the computation of defeat-status complicated if it were done for a single inference-node, but it is straightforward to recursively compute all of the defeat-statuses for the inference-graph simultaneously.

With the understanding that defeat-statuses will be computed as described, the *inference-graph* will consist of a set of inference-nodes and support-links. A support-link is a data-structure encoding an inference, and it has slots for the following information:

- support-link-target—the inference-node supported by the link;
- support-link-basis—the list of inference-nodes from which the inference is made;
- support-link-rule—the reason licensing the inference; this can be either a substantive reason or a string;
- support-link-defeaters—if the inference is defeasible, the set of inference-nodes having the syntactically appropriate form to defeat it (this ignores considerations of strength).

An inference-node N is a data-structure encoding the following information:

- the node-sequent
- support-links—the support-links supporting the node;
- node-justification—if the node has no support-links, this is a string describing its justification;
- consequent-links—the list of support-links for which this node is a member of the support-link-basis;
- node-defeatees—the list of support-links L such that N is a node-defeater of L;
- the defeat-status—the undefeated degree-of-support;

I.D.E.-Adequacy

Perhaps the greatest problem facing the designers of automated defeasible reasoners is that the set of warranted conclusions resulting from a set of premises and reason-schemas is not in general recursively enumerable. The solution embodied in OSCAR is to allow a defeasible reasoner to draw conclusions tentatively, sometimes retracting them later, and perhaps reinstating them still later, and so on. The set of conclusions drawn by such a reasoner cannot constitute a recursive enumeration of the set of warranted propositions, but I have proposed instead that it should systematically approximate the set of warranted conclusions in the following sense:

The rules for reasoning should be such that if the reasoner is interested in a proposition p then:
(1) if p is warranted, the reasoner will eventually reach a stage where p is justified and stays justified;
(2) if p is unwarranted, the reasoner will eventually reach a stage where p is unjustified and stays unjustified.

If these conditions are satisfied, the sequence of sets of justified conclusions at different stages of reasoning constitutes a "defeasible enumeration" of the subset of warranted propositions in which the reasoner is interested, and the reasoner is said to be "i.d.e.-adequate".

Because the set of warranted propositions is not recursively enumerable, an i.d.e.-adequate reasoner may never stop reasoning. In simple cases it may stop, by running out of things to do, but in complicated cases it will go on reasoning forever. The significance of such a reasoner, embedded in a rational agent, is that it tells the agent what to believe "given the current state of its reasoning", and if the agent has to take action, it does so on the basis of what it believes at that time, even if there is no guarantee that it would not change its beliefs later if it had more time to reason. This involves the conception of defeasible conclusions as "innocent until proven guilty". In other words, they are pefectly reasonable beliefs, and it is reasonable to act upon them, despite the fact that the agent cannot "prove" that they will never have to be retracted.

Flag-Based Reasoners
In the attempt to build an i.d.e.-adequate defeasible reasoner, a natural first inclination is to suppose that when a conclusion is defeated, the reasoner should stop reasoning from it unless or until it is subsequently reinstated. It turns out, however, that such a proposal cannot work. Consider two long arguments, and suppose the final step of each defeats an early step of the other. It follows from the analysis of defeat-status that both arguments are defeated. They undergo collective defeat. But a reasoner that stopped reasoning from a conclusion once it was defeated would never discover the collective defeat, because having completed one of the arguments, it would cease developing the other one. For this reason, an i.d.e.-adequate reasoner must continue reasoning from conclusions even when they are defeated. This suggests that such a reasoner should simply flag conclusions as defeated and go on reasoning. Defeat-status may affect the priorities that are assigned to performing various inference steps, so that undefeated conclusions

are given some precedence over defeated ones, but inferences from defeated conclusions must still go forth. Such a reasoner is said to be "flag-based". We can think of a flag-based reasoner as consisting of two largely autonomous modules: a "monotonic reasoner" that reasons and builds the inference-graph, without paying much attention (except in prioritizing inferences) to defeat-status, and a module that computes or recomputes defeat-statuses as new inferences are made. Such a reasoner has the form of a simple loop:

```
(loop
    (draw-a-conclusion)
    (recompute-defeat-statuses))
```

It was shown in chapter 3 that subject to some reasonable assumptions about the structure of prima facie reasons provided to the reasoner and the adequacy of the monotonic reasoner, the resulting flag-based reasoner will be i.d.e.-adequate.

Interest-Driven Reasoning

OSCAR's monotonic reasoner is based upon the deductive reasoner described in my [1990a]. That was an "interest-driven suppositional reasoner" for first-order logic. The reference to suppositional reasoning means that it can accommodate natural deduction rules like condition-alization, reasoning by cases, and *reductio ad absurdum*. For this purpose, the nodes of the *inference-graph* are taken to encode *sequents* rather than formulas. A sequent is a pair $\langle X,P \rangle$, where X is a set of formulas (the supposition of the sequent) and P is an individual formula. The sense in which the reasoner is interest-driven is that it reasons both backwards from the desired conclusions and forwards from the given premises. Reasoning backwards can be regarded as deriving interests from interests. This is related to backwards chaining and forwards chaining but it is not quite the same thing. The difference lies in the fact that different rules of inference and different reason-schemas are employed for backwards and for forwards reasoning. The motivation for this is that natural rules of inference are often very reasonable when applied in one direction but combinatorially explosive when applied in the other. For instance, the rule of *addition* tells us to infer the disjunction $(P \vee Q)$ from the disjunct P. As a rule of backwards reasoning, this is eminently reasonable. It tells us that if we want to establish a disjunction, one way is to try to get the first disjunct. But as a rule of forwards reasoning it would be catastrophic. It would have the reasoner infer every disjunction involving any conclusion it obtains.

We can think of interest-driven reasoning as consisting of three operations: (1) we reason forwards from previously drawn conclusions to new conclusions; (2) we reason backwards from interests to interests; (3) when we have reasoned backwards to a set of sequents as interests, and forwards to the same set of sequents as conclusions, then we *discharge interest* and conclude the sequent that led to those interests. For example, suppose we are given the premises P and $(P \supset Q)$ and are interested in the conclusion $(Q \vee R)$. From the latter, we could reason backwards to interest in Q and in R (using *addition* as our rule of inference). From the premises we could reason forwards to Q (using *modus ponens*). We then have Q as both a conclusion and an interest, so we can discharge interest. Our interest in Q derived from our interest in $(Q \vee R)$, so when we discharge interest, we conclude $(Q \vee R)$, and we are through.

As described in chapter 4, this reasoning proceeds in accordance with three procedures:

REASON-FORWARDS

If a set of sequents X is a forwards reason for a sequent S, some member of X is newly concluded, and the other members of X have already been concluded, then conclude S.

REASON-BACKWARDS

If interest is adopted in a sequent S, and a pair $\langle X, Y \rangle$ of sets of sequents is a backwards reason for S, where X is the set of forwards premises and Y is the set of backwards premises, then if every member of X has been concluded, adopt interest in any members of Y that have not already been concluded. If all members of both X and Y have been concluded, conclude S. If some members of X have not been concluded, then simply record $\langle X, Y \rangle$ as a potential reason for S, for use by DISCHARGE-INTEREST.

DISCHARGE-INTEREST

If interest was adopted in the members of Y as a way of getting the sequent S, and some member of Y is concluded and the other members of Y have already been concluded, then conclude S. If the pair $\langle X, Y \rangle$ has been recorded as a potential backwards reason for S, and some member of X is newly concluded and the other members of X have already been concluded, then adopt interest in any members of Y that have not already been concluded. If all members of both X and Y have been concluded, conclude S.

Reasoning forwards builds the *inference-graph*, and reasoning backwards builds the *interest-graph*. When the two graphs meet, interests are discharged, with the result that sequents that are of interest (as recorded in the *interest-graph*) are concluded and incorporated into the *inference-graph*. In the agent-architecture, queries posed by practical cognition form termini in the *interest-graph*. When OSCAR is treated as an isolated defeasible reasoner, these queries are supplied by the operator. When such queries are answered, the agent does something with the answers. What the agent does is determined by the purpose of the query. This is accomplished by storing instructions for what to do with an answer along with the query in *ultimate-epistemic-interests*.

As a deductive reasoner, this monotonic reasoner turns out to be surprisingly efficient, as I have documented in my [1990a]. However, the original motivation for developing it was to incorporate it into a system of defeasible reasoning. This is because standard deductive reasoners based upon resolution refutation cannot serve that purpose. Such systems, in effect, always reason by *reductio ad absurdum*, but *reductio ad absurdum* is invalid for reasoning involving prima facie reasons. If a contradiction is obtained from some premises by reasoning via prima facie reasons, that does not support an inference to the negation of the premises. Instead it defeats the defeasible inferences.

In deductive reasoning, all reasons are equally good (that is, perfect). But defeasible reasons can vary in strength, with important consequences for the behavior of a defeasible reasoner. For instance, given an argument for a conclusion and a stronger argument for its negation, the stronger argument wins. A common view in epistemology has been that argument strengths should behave like probabilities, but I have argued against that in chapter 3. OSCAR instead computes argument-strengths in terms of the "weakest link" principle. According to this principle, the strength of an argument, and the degree of support it confers on its conclusion, is the minimum of the (stipulated) degrees of justification of the input premises used and the strengths of the reasons used.

One of the main roles of degrees of support lies in the adjudication of disputes. Given an argument for P and another argument for $\sim P$, the stronger argument wins, that is, the conclusion of the stronger argument is justified and the weaker argument is defeated. If the arguments are equally strong, they defeat each other collectively, and neither conclusion is justified. More generally, given nodes α and β of the *inference-graph* where the sequent supported by α has the syntactical form of a rebutting or undercutting defeater for β, α defeats β iff the degree of support for α is at least as great as the degree of support for β.

Interests also come in degrees. A rational agent has practical goals, and this leads to queries regarding how to satisfy those goals being sent to the epistemic reasoner. The reasoner thus becomes interested in answering those queries, and that initiates backwards reasoning. But some of the goals will typically be more important than others, and this is reflected by differing degrees of interest in the queries deriving from those goals. Reasoning backwards from queries *ultimate-epistemic-interests* preserves the degree-of-interest. In general, if a sequent in the *interest-graph* is of interest for more than one reason (that is, there are branches of the *interest-graph* leading from it to more than one query in *ultimate-epistemic-interests*), the degree-of-interest in the sequent is the minimum of the degrees of interest in the queries from which it derives. This indicates the minimal degree of support an answer must have in order to satisfy (one source of) the interest.

The Interest-Graph

In the most general case, a backwards reason R has a list of forwards-premises, a list of backwards-premises, a desired-conclusion, and a list of variables to be used in pattern matching. If R is applicable to a desired-conclusion S, the reasoner matches S against the desired-conclusion, obtaining instantiations for some of the variables and thereby generating an *interest-scheme* $\langle X,Y,S \rangle$. The reasoner then looks for ways of instantiating the forwards-premise schemes X so that they are validated by conclusions that have already been drawn and are supported to the requisite degree of justification. A constraint on backwards reasons is that all the variables occur in the forwards premises and the conclusion, so once instances of the forwards-premises and the conclusion have been obtained, that uniquely determines the corresponding instance of the backwards-premises. Thus the reasoner obtains an instance $\langle X^*,Y^*,S \rangle$ of R where the members of X^* are validated to the requisite degree of justification. The reasoner then reasons backwards and adopts interest in the members of Y^*.

Subsequently, when a new conclusion C is drawn, DISCHARGE-INTEREST-SCHEMES checks the interest-scheme $\langle X,Y,S \rangle$ to see whether C can be used to instantiate some member of X, and if so whether the instantiation can be extended so that all members of X are instantiated to validated sequents. This yields a new instance $\langle X^{**}, Y^{**}, S \rangle$ of R where, once again, the forwards-premises X^{**} are validated to the requisite degree of justification, and then the reasoner reasons backwards and adopts interest in the members of Y^{**}.

To implement the above reasoning, the interest-scheme $\langle X, Y, S \rangle$ must be stored somewhere so that it can be accessed by DISCHARGE-INTEREST-SCHEMES. Along with it must be stored the list of variables remaining to be instantiated and the degree of justification required for validating instances. Accordingly, I will take an interest-scheme to be a data structure encoding the following information:

- the instantiated-reason.
- the forwards-basis—a list of formulas.
- the backwards-basis—a list of formulas.
- the instance-consequent—the sequent of interest.
- the target-interest—the *interest-graph* node recording interest in the instance-conclusion.
- the instance-variables—the set of variables to be used in finding instances of the forwards-basis by pattern matching.

Interest-schemes to be accessed by DISCHARGE-INTEREST-SCHEMES will be stored in the list *interest-schemes*.

In most backwards-reasons, the list of forwards-premises is empty (that is, they are "simple" backwards reasons). In that case, instantiating the reason-consequent uniquely determines the instantiation of the backwards-premises, and so no interest-schemes need be stored. The reasoner immediately adopts interest in the instantiated backwards-premises.

Reasoning backwards will build the *interest-graph*. The nodes of the *interest-graph* are either queries from *ultimate-epistemic-interests* or record sequents derivatively of interest. The latter will be referred to as "interests". The links either represent backwards reasons or connect sequents with queries for which they are answers. A link connects one node— the *resultant-interest*—with a list of sequents—the *basis*, in accordance with a backwards reason. The basis can be segregated into the forwards-basis and the backwards-basis, corresponding to the forwards-premises and backwards-premises of the reason. The members of the forwards-basis are already validated, so backwards reasoning begins with the resultant-interest and works backwards to the backwards-basis, adding its members to the *interest-graph* if necessary. Then further backwards reasoning from the backwards-basis will be initiated.

In the interest of efficiency, backwards reasoning from the backwards-basis will be done one element at a time. Only when an argument of adequate strength is found for the first element of the backwards-basis will the reasoner begin looking for an argument for the second member, and so forth. In this way, it will avoid expending its resources searching for arguments for some members when it is not possible to find arguments for other members.

When an argument is found for a member of the backwards-basis, the reasoner checks to see whether it is a deductive argument. A deductive argument is one in which none of the reasons employed are defeasible and no input states are used as premises. If the argument is deductive, the search for further arguments is cancelled. But if the argument is not deductive, then rather than cancelling the search for further arguments, the priority of the search is lowered.

To accommodate all of this, the *interest-graph-links* will be a set of links *L* encoding the following information:

- the resultant-interest—the *interest-graph* node from which the backwards reasoning proceeds, or the query in *ultimate-epistemic-interests* for which the link records an answer.
- the link-interests—the set of interests recording interest in members of the link-basis.
- the link-basis—if the resultant-interest is a query, this is the unit set of a sequent that answers it; otherwise this is the potential basis for an inference to the interest-sequent of the resultant-interest, this being the union of the backwards and forwards premises of an instance of a backwards reason whose conclusion is that interest-sequent.
- the link-rule—an indication of the rule of inference or substantive reason employed in such an inference, or "answer" if the resultant node is a query. In the latter case, the link is an "answer-link".
- the basis-remainder—if the resultant-interest is not a query, this is the list of elements of the backwards-premises that (1) are not validated by any nodes of the *inference-graph* of strength greater than or equal to the degree-of-interest, and (2) for which interests have not yet been constructed; if the resultant-interest is a query, this is an answer not validated by any nodes of the *inference-graph* of strength greater than or equal to the degree-of-interest and for which an interest has not yet been constructed.
- link-defeaters—if the link-rule is defeasible, this is the pair of c-lists for the rebutting-defeater and undercutting-defeater for the inference described by the link. When the link is created, these c-lists are created with empty lists of c-list-conclusions if they do not already exist.

- the link-defeat-status—T if some conclusion in the c-list-conclusions of one of the link-defeaters has a supposition contained in the resultant-supposition and a degree-of-justification greater than or equal to the degree-of-interest in the resultant-sequent; NIL otherwise. This represents a partial computation of defeat-status, proceeding just in terms of the validated members of the link-basis and the link-defeaters. It is used to lower the priority assigned to the backwards reasoning if L is defeated (according to this partial computation).
- link-strength—the maximum-degree-of-interest conveyed by the link.

Interests will encode the sequents related by the *interest-graph* links. This will not be taken to include the queries from *ultimate-epistemic-interests*. Thus the *interest-graph* actually includes both the members of *interests* and the queries from *ultimate-epistemic-interests*. An interest will be a data structure encoding the following information:

- the interest-sequent.
- the right-links—the list of *interest-graph-links* in which the interest-sequent is a member of the link-basis.
- the left-links—the list of *interest-graph-links* for which the present interest is the resultant-interest.
- the degree-of-interest in the interest-sequent—a number between 0 and 1; for non-terminal nodes this is the minimum of the degrees of interest of the interests to which the given interest is linked by right-links.
- the interest-defeat-status—NIL if the defeat-status of any of the right-links is NIL, T otherwise.

Some nodes of the *interest-graph* will be termini. They represent the starting points for backwards reasoning rather than being *for* something else. These will be either queries from *ultimate-epistemic-interests* or interests in defeaters for defeasible inference steps performed by the reasoner. Terminal nodes are distinguished by having empty lists of right-links.

The Inference-Queue

The basic control structure for these inference operations is the *inference-queue*. This is a queue of inferences (either backwards or forwards) waiting to be performed. The *inference-queue* will enqueue conclusions encoding input states (which will be percepts and primitive desires), new conclusions encoding the results of inferences, queries from *ultimate-epistemic-interests*, and new interests (*interest-graph* nodes). Accordingly, I will take the *inference-queue* to be an ordered list of data-structures called *inference-queue nodes*, each encoding the following information:

- the item enqueued—a conclusion, a query, or an *interest-graph* node;
- the item-kind—an indication of whether the enqueued item is a conclusion, a query, or an *interest-graph* node;
- item-complexity—discussed below;
- discounted-strength—discussed below;
- the degree-of-preference—discussed below.

The ordering of the nodes of the *inference-queue* will be done by the relation $\ulcorner x$ *is i-preferred to* $y \urcorner$. Specifying this relation is part of the process of programming OSCAR. A simple preference relation that is used as the default appeals to two properties of the enqueued item. The first will be referred to as the "discounted-strength" of the item and will be measured by a real number between 0 and 1. The discounted-strength of a desire is simply its desire-strength. The discounted-strength of a percept is its salience. The salience of a percept will, for now, be treated as a primitive property whose value is specified by the perceptual input systems to which OSCAR is attached. This may be treated in a more sophisticated way later. The discounted-strength of a conclusion of type "inference" will, in most cases, be measured by the degree-of-justification of the conclusion, but there are two complications. First, conclusions recording suppositions are generated by interests. For example, interest in a conditional will lead the reasoner to suppose the antecedent with the objective of inferring the consequent, and the supposition of the antecedent is recorded as an *inference-graph* node and a conclusion. The degree-of-justification of this conclusion will automatically be 1, but the priority assigned to reasoning from it should be a function of the discounted-strength of the generating interest. Accordingly, when a conclusion is generated by an interest, its discounted-strength will be taken to be the discounted-strength of the interest rather than the degree-of-justification. Second, it turns out to be desirable to give inferences in accordance with some inference rules (either backwards or forwards) low priority. This is accomplished by attaching a *discount-factor* (a real number between 0 and 1) to the rule and using that to lower the degree-of-preference. Accordingly, the discounted-strength of a conclusion of type "inference" that is not generated by an interest will, in general, be the maximum of the products of the degrees-of-support and the discount-factor of the node-rule for the undefeated nodes in its node-list, or some fixed number α_0 if all nodes on the node-list are defeated. The discounted-strength of an interest will be its interest-priority, which will be discussed below.

The second property to which the default preference relation appeals is "complexity". This is a measure of syntactic complexity, and the idea behind the preference ordering is that reasoning with simpler formulas is given precedence over reasoning with complex formulas. Accordingly, we define:

Where x is an enqueued item, *strength* is the discounted-strength of x, and *complexity* is the complexity of the sequent expressing the content of x, *the degree-of-preference of x* is *strength/complexity*.

The default preference relation is then:

x is i-preferred to y iff the degree-of-preference of x is greater than the degree-of-preference of y.

The default complexity measure simply counts the number of symbol tokens (not counting parentheses) occurring in the sequent expressing the content of the enqueued item. This has the effect of giving precedence to reasoning with short formulas. The only justification I have to offer for this complexity measure is that it seems to work reasonably well, and it is a rough reflection of the way human beings prioritize their reasoning.

The discounted-strength of an interest is its interest-priority. To understand this concept, it must first be realized that degrees of interest play two roles. They determine how justified an answer must be for it to be an acceptable answer, and they prioritize reasoning. Initially, the priority of backwards reasoning is determined directly by the degree-of-interest. If something is of interest ultimately for answering a certain query, and an answer is obtained for that query, this lowers the priority of backwards reasoning from that interest, but not the degree-of-interest itself (in its role of determining how good answers must be). So the *interest-priority* of an interest should be some function of (1) the degree-of-interest, (2) the discount-factor of the backwards reason used in its derivation, (3) whether the interest is ultimately aimed at answering a query none of whose query-answers are believed, (4) whether the interest derives from a defeated member of the *interest-graph*, and (5) whether the node-sequent is already supported by a conclusion whose degree-of-justification is greater than or equal to the degree-of-interest. The interest-priority must also be a number between 0 and 1. Supplying the exact definition of interest-priority will be part of the process of programming OSCAR, but a default definition is built into OSCAR. This definition is the following:

- The interest-priority of a query from *permanent-ultimate-epistemic-*

interests is its degree-of-interest.

- The interest-priority of any other query is α_0 if it has already been answered, and its degree-of-interest otherwise.
- The interest-priority of an *interest-graph* node having an empty set of right-links is α_0 (this represents interest in a defeater for a defeasible inference);
- The interest-priority of any other *interest-graph* node *node* is computed as follows. Let L be the set of its right-links having defeat-status NIL and resultant-interests with maximum-degrees-of-interest greater than the maximum degree-of-justification at which they have been discharged. If L is empty, the interest-priority of *node* is α_0; otherwise it is the maximum over L of the set of products of the discount-factor of the link-rule and the interest-priority of the resultant-interest.

α_0 serves as a base-level of interest-priority used for reasoning from defeated nodes and for the search for defeaters for *inference-graph* nodes. As long as $\alpha_0 > 0$, the reasoner will "eventually" get around to reasoning prioritized in this way, provided new environmental input does not continually delay it by inserting new items in front of it in the *inference-queue*. The higher the value of α_0, the more effort the reasoner is likely to expend on these matters.

The data-structures I have been describing are manipulated in epistemic cognition by THINK:

THINK

If the *inference-queue* is nonempty, let Q be the first member of the *inference-queue*:

- Remove Q from the *inference-queue*.
- Let *conclusion* be the item enqueued by Q if it is a conclusion:
  - insert *conclusion* into the list of *processed-conclusions*.
  - REASON-FORWARDS-FROM *conclusion*
- Let *query* be the item enqueued by Q if it is a query, and let *priority* be its interest-priority:
  - REASON-BACKWARDS-FROM-QUERY *query priority*.
- Let *interest* be the item enqueued by Q if it is an *interest-graph* node, and let *priority* be its interest-priority:
  - REASON-BACKWARDS-FROM *interest priority*.
  - FORM-EPISTEMIC-DESIRES-FOR *interest*.

For a detailed account of the operations performed by THINK, the reader is referred to *The OSCAR Manual*. This contains a complete description of the OSCAR architecture and details the LISP code implementing it.

3. Examples

OSCAR can be used without logic to deal with many of the reasoning problems that were discussed above. Consider the problem diagrammed in figure 2 of chapter 3. The following is a display of OSCAR's reasoning:

```
Problem #3
Figure 2
Given premises:
  A   justification = 1
  B   justification = 1
  C   justification = 1
Ultimate epistemic interests:
  J   interest = 1
  K   interest = 1
  L   interest = 1

  FORWARDS PRIMA FACIE REASONS
  pf-reason 1:  {A} ||=> D   strength = 1
  pf-reason 2:  {D} ||=> G   strength = 1
  pf-reason 3:  {B} ||=> E   strength = 1
  pf-reason 4:  {C} ||=> F   strength = 1
  pf-reason 5:  {I} ||=> L   strength = 1

  FORWARDS CONCLUSIVE REASONS
  con-reason 1:  {G} ||=> J   strength = 1
  con-reason 2:  {E} ||=> H   strength = 1
  con-reason 3:  {H} ||=> K   strength = 1
  con-reason 4:  {F} ||=> I   strength = 1
  con-reason 5:  {F} ||=> (B @ E)   strength = 1
  con-reason 6:  {H} ||=> (D @ G)   strength = 1
```

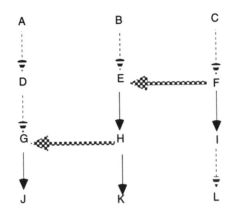

1
conclusion 1: A
by given
degree-of-support: 1
This node encodes a deductive argument.
2
conclusion 2: B
by given
degree-of-support: 1
This node encodes a deductive argument.
3
conclusion 3: C
by given
degree-of-support: 1
This node encodes a deductive argument.

Retrieving #<Query #1: J> from the inference-queue.
                         # 1
                         interest: J
                         This is of ultimate interest

Retrieving #<Query #2: K> from the inference-queue.
                         # 2
                         interest: K
                         This is of ultimate interest

Retrieving #<Query #3: L> from the inference-queue.
                         # 3
                         interest: L
                         This is of ultimate interest

Retrieving #<Conclusion #3: C> from the inference-queue.
4
conclusion 4: F
From { 3 } by pf-reason 4
degree-of-support: 1

This inference is defeasible.
         # 4
         interest: (C @ F)
         Of interest as defeater for inference-nodes (4)
         # 5
         interest: ~F
         Of interest as defeater for inference-nodes (4)

Retrieving #<Conclusion #4: F> from the inference-queue.
5
conclusion 5: I
From { 4 } by con-reason 4
degree-of-support: 1
This inference is not defeasible.
6
conclusion 6: (B @ E)
From { 4 } by con-reason 5
degree-of-support: 1
This inference is not defeasible.

Retrieving #<Conclusion #5: I> from the inference-queue.
7
conclusion 7: L
From { 5 } by pf-reason 5
degree-of-support: 1
This inference is defeasible.
         # 6
         interest: (I @ L)
         Of interest as defeater for inference-nodes (7)
         # 7
         interest: ~L
         Of interest as defeater for inference-nodes (7)

==

Justified belief in L
answers #<Query #3: L> affirmatively.

==

Retrieving #<Conclusion #7: L> from the inference-queue.

Retrieving #<Conclusion #2: B> from the inference-queue.
8
conclusion 8: E
From { 2 } by pf-reason 3
degree-of-support: 1
This inference is defeasible.
         # 8
         interest: (B @ E)
         Of interest as defeater for inference-nodes (8)
         # 9
         interest: ~E
         Of interest as defeater for inference-nodes (8)

vvvvvvvvvvvvvvvvvvvvvvvvvvvvvvvv
#<Node 8> has become defeated.

Retrieving #<Conclusion #8: E> from the inference-queue.
9
conclusion 9: H
From { 8 } by con-reason 2
degree-of-support: 1
This inference is not defeasible.
vvvvvvvvvvvvvvvvvvvvvvvvvvvvvvvv
#<Node 9> has become defeated.

Retrieving #<Conclusion #9: H> from the inference-queue.
10
conclusion 10: K
From { 9 } by con-reason 3
degree-of-support: 1
This inference is not defeasible.
vvvvvvvvvvvvvvvvvvvvvvvvvvvvvvvv
#<Node 10> has become defeated.

                    #<Conclusion #10: K> answers #<Query #2: K>

11
conclusion 11: (D @ G)
From { 9 } by con-reason 6
degree-of-support: 1
This inference is not defeasible.

                    vvvvvvvvvvvvvvvvvvvvvvvvvvvvvvvv
                    #<Node 11> has become defeated.

Retrieving #<Conclusion #10: K> from the inference-queue.

Retrieving #<Conclusion #1: A> from the inference-queue.
12
conclusion 12: D
From { 1 } by pf-reason 1
degree-of-support: 1
This inference is defeasible.
                              # 10
                              interest: (A @ D)
                              Of interest as defeater for inference-nodes (12)
                              # 11
                              interest: ~D
                              Of interest as defeater for inference-nodes (12)

Retrieving #<Conclusion #12: D> from the inference-queue.
13
conclusion 13: G
From { 12 } by pf-reason 2

degree-of-support: 1
This inference is defeasible.
     # 12
     interest: (D @ G)
     Of interest as defeater for inference-nodes (13)
     # 13
     interest: ~G
     Of interest as defeater for inference-nodes (13)

Retrieving #<Conclusion #13: G> from the inference-queue.
 # 14
conclusion 14: J
From { 13 } by con-reason 1
degree-of-support: 1
This inference is not defeasible.
     ==
     Justified belief in J
     answers #<Query #1: J> affirmatively.
     ==

Retrieving #<Conclusion #14: J> from the inference-queue.

Retrieving #<Conclusion #11: (D @ G)> from the inference-queue.

Retrieving #<Conclusion #6: (B @ E)> from the inference-queue.

Retrieving #<Interest 13: ~G supposing { }> from the inference-queue.

Retrieving #<Interest 11: ~D supposing { }> from the inference-queue.

Retrieving #<Interest 9: ~E supposing { }> from the inference-queue.

Retrieving #<Interest 7: ~L supposing { }> from the inference-queue.

Retrieving #<Interest 5: ~F supposing { }> from the inference-queue.

Retrieving #<Interest 12: (D @ G) supposing { }> from the inference-queue.

Retrieving #<Interest 10: (A @ D) supposing { }> from the inference-queue.

Retrieving #<Interest 8: (B @ E) supposing { }> from the inference-queue.

Retrieving #<Interest 6: (I @ L) supposing { }> from the inference-queue.

Retrieving #<Interest 4: (C @ F) supposing { }> from the inference-queue.

================ ULTIMATE EPISTEMIC INTERESTS ==================
Interest in L
is answered affirmatively by #<Conclusion #7: L>

Interest in K
is unsatisfied.

Interest in J
is answered affirmatively by #<Conclusion #14: J>
===
ARGUMENT #1
This is an undefeated argument for:
   L
which is of ultimate interest.

3. C   given
4. F   pf-reason 4 from { 3 }
5. I   con-reason 4 from { 4 }
7. L   pf-reason 5 from { 5 }
===
ARGUMENT #2
This is a defeated argument for:
   K
which is of ultimate interest.

2. B   given
8. E   pf-reason 3 from { 2 }
9. H   con-reason 2 from { 8 }
10. K   con-reason 3 from { 9 }
===
ARGUMENT #3
This is an undefeated argument for:
   (B @ E)
and it defeats argument #2

3. C   given
4. F   pf-reason 4 from { 3 }
6. (B @ E)   con-reason 5 from { 4 }
===
ARGUMENT #4
This is an undefeated argument for:
   J
which is of ultimate interest.

1. A   given
12. D   pf-reason 1 from { 1 }
13. G   pf-reason 2 from { 12 }
14. J   con-reason 1 from { 13 }
===
ARGUMENT #5
This is a defeated argument for:
   (D @ G)
and it defeats argument #4

2. B   given

8. E   pf-reason 3 from { 2 }
9. H   con-reason 2 from { 8 }
11. (D @ G)   con-reason 6 from { 9 }

This argument is defeated by argument #3
==
Elapsed time = 0.08 sec
Cumulative size of arguments = 14
Size of inference-graph = 14
100% of the inference-graph was used in the argument.

For a second example, consider a simple case of collective defeat:

Problem #2
This is a case of collective defeat.
Given premises:
    P   justification = 1
    A   justification = 1
Ultimate epistemic interests:
    R   interest = 1

    FORWARDS PRIMA FACIE REASONS
    pf-reason 1:   {P} ||=> Q   strength = 1
    pf-reason 2:   {Q} ||=> R   strength = 1
    pf-reason 3:   {A} ||=> B   strength = 1

    BACKWARDS PRIMA FACIE REASONS
    pf-reason 4:   {} {C} ||=> ~R   strength = 1
    pf-reason 5:   {} {B} ||=> C   strength = 1

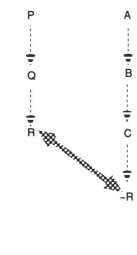

1
conclusion 1: P
by given
degree-of-support: 1
This node encodes a deductive argument.
2
conclusion 2: A
by given
degree-of-support: 1
This node encodes a deductive argument.

Retrieving #<Query #1: R> from the inference-queue.
      # 1
      interest: R
      This is of ultimate interest

Retrieving #<Conclusion #2: A> from the inference-queue.
3
conclusion 3: B
From { 2 } by pf-reason 3
degree-of-support: 1
This inference is defeasible.
      # 2
      interest: (A @ B)
      Of interest as defeater for inference-nodes (3)
      # 3
      interest: ~B
      Of interest as defeater for inference-nodes (3)

Retrieving #<Conclusion #3: B> from the inference-queue.

Retrieving #<Conclusion #1: P> from the inference-queue.
4
conclusion 4: Q
From { 1 } by pf-reason 1
degree-of-support: 1
This inference is defeasible.
      # 4
      interest: (P @ Q)
      Of interest as defeater for inference-nodes (4)
      # 5
      interest: ~Q
      Of interest as defeater for inference-nodes (4)

Retrieving #<Conclusion #4: Q> from the inference-queue.
5
conclusion 5: R
From { 4 } by pf-reason 2
degree-of-support: 1

This inference is defeasible.
                # 6
                interest: (Q @ R)
                Of interest as defeater for inference-nodes (5)
                # 7
                interest: ~R
                Of interest as defeater for inference-nodes (5)
==
Justified belief in R
answers #<Query #1: R> affirmatively.
==

Retrieving #<Conclusion #5: R> from the inference-queue.

Retrieving #<Interest 7: ~R supposing { }> from the inference-queue.
                # 8
                interest: C
                For interest 7 by pf-reason 4

Retrieving #<Interest 8: C supposing { }> from the inference-queue.
                # 9
                interest: B
                For interest 8 by pf-reason 5
6
conclusion 6: C
From { 3 } by pf-reason 5
degree-of-support: 1
This inference is defeasible.
                # 10
                interest: (B @ C)
                Of interest as defeater for inference-nodes (6)
                # 11
                interest: ~C
                Of interest as defeater for inference-nodes (6)
7
conclusion 7: ~R
From { 6 } by pf-reason 4
degree-of-support: 1
This inference is defeasible.
                # 12
                interest: (C @ ~R)
                Of interest as defeater for inference-nodes (7)
                Readopting interest in:
                # 1
                interest: R
                Of interest as defeater for inference-nodes (7)

Recomputed assignment-tree:
assignment-tree 0:
. ((#<Node 6>) (#<Node 4>) (#<Node 3>) (#<Node 2>) (#<Node 1>))
. triangle 1:
. . (#<Node 7> #<Node 5>)
. . . . assignment-tree 1:
. . . . . ((#<Node 5> . T) (#<Node 7>))
. . . . assignment-tree 2:
. . . . . ((#<Node 5>) (#<Node 7> . T))
           vvvvvvvvvvvvvvvvvvvvvvvvvvvvvvv
           #<Node 7> has become defeated.
           vvvvvvvvvvvvvvvvvvvvvvvvvvvvvvv
           #<Node 5> has become defeated.
           ===
           Lowering the degree of justification of R
           retracts the previous answer to #<Query #1: R>
           ===

Retrieving #<Conclusion #6: C> from the inference-queue.

Retrieving #<Conclusion #7: ~R> from the inference-queue.

Retrieving #<Interest 9: B supposing { }> from the inference-queue.

Retrieving #<Interest 11: ~C supposing { }> from the inference-queue.

Retrieving #<Interest 5: ~Q supposing { }> from the inference-queue.

Retrieving #<Interest 3: ~B supposing { }> from the inference-queue.

Retrieving #<Interest 10: (B @ C) supposing { }> from the inference-queue.

Retrieving #<Interest 6: (Q @ R) supposing { }> from the inference-queue.

Retrieving #<Interest 4: (P @ Q) supposing { }> from the inference-queue.

Retrieving #<Interest 2: (A @ B) supposing { }> from the inference-queue.

Retrieving #<Interest 12: (C @ ~R) supposing { }> from the inference-queue.

================ ULTIMATE EPISTEMIC INTERESTS ==================
Interest in R
is unsatisfied.
===
ARGUMENT #1
This is a defeated argument for:
    R
which is of ultimate interest.

1. P   given
4. Q   pf-reason 1 from { 1 }
5. R   pf-reason 2 from { 4 }
==
ARGUMENT #2
This is a defeated argument for:
   ~R
and it defeats argument #1

2. A   given
3. B   pf-reason 3 from { 2 }
6. C   pf-reason 5 from { 3 }
7. ~R   pf-reason 4 from { 6 }

This argument is defeated by argument #1
==

Elapsed time = 0.05 sec
Cumulative size of arguments = 7
Size of inference-graph = 7
100% of the inference-graph was used in the argument.

Figure 8 of chapter 3 diagrammed the lottery paradox paradox.
The following is a display of OSCAR's reasoning applied to that problem
for the simplified case of three tickets:

Problem #8
Figure 8 -- the lottery paradox paradox
Given premises:
   P   justification = 1
Ultimate epistemic interests:
   ~T1   interest = 1
   ~T2   interest = 1
   ~T3   interest = 1

   FORWARDS PRIMA FACIE REASONS
   pf-reason 1: {R} ||=> ~T1   strength = 1
   pf-reason 2: {R} ||=> ~T2   strength = 1
   pf-reason 3: {R} ||=> ~T3   strength = 1
   pf-reason 4: {P} ||=> R   strength = 1

   FORWARDS CONCLUSIVE REASONS
   con-reason 1: {R , ~T1 , ~T2} ||=> T3   strength = 1
   con-reason 2: {R , ~T2 , ~T3} ||=> T1   strength = 1
   con-reason 3: {R , ~T1 , ~T3} ||=> T2   strength = 1
   con-reason 4: {~T1 , ~T2 , ~T3} ||=> ~R   strength = 1

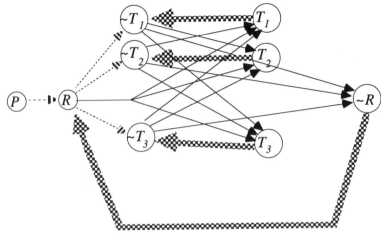

1
conclusion 1: P
by given
degree-of-support: 1
This node encodes a deductive argument.

Retrieving #<Conclusion #1: P> from the inference-queue.
 # 2
conclusion 2: R
From { 1 } by pf-reason 4
degree-of-support: 1
This inference is defeasible.
                    # 1
                    interest: (P @ R)
                    Of interest as defeater for inference-nodes (2)
                    # 2
                    interest: ~R
                    Of interest as defeater for inference-nodes (2)

Retrieving #<Conclusion #2: R> from the inference-queue.
 # 3
conclusion 3: ~T1
From { 2 } by pf-reason 1
degree-of-support: 1
This inference is defeasible.
                    # 3
                    interest: (R @ ~T1)
                    Of interest as defeater for inference-nodes (3)
                    # 4
                    interest: T1
                    Of interest as defeater for inference-nodes (3)

4
conclusion 4: ~T2
From { 2 } by pf-reason 2
degree-of-support: 1
This inference is defeasible.

> # 5
> interest: (R @ ~T2)
> Of interest as defeater for inference-nodes (4)
> # 6
> interest: T2
> Of interest as defeater for inference-nodes (4)

5
conclusion 5: ~T3
From { 2 } by pf-reason 3
degree-of-support: 1
This inference is defeasible.

> # 7
> interest: (R @ ~T3)
> Of interest as defeater for inference-nodes (5)
> # 8
> interest: T3
> Of interest as defeater for inference-nodes (5)

Retrieving #<Conclusion #5: ~T3> from the inference-queue.

Retrieving #<Interest 8: T3 supposing { }> from the inference-queue.

Retrieving #<Conclusion #4: ~T2> from the inference-queue.
6
conclusion 6: T1
From { 4 , 5 , 2 } by con-reason 2
degree-of-support: 1
This inference is not defeasible.

Recomputed assignment-tree:
assignment-tree 0:
. ((#<Node 3> . T) (#<Node 6>) (#<Node 5>) (#<Node 4>) (#<Node 2>)
. (#<Node 1>))
    vvvvvvvvvvvvvvvvvvvvvvvvvvvvvvvvvvvvv
    #<Node 3> has become defeated.

Retrieving #<Conclusion #6: T1> from the inference-queue.

Retrieving #<Interest 6: T2 supposing { }> from the inference-queue.

Retrieving #<Interest 4: T1 supposing { }> from the inference-queue.

Retrieving #<Query #1: ~T1> from the inference-queue.

> # 9
> interest: ~T1
> This is of ultimate interest

```
----------------------------------------
#<Conclusion #3:  ~T1> answers #<Query #1: ~T1>
----------------------------------------
```

```
-------------------------------------------------------------------------
Retrieving #<Query #2: ~T2> from the inference-queue.
          # 10
          interest: ~T2
          This is of ultimate interest
     =============================================
     Justified belief in ~T2
     answers #<Query #2: ~T2> affirmatively.
     =============================================
```

```
-------------------------------------------------------------------------
Retrieving #<Query #3: ~T3> from the inference-queue.
          # 11
          interest: ~T3
          This is of ultimate interest
     =============================================
     Justified belief in ~T3
     answers #<Query #3: ~T3> affirmatively.
     =============================================
```

```
-------------------------------------------------------------------------
Retrieving #<Conclusion #3:  ~T1> from the inference-queue.
# 7
conclusion 7: T3
From { 3 , 4 , 2 } by con-reason 1
degree-of-support: 1
This inference is not defeasible.
-------------------------------------------------------------------------
Recomputed assignment-tree:
assignment-tree 0:
. ((#<Node 4>) (#<Node 2>) (#<Node 1>))
. triangle 1:
. . (#<Node 5> #<Node 6> #<Node 3> #<Node 7>)
. . . . assignment-tree 1:
. . . . . ((#<Node 7> . T) (#<Node 3> . T) (#<Node 6>) (#<Node 5>))
. . . . assignment-tree 2:
. . . . . ((#<Node 7>) (#<Node 3>) (#<Node 6> . T) (#<Node 5> . T))
          vvvvvvvvvvvvvvvvvvvvvvvvvvvvvvvvvv
          #<Node 5> has become defeated.
          vvvvvvvvvvvvvvvvvvvvvvvvvvvvvvvvvv
          #<Node 6> has become defeated.
          vvvvvvvvvvvvvvvvvvvvvvvvvvvvvvvvvv
          #<Node 7> has become defeated.
          =========================================
          Lowering the degree of justification of ~T3
          retracts the previous answer to #<Query #3: ~T3>
          =========================================
# 8
conclusion 8: T2
From { 3 , 5 , 2 } by con-reason 3
```

degree-of-support: 1
This inference is not defeasible.

Recomputed assignment-tree:
assignment-tree 0:
. ((#<Node 2>) (#<Node 1>))
. triangle 2:
. . (#<Node 5> #<Node 6> #<Node 8> #<Node 4> #<Node 3>
. . #<Node 7>)
. . . . assignment-tree 3:
. . . . . ((#<Node 7> . T) (#<Node 8> . T) (#<Node 3> . T) (#<Node 6>) (#<Node 4>)
. . . . . (#<Node 5>))
. . . . assignment-tree 4:
. . . . . ((#<Node 8>) (#<Node 3>) (#<Node 6> . T) (#<Node 7> . T) (#<Node 4> . T)
. . . . . (#<Node 5>))
. . . . assignment-tree 5:
. . . . . ((#<Node 7>) (#<Node 4>) (#<Node 3>) (#<Node 6> . T) (#<Node 8> . T)
. . . . . (#<Node 5> . T))
                vvvvvvvvvvvvvvvvvvvvvvvvvvvvvvvvvv
                #<Node 4> has become defeated.
                vvvvvvvvvvvvvvvvvvvvvvvvvvvvvvvvvv
                #<Node 8> has become defeated.

                ==
                Lowering the degree of justification of ~T2
                retracts the previous answer to #<Query #2: ~T2>
                ==
9
conclusion 9: ~R
From { 3 , 5 , 4 } by con-reason 4
degree-of-support: 1
This inference is not defeasible.

Recomputed assignment-tree:
assignment-tree 0:
. ((#<Node 1>))
. triangle 3:
. . (#<Node 2> #<Node 6> #<Node 7> #<Node 8> #<Node 4>
. . #<Node 5> #<Node 3> #<Node 9>)
. . . . assignment-tree 6:
. . . . . ((#<Node 6> . T) (#<Node 8> . T) (#<Node 9> . T) (#<Node 5> . T) (#<Node 7>)
. . . . . (#<Node 4>) (#<Node 3>) (#<Node 2>))
. . . . assignment-tree 7:
. . . . . ((#<Node 8>) (#<Node 5>) (#<Node 6> . T) (#<Node 7> . T) (#<Node 9> . T)
. . . . . (#<Node 4> . T) (#<Node 3>) (#<Node 2>))
. . . . assignment-tree 8:
. . . . . ((#<Node 6>) (#<Node 4>) (#<Node 5>) (#<Node 7> . T) (#<Node 8> . T)
. . . . . (#<Node 9> . T) (#<Node 3> . T) (#<Node 2>))
                vvvvvvvvvvvvvvvvvvvvvvvvvvvvvvvvvv
                #<Node 9> has become defeated.

Retrieving #<Conclusion #8: T2> from the inference-queue.

Retrieving #<Conclusion #7: T3> from the inference-queue.

Retrieving #<Conclusion #9: ~R> from the inference-queue.

Retrieving #<Interest 2: ~R supposing { }> from the inference-queue.

Retrieving #<Interest 1: (P @ R) supposing { }> from the inference-queue.

Retrieving #<Interest 7: (R @ ~T3) supposing { }> from the inference-queue.

Retrieving #<Interest 5: (R @ ~T2) supposing { }> from the inference-queue.

Retrieving #<Interest 3: (R @ ~T1) supposing { }> from the inference-queue.

================ ULTIMATE EPISTEMIC INTERESTS =================
Interest in ~T3
is unsatisfied.

Interest in ~T2
is unsatisfied.

Interest in ~T1
is unsatisfied.
==
ARGUMENT #1
This is a defeated argument for:
    ~T3
which is of ultimate interest.

1. P   given
2. R   pf-reason 4 from { 1 }
5. ~T3   pf-reason 3 from { 2 }
==
ARGUMENT #2
This is a defeated argument for:
    T3
and it defeats argument #1

1. P   given
2. R   pf-reason 4 from { 1 }
4. ~T2   pf-reason 2 from { 2 }
3. ~T1   pf-reason 1 from { 2 }
7. T3   con-reason 1 from { 3 , 4 , 2 }
==
ARGUMENT #3
This is a defeated argument for:
    T2
and it defeats argument #2

1. P   given
2. R   pf-reason 4 from { 1 }
5. ~T3   pf-reason 3 from { 2 }
3. ~T1   pf-reason 1 from { 2 }
8. T2   con-reason 3 from { 3 , 5 , 2 }

This argument is defeated by argument #2

===
ARGUMENT #4
This is a defeated argument for:
    T1
and it defeats arguments #2 , #3

1. P   given
2. R   pf-reason 4 from { 1 }
5. ~T3   pf-reason 3 from { 2 }
4. ~T2   pf-reason 2 from { 2 }
6. T1   con-reason 2 from { 4 , 5 , 2 }

This argument is defeated by arguments #2 , #3

===
ARGUMENT #5
This is a defeated argument for:
    ~R
and it defeats arguments #1 , #2 , #3 , #4 , #5

1. P   given
2. R   pf-reason 4 from { 1 }
4. ~T2   pf-reason 2 from { 2 }
5. ~T3   pf-reason 3 from { 2 }
3. ~T1   pf-reason 1 from { 2 }
9. ~R   con-reason 4 from { 3 , 5 , 4 }

This argument is defeated by arguments #2 , #3 , #4 , #5

===
ARGUMENT #6
This is a defeated argument for:
    ~T2
which is of ultimate interest.

1. P   given
2. R   pf-reason 4 from { 1 }
4. ~T2   pf-reason 2 from { 2 }

===
ARGUMENT #7
This is a defeated argument for:
    ~T1
which is of ultimate interest.

1. P   given
2. R   pf-reason 4 from { 1 }

3. ~T1   pf-reason 1 from { 2 }
===

Elapsed time = 0.14 sec
Cumulative size of arguments = 9
Size of inference-graph = 9
100% of the inference-graph was used in the argument.

Given suitable inference rules (in the form of conclusive reasons),
OSCAR can also prove theorems in logic. The following is a simple
example:

Problem #30

Given premises:
   (q -> r)   justification = 1
   (r -> (p & q))   justification = 1
   (p -> (q v r))   justification = 1
Ultimate epistemic interests:
   (p <-> q)   interest = 1

1
conclusion 1: (q -> r)
by given
degree-of-support: 1
This node encodes a deductive argument.
2
conclusion 2: (r -> (p & q))
by given
degree-of-support: 1
This node encodes a deductive argument.
3
conclusion 3: (p -> (q v r))
by given
degree-of-support: 1
This node encodes a deductive argument.

Retrieving #<Query #1: (p <-> q)> from the inference-queue.
            # 1
            interest: (p <-> q)
            This is of ultimate interest
            # 2
            interest: (q -> p)
            For interest 1 by bicondit-intro

Retrieving #<Interest 2: (q -> p) supposing { }> from the inference-queue.
4
conclusion 4: q   supposition: { q }

by supposition
degree-of-support: 1
This node encodes a deductive argument.
                              # 3
                              interest: p   supposition: { q }
                              For interest 2 by conditionalization
5
conclusion 5: ~(q -> p)   supposition: { ~(q -> p) }
by supposition
degree-of-support: 1
This node encodes a deductive argument.

Retrieving #<Interest 3: p supposing { q }> from the inference-queue.
6
conclusion 6: ~p   supposition: { q , ~p }
by supposition
degree-of-support: 1
This node encodes a deductive argument.

Retrieving #<Conclusion #4: q supposing { q }> from the inference-queue.
                              # 4
                              interest: ~q   supposition: { q , ~p }
                              For interest 3 by reductio using conclusion 4

Retrieving #<Conclusion #1: (q -> r)> from the inference-queue.
7
conclusion 7: r   supposition: { q }
From { 1 , 4 } by modus-ponens1
degree-of-support: 1
This node encodes a deductive argument.
                              # 5
                              interest: ~(q -> r)   supposition: { q , ~p }
                              For interest 3 by reductio using conclusion 1
                              # 6
                              interest: ~(q -> r)   supposition: { ~(q -> p) }
                              For interest 2 by reductio using conclusion 1

Retrieving #<Conclusion #7: r supposing { q }> from the inference-queue.
                              # 7
                              interest: ~r   supposition: { q , ~p }
                              For interest 3 by reductio using conclusion 7

Retrieving #<Interest 7: ~r supposing { q , ~p }> from the inference-queue.

Retrieving #<Interest 4: ~q supposing { q , ~p }> from the inference-queue.

Retrieving #<Conclusion #6: ~p supposing { q , ~p }> from the inference-queue.
                              # 8
                              interest: p   supposition: { q , ~p }
                              For interest 3 by reductio using conclusion 6

Retrieving #<Interest 8: p supposing { q , ~p }> from the inference-queue.

Retrieving #<Conclusion #3: (p -> (q v r))> from the inference-queue.

          # 9

          interest: ~(p -> (q v r))   supposition: { q , ~p }

          For interest 3 by reductio using conclusion 3

          # 10

          interest: ~(p -> (q v r))   supposition: { ~(q -> p) }

          For interest 2 by reductio using conclusion 3

Retrieving #<Conclusion #2: (r -> (p & q))> from the inference-queue.

8

conclusion 8: (p & q)   supposition: { q }

From { 2 , 7 } by modus-ponens1

degree-of-support: 1

This node encodes a deductive argument.

          # 11

          interest: ~(r -> (p & q))   supposition: { q , ~p }

          For interest 3 by reductio using conclusion 2

          # 12

          interest: ~(r -> (p & q))   supposition: { ~(q -> p) }

          For interest 2 by reductio using conclusion 2

Retrieving #<Conclusion #8: (p & q) supposing { q }> from the inference-queue.

9

conclusion 9: p   supposition: { q }

From { 8 } by simp

degree-of-support: 1

This node encodes a deductive argument.

....

Cancelling #<Interest 8: p supposing { q , ~p }>

....

10

conclusion 10: (q -> p)

From { 9 } by conditionalization

degree-of-support: 1

This node encodes a deductive argument.

          # 13

          interest: (p -> q)

          For interest 1 by bicondit-intro using conclusion 10

....

Cancelling #<Interest 2: (q -> p) supposing { }>

. Cancelling #<Node 5>

. Cancelling #<Node 4>

. . Cancelling #<Node 7>

. . . Cancelling #<Node 8>

. . . . Cancelling #<Node 9>

. Cancelling #<Interest 12: ~(r -> (p & q)) supposing { ~(q -> p) }>

. Cancelling #<Interest 10: ~(p -> (q v r)) supposing { ~(q -> p) }>

. Cancelling #<Interest 6: ~(q -> r) supposing { ~(q -> p) }>

. Cancelling #<Interest 3: p supposing { q }>

. . Cancelling #<Node 6>
. . Cancelling #<Interest 11: ~(r -> (p & q)) supposing { q , ~p }>
. . Cancelling #<Interest 9: ~(p -> (q v r)) supposing { q , ~p }>
. . Cancelling #<Interest 8: p supposing { q , ~p }>
. . Cancelling #<Interest 7: ~r supposing { q , ~p }>
. . Cancelling #<Interest 5: ~(q -> r) supposing { q , ~p }>
. . Cancelling #<Interest 4: ~q supposing { q , ~p }>
....

Retrieving #<Interest 13: (p -> q) supposing { }> from the inference-queue.
11
conclusion 11: p   supposition: { p }
by supposition
degree-of-support: 1
This node encodes a deductive argument.
                # 14
                interest: q   supposition: { p }
                For interest 13 by conditionalization
12
conclusion 12: ~(p -> q)   supposition: { ~(p -> q) }
by supposition
degree-of-support: 1
This node encodes a deductive argument.
                # 15
                interest: ~(r -> (p & q))   supposition: { ~(p -> q) }
                For interest 13 by reductio using conclusion 2
                # 16
                interest: ~(p -> (q v r))   supposition: { ~(p -> q) }
                For interest 13 by reductio using conclusion 3
                # 17
                interest: ~(q -> r)   supposition: { ~(p -> q) }
                For interest 13 by reductio using conclusion 1

Retrieving #<Interest 14: q supposing { p }> from the inference-queue.
13
conclusion 13: ~q   supposition: { p , ~q }
by supposition
degree-of-support: 1
This node encodes a deductive argument.
                # 18
                interest: ~(r -> (p & q))   supposition: { p , ~q }
                For interest 14 by reductio using conclusion 2
                # 19
                interest: ~(p -> (q v r))   supposition: { p , ~q }
                For interest 14 by reductio using conclusion 3
                # 20
                interest: ~(q -> r)   supposition: { p , ~q }
                For interest 14 by reductio using conclusion 1

Retrieving #<Conclusion #11: p supposing { p }> from the inference-queue.
14

conclusion 14: (q v r)   supposition: { p }
From { 11 , 3 } by modus-ponens2
degree-of-support: 1
This node encodes a deductive argument.
       # 21
       interest: ~p   supposition: { p , ~q }
       For interest 14 by reductio using conclusion 11

Retrieving #<Conclusion #10: (q -> p)> from the inference-queue.
       # 22
       interest: ~(q -> p)   supposition: { p , ~q }
       For interest 14 by reductio using conclusion 10
       # 23
       interest: ~(q -> p)   supposition: { ~(p -> q) }
       For interest 13 by reductio using conclusion 10

Retrieving #<Conclusion #14: (q v r) supposing { p }> from the inference-queue.

Retrieving #<Interest 21: ~p supposing { p , ~q }> from the inference-queue.

Retrieving #<Conclusion #13: ~q supposing { p , ~q }> from the inference-queue.
       # 15
conclusion 15: r   supposition: { p , ~q }
From { 13 , 14 } by disj-syl21
degree-of-support: 1
This node encodes a deductive argument.
       # 24
       interest: q   supposition: { p , ~q }
       For interest 14 by reductio using conclusion 13

Retrieving #<Interest 24: q supposing { p , ~q }> from the inference-queue.

Retrieving #<Conclusion #15: r supposing { p , ~q }> from the inference-queue.
       # 16
conclusion 16: (p & q)   supposition: { p , ~q }
From { 15 , 2 } by modus-ponens2
degree-of-support: 1
This node encodes a deductive argument.
       # 25
       interest: ~r   supposition: { p , ~q }
       For interest 14 by reductio using conclusion 15

Retrieving #<Interest 25: ~r supposing { p , ~q }> from the inference-queue.

Retrieving #<Conclusion #16: (p & q) supposing { p , ~q }> from the inference-queue.
       # 17
conclusion 17: q   supposition: { p , ~q }
From { 16 } by simp
degree-of-support: 1
This node encodes a deductive argument.

18
conclusion 18: q   supposition: { p }
From { 13 , 17 } by reductio
degree-of-support: 1
This node encodes a deductive argument.
19
conclusion 19: (p -> q)
From { 18 } by conditionalization
degree-of-support: 1
This node encodes a deductive argument.
20
conclusion 20: (p <-> q)
From { 10 , 19 } by bicondit-intro
degree-of-support: 1
This node encodes a deductive argument.

==
Justified belief in (p <-> q)
answers #<Query #1: (p <-> q)> affirmatively.
==
ALL QUERIES HAVE BEEN ANSWERED DEDUCTIVELY.

================= ULTIMATE EPISTEMIC INTERESTS =================
Interest in (p <-> q)
is answered affirmatively by conclusion 20
==
ARGUMENT #1
This is a deductive argument for:
   (p <-> q)
which is of ultimate interest.

3. (p -> (q v r))   given
1. (q -> r)   given
2. (r -> (p & q))   given
   |---
   | Suppose: { q }
   |---
   | 4. q   supposition
   | 7. r   modus-ponens1 from { 1 , 4 }
   | 8. (p & q)   modus-ponens1 from { 2 , 7 }
   | 9. p   simp from { 8 }
10. (q -> p)   conditionalization from { 9 }
   |---
   | Suppose: { p }
   |---
   | 11. p   supposition
   | 14. (q v r)   modus-ponens2 from { 11 , 3 }
      |---
      | Suppose: { p , ~q }
      |---
      | 13. ~q   supposition
      | 15. r   disj-syl21 from { 13 , 14 }

```
    | 16. (p & q)    modus-ponens2 from { 15 , 2 }
    | 17. q    simp from { 16 }
    | 18. q    reductio from { 13 , 17 }
    19. (p -> q)    conditionalization from { 18 }
    20. (p <-> q)    bicondit-intro from { 10 , 19 }
==================================================================
```

Elapsed time = 0.17 sec
Cumulative size of arguments = 17
Size of inference-graph = 20
85% of the inference-graph was used in the argument.
25 interests were adopted.

Some problems require the use of both defeasible and deductive reasoning. For instance, the lottery paradox paradox was formulated above so as to avoid the use of logic, but it is more natural to formulate it as follows:

Problem #9
Figure 8 -- the lottery paradox paradox using logic
Given premises:
    P   justification = 1
Ultimate epistemic interests:
    ~T1   interest = 1
    ~T2   interest = 1
    ~T3   interest = 1

FORWARDS PRIMA FACIE REASONS
    pf-reason 1: {R} ||=> ~T1   strength = 1
    pf-reason 2: {R} ||=> ~T2   strength = 1
    pf-reason 3: {R} ||=> ~T3   strength = 1
    pf-reason 4: {P} ||=> R   strength = 1

FORWARDS CONCLUSIVE REASONS
    con-reason 1: {R} ||=> (T1 v (T2 v T3))   strength = 1

```
================ ULTIMATE EPISTEMIC INTERESTS =================
Interest in ~T3
is unsatisfied.
-----------------------------------------------------
Interest in ~T2
is unsatisfied.
-----------------------------------------------------
Interest in ~T1
is unsatisfied.
==================================================================
```

ARGUMENT #1
This is a defeated argument for:
~T3
which is of ultimate interest.

1. P   given
2. R   pf-reason 4 from { 1 }
6. ~T3   pf-reason 3 from { 2 }
==
ARGUMENT #2
This is a defeated argument for:
T3
and it defeats argument #1

1. P   given
2. R   pf-reason 4 from { 1 }
5. ~T2   pf-reason 2 from { 2 }
3. (T1 v (T2 v T3))   con-reason 1 from { 2 }
4. ~T1   pf-reason 1 from { 2 }
15. (T2 v T3)   disj-syl11 from { 3 , 4 }
16. T3   disj-syl11 from { 15 , 5 }
==
ARGUMENT #3
This is a defeated argument for:
T2
and it defeats argument #2

1. P   given
2. R   pf-reason 4 from { 1 }
6. ~T3   pf-reason 3 from { 2 }
3. (T1 v (T2 v T3))   con-reason 1 from { 2 }
4. ~T1   pf-reason 1 from { 2 }
15. (T2 v T3)   disj-syl11 from { 3 , 4 }
17. T2   disj-syl12 from { 15 , 6 }

This argument is defeated by argument #2
==
ARGUMENT #4
This is a defeated argument for:
~R
and it defeats arguments #1 , #2 , #3 , #4

1. P   given
2. R   pf-reason 4 from { 1 }
4. ~T1   pf-reason 1 from { 2 }
5. ~T2   pf-reason 2 from { 2 }
6. ~T3   pf-reason 3 from { 2 }
19. ~(T2 v T3)   i-neg-disj from { 6 , 5 }
    |---
    | Suppose: { R }
    |---

| 13. R   reductio-supposition
| 44. (T1 v (T2 v T3))   con-reason 1 from { 13 }
| 46. T1   disj-syl12 from { 44 , 19 }
47. ~R   reductio from { 46 , 4 }

This argument is defeated by arguments #2 , #3 , #4

===
ARGUMENT #5
This is a defeated argument for:
  T1
and it defeats arguments #2 , #3 , #4

1. P   given
2. R   pf-reason 4 from { 1 }
3. (T1 v (T2 v T3))   con-reason 1 from { 2 }
6. ~T3   pf-reason 3 from { 2 }
5. ~T2   pf-reason 2 from { 2 }
19. ~(T2 v T3)   i-neg-disj from { 6 , 5 }
25. T1   disj-syl22 from { 19 , 3 }

This argument is defeated by arguments #2 , #3 , #4

===
ARGUMENT #6
This is a defeated argument for:
  ~T2
which is of ultimate interest.

1. P   given
2. R   pf-reason 4 from { 1 }
5. ~T2   pf-reason 2 from { 2 }

===
ARGUMENT #7
This is a defeated argument for:
  ~T1
which is of ultimate interest.

1. P   given
2. R   pf-reason 4 from { 1 }
4. ~T1   pf-reason 1 from { 2 }
===

Elapsed time = 0.69 sec
Cumulative size of arguments = 15
Size of inference-graph = 51
29% of the inference-graph was used in the argument.
15 interests were adopted.

Another example of interest is the paradox of the preface, as diagrammed in figure 18 of chapter 3:

Problem #17
Figure 18 -- the paradox of the preface, using logic.
Given premises:
    P1   justification = 1
    P2   justification = 1
    P3   justification = 1
    S   justification = 1
    T   justification = 1
Ultimate epistemic interests:
    (Q1 & (Q2 & Q3))   interest = 1

FORWARDS PRIMA FACIE REASONS
    pf-reason 1: {P1} ||=> Q1   strength = 1
    pf-reason 2: {P2} ||=> Q2   strength = 1
    pf-reason 3: {P3} ||=> Q3   strength = 1
    pf-reason 4: {S} ||=> R   strength = 1
    pf-reason 5: {T} ||=> ~(Q1 & (Q2 & Q3))   strength = 1
    pf-reason 6: {S1} ||=> (T @ ~(Q1 & (Q2 & Q3)))   strength = 1
    pf-reason 7: {S2} ||=> (T @ ~(Q1 & (Q2 & Q3)))   strength = 1
    pf-reason 8: {S3} ||=> (T @ ~(Q1 & (Q2 & Q3)))   strength = 1

FORWARDS CONCLUSIVE REASONS
    con-reason 4: {R , Q1 , Q3} ||=> S2   strength = 1
    con-reason 5: {R , Q2 , Q3} ||=> S1   strength = 1
    con-reason 6: {R , Q1 , Q2} ||=> S3   strength = 1

=============== ULTIMATE EPISTEMIC INTERESTS =================
Interest in (Q1 & (Q2 & Q3))
is answered affirmatively by conclusion 28
==
ARGUMENT #1
This is an undefeated argument for:
    (Q1 & (Q2 & Q3))
which is of ultimate interest.

1. P1   given
12. Q1   pf-reason 1 from { 1 }
3. P3   given
2. P2   given
8. Q3   pf-reason 3 from { 3 }
9. Q2   pf-reason 2 from { 2 }
29. (Q2 & Q3)   adjunction from { 8 , 9 }
30. (Q1 & (Q2 & Q3))   adjunction from { 29 , 12 }
==

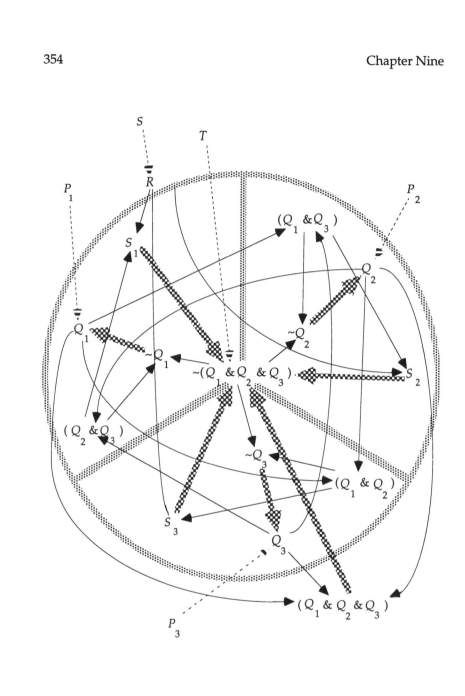

ARGUMENT #2
This is a defeated argument for:
  ~Q2
and it defeats argument #1

3. P3   given
8. Q3   pf-reason 3 from { 3 } 1. P1   given
12. Q1   pf-reason 1 from { 1 }
5. T   given
6. ~(Q1 & (Q2 & Q3))   pf-reason 5 from { 5 }
38. (~Q1 v ~(Q2 & Q3))   DM from { 6 }
39. ~(Q2 & Q3)   disj-syl11 from { 38 , 12 }
41. (~Q2 v ~Q3)   DM from { 39 }
43. ~Q2   disj-syl12 from { 41 , 8 }

This argument is defeated by argument #1
==
ARGUMENT #3
This is a defeated argument for:
  ~Q3
and it defeats arguments #1 , #2

2. P2   given
9. Q2   pf-reason 2 from { 2 }
1. P1   given
12. Q1   pf-reason 1 from { 1 }
5. T   given
6. ~(Q1 & (Q2 & Q3))   pf-reason 5 from { 5 }
38. (~Q1 v ~(Q2 & Q3))   DM from { 6 }
39. ~(Q2 & Q3)   disj-syl11 from { 38 , 12 }
41. (~Q2 v ~Q3)   DM from { 39 }
42. ~Q3   disj-syl11 from { 41 , 9 }

This argument is defeated by arguments #1 , #2
==
ARGUMENT #4
This is a defeated argument for:
  ~Q1
and it defeats arguments #1 , #2 , #3

3. P3   given
2. P2   given
8. Q3   pf-reason 3 from { 3 }
9. Q2   pf-reason 2 from { 2 }
29. (Q2 & Q3)   adjunction from { 8 , 9 }
5. T   given
6. ~(Q1 & (Q2 & Q3))   pf-reason 5 from { 5 }
38. (~Q1 v ~(Q2 & Q3))   DM from { 6 }
40. ~Q1   disj-syl12 from { 38 , 29 }

This argument is defeated by arguments #1 , #2 , #3

===

ARGUMENT #5
This is an undefeated argument for:
    (T @ ~(Q1 & (Q2 & Q3)))
and it defeats arguments #2 , #3 , #4

2. P2   given
3. P3   given
4. S   given
9. Q2   pf-reason 2 from { 2 }
8. Q3   pf-reason 3 from { 3 }
7. R   pf-reason 4 from { 4 }
10. S1   con-reason 5 from { 9 , 8 , 7 }
11. (T @ ~(Q1 & (Q2 & Q3)))   pf-reason 6 from { 10 }

This argument is defeated by arguments #2 , #3
===

ARGUMENT #6
This is an undefeated argument for:
    (T @ ~(Q1 & (Q2 & Q3)))
and it defeats arguments #2 , #3 , #4

1. P1   given
2. P2   given
4. S   given
12. Q1   pf-reason 1 from { 1 }
9. Q2   pf-reason 2 from { 2 }
7. R   pf-reason 4 from { 4 }
14. S3   con-reason 6 from { 12 , 9 , 7 }
15. (T @ ~(Q1 & (Q2 & Q3)))   pf-reason 8 from { 14 }

This argument is defeated by arguments #2 , #4
===

ARGUMENT #7
This is an undefeated argument for:
    (T @ ~(Q1 & (Q2 & Q3)))
and it defeats arguments #2 , #3 , #4

1. P1   given
3. P3   given
4. S   given
12. Q1   pf-reason 1 from { 1 }
8. Q3   pf-reason 3 from { 3 }
7. R   pf-reason 4 from { 4 }
13. S2   con-reason 4 from { 12 , 8 , 7 }
16. (T @ ~(Q1 & (Q2 & Q3)))   pf-reason 7 from { 13 }

This argument is defeated by arguments #3 , #4
===

Elapsed time = 1.24 sec

Cumulative size of arguments = 24
Size of inference-graph = 82
29% of the inference-graph was used in the argument.
28 interests were adopted.

OSCAR can also perform deductive reasoning in the predicate calculus and combine such first-order reasoning with defeasible reasoning.
The following is an example of first-order deductive reasoning:

Problem #58
Pelletier's problem 36
Given premises:
  ($\forall$ x)($\exists$ y)(F x y)   justification = 1
  ($\forall$ x)($\exists$ z)(G x z)   justification = 1
  ($\forall$ x)($\forall$ y)(((F x y) v (G x y)) -> ($\forall$ z)(((F y z) v (G y z)) -> (H x z))) justification = 1
Ultimate epistemic interests:
  ($\forall$ x)($\exists$ y)(H x y)   interest = 1

================ ULTIMATE EPISTEMIC INTERESTS =================
Interest in ($\forall$ x)($\exists$ y)(H x y)
is answered affirmatively by conclusion 24
===
ARGUMENT #1
This is a deductive argument for:
  ($\forall$ x)($\exists$ y)(H x y)
which is of ultimate interest.

3. ($\forall$ x)($\forall$ y)(((F x y) v (G x y)) -> ($\forall$ z)(((F y z) v (G y z)) -> (H x z)))   given
10. ($\forall$ y)(((F x7 y) v (G x7 y)) -> ($\forall$ z)(((F y z) v (G y z)) -> (H x7 z)))   UI from{3 }
1. ($\forall$ x)($\exists$ y)(F x y)   given
8. ($\exists$ y)(F x5 y)   UI from { 1 }
9. (F x5 (@y6 x5))   EI from { 8 }
17. (~(G x8 (@y6 x8)) -> (F x8 (@y6 x8)))   conditionalization from { 9 }
18. ((F x8 (@y6 x8)) v (G x8 (@y6 x8)))   disj-cond-2 from { 17 }
11. (((F x7 x8) v (G x7 x8)) -> ($\forall$ z)(((F x8 z) v (G x8 z)) -> (H x7 z)))   UI from{ 10}
  |---
  | Suppose: { ~($\exists$ y)(H ^x0 y) }
  |---
  | 4. ~($\exists$ y)(H ^x0 y)   reductio-supposition
  | 12. ($\forall$ y)~(H ^x0 y)   neg-eg from { 4 }
  | 13. ~(H ^x0 x22)   UI from { 12 }
  | 19. ~(((F x8 (@y6 x8)) v (G x8 (@y6 x8))) -> (H ^x0 (@y6 x8)))
      i-neg-condit from { 18 , 13 }
  | 20. ($\exists$ z)~(((F x8 z) v (G x8 z)) -> (H ^x0 z))   EG from { 19 }
  | 21. ~($\forall$ z)(((F x8 z) v (G x8 z)) -> (H ^x0 z))   i-neg-ug from { 20 }
  | 22. ~(((F ^x0 (@y6 ^x0)) v (G ^x0 (@y6 ^x0)))) ->
            ($\forall$ z)(((F (@y6 ^x0) z) v (G (@y6 ^x0) z)) -> (H ^x0 z)))
      i-neg-condit from { 18 , 21 }
23. ($\exists$ y)(H ^x0 y)   reductio from { 22 , 11 }
24. ($\forall$ x)($\exists$ y)(H x y)   UG from { 23 }

==

Elapsed time = 0.64 sec
Cumulative size of arguments = 17
Size of inference-graph = 24
70% of the inference-graph was used in the argument.
15 interests were adopted.

4. The Status of the OSCAR Project

The objective of the OSCAR project is to produce a theory of rationality
of sufficient detail that it can provide the basis for the construction of
an artilect. This book has described an architecture for rational thought.
This architecture provides the framework for a system of epistemic
and practical cognition and it has been implemented in the program
OSCAR. "OSCAR" is also the name of the resulting artilect. It is a
consequence of this architecture that the difficult tasks all get relegated
to epistemic cognition. The architecture describes the general structure
of epistemic cognition but does not attempt to describe all of the details
of the reasoning required for answering the queries posed by practical
cognition. If the general theory embodied in this architecture is correct,
such reasoning can be implemented by providing the artilect with an
appropriate system of mental representation, an array of reason-
schemas (including conclusive reasons, prima facie reasons, and defeaters) segregated into backwards and forwards reason-schemas, and
a prioritizing scheme for the *inference-queue*. If this is done properly,
the artilect should be able to do all of the reasoning required. This is a
rather grand claim, and I would not go so far as to say that I am
confident that it is correct. But the only way to find out is to make a
concerted effort to incorporate such reasoning into OSCAR and test
the result. That is the objective of the next stage of the OSCAR project.

OSCAR must be provided with both reason-schemas and Q&I modules, neither of which involves further programming at the level of the
architecture. If the theory is correct, the programming task is finished,
at least in principle. The program described above is all the program
required for building an artilect.[2] The rest of what is involved is a

---

[2] This claim should be qualified in one way. For designing an artilect, perception
can, for the most part, be treated as an unanalyzed module providing input to
epistemic cognition. But there is one respect in which that is inadequate. I have
lumped the kind of introspection involved in reflexive cognition into perception, but
such introspection is entirely internal to epistemic cognition and should be given a

matter of providing appropriate data structures for use by the program
rather than a matter of extending the program. The task becomes one
of providing a logical analysis of the various kinds of reasoning and
Q&I modules required for answering the queries posed by practical
cognition.

Let us look more closely at the task of enabling OSCAR to do the
kinds of reasoning required of a rational agent. We have three degrees
of freedom in the control of OSCAR's reasoning. First, we control the
order in which reasoning is performed by stipulating how tasks are
prioritized in the *inference-queue*. In the current LISP implementation,
this is done in rather simple ways, but in principle, this can be a
matter of great complexity and sophistication. This also provides one
of the main handles the reflexive reasoner can use to control its own
reasoning. The second degree of freedom concerns the contents of
permanent-ultimate-epistemic-interests. These are, in effect, the set of
instructions that drive the whole system. The third degree of freedom
concerns the reason-schemas provided for the reasoner. Part of the
problem of providing reason-schemas concerns constructing a system
of mental representation that allows for efficient encoding of the reasoning. This has not been a topic of traditional philosophical interest,
but it has been a matter of great concern in both AI and cognitive
psychology. The reason-schemas currently employed by OSCAR are
formulated entirely in first-order logic, but that is almost certainly too
simple. However, it can be changed without changing the architecture,
simply by writing new reason-schemas. The next part of the problem
of providing reason-schemas concerns formulating the schemas themselves. This requires describing the schemas in complete logical detail,
specifying whether they formulate conclusive reasons or prima facie
reasons, and determining their directionality (backwards or forwards
reasons). For prima facie reasons, defeaters must be described, which
is a matter of providing more reason-schemas.

Finding a correct formulation of the reason-schemas involved in
various kinds of reasoning is to a large extent a traditional philosophical
problem. Topics of particular interest include induction, abduction,
direct inference, probabilistic acceptance rules, and perceptual knowledge. There is an immense philosophical literature on each of these

---

computational account. This is just a matter of inserting into the *inference-queue*
various beliefs about what is transpiring in cognition. But design decisions must be
made about which states should be introspectible and under what circumstances
introspection occurs. The programming problems here are trivial, but the design
problems may involve some subtle complexities.

topics. There are other philosophical problems that are less obviously connected with all of this, but which must nevertheless be dealt with in order to complete the project. An example is the liar paradox. It was noted in chapter 1 that a reflexive cognizer will encounter the liar paradox and must be capable of handling it in some non-crippling fashion. I suspect that a great many traditional philosophical problems may eventually turn out to be relevant to the enterprise of choosing reason-schemas for an artilect. AI itself has spawned a large literature on reasoning about time, change, causation, and so forth, all of which are of direct relevance to planning. This research is, in fact, of a traditional philosophical sort, although it has been carried out largely by nonphilosophers. The AI literature on automated theorem proving is also of direct relevance to the selection of reason-schemas. Any automated theorem prover could be implemented within OSCAR by selecting the proper reason-schemas and prioritizing relation.

One of the main functions of epistemic cognition in OSCAR is to construct plans. Planning has, of course, been one of the prominent subfields of AI. It is a familiar point that planning can be viewed as search through a space of possible plans, and most of the research in planning theory has been directed at controlling search to make it more efficient. In OSCAR, the search is carried out in the epistemic reasoner. In the OSCAR plan representation scheme, plans are set-theoretic objects. The task of finding a plan that meets certain criteria is analogous to that of proving mathematical existence theorems by making constructions.

A rational agent cannot live by reasoning alone. In order to survive in a fast-moving and hostile environment, a rational agent must have a liberal endowment of Q&I modules. That is as true of an artilect as of a natural rational agent. Designing truly sophisticated Q&I modules may prove more difficult than analyzing reasoning, because we can introspect much of what goes on in reasoning and use that to guide us in constructing theories of reasoning. That is the traditional method of philosophy. Q&I modules, on the other hand, are black boxes from the perspective of introspection. The design of appropriate Q&I modules is an engineering problem, pure and simple. Of course, we can also think of the design of reasoning systems as an engineering problem, but it is made simpler by the fact that we can observe and copy many of the details of a working reasoning system (human cognition) in action.

To summarize, the OSCAR project has proposed a general architecture for rational cognition, and this architecture has been implemented in a LISP program. But many of the most difficult problems remain. These consist of implementing specific kinds of reasoning within the architecture. The next stage of the OSCAR project will undertake this task.

OSCAR has been provided with a user interface that allows one to use it and experiment with it without doing any programming. Reason-schemas and problem sets can be typed into the system in a simple and perspicuous form, to encourage would-be cognitive carpenters to use OSCAR as a tool in their investigations. For instance, an epistemologist investigating inductive reasoning or inference to the best explanation can test proposed reason-schemas by loading them into OSCAR and seeing how they work on a variety of concrete problems. Readers are encouraged to obtain a copy of OSCAR and *The OSCAR Manual*, and experiment with them. These are available electronically, by anonymous FTP, from aruba.ccit.arizona.edu, in the directory pub/oscar. Help in obtaining the files by FTP or in running OSCAR can be secured by sending an email message to oscar-help@arizona.edu. Both *The OSCAR Manual* and the code will be updated periodically to reflect advances in the OSCAR project. In order to run OSCAR, all that is needed is access to a computer running Common LISP. Eventually, standalone versions of OSCAR will be produced that will not require the user to have LISP.

References

Agre, P. E., and Chapman, D.
1987   Pengi: an implementation of a theory of activity. *Proceedings of AAAI-87*, 268–272.

Allen, J., Hendler, J., and Tate, A.
1990   *Readings in Planning*. Los Altos, Calif.: Morgan Kaufmann.

Bacchus, Fahiem
1990   *Representing and Reasoning with Probabilistic Knowledge*. Cambridge, Mass.: MIT Press.

Baker, A., and Ginsberg, M.
1989   A theorem prover for prioritized circumscription. *Proceedings IJCAI-89*, 463–467.

Bratman, Michael
1987   *Intention, Plans, and Practical Reason*. Cambridge, Mass.: Harvard University Press.
1989   Intention and personal policies. *Philosophical Perspectives* **3**, 443–469.
1992   Planning and the stability of intention. *Minds and Machines* **2**, 1–16.

Bratman, Michael, Israel, D., and Pollack, M.
1991   Plans and resource-sounded practical reasoning. In *Philosophy and AI*, ed. Robert Cummins and John Pollock. Cambridge, Mass.: Bradford Books/MIT Press.

Bundy, Alan
1983   *The Computer Modeling of Mathematical Reasoning*. London: Academic Press.

Carnap, Rudolph
1950   *The Logical Foundations of Probability*. Chicago: University of Chicago Press.
1952   *The Continuum of Inductive Methods*. Chicago: University of Chicago Press.

Chang, C., and Lee, R.
1973   *Symbolic Logic and Mechanical Theorem Proving*. London: Academic Press.

Cheng, P. W., and Holyoak, K. J.
1985   Pragmatic reasoning schemas. *Cognitive Psychology* **17**, 391–406.

Chisholm, Roderick
1957   *Perceiving*. Ithaca: Cornell University Press.

1966   *Theory of Knowledge.* 1st ed. Englewood Cliffs, NJ.: Prentice-Hall.

1977   *Theory of Knowledge.* 2nd ed. Englewood Cliffs, NJ.: Prentice-Hall.

Cohn, A.

1985   On the solution of Schubert's steamroller in many sorted logic. *Proceedings IJCAI-85.*

Daniel, L.

1983   Planning and operations research. In *Artificial Intelligence: Tools, Techniques, and Applications.* New York: Harper & Row.

Dean, T., Firby, J., and Miller, D.

1988   Hierarchical planning involving deadlines, travel time, and resources. *Computational Intelligence* **4**, 381–398.

de Garis, Hugo

1989   What if AI succeeds?: the rise of the 21st century artilect. *AI Magazine* **10**, 16–27.

Delgrande, J. P.

1988   An approach to default reasoning based on a first-order conditional logic: revised report. *Artificial Intelligence* **36**, 63–90.

Dennett, Daniel

1987   *The Intentional Stance.* Cambridge, Mass.: Bradford/MIT Press.

DiFinetti, Bruno

1975   *Theory of Probability.* New York: Wiley.

Doyle, Jon

1979   A truth-maintenance system. *Artificial Intelligence* **12**, 231–272.

1988   On universal theories of default. Technical report CMU-CS-88-111. Carnegie Mellon Computer Science Department.

1988a   Artificial intelligence and rational self-government. Technical report CMU-CS-88-124. Carnegie Mellon Computer Science Department.

Drummond, M.

1985   Refining and extending the procedural net. *Proceedings IJCAI-85*, 1010–1012.

Etherington, David

1987   Formalizing nonmonotonic reasoning systems. *Artificial Intelligence* **31**, 41–86.

Etherington, D., Kraus, S., and Perlis, D.

1991   Nonmonotonicity and the scope of reasoning. *Artificial Intelligence* **52**, 221–261.

Etherington, D., and Reiter, R.

1983   On inheritance hierarchies with exceptions. *Proceedings of AAAI-83.*

Fodor, Jerry
1975   *The Language of Thought.* New York: Thomas Y. Crowell.
Fox, M. S., Allen, B., and Strohm, G.
1981   Job shop scheduling: an investigation in constraint-based reasoning. *Proceedings IJCAI-81.*
Gabbay, Dob
1985   *Theoretical Foundations for Non-monotonic Reasoning in Expert Systems.* Berlin: Springer-Verlag.
1991   Theoretical foundations for nonmonotonic reasoning Part 2: structured nonmonotonic theories. *Proceedings of the Scandinavian Conference on Artificial Intelligence.* Roskilde, Denmark: IOS Press.
Gauthier, David
1986   *Morals by Agreement.* Oxford: Oxford University Press.
Geffner, Hector
1990   Conditional entailment: closing the gap between defaults and conditionals. *Proceedings of the Third International Workshop on Non-Monotonic Reasoning,* 58–72.
Georgeff, Michael P.
1987   Planning. *Annual Review of Computer Science 1987,* 2, 359–400.
Georgeff, M., and Lansky, A.
1986   *Reasoning about Actions and Plans.* Los Altos, Calif.: Morgan Kaufmann.
Ginsberg, M. L.
1989   A circumscriptive theorem prover. *Artificial Intelligence* 39, 209–230.
Gold, E. M.
1965   Limiting recursion. *Journal of Symbolic Logic* 30, 28–48.
Goodman, Nelson
1955   *Fact, Fiction, and Forecast.* Cambridge, Mass.: Harvard University Press.
Halpern, J. Y.
1990   An analysis of first-order logics of probability. *Artificial Intelligence* 46, 311–350.
Harman, Gilbert
1986   *Change in View.* Cambridge, Mass.: MIT Press.
Horty, J.
1992   Some direct theories of nonmonotonic inheritance. In *Handbook of Logic in Artificial Intelligence and Logic Programming,* ed. D. Gabbay and C. Hogger. Oxford: Oxford University Press.

Horty, J., and R. Thomason
1990   Boolean extensions of inheritance networks. *Proceedings of AAI-90*, 633–639.
Horty, J., Thomason, R., and Touretzky, D.
1990   A skeptical theory of inheritance in nonmonotonic semantic networks. *Artificial Intelligence* **42**, 311–348.
Israel, David
1980   What's wrong with non-monotonic logic? *Proceedings of the First Annual National Conference on Artificial Intelligence.* 99–101.
Jeffrey, Richard
1983   *The Logic of Decision,.* 2nd Edition. Chicago: University of Chicago Press.
Kraus, S., Lehmann, D., and Magidor, M.
1990   Nonmonotonic reasoning, preferential models, and cumulative logics. *Artificial Intelligence* **44**, 167–204.
Kyburg, Henry, Jr.
1961   *Probability and the Logic of Rational Belief.* Middletown, Conn.: Wesleyan University Press.
1970   Conjunctivitis. In *Induction, Acceptance, and Rational Belief*, ed. Marshall Swain. Dordrecht: Reidel.
1974   *The Logical Foundations of Statistical Inference.* Dordrecht: Reidel.
1983   The reference class. *Philosophy of Science* **50**, 374–397.
Lackner, J. R., and Garrett, M. F.
1972   Resolving ambiguity: effects of biasing context in the unattended ear. *Cognition* **1**, 359–372.
Levesque, H. J.
1990   All I know: a study in autoepistemic logic. *Artificial Intelligence* **42**, 263–310.
Levi, Isaac
1980   *The Enterprise of Knowledge.* Cambridge, Mass.: MIT Press.
Lin, Fangzhen, and Shoham, Yoav
1990   Argument systems: a uniform basis for nonmonotonic reasoning. Technical report STAN-CS-89-1243. Stanford University, Dept. of Computer Science.
Loui, Ron
1987   Defeat among arguments: a system of defeasible inference. *Computational Intelligence* **3**, 100–106.
McCarthy, J.
1980   Circumscription—a form of non-monotonic reasoning. *Artificial Intelligence* **13**, 27–39.
1984   Applications of circumscription to formalizing common sense

knowledge. *Proceedings of the Workshop on Nonmonotonic Reasoning, 1984.*

McCarthy, J., and Hayes, P.

1969   Some philosophical problems from the standpoint of artificial intelligence. *Machine Intelligence* **4**, 463–502.

McDermott, Drew

1991   A general framework for reason maintenance. *Artificial Intelligence* **50**, 289–329.

McDermott, Drew, and Doyle, Jon

1980   Non-monotonic logic I. *Artificial Intelligence* **13**, 41–72.

Makinson, David

1965   The paradox of the preface. *Analysis* **25**, 205–207.

1988   General theory of cumulative inference. *Proceedings of the 2nd Workshop on Nonmonotonic Reasoning*, 1–18. Grassau, FRG. Springer Verlag.

Manna, Z., and Waldinger, R. J.

1987   A theory of plans. In *Reasoning about Actions and Plans: Proceedings of the 1986 Workshop*. 11–45. Los Altos, Calif.: Morgan Kaufmann.

Martin, Robert L.

1970   *The Paradox of the Liar.* New Haven: Yale University Press.

1984   *Recent Essays on Truth and the Liar Paradox.* New York: Oxford University Press.

Moore, R.

1985   Semantical considerations on nonmonotonic logic. *Artificial Intelligence* **25**, 75–94.

Nagel, Thomas

1970   *The Possibility of Altruism.* Oxford: Oxford University Press.

Nute, Donald

1988   Defeasible reasoning: a philosophical analysis in PROLOG. *Aspects of AI*, ed. J. Fetzer. Reidel.

1992   Basic defeasible logic. In *Intensional Logics for Programming*, ed. L. Farinas del Cerro and M. Pentonnen, 125-154. Oxford: Oxford University Press.

Nute, Donald and Lewis, M.

1986   A users manual for d-Prolog. ACMC Research Report 01-0016. University of Georgia.

Osherson, Daniel, Stern, Joshua, Wilkie, Ormond, and Barto, Andrew

1991   Default probability. *Cognitive Science* **15**, 251–270.

Parfit, Derek

1984   *Reasons and Persons.* Oxford: Oxford University Press.

Pearl, Judea
1988   *Probabilistic Reasoning in Intelligent Systems: Networks of Plausible Inference.* Los Altos, Calif.: Morgan Kaufmann.

Pednault, E. P. D.
1987   Solving multiagent dynamic world problems in the classical planning framework. In *Reasoning about Actions and Plans: Proceedings of the 1986 Workshop.* 42–87. Los Altos, Calif.: Morgan Kaufmann.

Pelletier, F. J.
1986   Seventy-five problems for testing automatic theorem provers. *Journal of Automated Reasoning* **2**, 191–216. See the errata in *Journal of Automated Reasoning* **4** (1988), 235–6.

Perlis, Donald
1985   Languages with self-reference I: foundations. *Artificial Intelligence* **25**, 301–322.

Pettit, Philip
1991   Decision theory and folk psychology. In *Foundations of Decision Theory*, ed. M. Bacharach and S. Hurley. Oxford: Oxford University Press.

Pollock, John L.
1965   *Analyticity and Implication.* PhD dissertation, University of California, Berkeley.
1967   Criteria and our knowledge of the material world. *Philosophical Review* **76**, 28–60.
1970   The structure of epistemic justification. *American Philosophical Quarterly*, monograph series **4**, 62–78.
1971   Perceptual Knowledge. *Philosophical Review* **83**, 287–319.
1974   *Knowledge and Justification.* Princeton: Princeton University Press.
1979   Reasons and reasoning. American Philosophical Association Symposium.
1983   How do you maximize expectation value? *Nous* **17**, 409–423.
1983a   Epistemology and probability. *Synthese* **55**, 231–252.
1986   *Contemporary Theories of Knowledge.* Totowa, N.J.: Rowman and Littlefield.
1986a   A theory of moral reasoning. *Ethics* **96**, 506–523.
1987   Defeasible reasoning. *Cognitive Science* **11**, 481–518.
1989   *How to Build a Person; a Prolegomenon.* Cambridge, Mass.: Bradford/MIT Press.
1990   *Nomic Probability and the Foundations of Induction.* New York: Oxford University Press.

1990a   Interest driven suppositional reasoning. *Journal of Automated Reasoning* **6**, 419–462.

1990b   OSCAR: a general theory of rationality. *Journal of Experimental and Theoretical AI* **1**, 209-226.

1990c   A theory of defeasible reasoning. *International Journal of Intelligent Systems* **6**, 33–54.

1991   Self-defeating arguments. *Minds and Machines* **1**, 367–392.

1992   New foundations for practical reasoning. *Minds and Machines* **2**, 113–144.

1992a   How to reason defeasibly. *Artificial Intelligence* **57**, 1–42.

1993   The phylogeny of rationality. *Cognitive Science* **17**, 563–588.

1994   Justification and defeat. *Artificial Intelligence* **67**, 377–408.

1995   OSCAR – a general purpose defeasible reasoner. *Journal of Applied Non-Classical Logics*, forthcoming.

1995a   Practical Reasoning in OSCAR. *Philosophical Perspectives* **9**, forthcoming.

Poole, D.

1985   On the comparison of theories: preferring the most specific explanation. *Proceedings of Proceedings IJCAI-85*.

1988   A logical framework for default reasoning. *Artificial Intelligence* **36**, 27-48.

Putnam, Hilary

1965   Trial and error predicates and the solution to a problem of Mostowski. *Journal of Symbolic Logic* **30**, 49–57.

Ramsey, Frank

1926   Truth and probability. In*The Foundations of Mathematics*, ed. R. B. Braithwaite. Paterson, NJ.: Littlefield, Adams.mework for default reasoning. *Artificial Intelligence* **36**, 27–48.

Reichenbach, Hans

1949   *A Theory of Probability*. Berkeley: University of California Press. (Original German edition 1935).

Reiter, Raymond

1980   A logic for default reasoning. *Artificial Intelligence* **13**, 81–132.

Reiter, R., and Criscuolo, G.

1981   On interacting defaults. *Proceedings IJCAI-81*, 270–276.

Rips, Lance

1983   Cognitive processes in propositional reasoning. *Psychological Review* **90**: 38–71.

1994   *The Psychology of Proof*. Cambridge, Mass.: Bradford/MIT Press.

Sacerdotti, E. D.

1975   The non-linear nature of plans. *Proceedings IJCAI-75*.

1977   *A Structure of Plans and Behavior.* Amsterdam: Elsevier-North Holland.

Savage, Leonard

1972   *The Foundations of Statistics.* 2nd Edition. New York: Dover.

Simari, G. R., and Loui, R. P.

1992   A mathematical treatment of defeasible reasoning and its implementation. *Artificial Intelligence* **53**, 125–158.

Simon, Herbert A.

1977   *Models of Discovery.* Dordrecht: Reidel.

Skyrms, Brian

1980   *Causal Necessity.* New Haven: Yale University Press.

Smith, E. E., Langston, C., and Nisbett R.

1992   The case for rules of reasoning. *Cognitive Science* **16**, 1–40.

Smith, George

1992   Strategies, scheduling effects, and the stability of intentions (comments on Bratman). *Minds and Machines* **2**, 17–26.

Stickel, M. E.

1985   Schubert's steamroller problem: formulations and solutions. *Journal of Automated Reasoning* **2**, 89–101.

Strong, H. R.

1971   Translating recursive equations into flowcharts. *Journal of Computer Systems Science* **5**: 254–285.

Sussman, G. J.

1973   *A Computational Model of Skill Acquisition.* Technical report AI TR-297. Cambridge, Mass.: Artificial Intelligence Lab, MIT.

Tarski, Alfred

1956   The concept of truth in formalized languages. *Logic, Semantics, and Metamathematics, Papers from 1923 to 1938, by Alfred Tarski.* Oxford: Clarendon Press.

Tate, A.

1974   *INTERPLAN: A plan generation system which can deal with interactions between goals.* Memo MIP-R-109. Edinburgh: Machine Intelligence Research Unit, University of Edinburgh.

1977   Generating project networks. *Proceedings IJCAI-77.*

Tate, A., Hendler, J., and Drummond, M.

1990   A review of AI planning techniques. In Allen, Hendler, and Tate [1990], 26–49.

Tate, A., and Whiter, A. M.

1984   Planning with multiple resource constraints and an application to a Naval planning problem. *First Conference on the Applications of Artificial Intelligence, Denver.*

Thomason, R.
1987   NETL and subsequent path-based inheritance theories. In *Computers and Mathematics with Applications*, ed. E. Y. Rodin. Elmsford, NY: Pergamon Press.

Touretzky, D.
1984   Implicit orderings of defaults in inheritance systems. *Proceedings of AAAI-84.*

Touretzky, D., Horty, J., and Thomason, R.
1987   A clash of intuitions: the current state of nonmonotonic multiple inheritance systems. In *Proceedings of the Tenth International Joint Conference on Artificial Intelligence (Proceedings IJCAI-87)*, Los Altos, Calif.: Morgan Kaufmann Publishers, 476–482.

Tversky, A.
1977   Features of similarity. *Psychological Review* **84**, 327–352.

Tversky, A., and Kahneman, D.
1974   Judgment under uncertainty: heuristics and biases. *Science* **185**, 1124–1131.

von Neumann, J., and Morgenstern, O.
1944   *Theory of Games and Economic Behavior.* New York: Wiley.

Waldinger, R.
1977   Achieving several goals simultaneously. *Machine Intelligence* **8**, 94–136.

Warren, D. H. D.
1976   Generating conditional plans and programs. In Proceedings of the AISB Summer Conference, 344–35. University of Edinburgh, UK4.

Wason, P.
1966   Reasoning. In B. Foss (ed.), *New Horizons in Psychology.* Harmondsworth, England: Penguin.

Wilson, G. A., and Minker, J.
1976   Resolution, refinements, and search strategies: a comparative study. *IEEE Transactions on Computers* **C-25** , 782–801.

Wos, L., Overbeek, R., Lusk, E., and Boyle, J.
1984   *Automated Reasoning.* Englewood Cliffs, NJ.: Prentice Hall.

Index